PRENTICE HALL
LITERATURE

P E N G U I N   E D I T I O N

Reader's Notebook

Grade Eleven

PEARSON

Prentice
Hall

Upper Saddle River, New Jersey
Boston, Massachusetts

ISBN 0-13-190793-X

7 8 9 10   09 08

ACKNOWLEDGMENTS

Grateful acknowledgment is made to the following for copyrighted material:

Sandra Dijkstra Literary Agency
"Mother Tongue" by Amy Tan. Copyright © 1990 by Amy Tan. First appeared in *The Threepenny Review*. Reprinted by permission.

The Echo Foundation
"The Echo Foundation Brings Henry Gates, Jr. to Charlotte" from *The Echo Foundation*.

Farrar, Straus & Giroux, LLC
"The First Seven Years" by Bernard Malamud from *The Magic Barrel*. Copyright © 1950, 1958 and copyright renewed © 1977, 1986 by Bernard Malamud.

Harcourt, Inc.
"A Worn Path" from A CURTAIN OF GREEN AND OTHER STORIES, copyright 1941 and renewed 1969 by Eudora Welty. "Everyday Use" from *In Love & Trouble: Stories of Black Women*, copyright © 1973 by Alice Walker. Reprinted by permission of Harcourt, Inc. This material may not be reproduced in any form or by any means without the prior written permission of publisher.

Museum of Afro American History
"Museum of Afro-American History Mission Statement" from *www.afroammuseum.org/about.htm*.

The New York Times
"Review of the Crucible" by Brooks Atkinson from *New York Times, Published: January 23, 1953*. Used with permission.

Plimoth Plantation, Inc.
"Plimoth Plantation" from *www.plimoth.org/index.html*. Reprinted by permission of Plimoth Plantation, Inc.

Princeton University Press
From *Walden* by Henry David Thoreau. Copyright © 1971 by Princeton University Press. All rights reserved. Used by permission of Princeton University Press.

Scribner, a Division of Simon & Schuster, Inc.
"The Far and the Near" from *Death to Morning* by Thomas Wolfe. Copyright 1935 by Charles Scribner's Sons; copyright renewed © 1963 by Paul Gitlin. "In Another Country" from *Men Without Woman* by Ernest Hemingway. Copyright 1927 by Charles Scribner's Sons. Copyright renewed 1955 by Ernest Hemingway. Used by permission of Scribner, a Division of Simon & Schuster, Inc.

Sterling Lord Literistic, Inc.
"The Crisis, Number 1" by Thomas Paine from *Citizen Tom Paine*. Copyright by Howard Fast. Used by permission of Sterling Lord Literistic, Inc.

Syracuse University Press
"The Iroquois Constitution" from *Parker on the Iroquois: Iroquois Uses of Maize and Other Food Plants; The Code of Handsome Lake; The Seneca Prophet; The Constitution of the Five Nations* by Arthur C. Parker, edited by William N. Fenton (Syracuse University Press, Syracuse, NY, 1981).

Viking Penguin, Inc.
From *The Grapes of Wrath* by John Steinbeck, copyright 1939, renewed © 1967 by John Steinbeck.

Yale University Press
Excerpt from "Sinners in the Hands of an Angry God" from *The Sermons of Jonathan Edwards: A Reader* published by Yale University Press. Copyright © 1999 by Yale University Press. Used with permission.

Note: Every effort has been made to locate the copyright owner of material reproduced on this component. Omissions brought to our attention will be corrected in subsequent editions.

Contents

UNIT 3 A Growing Nation: Nineteenth-Century Literature (1800–1870)

© Pearson Education, Inc., publishing as Pearson Prentice Hall.

UNIT 5 Disillusion, Defiance, and Discontent: The Modern Age (1914–1946)

READING INFORMATIONAL MATERIALS

UNIT 6 Prosperity and Protest: The Contemporary Period (1946–Present)

PART 2 Turbo Vocabulary

INTERACTING WITH THE TEXT

As you read your hardcover student edition of *Prentice Hall Literature* use the **Reader's Notebook** to guide you in learning and practicing the skills presented. In addition, many selections in your student edition are presented here in an interactive format. The notes and instruction will guide you in applying reading and literary skills and in thinking about the selection. The examples on these pages show you how to use the notes as a companion when you read.

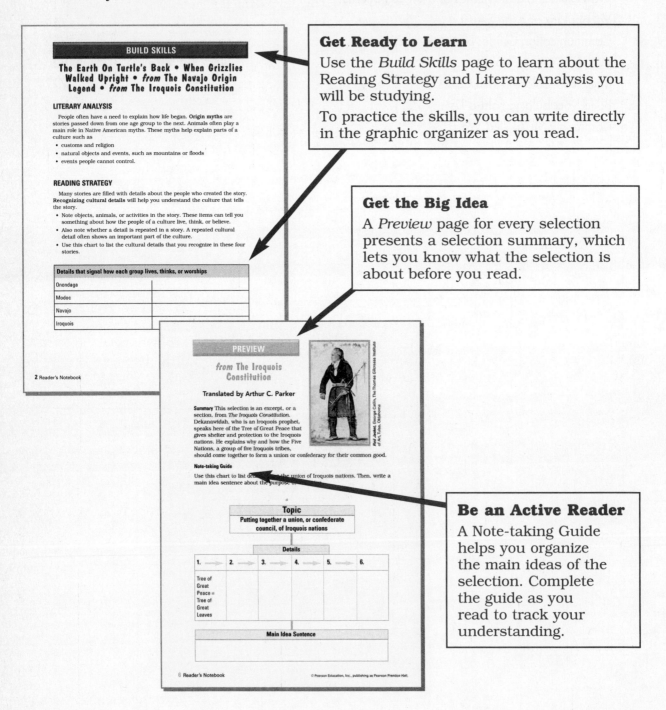

BUILD SKILLS

The Earth On Turtle's Back • When Grizzlies Walked Upright • *from* The Navajo Origin Legend • *from* The Iroquois Constitution

LITERARY ANALYSIS

People often have a need to explain how life began. **Origin myths** are stories passed down from one age group to the next. Animals often play a main role in Native American myths. These myths help explain parts of a culture such as

• customs and religion
• natural objects and events, such as mountains or floods
• events people cannot control.

READING STRATEGY

Many stories are filled with details about the people who created the story. **Recognizing cultural details** will help you understand the culture that tells the story.

• Note objects, animals, or activities in the story. These items can tell you something about how the people of a culture live, think, or believe.
• Also note whether a detail is repeated in a story. A repeated cultural detail often shows an important part of the culture.
• Use this chart to list the cultural details that you recognize in these four stories.

Details that signal how each group lives, thinks, or worships		
Onondaga		
Modoc		
Navajo		
Iroquois		

2 Reader's Notebook

PREVIEW

from The Iroquois Constitution

Translated by Arthur C. Parker

Summary This selection is an excerpt, or a section, from *The Iroquois Constitution*. Dekanawidah, who is an Iroquois prophet, speaks here of the Tree of Great Peace that gives shelter and protection to the Iroquois nations. He explains why and how the Five Nations, a group of five Iroquois tribes, should come together to form a union or confederacy for their common good.

Note-taking Guide

Use this chart to list details about the union of Iroquois nations. Then, write a main idea sentence about the purpose of the union.

Topic
Putting together a union, or confederate council, of Iroquois nations

Details

1.	2.	3.	4.	5.	6.
Tree of Great Peace = Tree of Great Leaves					

Main Idea Suntence

6 Reader's Notebook   © Pearson Education, Inc., publishing as Pearson Prentice Hall.

Get Ready to Learn

Use the *Build Skills* page to learn about the Reading Strategy and Literary Analysis you will be studying.

To practice the skills, you can write directly in the graphic organizer as you read.

Get the Big Idea

A *Preview* page for every selection presents a selection summary, which lets you know what the selection is about before you read.

Be an Active Reader

A Note-taking Guide helps you organize the main ideas of the selection. Complete the guide as you read to track your understanding.

from The Iroquois Constitution
Translated by Arthur C. Parker

As people form a new group, they often choose something to represent their values. As the Iroquois nations in this selection come together, they choose a tree as their symbol. The roots of the tree are all part of one tree, but they are also individual and separate. The roots also reach in different directions from one starting point—the tree. The Tree of the Great Peace, then, is a symbol for the peace that all the Iroquois nations want to create.

I am Dekanawidah and with the Five Nations' confederate lords I plant the Tree of the Great Peace. I name the tree the Tree of the Great Long Leaves. Under the shade of this Tree of the Great Peace we spread the soft white feathery down of the globe thistle as seats for you, Adodarhoh, and your cousin lords.

We place you upon those seats, spread soft with the feathery down of the globe thistle, there beneath the shade of the spreading branches of the Tree of Peace. There shall you sit and watch the council fire of the confederacy of the Five Nations, and all the affairs of the Five Nations shall be transacted at this place before you.

Roots have spread out from the Tree of the Great Peace, one to the north, one to the east, one to the south and one to the west. The name of these roots is the Great White Roots and their nature is peace and strength.

If any man or any nation outside the Five Nations shall obey the laws of the Great Peace and make known their disposition to the lords of the confederacy, they may trace the roots to the tree and if their minds are clean and they are obedient and promise to obey the wishes of the confederate council, they shall be welcomed to take shelter beneath the Tree of the Long Leaves.

We place at the top of the Tree of the Long Leaves an eagle who is able to see afar. If he sees in the distance any evil approaching or any danger threatening he will at once warn the people of the confederacy.

The smoke of the confederate council fire shall ever ascend and pierce the sky so that other nations who may be allies may see the council fire of the Great Peace . . .

Vocabulary Development: confederate (kon FED er it) *adj.* united with others for a common purpose **disposition** (dis puh ZISH uhn) *n.* an inclination or tendency

1. **Five Nations** the Mohawk, Oneida, Onondaga, Cayuga, and Seneca tribes. Together, these tribes formed the Iroquois Confederation.

© Pearson Education, Inc., publishing as Pearson Prentice Hall.

TAKE NOTES

Activate Prior Knowledge

Groups and organizations often use rituals or ceremonies to mark important occasions. Write down two or three facts about a ritual you have seen or participated in, like a graduation or a wedding. As you read, compare that ritual to the one described here.

1. _____
2. _____
3. _____

Reading Strategy

Underline the two names of the tree and the name of the roots. What **cultural details**, orig... about the way the people of a c... do you learn about the Iroquois ... Dekanawidah names the tre... its roots?

_____
_____
_____

Reading Check

What do the Tree of Great Peace and the eagle stand for?

_____
_____
_____

from The Iroquois Constitution **7**

Take Notes
Side-column questions accompany the selections that appear in the Reader's Notebooks. These questions are a built-in tutor to help you practice the skills and understand what you read.

Mark the Text
Use write-on lines to answer questions in the side column. You may also want to use the lines for your own notes.

When you see a pencil, you should underline, circle, or mark the text as indicated.

APPLY THE SKILLS

The Earth on Turtle's Back • When Grizzlies Walked Upright • *from* The Navajo Origin Legend • *from* The Iroquois Constitution

1. **Infer:** Why do the Navajo people believe that spirits are kind?
   _____

2. **Infer:** Why do the Modoc people believe that spirits are mean?
   _____

3. **Literary Analysis:** Use this chart to list three aspects or parts of nature. Write the role each plays in Native American life.

Aspect of Nature	Connection to Native American Life

4. **Reading Strategy:** Write one **cultural detail** that you recognize from "The Earth on Turtle's Back." Write another cultural detail you recognize from "When Grizzlies Walked Upright." What does each detail tell you about the culture that tells the story?
   _____
   _____

5. **Reading Strategy:** Write one **cultural detail** that you recognize from "The Navajo Origin Legend." Write another cultural detail that you recognize from "The Iroquois Constitution." What does each detail tell you about the culture that tells the story?
   _____
   _____

10 Reader's Notebook

© Pearson Education, Inc., publishing as Pearson Prentice Hall.

Check Your Understanding
Questions after every selection help you think about the selection. You can use the write-on lines and charts to answer the questions. Then, share your ideas in class discussions.

PART 1

The Earth on Turtle's Back • When Grizzlies Walked Upright • *from* The Navajo Origin Legend • *from* The Iroquois Constitution

LITERARY ANALYSIS

People often have a need to explain how life began. **Origin myths** are stories passed down from one age group to the next. Animals often play a main role in Native American myths. These myths help explain parts of a culture such as

- customs and religion
- natural objects and events, such as mountains or floods
- events people cannot control.

READING STRATEGY

Many stories are filled with details about the people who created the story. **Recognizing cultural details** will help you understand the culture that tells the story.

- Note objects, animals, or activities in the story. These items can tell you something about how the people of a culture live, think, or believe.
- Also note whether a detail is repeated in a story. A repeated cultural detail often shows an important part of the culture.
- Use this chart to list the cultural details that you recognize in these four stories.

Details that signal how each group lives, thinks, or worships	
Onondaga	
Modoc	
Navajo	
Iroquois	

The Earth on Turtle's Back

from the Onondaga

Summary The Onondaga are one of the Iroquois tribes. In this story, they tell about a time before Earth was above water. A brave muskrat brings a tiny piece of earth out of the water to help a woman who falls from the sky. A turtle's back then becomes the base for Earth. Then, life on Earth begins. A story such as this helps the reader understand the beliefs and thinking of the Onondaga people.

Note-taking Guide

Use this diagram to record events in the order in which they happen in this story.

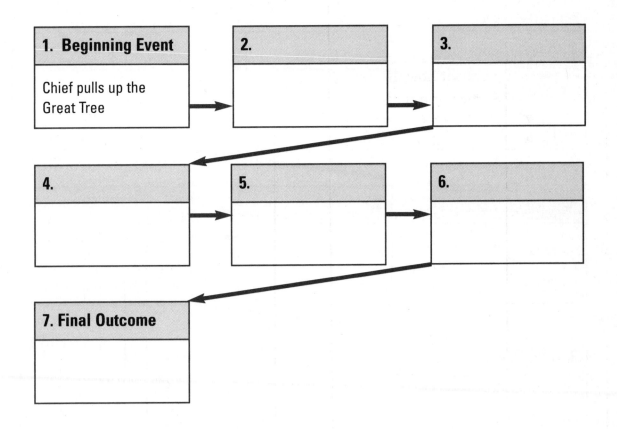

1. Beginning Event	2.	3.
Chief pulls up the Great Tree		

4.	5.	6.

7. Final Outcome

When Grizzlies Walked Upright

from the Modoc

Summary The Modoc lived in areas that became part of the western United States. They tell a story that explains where the first Native Americans come from. A daughter of the Chief of the Sky Spirits comes to Earth and marries a grizzly bear. Their children become the first Native Americans.

Note-taking Guide

Use this diagram to record events in the order in which they happen in this story.

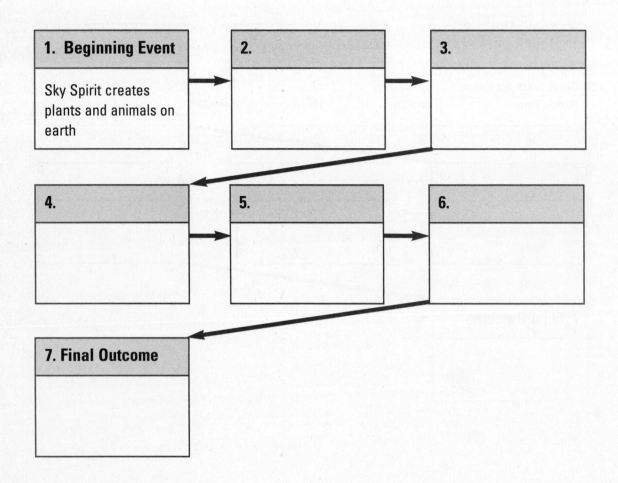

1. Beginning Event	2.	3.
Sky Spirit creates plants and animals on earth		

4.	5.	6.

7. Final Outcome

from The Navajo Origin Legend

Summary This part of the Navajo legend tells how the wind breathes life into corn to create the First Man and First Woman. This creation myth shows how important nature, corn, animal skins, feathers, and the wind are to the Navajo.

Note-taking Guide

Use this diagram to record events in the order in which they happen in this story.

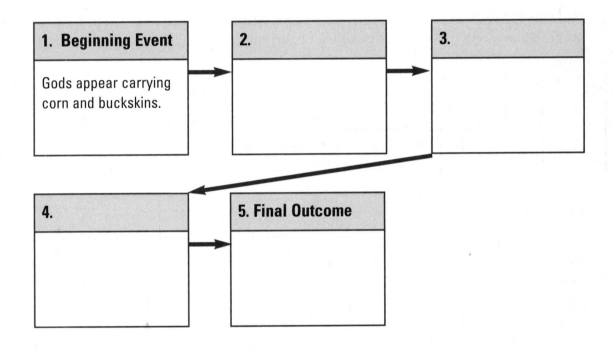

1. Beginning Event
Gods appear carrying corn and buckskins.

2.

3.

4.

5. Final Outcome

from The Iroquois Constitution

Translated by Arthur C. Parker

Summary This selection is an excerpt, or a section, from *The Iroquois Constitution*. Dekanawidah, who is an Iroquois prophet, speaks here of the Tree of Great Peace that gives shelter and protection to the Iroquois nations. He explains why and how the Five Nations, a group of five Iroquois tribes, should come together to form a union or confederacy for their common good.

Red Jacket, George Catlin, The Thomas Gilcrease Institute of Art, Tulsa, Oklahoma

Note-taking Guide

Use this chart to list details about the union of Iroquois nations. Then, write a main idea sentence about the purpose of the union.

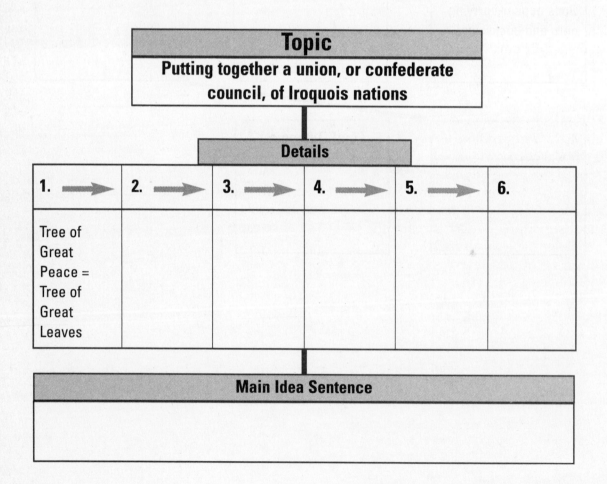

Topic

Putting together a union, or confederate council, of Iroquois nations

Details

1. →	2. →	3. →	4. →	5. →	6.
Tree of Great Peace = Tree of Great Leaves					

Main Idea Sentence

from The Iroquois Constitution
Translated by Arthur C. Parker

As people form a new group, they often choose something to represent their values. As the Iroquois nations in this selection come together, they choose a tree as their symbol. The roots of the tree are all part of one tree, but they are also individual and separate. The roots also reach in different directions from one starting point—the tree. The Tree of the Great Peace, then, is a symbol for the peace that all the Iroquois nations want to create.

I am Dekanawidah and with the Five Nations[1] <u>confederate</u> lords I plant the Tree of the Great Peace. I name the tree the Tree of the Great Long Leaves. Under the shade of this Tree of the Great Peace we spread the soft white feathery down of the globe thistle as seats for you, Adodarhoh, and your cousin lords.

We place you upon those seats, spread soft with the feathery down of the globe thistle, there beneath the shade of the spreading branches of the Tree of Peace. There shall you sit and watch the council fire of the confederacy of the Five Nations, and all the affairs of the Five Nations shall be transacted at this place before you.

Roots have spread out from the Tree of the Great Peace, one to the north, one to the east, one to the south and one to the west. The name of these roots is the Great White Roots and their nature is peace and strength.

If any man or any nation outside the Five Nations shall obey the laws of the Great Peace and make known their <u>disposition</u> to the lords of the confederacy, they may trace the roots to the tree and if their minds are clean and they are obedient and promise to obey the wishes of the confederate council, they shall be welcomed to take shelter beneath the Tree of the Long Leaves.

We place at the top of the Tree of the Long Leaves an eagle who is able to see afar. If he sees in the distance any evil approaching or any danger threatening he will at once warn the people of the confederacy.

The smoke of the confederate council fire shall ever ascend and pierce the sky so that other nations who may be allies may see the council fire of the Great Peace . . .

Vocabulary Development: confederate (kon FED er it) *adj.* united with others for a common purpose
disposition (dis puh ZISH uhn) *n.* an inclination or tendency

---

1. **Five Nations** the Mohawk, Oneida, Onondaga, Cayuga, and Seneca tribes. Together, these tribes formed the Iroquois Confederation.

TAKE NOTES

Activate Prior Knowledge

Groups and organizations often use rituals or ceremonies to mark important occasions. Write down two or three facts about a ritual you have seen or participated in, like a graduation or a wedding. As you read, compare that ritual to the one described here.

1. _____

2. _____

3. _____

Reading Strategy

Underline the two names of the tree and the name of the roots. What **cultural details,** or signals about the way the people of a culture live, do you learn about the Iroquois when Dekanawidah names the tree and its roots?

_____
_____
_____
_____

Reading Check

What do the Tree of Great Peace and the eagle stand for?

_____
_____
_____
_____

Reading Strategy

Reread the bracketed paragraphs. Why is it so important for the lords of the confederacy to be honest?

_____

_____

_____

_____

Literary Analysis

Much of what we know about Native American culture comes from an **oral tradition,** meaning that stories are passed from generation to generation by word of mouth. Circle the phrases on this page that would be particularly effective if spoken aloud.

Whenever the confederate lords shall assemble for the purpose of holding a council, the Onondaga lords shall open it by expressing their gratitude to their cousin lords and greeting them, and they shall make an address and offer thanks to the earth where men dwell, to the streams of water, the pools, the springs and the lakes, to the maize and the fruits, to the medicinal herbs and trees, to the forest trees for their usefulness, to the animals that serve as food and give their pelts for clothing, to the great winds and the lesser winds, to the thunderers, to the sun, the mighty warrior, to the moon, to the messengers of the Creator who reveal his wishes and to the Great Creator who dwells in the heavens above, who gives all the things useful to men, and who is the source and the ruler of health and life.

Then shall the Onondaga lords declare the council open . . .

All lords of the Five Nations' Confederacy must be honest in all things . . . It shall be a serious wrong for anyone to lead a lord into trivial affairs, for the people must ever hold their lords high in estimation out of respect to their honorable positions.

When a candidate lord is to be installed he shall furnish four strings of shells (or wampum)[2] one span in length bound together at one end. Such will constitute the evidence of his pledge to the confederate lords that he will live according to the constitution of the Great Peace and exercise justice in all affairs.

When the pledge is furnished the speaker of the council must hold the shell strings in his hand and address the opposite side of the council fire and he shall commence his address saying: "Now behold him. He has now become a confederate lord. See how splendid he looks." An address may then follow. At the end of it he shall send the bunch of shell strings to the opposite side and they shall be received as evidence of the pledge. Then shall the opposite side say:

"We now do crown you with the sacred emblem of the deer's antlers, the emblem of your lordship. You shall now become a mentor of the people of the Five Nations. The thickness of your skin shall be seven spans—which is to say that you shall be proof against anger, offensive actions and criticism. Your heart shall be filled with peace and good will and your mind filled with a yearning for the welfare of the people of the confederacy. With endless patience you shall carry out your duty and your firmness shall be tempered

---

2. **wampum** (WAHM puhm) *n.* small beads made of shells.

with tenderness for your people. Neither anger nor fury shall find lodgement in your mind and all your words and actions shall be marked with calm <u>deliberation</u>. In all of your deliberations in the confederate council, in your efforts at law making, in all your official acts, self-interest shall be cast into oblivion. Cast not over your shoulder behind you the warnings of the nephews and nieces should they chide you for any error or wrong you may do, but return to the way of the Great Law which is just and right. Look and listen for the welfare of the whole people and have always in view not only the present but also the coming generations, even those whose faces are yet beneath the surface of the ground—the unborn of the future nation."

Vocabulary Development: deliberation (di lib uh RAY shuhn) *n.*
careful consideration

Reader's Response: What words would you use to describe the kind of union or confederacy that Dekanawidah announces in this selection?

_____

_____

_____

Thinking About the Skill: How did thinking about the **cultural details** in this selection help you to understand and enjoy your reading?

_____

_____

_____

Reading Strategy

The word *deliberation* is formed by adding the **Latin suffix** *–tion* to the word *deliberate* after dropping the *te.* Create new words by doing the same thing to the words *estimate* and *constitute.* Then, underline these words in the bracketed paragraphs on page 6.

1. _____

_____

2. _____

_____

Reading Check

What does it mean to be a lord of the Five Nations?

_____

_____

_____

_____

_____

The Earth on Turtle's Back • When Grizzlies Walked Upright • *from* The Navajo Origin Legend • *from* The Iroquois Constitution

1. **Infer:** Why do the Navajo people believe that spirits are kind?

   _____

2. **Infer:** Why do the Modoc people believe that spirits are mean?

   _____

3. **Literary Analysis:** Use this chart to list three aspects or parts of nature. Write the role each plays in Native American life.

Aspect of Nature	Connection to Native American Life

4. **Reading Strategy:** Write one **cultural detail** that you recognize from "The Earth on Turtle's Back." Write another cultural detail you recognize from "When Grizzlies Walked Upright." What does each detail tell you about the culture that tells the story?

   _____

   _____

5. **Reading Strategy:** Write one **cultural detail** that you recognize from "The Navajo Origin Legend." Write another cultural detail that you recognize from "The Iroquois Constitution." What does each detail tell you about the culture that tells the story?

   _____

   _____

A Journey Through Texas • Boulders Taller Than the Great Tower of Seville

LITERARY ANALYSIS

Early European explorers often wrote about their travels in the Americas. These stories are called **exploration narratives**. Exploration narratives use details to describe the places explorers visit and the people they meet. Explorers write narratives to help people back home imagine what a place is like.

Authors write with different styles. An **author's style** is his or her choice of words, detail, and focus. For example, the authors of these two narratives provide different details to tell about their explorations. They focus on events, people, and places in different ways. Fill out this Venn diagram with the similarities and differences in the writing styles of these two authors.

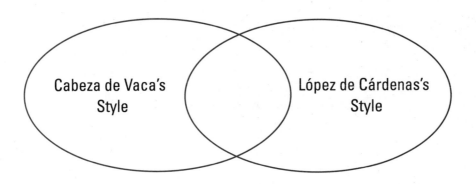

Cabeza de Vaca's Style

López de Cárdenas's Style

READING STRATEGY

To follow the order of events, pay close attention to **signal words**—words that highlight the relationships among ideas. Look at these examples:

- **time:** *After five days*, they had not *yet* returned.
- **contrast:** . . . *although* this was the warm season, no one could live in this canyon because of the cold.

As you read, take note of signal words and the relationships they indicate.

A Journey Through Texas

Alvar Núñez Cabeza de Vaca

Summary In this narrative, the author describes his journey into what is now the state of Texas. There, he meets many Native Americans who help him on his journey. The Native Americans share food with him and help him find his way. The author learns to appreciate the different ways people have found to live.

Note-taking Guide

Use this diagram to record details about the author's experiences.

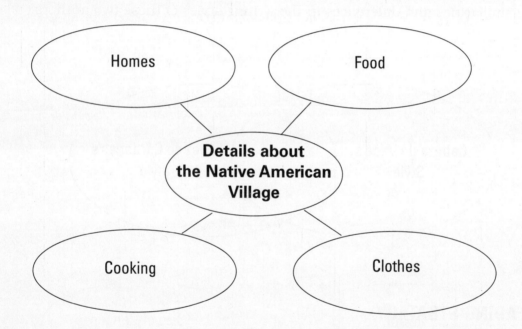

Boulders Taller Than the Great Tower of Seville

García López de Cárdenas

Summary This narrative tells about the first time that Europeans come to the Grand Canyon. The author describes the canyon's vast size, difficult landscape, and cold weather. He explains what happens when his group tries to explore the canyon.

Note-taking

Use this diagram to record details about the author's experiences.

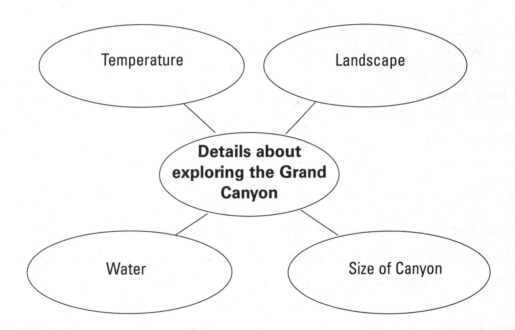

Temperature

Landscape

Details about exploring the Grand Canyon

Water

Size of Canyon

A Journey Through Texas • Boulders Taller Than the Great Tower of Seville

1. **Draw Conclusions**: Cabeza de Vaca explains that many Native Americans fell sick and eight of them died. What do the Native Americans believe caused the sickness?

   _____

2. **Infer:** Why does Coronado send López de Cárdenas and his group on a mission north?

   _____

3. **Literary Analysis: Compare and contrast** the way Cabeza de Vaca and López de Cárdenas react to the Native Americans. Use this chart to record your ideas.

Writer	Landscape and Cultural Details	Writer's Reaction
Cabeza de Vaca		
López de Cárdenas		

4. **Reading Strategy: Signal words** show the relationships among ideas. Read the sentence below. Determine whether the underlined signal word shows a relationship of time or contrast. Write your answer on the line provided.

   These explorers had many adventures. <u>Then</u>, they wrote detailed reports of their journeys. _____

5. **Reading Strategy:** Read the sentence below. Determine whether the underlined signal word shows a relationship of time or contrast. Write your answer on the line provided.

   The Native Americans sometimes had to deal with their enemies while helping the explorers, <u>but</u> they helped the explorers anyway. _____

from Journal of the First Voyage to America

LITERARY ANALYSIS

A **journal** is a written account of what happens in a person's life each day. European explorers who came to the Americas kept details of their expeditions in daily journals.

- Journals provide details from eyewitnesses, or spectators who can describe what actually happened.
- Journals are accounts of the writer's personal reactions. A journal can reveal much about the writer's feelings, thoughts, and values.

READING STRATEGY

Authors have many different reasons for writing. **Recognizing the author's purpose** can help you understand why a work was written. If you know the author's purpose, you can also understand the word choices and ideas included in the written work.

Use this chart as you read Columbus's journal. List Columbus's favorable descriptions of objects, people, and events. Then explain his purpose for writing those descriptions.

Favorable Descriptions	Author's Purpose

from Journal of the First Voyage to America

Summary Columbus writes in his journal about his exploration of a beautiful island. He describes spectacular trees, flowers, and birds. He also tells how the native people respond to him and his crew. Columbus wants to impress the people who are paying for his trip, so he describes the exotic objects he is bringing home.

Note-taking Guide

Use this diagram to record the events in the order in which they happen in this journal.

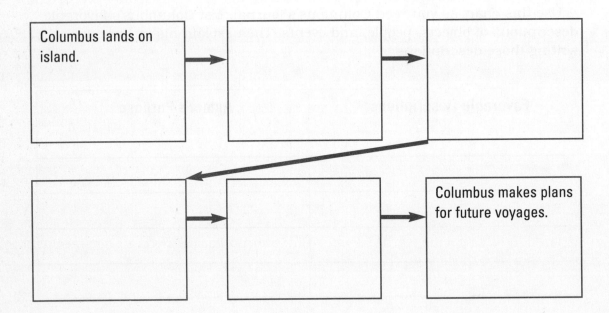

from Journal of the First Voyage to America

1. **Literary Analysis**: Identify three details from Columbus's **journal** that could only be provided by someone who was on the trip, that is, an eyewitness. List the details in a chart like this one.

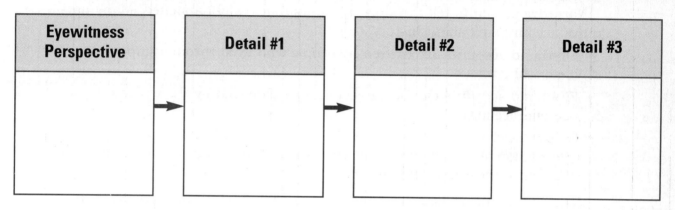

Eyewitness Perspective	Detail #1	Detail #2	Detail #3

2. **Literary Analysis**: What does Columbus think about each of the details you listed in the chart?

_____

_____

3. **Reading Strategy**: What is the **author's purpose** for writing this journal?

_____

_____

4. **Support**: Identify specific words, details, and events that help you understand what the author's purpose is in this journal.

_____

_____

5. **Hypothesize**: How would this journal be different if it had been written by a Native American who was there watching?

_____

_____

from The General History of Virginia •
from Of Plymouth Plantation

LITERARY ANALYSIS

Narrative accounts tell the story of events that really happened. Many narrative accounts tell about history.

- Firsthand accounts are written by people who lived through important historical events.
- Firsthand accounts can be subjective, or influenced by the writer's personal feelings.
- Secondhand accounts are written by people who have gathered information about an event. However, these writers did not actually experience the events themselves.

John Smith and William Bradford both provide firsthand observations in their narrative accounts.

READING STRATEGY

Breaking down sentences can help you understand sentences that are long and complicated.

- Look at one section of the sentence at a time. Separate the most important parts of the sentence from any difficult language.
- Use punctuation to help you decide where to break sentences into smaller parts.
- Use a chart like this one to help you break down sentences and figure out their meaning.

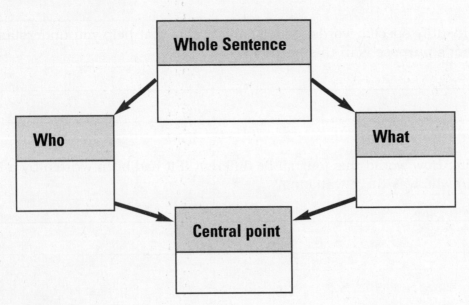

from The General History of Virginia

John Smith

Summary This excerpt tells of the hardships of the Jamestown colony. Fifty colonists die between May and September. When Captain John Smith goes on an expedition, he and his men are attacked by Indians. Smith's life is spared because he gives the Indians his compass and because Pocahontas, Chief Powhatan's daughter, saves him. After six weeks as a captive, Smith is allowed to return to Jamestown. Pocahontas brings the settlers food, saving their lives.

Note-taking Guide

Use this chart to record four important events.

Topic			
The first months of the Jamestown settlement			
1. ➡	2. ➡	3. ➡	4. ➡
After the ship leaves, the settlers do not have enough food.	The settlers work so hard that they become weak.		

Main Idea Sentence
Despite great challenges, the settlement survives.

You may have learned about
Pocahontas in your social studies
classes, or you may have seen the
film about Pocahontas, heard the
music, or seen the related toys.
Write two facts you know about
Pocahontas.

1. _____

_____

2. _____

_____

Reading Strategy

Read this selection
slowly, one sentence
at a time. As you read, **break each
sentence down** and think carefully
about what it means. Use the footnotes to help you. Start with the
first sentence. Circle the words
that tell you what happens to the
settlers after ten days.

Reading Check

Why are the settlers so miserable?

_____

_____

_____

_____

from The General History of Virginia
John Smith
What Happened Till the First Supply

*John Smith himself wrote this account of the early months of the
Jamestown settlement. For that reason, he may be trying to make his
actions seem even braver and more selfless than they were. As you
read, stay alert for evidence of exaggerating by Smith.*

Being thus left to our fortunes, it fortuned[1] that within ten
days, scarce ten amongst us could either go[2] or well stand,
such extreme weakness and sickness oppressed us. And
thereat none need marvel if they consider the cause and
reason, which was this: While the ships stayed, our allowance
was somewhat bettered by a daily proportion of biscuit which
the sailors would <u>pilfer</u> to sell, give, or exchange with us for
money, sassafras,[3] or furs. But when they departed, there
remained neither tavern, beer house, nor place of relief but the
common kettle.[4] Had we been as free from all sins as gluttony
and drunkenness we might have been canonized for saints,
but our President[5] would never have been admitted for
engrossing to his private,[6] oatmeal, sack,[7] oil, aqua vitae,[8] beef,
eggs, or what not but the kettle; that indeed he allowed equally
to be distributed, and that was half a pint of wheat and as
much barley boiled with water for a man a day, and this,
having fried some twenty-six weeks in the ship's hold,
contained as many worms as grains so that we might truly call
it rather so much bran than corn; our drink was water, our
lodgings castles in the air.

With this lodging and diet, our extreme toil in bearing and
planting <u>palisades</u> so strained and bruised us and our
continual labor in the extremity of the heat had so weakened
us, as were cause sufficient to have made us as miserable in
our native country or any other place in the world.

From May to September, those that escaped lived upon
sturgeon and sea crabs. Fifty in this time we buried; the rest

---

Vocabulary Development: pilfer (PIL fer) *v.* steal
palisades (PAL uh saydz) *n.* large,
pointed stakes set in the ground to
form a fence used for defense

---

1. **fortuned** *v.* happened.
2. **go** *v.* be active.
3. **sassafras** (SAS uh fras) *n.* a tree, the root of which was valued for its supposed
   medicinal qualities.
4. **common kettle** communal cooking pot.
5. **President** Wingfield, the leader of the colony.
6. **engrossing to his private** taking for his own use.
7. **sack** *n.* type of white wine.
8. **aqua vitae** (AK wuh VY tee) brandy.

seeing the President's projects to escape these miseries in our pinnace[9] by flight (who all this time had neither felt want nor sickness) so moved our dead spirits as we deposed him and established Ratcliffe in his place . . .

But now was all our provision spent, the sturgeon gone, all helps abandoned, each hour expecting the fury of the savages; when God, the patron of all good endeavors, in that desperate extremity so changed the hearts of the savages that they brought such plenty of their fruits and provision as no man wanted.

And now where some affirmed it was ill done of the Council[10] to send forth men so badly provided, this incontradictable reason will show them plainly they are too ill advised to nourish such ill <u>conceits</u>: First, the fault of our going was our own; what could be thought fitting or necessary we had, but what we should find, or want, or where we should be, we were all ignorant and supposing to make our passage in two months, with victual to live and the advantage of the spring to work; we were at sea five months where we both spent our victual and lost the opportunity of the time and season to plant, by the unskillful presumption of our ignorant transporters that understood not at all what they undertook.

Such actions have ever since the world's beginning been subject to such accidents, and everything of worth is found full of difficulties, but nothing so difficult as to establish a commonwealth so far remote from men and means and where men's minds are so untoward[11] as neither do well themselves nor suffer others. But to proceed.

The new President and Martin, being little beloved, of weak judgment in dangers, and less industry in peace, committed the managing of all things abroad[12] to Captain Smith, who, by his own example, good words, and fair promises, set some to mow, others to bind thatch, some to build houses, others to thatch them, himself always bearing the greatest task for his own share, so that in short time he provided most of them lodgings, neglecting any for himself. . . .

Leading an expedition on the Chickahominy River, Captain Smith and his men are attacked by Indians, and Smith is taken prisoner.

When this news came to Jamestown, much was their sorrow for his loss, few expecting what ensued.

Vocabulary Development: conceits (kuhn SEETZ) *n.* strange or fanciful ideas

---

9. **pinnace** (PIN is) *n.* small sailing ship.
10. **Council** the seven persons in charge of the expedition.
11. **untoward** *adj.* stubborn.
12. **abroad** *adv.* outside the palisades.

from The General History of Virginia **21**

This selection is a **narrative account,** or a story of real-life events. It is told by John Smith, who actually participated in the events. Reread the underlined words. How can you tell that Smith's account may not be completely objective—that he may be making himself look good?

_____

_____

_____

_____

_____

_____

How many bowmen do the Indians have?

_____

_____

What happens to Robinson and Emry?

_____

_____

What does Smith give to Opechancanough, King of Pamunkee?

_____

_____

_____

Six or seven weeks those barbarians kept him prisoner, many strange triumphs and conjurations they made of him, yet he so demeaned himself amongst them, <u>as he not only diverted them from surprising the fort, but procured his own liberty, and got himself and his company such estimation amongst them, that those savages admired him.</u>

The manner how they used and delivered him is as followeth: The savages having drawn from George Cassen whither Captain Smith was gone, prosecuting that opportunity they followed him with three hundred bowmen, conducted by the King of Pamunkee,[13] who in divisions searching the turnings of the river found Robinson and Emry by the fireside; those they shot full of arrows and slew. Then finding the Captain, as is said, that used the savage that was his guide as his shield (three of them being slain and divers[14] others so galled),[15] all the rest would not come near him. Thinking thus to have returned to his boat, regarding them, as he marched, more than his way, slipped up to the middle in an oozy creek and his savage with him; yet dared they not come to him till being near dead with cold he threw away his arms. Then according to their compositions[16] they drew him forth and led him to the fire where his men were slain. Diligently they chafed his benumbed limbs.

He demanding for their captain, they showed him Opechancanough, King of Pamunkee, to whom he gave a round ivory double compass dial. Much they marveled at the playing of the fly and needle,[17] which they could see so plainly and yet not touch it because of the glass that covered them. <u>But when he demonstrated by that globe-like jewel the roundness of the earth and skies, the sphere of the sun, moon, and stars, and how the sun did chase the night round about the world continually, the greatness of the land and sea, the diversity of nations, variety of complexions, and how we were to them antipodes[18] and many other such like matters, they all stood as amazed with admiration.</u>

Nothwithstanding, within an hour after, they tied him to a tree, and as many as could stand about him prepared to shoot him, but the King holding up the compass in his hand, they all laid down their bows and arrows and in a triumphant manner led him to Orapaks where he was after their manner kindly feasted and well used. . . .

At last they brought him to Werowocomoco, where was Powhatan, their Emperor. Here more than two hundred of those grim courtiers stood wondering at him, as he had been a monster, till Powhatan and his train had put themselves in their

13. **Pamunkee** Pamunkee River.
14. **divers** (DY vuhrz) *adj.* several.
15. **galled** *v.* wounded.
16. **composition** *n.* ways.
17. **fly and needle** *n.* parts of a compass.
18. **antipodes** (an TIP uh deez´) *n.* two places on opposite sides of the Earth.

greatest braveries. Before a fire upon a seat like a bedstead, he sat covered with a great robe made of raccoon skins and all the tails hanging by. <u>On either hand did sit a young wench of sixteen or eighteen years and along on each side the house, two rows of men and behind them as many women, with all their heads and shoulders painted red, many of their heads bedecked with the white down of birds, but every one with something, and a great chain of white beads about their necks.</u>

At his entrance before the King, all the people gave a great shout. The queen of Appomattoc was appointed to bring him water to wash his hands, and another brought him a bunch of feathers, instead of a towel, to dry them; having feasted him after their best barbarous manner they could, a long consultation was held, but the conclusion was, two great stones were brought before Powhatan: then as many as could, laid hands on him, dragged him to them, and thereon laid his head and being ready with their clubs to beat out his brains, Pocahontas, the King's dearest daughter, when no entreaty could prevail, got his head in her arms and laid her own upon his to save him from death; whereat the Emperor was contented he should live to make him hatchets, and her bells, beads, and copper, for they thought him as well of all occupations as themselves.[19] For the King himself will make his own robes, shoes, bows, arrows, pots; plant, hunt, or do anything so well as the rest.

Two days after, Powhatan, having disguised himself in the most fearfulest manner he could, caused Captain Smith to be brought forth to a great house in the woods and there upon a mat by the fire to be left alone. Not long after, from behind a mat that divided the house, was made the most dolefulest noise he ever heard; then Powhatan more like a devil than a man, with some two hundred more as black as himself, came unto him and told him now they were friends, and presently he should go to Jamestown to send him two great guns and a grindstone for which he would give him the country of Capahowasic and forever esteem him as his son Nantaquond.

So to Jamestown with twelve guides Powhatan sent him. That night they quartered in the woods, he still expecting (as he had done all this long time of his imprisonment) every hour to be put to one death or other, for all their feasting. But almighty God (by His divine providence) had <u>mollified</u> the hearts of those stern barbarians with compassion. The next morning betimes they came to the fort, where Smith having used the savages with what kindness he could, he showed Rawhunt, Powhatan's trusty servant, two

> **Vocabulary Development: mollified** (MAHL uh fyd) *v.* soothed; calmed

---

19. **as well . . . themselves** capable of making them just as well as they could themselves.

TAKE NOTES

Reading Strategy

Reread the underlined sentence. **Break the sentence down** and answer the following questions about it.

1. How old are the young wenches?

_____

_____

2. What color are the heads and shoulders of the men and women painted?

_____

_____

3. What do many of them have on their heads?

_____

_____

4. What do they have around their necks?

_____

_____

Reading Check

How does Pocahontas save Smith's life?

_____

_____

Reading Check

What does Powhatan do to frighten Smith?

_____

_____

_____

Reread the bracketed sentence.
Break the sentence down and
answer the following questions
about it.

1. What are the strongest settlers
getting ready to do?

_____

_____

2. How does Smith stop them?

_____

_____

_____

How does Pocahontas save the
lives of the settlers?

_____

_____

_____

_____

_____

_____

demiculverins[20] and a millstone to carry Powhatan; they
found them somewhat too heavy, but when they did see him
discharge them, being loaded with stones, among the boughs
of a great tree loaded with icicles, the ice and branches came
so tumbling down that the poor savages ran away half dead
with fear. But at last we regained some conference with them
and gave them such toys and sent to Powhatan, his women,
and children such presents as gave them in general full
content.

Now in Jamestown they were all in combustion,[21] the
strongest preparing once more to run away with the pinnace;
which, with the hazard of his life, with saker falcon[22] and
musket shot, Smith forced now the third time to stay or sink.

Some, no better than they should be, had plotted with the
President the next day to have him put to death by the
Levitical law,[23] for the lives of Robinson and Emry; pretending
the fault was his that had led them to their ends: but he
quickly took such order with such lawyers that he laid them
by their heels till he sent some of them prisoners for England.

Now every once in four or five days, Pocahontas with her
attendants brought him so much provision that saved many
of their lives, that else for all this had starved with hunger.

His relation of the plenty he had seen, especially at
Werowocomoco, and of the state and bounty of Powhatan (which till
that time was unknown), so revived their dead spirits (especially the
love of Pocahontas) as all men's fear was abandoned.

Thus you may see what difficulties still crossed any good
endeavor; and the good success of the business being thus
oft brought to the very period of destruction; yet you see by
what strange means God hath still delivered it.

---

20. **demiculverins** (dem ee KUL vuhr inz) large cannons.
21. **combustion** (kuhm BUS chuhn) *n.* tumult.
22. **saker falcon** small cannon.
23. **Levitical law** "He that killeth man shall surely be put to death" (Leviticus 24:17).

Reader's Response: If you had the opportunity to travel to a
new country where you might face many difficulties, would you
go? Why?

_____

_____

Thinking About the Skill: How did knowing that this is a **narrative account** written by John Smith himself affect the way
you read this selection?

_____

_____

from Of Plymouth Plantation

Summary This **narrative account** tells of the Puritans' first journey to the New World. The first part of the narrative describes their voyage. The second section describes the hardships of their first winter in Massachusetts. The third part tells how the Puritans received help from Native Americans and made a peace treaty with them.

Note-taking Guide

Use this table to record how the settlers survived hardship and danger.

Section of text	Hardships the settlers faced	What the settlers did
Of Their Voyage		
The Starving Time		
Indian Relations		

from The General History of Virginia •
from Of Plymouth Plantation

1. **Literary Analysis**: Find examples in the selections of these important characteristics of **narrative accounts**. Write your answers in the chart.

What the Writer Saw

Selection

Factual Information

What the Writer Heard

Subjective Bias

2. **Literary Analysis**: What was Smith's purpose in writing his **narrative account** of exploring Virginia?

_____

_____

3. **Literary Analysis**: What was Bradford's purpose in writing his narrative account of Plymouth Plantation?

_____

_____

4. **Reading Strategy**: Choose a sentence in the narratives that you found difficult to understand. Try **breaking down the sentence** to separate the hard language from the key parts. Write what the sentence means in your own words.

Original sentence: _____

Your interpretation of the sentence: _____

5. **Hypothesize**: Explain how Bradford's account might have been different if the Pilgrims had successfully settled at their original destination farther south.

_____

_____

WEB SITES

About Web Sites

A **Web site** is a collection of Web pages—words and pictures on a topic that can be found on the Internet. Each page has its own URL, or "address." Web sites feature underlined words and icons that serve as links to other sites or pages. You can find more information by clicking on these words.

The Web can be a wonderful tool for business or learning. You can buy, sell, or trade things on the Web. It also offers great ways to learn.

Reading Strategy

Learn how to locate appropriate information to get the most out of Internet research. Use a search engine. It will list any page on the Web that has words matching a search term you type in. Use specific words when you use a search engine. If you are looking for information on the Puritans who settled in America, search for the word *Pilgrim*. Too broad a term, such as *colony,* will give you a list that is too long.

The box below lists a few of the features found on Web sites. Not every feature will be useful. Keep your purpose in mind as you explore.

Elements of Web Sites

- **Links, hotspotted text**, and other **navigation elements** help you move around the site quickly. Click on any area of the page over which your cursor changes to a hand, and you will be brought to a linked page.

- **A SEARCH function** helps you locate information anywhere on the site, using search terms.

- **Photos, videos, and audio clips** are added to many sites. You may need to download additional software to use these resources.

- **Links** connect you to other pages within the site and to other related Web sites.

- **Contact information** tells you who sponsored the site. An e-mail address to which you may send questions or comments may be included.

Build Understanding

Knowing this term will help you understand the information on this Web site.

virtual tour (VER choo uhl TOOR) tour that is taken through a computer

---

Stop to Reflect

Web designers work to create home pages that look good so that visitors will want to explore the site further. Do you think the designers of this site were successful? Why or why not?

_____

_____

_____

Reading Web Pages

The words at the top of the pictures contain information. Circle the link you would click on if you wanted to get directions to Plimoth Plantation.

_____

_____

_____

Reading Strategy

A Web site's home page often contains many links to other pages within the site. These links help you find **appropriate information**. Links can be text or images. Circle the text link that will tell you how to contact the site's sponsor, Plimoth Plantation.

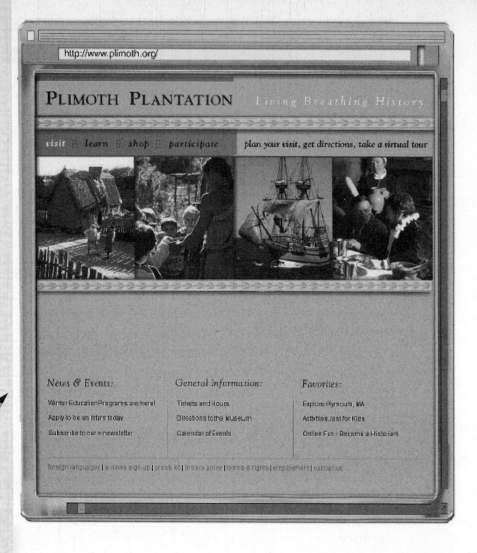

http://www.plimoth.org/

PLIMOTH PLANTATION *Living Breathing History*

visit :: learn :: shop :: participate   plan your visit, get directions, take a virtual tour

News & Events:
Winter Education Programs are here!
Apply to be an intern today
Subscribe to our e-newsletter

General Information:
Tickets and Hours
Directions to the Museum
Calendar of Events

Favorites:
Explore Plymouth, MA
Activities Just for Kids
Online Fun - Become a Historian!

foreign language | e-news sign-up | press kit | privacy policy | terms & rights | employment | contact us

http://www.plimoth.org/visit/what/1627.asp

PLIMOTH PLANTATION *Living Breathing History*

virtual tour : what to see & do : plan your visit : explore plymouth, ma : calendar of events : group tours : functions

what to see & do

1627 pilgrim village

hobbamock's homesite

mayflower II

crafts center

nye barn

thanksgiving exhibit

dining

practical questions
about visiting

Featured Item in
Our Shop :
Making of a Colony Video

*"Welcome to the town! How do you
fare?
Are you just passing through, or
mayhaps you are desiring to settle in
this wilderness?"*

1627 Pilgrim Village

This is one of the ways you may be greeted in the 1627 Pilgrim Village,
a re-creation of the small farming town built by English colonists in the
midst of the Wampanoag homeland. Find yourself immersed in the year
1627, just seven years after the voyage of the Mayflower. In the village
you will be surrounded by the modest timber-framed houses, fragrant
raised-bed gardens, well-tended livestock and fascinating townspeople
of Plymouth Colony, the first permanent English settlement in New
England.

The people you will meet are costumed role players who have taken on
the names, viewpoints and life histories of the people who actually lived
in the colony in 1627, popularly known as the 'Pilgrims' today. Each
one has a unique story to tell. Learn about the colony's difficult begin-
nings or discover the gossip of the day. Ask about religious beliefs,
medical practices or relations with the local Wampanoag People. Talk
to a housewife and learn what a "pottage" is, or see how a duck or
bluefish is cooked on the hearth. Help a young colonist pull up a few
weeds in a cornfield, mix daub with your feet for a house under con-
struction, or just relax on a bench enjoying the unique atmosphere of
17th-century New Plymouth.

Stop to Reflect

Why do you think the navigation
bar, which is bracketed, appears
not just on the home page but also
on this interior page?

_____

_____

_____

Reading Strategy

Circle the text you
would click on if you
wanted to **locate information** about
the Mayflower II.

Reading Informational Materials

List five key words you could use to
access this **Web site**.

1. _____

2. _____

3. _____

4. _____

5. _____

THINKING ABOUT THE WEB SITE

1. What should you do to get the Web site's information in Spanish?

_____

2. Why are pictures on the home page used as links?

_____

READING STRATEGY

3. How can you use the Web site to buy books about seventeenth-century New England?

_____

4. On the home page, under what category do you find a link to Plimoth Plantation's calendar of events?

_____

TIMED WRITING: EVALUATION (20 minutes)

Use this cluster diagram to brainstorm the features of a well-organized Web site. Think about the features of a Web site, such as links, hotspotted text, photos, videos, and SEARCH functions. Does the Web site offer these things? Use the cluster diagram to write your evaluation.

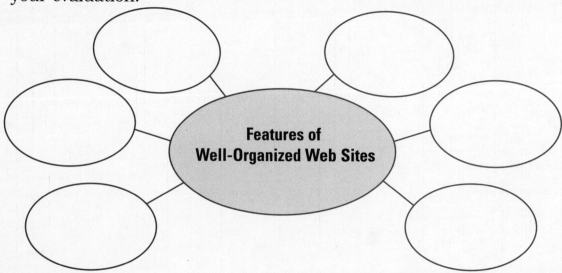

Features of
Well-Organized Web Sites

Huswifery • To My Dear and Loving Husband

LITERARY ANALYSIS

Puritan Plain Style is a writing style used by many Puritan writers. This style reflects the simple, straightforward Puritan lifestyle. Characteristics of Puritan Plain Style include

- short words
- direct statements
- references to everyday, ordinary objects.

Puritans believed that poetry should be written about religious subjects in order to serve God.

READING STRATEGY

- When you **paraphrase** a written work, you restate the main ideas in your own words. Paraphrasing is a good skill to use when reading poetry. For example, Puritan poetry may be written in a simple style, but it can still be difficult to understand. Paraphrasing can help you clarify complicated ideas expressed by these Puritan poets.
- When you read a line from these poems that you do not understand, try to paraphrase it. Use a diagram like this one to organize your paraphrases.

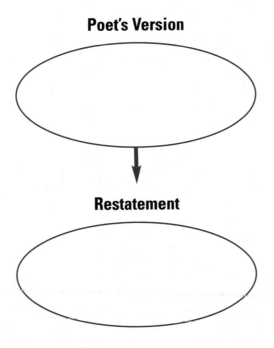

Poet's Version

Restatement

Huswifery • To My Dear and Loving Husband

Summaries Taylor's poem is addressed to God. The speaker in the poem compares himself to a spinning wheel that turns yarn into cloth. The speaker wants to be changed by God into a person who is worthy of being saved. In Bradstreet's poem, the speaker addresses her husband. She expresses her deep love for him, which will endure even after their lives on earth are over.

Note-taking Guide

Use this chart to help you compare elements of these two poems.

Taylor		Bradstreet
	The poet is speaking to...?	
	Images in poem	
	Religious references	

Huswifery • To My Dear and Loving Husband

1. **Literary Analysis: Puritan Plain Style** reflects the Puritans' plain, simple lives. Use this chart to list words, phrases, and references in each poem that represent Puritan Plain Style.

Concept **Thy spinning wheel complete**		*Perception* **References to household objects reflect plain lives**
	→	

2. **Analyze:** Analyze each poem to identify characteristics that are not typical of Puritan Plain Style.

   Taylor's poem: _____

   Bradstreet's poem: _____

3. **Reading Strategy: Paraphrase** these passages from "To My Dear and Loving Husband" by restating in your own words what the passages mean.

   a. Lines 5-6: _____

   b. Lines 9-12: _____

4. **Reading Strategy: Paraphrase** these passages from "Huswifery" by restating in your own words what the passages mean.

   a. Lines 9-12: _____

   b. Lines 13-16: _____

5. **Interpret:** What images in "To My Dear and Loving Husband" suggest the richness of the love that the speaker and her husband share?

   _____

from Sinners in the Hands of an Angry God

LITERARY ANALYSIS

A **sermon** is a speech given by a preacher in a house of worship. A sermon is a type of **oratory,** or formal public speaking. As you read, keep in mind these features of an oratory:

• It is persuasive.

• It appeals to the emotions of listeners.

• It addresses the needs of listeners.

• It calls for listeners to take action.

• It uses colorful language.

READING STRATEGY

Context clues help you understand the meanings of unfamiliar words. A word's context is its surrounding words, phrases, and sentences. Look for context clues to find the meaning of *abominable* in the following sentence:

> You are ten thousand times more abominable in his [God's] eyes than the most hateful venomous serpent is in ours. . . .

The context clue here is in the comparison. Edwards says that the way a sinner looks in God's eyes is like the way a hateful snake looks in our eyes. From this clue, you can guess that *abominable* must be close in meaning to *horrible* or *disgusting*.

Use this chart to help you find the meaning of unfamiliar words.

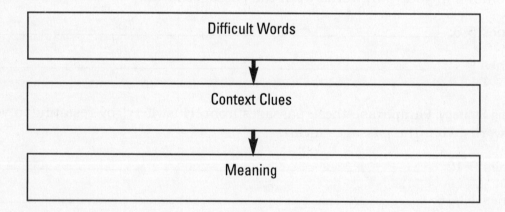

Difficult Words

↓

Context Clues

↓

Meaning

from Sinners in the Hands of an Angry God

Jonathan Edwards

Summary This excerpt from Edwards's sermon describes God's rising anger against the sinners in the congregation. These sinners, Edwards says, are like spiders that their angry God holds over hell. Edwards tells his listeners that they can save their souls from everlasting suffering only if they beg God for forgiveness now and experience the saving grace of conversion, which will give them a place among the elect, or those chosen by God.

Note-taking Guide

Use this chart to record details of what Edwards tells the sinners in his audience.

Purpose	Details to Achieve This Purpose
To motivate listeners to convert and save their souls	• Only the power of God holds you up.

Think about sermons or speeches you have heard that have had a strong effect on you. Were the speakers appealing to your emotions or to your mind?

_____

_____

_____

_____

Literary Analysis

This selection is a **sermon,** or a speech given in a house of worship. Circle two or more words on this page that make it clear that this speech has a religious purpose.

Reading Check

What would happen to the members of Edwards's audience if God let them go?

_____

_____

_____

_____

_____

_____

_____

from Sinners in the Hands of an Angry God
Jonathan Edwards

The complete version of this sermon lasted six hours and caused fear and hysteria in the Connecticut church where Edwards preached. Edwards's conservative religious views made him quite a controversial figure.

This is the case of every one of you that are out of Christt:[1] That world of misery, that lake of burning brimstone, is extended abroad under you. There is the dreadful pit of the glowing flames of the wrath of God; there is Hell's wide gaping mouth open; and you have nothing to stand upon, nor anything to take hold of; there is nothing between you and Hell but the air; it is only the power and mere pleasure of God that holds you up.

You probably are not sensible of this; you find you are kept out of Hell, but do not see the hand of God in it; but look at other things, as the good state of your bodily constitution, your care of your own life, and the means you use for your own preservation. But indeed these things are nothing; if God should withdraw his hand, they would avail no more to keep you from falling than the thin air to hold up a person that is suspended in it.

Your wickedness makes you as it were heavy as lead, and to tend downwards with great weight and pressure towards Hell; and if God should let you go, you would immediately sink and swiftly descend and plunge into the bottomless gulf, and your healthy constitution, and your own care and prudence, and best contrivance, and all your righteousness, would have no more influence to uphold you and keep you out of Hell, than a spider's web would have to stop a fallen rock. Were it not for the sovereign pleasure of God, the earth would not bear you one moment . . . The world would spew you out, were it not for the sovereign hand of Him who hath subjected it in hope. There are black clouds of God's wrath now hanging directly over your heads, full of the dreadful storm, and big with thunder; and were it not for the restraining hand of God, it would immediately burst forth upon you. The sovereign pleasure of God, for the present, stays[2] his rough wind; otherwise it would come with fury, and your destruction would come like a

---

1. **out of Christ** not in God's grace.
2. **stays** restrains.

whirlwind, and you would be like the chaff of the summer threshing floor.

The wrath of God is like great waters that are dammed for the present; they increase more and more, and rise higher and higher, till an outlet is given; and the longer the stream is stopped, the more rapid and mighty is its course, when once it is let loose. It is true, that judgment against your evil works has not been executed hitherto; the floods of God's vengeance have been withheld; but your guilt in the meantime is constantly increasing, and you are every day treasuring up more wrath; the waters are constantly rising, and waxing more and more mighty; and there is nothing but the mere pleasure of God, that holds the waters back, that are unwilling to be stopped, and press hard to go forward. If God should only withdraw his hand from the floodgate, it would immediately fly open, and the fiery floods of the fierceness and wrath of God, would rush forth with inconceivable fury, and would come upon you with <u>omnipotent</u> power; and if your strength were ten thousand times greater than it is, yea, ten thousand times greater than the strength of the stoutest, sturdiest devil in Hell, it would be nothing to withstand or endure it.

The bow of God's wrath is bent, and the arrow made ready on the string, and justice bends the arrow at your heart, and strains the bow, and it is nothing but the mere pleasure of God, and that of an angry God, without any promise or obligation at all, that keeps the arrow one moment from being made drunk with your blood. Thus all you that never passed under a great change of heart, by the mighty power of the spirit of God upon your souls; all you that were never born again, and made new creatures, and raised from being dead in sin, to a state of new, and before altogether unexperienced light and life, are in the hands of an angry God. However you may have reformed your life in many things, and may have had religious affections, and may keep up a form of religion in your families and closets,[3] and in the house of God, it is nothing but His mere pleasure that keeps you from being this moment swallowed up in everlasting destruction. However unconvinced you may now be of the truth of what you hear, by and by you will be fully convinced of it.

Vocabulary Development: omnipotent (ahm NIP uh tuhnt) *adj.*
all-powerful

---

3. **closets** *n.* small, private rooms for meditation.

TAKE NOTES

Reading Strategy

Notice the underlined word, *omnipotent*. This word is formed with the **Latin prefix** *omni-*, meaning "all," and the root *potent*, meaning "powerful." Use a dictionary to find two other words with the same Latin prefix. Write the words and a brief definition of each word below.

_____

_____

_____

Reading Strategy

Reread the bracketed sentence. Which listeners are in the hands of an angry God?

_____

_____

_____

Literary Analysis

This sermon is a form of **oratory**, or public speaking that is formal, persuasive, and emotionally appealing. From accounts of this sermon, Edwards read it in a calm, level voice. The emotional appeal of the oratory came, then, from the images, or word pictures, that Edwards used. Circle two striking images on this page.

One technique of **oratory** is repetition, or repeating the same idea for effect. Read the bracketed sentence and circle the repeated word. What effect does this repeated word have on you as a reader?

_____

_____

_____

_____

Reading Strategy

Write three adjectives to describe God as pictured by Edwards on this page.

1. _____

2. _____

3. _____

Reading Check

What will happen to listeners who continue in an unconverted state?

_____

_____

_____

_____

_____

_____

Those that are gone from being in the like circumstances with you, see that it was so with them; for destruction came suddenly upon most of them; when they expected nothing of it, and while they were saying, peace and safety: now they see, that those things on which they depended for peace and safety, were nothing but thin air and empty shadows.

The God that holds you over the pit of Hell, much as one holds a spider, or some loathsome insect over the fire, abhors you, and is dreadfully provoked: his wrath towards you burns like fire; he looks upon you as worthy of nothing else, but to be cast into the fire; he is of purer eyes than to bear to have you in his sight; you are ten thousand times more abominable in his eyes, than the most hateful venomous serpent is in ours. . . .

O sinner! Consider the fearful danger you are in: it is a great furnace of wrath, a wide and bottomless pit, full of the fire of wrath, that you are held over in the hand of that God, whose wrath is provoked and incensed as much against you, as against many of the damned in Hell. You hang by a slender thread, with the flames of divine wrath flashing about it, and ready every moment to singe it, and burn it asunder; and you have no interest in any mediator, and nothing to lay hold of to save yourself, nothing to keep off the flames of wrath, nothing of your own, nothing that you ever have done, nothing that you can do, to induce God to spare you one moment. . . .

When God beholds the <u>ineffable</u> extremity of your case, and sees your torment to be so vastly disproportioned to your strength, and sees how your poor soul is crushed, and sinks down, as it were, into an infinite gloom; he will have no compassion upon you, he will not forbear the executions of his wrath, or in the least lighten his hand; there shall be no moderation or mercy, nor will God then at all stay his rough wind; he will have no regard to your welfare, nor be at all careful lest you should suffer too much in any other sense, than only that you shall *not suffer beyond what strict justice requires*. . . .

God stands ready to pity you; this is a day of mercy; you may cry now with some encouragement of obtaining mercy. But once the day of mercy is past, your most lamentable and <u>dolorous</u> cries and shrieks will be in vain; you will be wholly lost and thrown away of God, as

---

Vocabulary Development: ineffable (In EF uh buhl) *adj.* inexpressible; unable to be spoken
dolorous (DOH luhr uhs) *adj.* sad; mournful

to any regard to your welfare. God will have no other use to put you to, but to suffer misery; you shall be continued in being to no other end; for you will be a vessel of wrath fitted to destruction; and there will be no other use of this vessel, but to be filled full of wrath. . . .

Thus it will be with you that are in an unconverted state, if you continue in it; the infinite might, and majesty, and terribleness of the omnipotent God shall be magnified upon you, in the ineffable strength of your torments. You shall be tormented in the presence of the holy angels, and in the presence of the Lamb,[4] and when you shall be in this state of suffering, the glorious inhabitants of Heaven shall go forth and look on the awful spectacle, that they may see what the wrath and fierceness of the Almighty is; and when they have seen it, they will fall down and adore that great power and majesty. . . .

It would be dreadful to suffer this fierceness and wrath of Almighty God one moment; but you must suffer it to all eternity. There will be no end to this exquisite horrible misery. When you look forward, you shall see a long forever, a boundless duration before you, which will swallow up your thoughts and amaze your soul; and you will absolutely despair of ever having any deliverance, any end, any mitigation, any rest at all. . . .

How dreadful is the state of those that are daily and hourly in the danger of this great wrath and infinite misery! But this is the dismal case of every soul in this congregation that has not been born again, however moral and strict, sober and religious, they may otherwise be. Oh that you would consider it, whether you be young or old! . . . Those of you that finally continue in a natural condition, that shall keep you out of Hell longest will be there in a little time! Your damnation does not slumber; it will come swiftly, and, in all probability, very suddenly upon many of you. You have reason to wonder that you are not already in Hell. It is doubtless the case of some whom you have seen and known, that never deserved Hell more than you, and that heretofore appeared as likely to have been now alive as you. Their case is past all hope; they are crying in extreme misery and perfect despair; but here you are in the land of the living and in the house of God, and have an opportunity to obtain salvation. What would not those poor damned hopeless souls give for one day's opportunity such as you now enjoy!

4. **the Lamb** Jesus.

from Sinners in the Hands of an Angry God **39**

TAKE NOTES

Reading Strategy

Look at the word *mitigation*, underlined in blue. To find the meaning of a word you do not know, look at the words and phrases around that word, or the **context clues**. Circle the words around *mitigation* that are **context clues**. Now write a definition of *mitigation* below.

_____

_____

_____

Reading Strategy

Reread the bracketed paragraph and **summarize** it on separate paper. Be sure that your summary answers these questions: What should all members of the congregation consider? How fast will damnation come? What opportunity do the members of the congregation have?

Stop to Reflect

Throughout this **sermon**, Edwards has painted a frightening picture of God's power and anger. In the last paragraph on this page, he begins to talk to the congregation about mercy and the opportunity for hope. Why does he do this?

Literary Analysis

As an example of persuasive **oratory,** this section of the **sermon** ends with a call to action. What does Edwards encourage his listeners to do?

_____

_____

_____

_____

_____

_____

And now you have an extraordinary opportunity, a day wherein Christ has thrown the door of mercy wide open, and stands in calling and crying with a loud voice to poor sinners; a day wherein many are flocking to him, and pressing into the kingdom of God. Many are daily coming from the east, west, north and south; many that were very lately in the same miserable condition that you are in, are now in a happy state, with their hearts filled with love to him who has loved them, and washed them from their sins in his own blood, and rejoicing in hope of the glory of God. How awful is it to be left behind at such a day! To see so many others feasting, while you are pining and perishing! To see so many rejoicing and singing for joy of heart, while you have cause to mourn for sorrow of heart, and howl for vexation of spirit! . . .

Therefore, let everyone that is out of Christ now awake and fly from the wrath to come. The wrath of Almighty God is now undoubtedly hanging over a great part of this congregation: let everyone fly out of Sodom.[5] "Haste and escape for your lives, look not behind you, escape to the mountain, lest you be consumed."[6]

---

5. **Sodom** (SAHD uhm) in the Bible, a city destroyed by fire because of the sinfulness of its people.
6. **"Haste . . . consumed"** from Genesis 19:17, the angels' warning to Lot, the only virtuous man in Sodom, to flee the city before they destroy it.

Reader's Response: What would your reaction be if your principal began the school year with a speech as frightening as Edwards's sermon?

_____

_____

_____

Thinking About the Skill: How did knowing that this selection is an example of **oratory** help you to understand the techniques that Edwards uses?

_____

_____

_____

from Sinners in the Hands of an Angry God

1. **Literary Analysis:** What is the main message of Edwards's **sermon**?

   _____

   _____

   _____

2. **Literary Analysis:** Edwards uses fear in his **sermon** to motivate his congregation. Why do you think that this strategy works well for his purpose?

   _____

   _____

   _____

3. **Connect:** Identify five symbols that Edwards uses to describe God's wrath. Use this chart.

4. **Reading Strategy:** Use **context clues** to define the underlined word: "you are every day treasuring up more wrath; the waters are constantly rising, and waxing more and more mighty . . ."

   _____

   _____

   _____

from Sinners in the Hands of an Angry God (cont'd)

5. **Evaluate:** Given his purpose and his audience, do you think Edwards's sermon was effective? Why or why not?

_____

_____

_____

_____

_____

from The Autobiography • *from* Poor Richard's Almanack

LITERARY ANALYSIS

An **autobiography** is the story of a person's life, told by the person. Autobiography was a new form of literature when Benjamin Franklin wrote *The Autobiography*. His work set a standard for this new type of writing.

- An autobiography presents events in a person's life according to how that person sees them.
- An autobiography can give personal views of history. Information about the politics, habits, ideas, and values of a society can be found in autobiographies.

Use this chart to record details from *The Autobiography*. These details will tell you about Franklin's attitudes and his world.

Details About Franklin's Life	Details About Franklin's Attitudes	Details About Franklin's Times

READING STRATEGY

Franklin presents many details about his life, his goals, and his interests. You can **draw conclusions** about Franklin and his life by using evidence from the text and from your own experiences. A conclusion is an opinion you reach by pulling together facts and details.

As you read, follow this pattern for drawing conclusions about Franklin's character:

- **Details:** Franklin changes his plan when he sees he is not doing what he expected to do.
- **Personal Experience:** You thought of a different approach when you failed to meet a certain goal.
- **Conclusion:** Franklin is likely to make adjustments to meet his goals.

from The Autobiography

Benjamin Franklin

Summary In this section of his autobiography, Franklin explains how he plans to reach moral perfection. He lists thirteen virtues, or qualities, that he will work on one by one. To keep track of his progress, Franklin writes the virtues in a special notebook. He places a black mark beside a virtue every time he forgets to follow it. Each week he works on a different virtue. Franklin finds that his plan is helpful but not completely successful.

Note-taking Guide

Use this chart to keep track of the different virtues that Franklin works on. List the virtues in order from most important to least important.

Virtues to Help Franklin Reach His Goal
• Temperance
•
•
•
•
•
•
•
•
•
•
•
•

from The Autobiography
Benjamin Franklin

You probably know Benjamin Franklin as a statesman and a signer of the Declaration of Independence. This selection shows a more personal side of Franklin. Franklin describes his carefully planned project to achieve moral perfection.

It was about this time I conceived the bold and <u>arduous</u> project of arriving at moral perfection. I wished to live without committing any fault at any time; I would conquer all that either natural inclination, custom, or company might lead me into. As I knew, or thought I knew, what was right and wrong, I did not see why I might not always do the one and avoid the other. But I soon found I had undertaken a task of more difficulty than I had imagined. While my care was employed in guarding against one fault, I was often surprised by another; habit took the advantage of inattention; inclination was sometimes too strong for reason. I concluded, at length, that the mere speculative conviction that it was our interest to be completely virtuous was not sufficient to prevent our slipping; and that the contrary habits must be broken, and good ones acquired and established, before we can have any dependence on a steady, uniform rectitude of conduct. For this purpose I therefore contrived the following method.

In the various enumerations of the moral virtues I had met with in my reading, I found the catalog more or less numerous, as different writers included more or fewer ideas under the same name. *Temperance*, for example, was by some confined to eating and drinking, while by others it was extended to mean the moderating every other pleasure, appetite, inclination, or passion, bodily or mental, even to our <u>avarice</u> and ambition. I proposed to myself, for the sake of clearness, to use rather more names, with fewer ideas annexed to each, than a few names with more ideas; and I included under thirteen names of virtues all that at that time occurred to me as necessary or desirable, and annexed to each a short precept, which fully expressed the extent I gave to its meaning.

These names of virtues, with their precepts, were:

1. TEMPERANCE Eat not to dullness; drink not to elevation.
2. SILENCE Speak not but what may benefit others or yourself; avoid trifling conversation.
3. ORDER Let all your things have their places; let each part of your business have its time.

Vocabulary Development: arduous (AHR joo wuhs) *adj.* difficult
avarice (AV uhr is) *n.* greed

TAKE NOTES

Activate Prior Knowledge

Many people take time to make New Year's resolutions every year. As you read this selection, remind yourself of any plans or resolutions you have made. As you read, think about how they are like or unlike Franklin's project to achieve moral perfection.

Literary Analysis

This selection is a form of nonfiction called **autobiography**. In an autobiography, a person tells the story of his or her own life, using the pronoun I. In the first paragraph, circle the pronoun I every time it appears.

Reading Strategy

Read this selection slowly, one sentence at a time. As you read, **make inferences,** or read between the lines for information. For example, what inferences can you make about Franklin's character from reading the bracketed sentence in the first paragraph?

_____

_____

_____

How many virtues does Franklin commit himself to?

_____

_____

_____

As you read, you often encounter **words with multiple meanings**—that is, words that mean different things in different situations or contexts. Franklin uses the word *industry,* for example, to mean working hard and wasting no time. Use a dictionary to find another meaning for the word *industry* and write the meaning below.

_____

_____

_____

Franklin decides to work on his virtues one at a time. Why does he start with temperance? Circle the sentence that answers this question and write the answer below in your own words.

_____

_____

_____

4. RESOLUTION Resolve to perform what you ought; perform without fail what you resolve.
5. FRUGALITY Make no expense but to do good to others or yourself; i.e., waste nothing.
6. INDUSTRY Lose no time; be always employed in something useful; cut off all unnecessary actions.
7. SINCERITY Use no hurtful deceit; think innocently and justly, and, if you speak, speak accordingly.
8. JUSTICE Wrong none by doing injuries, or omitting the benefits that are your duty.
9. MODERATION Avoid extremes; forebear resenting injuries so much as you think they deserve.
10. CLEANLINESS Tolerate no uncleanliness in body, clothes, or habitation.
11. TRANQUILLITY Be not disturbed at trifles, or at accidents common or unavoidable.
12. CHASTITY
13. HUMILITY Imitate Jesus and Socrates.[1]

My intention being to acquire the *habitude* of all these virtues, I judged it would be well not to distract my attention by attempting the whole at once but to fix it on one of them at a time; and, when I should be master of that, then to proceed to another, and so on, till I should have gone through the thirteen; and, as the previous acquisition of some might facilitate the acquisition of certain others, I arranged them with that view, as they stand above. *Temperance* first, as it tends to procure that coolness and clearness of head, which is so necessary where constant vigilance was to be kept up, and guard maintained against the unremitting attraction of ancient habits and the force of perpetual temptations. This being acquired and established, *Silence* would be more easy; and my desire being to gain knowledge at the same time that I improved in virtue, and considering that in conversation it was obtained rather by the use of the ears than of the tongue, and therefore wishing to break a habit I was getting into of prattling, punning, and joking, which only made me acceptable to trifling company, I gave *Silence* the second place. This and the next, *Order,* I expected would allow me more time for attending to my project and my studies. *Resolution,* once become habitual, would keep me firm in my endeavors to obtain all the subsequent virtues; *Frugality* and *Industry* freeing me from my remaining debt and producing affluence and independence, would make more easy the practice of *Sincerity* and *Justice,* etc., etc. Conceiving then, that,

---

Vocabulary Development: vigilance (VIJ uh luhns) *n.* watchfulness

---

1. **Socrates** (SAHK ruh teez) Greek philosopher and teacher (470?–399 B.C.).

agreeably to the advice of Pythagoras[2] in his *Golden Verses*, daily examination would be necessary, I contrived the following method for conducting that examination.

I made a little book, in which I allotted a page for each of the virtues. I ruled each page with red ink, so as to have seven columns, one for each day of the week, marking each column with a letter for the day. I crossed these columns with thirteen red lines, marking the beginning of each line with the first letter of one of the virtues, on which line and in its proper column I might mark, by a little black spot, every fault I found upon examination to have been committed respecting that virtue upon that day.

I determined to give a week's strict attention to each of the virtues successively. Thus, in the first week, my great guard was to avoid every[3] the least offense against *Temperance*, leaving the other virtues to their ordinary chance, only marking every evening the faults of the day. Thus, if in the first week I could keep my first line, marked *T.* clear of spots, I supposed the habit of that virtue so much strengthened, and its opposite weakened, that I might venture extending my attention to include the next, and for the following week keep both lines clear of spots. Proceeding thus to the last, I could go through a course complete in thirteen weeks, and four courses in a year. And like him who, having a garden to weed, does not attempt to eradicate all the bad herbs at once, which would exceed his reach and his strength, but works on one of the beds at a time, and, having accomplished the first, proceeds to a second, so I should have, I hoped, the encouraging pleasure of seeing on my pages the progress I made in virtue, by clearing successively my lines of their spots, till in the end, by a number of courses, I should be happy in viewing a clean book, after a thirteen weeks' daily examination. . . .

The precept of *Order* requiring that *every part of my business should have its allotted time*, one page in my little book contained the following scheme of employment for the twenty-four hours of a natural day.

The Morning.
Question. What good shall I do this day?

5
6

Rise, wash, and address *Powerful Goodness!* Contrive day's business, and take the resolution of the

7 day; prosecute the present study, and breakfast.

8

---

2. **Pythagoras** (pi THAG uh ruhs) Greek philosopher and mathematician who lived in the sixth century B.C.
3. **every** even.

TAKE NOTES

Reading Strategy

Continue to **make inferences,** or read between the lines for information. What additional inferences can you make about Franklin now that you have read his list of virtues and his explanation of each one?

_____

_____

Reading Strategy

Reread the bracketed paragraph. Choose one of Franklin's virtues. On a blank sheet of paper, make a page for that virtue, using Franklin's description of his "little book." You will need a red pen or pencil. Now **make an inference** about why this "little book" is a good way for Franklin to keep track of his progress.

_____

_____

_____

Reading Strategy

Making inferences as you read helps you **draw conclusions** about what you are reading, or make general statements based on details from what you've read. What conclusion can you draw about Franklin at this point?

_____

_____

_____

Why does Franklin choose to work on the virtues one at a time?

_____

_____

_____

_____

_____

Because this selection is an **autobiography**, Franklin is giving information about himself and his daily life. He even gives you a schedule for a usual day in his life. What are the similarities between Franklin's day and yours? What are the differences?

_____

_____

_____

Reread the bracketed paragraph. **Draw** one or two **conclusions** about Franklin based on the fact that Franklin eventually stops his plan for acquiring the virtues.

_____

_____

_____

	9	Work.
	10	
	11	
NOON.	12	Read, or overlook
	1	my accounts, and
		dine.
	2	
	3	Work.
	4	
	5	
EVENING.	6	Put things in
Question. What good have I	7	their places.
done today?	8	Supper. Music or
	9	diversion, or
		conversation.
		Examination of the
		day.
	10	
NIGHT.	11	
	12	
	1	Sleep.
	2	
	3	
	4	

I entered upon the execution of this plan for self-examination, and continued it with occasional intermissions for some time. I was surprised to find myself so much fuller of faults than I had imagined; but I had the satisfaction of seeing them diminish. To avoid the trouble of renewing now and then my little book, which, by scraping out the marks on the paper of old faults to make room for new ones in a new course, became full of holes, I transferred my tables and precepts to the ivory leaves of a memorandum book, on which the lines were drawn with red ink that made a durable stain, and on those lines I marked my faults with a black-lead pencil, which marks I could easily wipe out with a wet sponge. After a while I went through one course only in a year, and afterward only one in several years, till at length I omitted them entirely, being employed in voyages and business abroad, with a multiplicity of affairs that interfered; but I always carried my little book with me.

My scheme of *Order* gave me the most trouble; and I found that, though it might be practicable where a man's business was such as to leave him the <u>disposition</u> of his time, that of a journeyman printer, for instance, it was not possible to be exactly observed by a master, who must mix with the world and often receive people of business at their

---

Vocabulary Development: disposition (dis puh ZISH uhn) *n.* management

---

own hours. *Order*, too, with regard to places for things, papers, etc., I found extremely difficult to acquire. I had not been early accustomed to it, and, having an exceeding good memory, I was not so sensible of the inconvenience attending want of method. This article, therefore, cost me so much painful attention, and my faults in it vexed me so much, and I made so little progress in amendment, and had such frequent relapses, that I was almost ready to give up the attempt, and content myself with a faulty character in that respect, like the man who, in buying an ax of a smith, my neighbor, desired to have the whole of its surface as bright as the edge. The smith consented to grind it bright for him if he would turn the wheel; he turned, while the smith pressed the broad face of the ax hard and heavily on the stone, which made the turning of it very fatiguing. The man came every now and then from the wheel to see how the work went on, and at length would take his ax as it was, without farther grinding. "No," said the smith, "turn on, turn on; we shall have it bright by and by; as yet, it is only speckled." "Yes," says the man, *"but I think I like a speckled ax best."* And I believe this may have been the case with many, who, having, for want of some such means as I employed, found the difficulty of obtaining good and breaking bad habits in other points of vice and virtue, have given up the struggle, and concluded that *"a speckled ax was best"*; for something, that pretended to be reason, was every now and then suggesting to me that such extreme nicety as I exacted of myself might be a kind of <u>foppery</u> in morals, which, if it were known, would make me ridiculous; that a perfect character might be attended with the inconvenience of being envied and hated; and that a benevolent man should allow a few faults in himself, to keep his friends in countenance.

In truth, I found myself incorrigible with respect to *Order*; and now I am grown old, and my memory bad, I feel very sensibly the want of it. But, on the whole, though I never arrived at the perfection I had been so ambitious of obtaining, but fell far short of it, yet I was, by the endeavor, a better and a happier man than I otherwise should have been if I had not attempted it; as those who aim at perfect writing by imitating the engraved copies, though they never reached the wished-for excellence of those copies, their hand is mended by the endeavor, and is tolerable while it continues fair and legible.

TAKE NOTES

Stop to Reflect

Franklin begins his project to acquire virtues with energy and good intentions. He does well with the project for several years, but eventually he goes through his course less often. Finally he stops doing it at all. Think about a project you began with high energy and positive intentions, like keeping your room neat or learning to play the piano. How long were you able to continue? Why do you think people often have trouble keeping their projects going over time?

_____

_____

Reading Check

Why is Franklin tempted to give up his efforts to acquire the virtue of Order?

_____

_____

_____

Reading Strategy

Reread the bracketed paragraph slowly. **Draw a conclusion** about the connection between the grinding of the ax and Franklin's problems with Order. You can reach your conclusion by **making inferences** as you read each sentence.

_____

_____

_____

Vocabulary Development: foppery (FAHP uhr ee) *n.* foolishness

Reading Strategy

Notice the word *best,* used several times in this paragraph. *Best* is the superlative form of *good.* It is an example of an **irregular comparison of adjectives and adverbs.** *Good* is the positive form, *better* is the comparative form, and *best* is the superlative form. Other examples of irregular comparisons include *well, bad,* and *little.* Write the comparative and superlative forms of *well, bad,* and *little* below.

_____

_____

Reading Check

Why does Franklin think trying for perfection is worth it, even though he does not completely succeed?

_____

_____

_____

Reading Check

Franklin feels that many of the good things in his life have come from trying to reach moral perfection. List three positive aspects of Franklin's life for which he credits his pursuit of virtue.

1. _____

_____

2. _____

_____

3. _____

_____

It may be well my posterity should be informed that to this little artifice, with the blessing of God, their ancestor owed the constant <u>felicity</u> of his life, down to his seventy-ninth year in which this is written. What reverses may attend the remainder is in the hand of Providence; but, if they arrive, the reflection on past happiness enjoyed ought to help his bearing them with more resignation. To *Temperance* he ascribes his long-continued health, and what is still left to him of a good constitution; to *Industry* and *Frugality,* the early easiness of his circumstances and acquisition of his fortune, with all that knowledge that enabled him to be a useful citizen, and obtained for him some degree of reputation among the learned; to *Sincerity* and *Justice,* the confidence of his country, and the honorable employs it conferred upon him; and to the joint influence of the whole mass of the virtues, <u>even in the imperfect state he was able to acquire them, all that evenness of temper, and that cheerfulness in conversation, which makes his company still sought for, and agreeable even to his younger acquaintance.</u> I hope, therefore, that some of my descendants may follow the example and reap the benefit.

Vocabulary Development: felicity (fuh LIS uh tee) *n.* happiness; bliss

Reader's Response: Franklin has most of his problems with the virtue of Order. Which of Franklin's thirteen virtues do you think you would have the most trouble with? Why?

_____

_____

Thinking About the Skill: How will **making inferences** and **drawing conclusions** help you read other nonfiction and fiction selections?

_____

_____

from Poor Richard's Almanack

Benjamin Franklin

Summary Franklin gives advice about how people should behave. He presents his thoughts in **aphorisms,** or short sayings with a message. Many of his aphorisms come from traditional folk sayings. Sayings such as "Well done is better than well said" tell something about Franklin and what he values.

Note-taking Guide

Aphorisms can sometimes mean more than one thing. Use this chart to examine some of Franklin's sayings. Write down any second meanings.

Saying	Meaning
Keep thy shop, and thy shop will keep thee.	Work hard and your work will earn you money.

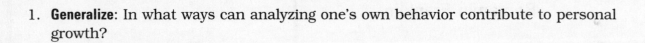
from The Autobiography • from Poor Richard's Almanack

1. **Generalize:** In what ways can analyzing one's own behavior contribute to personal growth?

_____

_____

2. **Literary Analysis:** Franklin's **autobiography** shows that he wants to improve his moral virtues. What does this goal tell you about the time period in which he lived?

_____

_____

3. **Literary Analysis:** Connect an **aphorism** from *Poor Richard's Almanack* to a virtue listed in *The Autobiography*. Explain the connection you make. Use this chart to record your response.

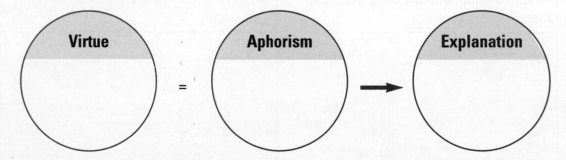

4. **Reading Strategy:** In *The Autobiography*, Franklin keeps track of how much he improves his moral virtues. He explains that he had to adjust his record-keeping system as his plan moved forward. What **conclusion** can you draw about his character based on these adjustments?

_____

_____

from The Interesting Narrative of the Life of Olaudah Equiano

LITERARY ANALYSIS

A **slave narrative** is an autobiographical account of the life of a slave. Slave narratives often show the horrors of slavery, telling about a slave's experiences from his or her point of view. In the following example, Olaudah Equiano describes the conditions on the ship that brought him to Barbados. He uses **emotional appeals**, persuasive statements that inspire sympathy in his readers.

The shrieks of the women, and the groans of the dying, rendered the whole a scene of horror almost inconceivable.
As you read, look for other details that describe the horrors of the voyage.

READING STRATEGY

It is helpful to **summarize** the main points of a challenging text. When you summarize, you state briefly in your own words the main ideas and key details of the text. The following chart will help you summarize Equiano's first paragraph. As you read, write notes in the boxes to help you summarize Equiano's ideas.

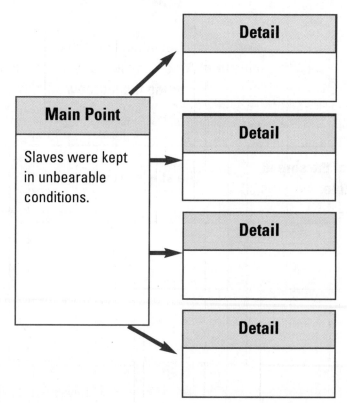

from The Interesting Narrative of the Life of Olaudah Equiano

Summary Olaudah Equiano recalls his experiences aboard a slave ship. He describes the crowded conditions, the sickening smells, and the slaves' despair. He explains that the ship's crew chained, starved, and beat their captives. Many people did not survive the terrible journey. Those who lived were examined and sold when they reached Barbados.

Note-taking Guide

Use this chart to summarize the conditions on a slave ship.

Main Idea

Conditions on slave ships from Africa cause many slaves to die during the journey.

The smell of the ship is terrible.	The ship's crew is cruel.	Many slaves die.

from The Interesting Narrative of the Life of Olaudah Equiano

Olaudah Equiano

Several early editions of The Interesting Narrative of Olaudah Equiano *were published with the poems of Phillis Wheatley, another former slave. Wheatley and Equiano are among the earliest writers in a rich African American literary tradition.*

At last when the ship we were in, had got in all her cargo, they made ready with many fearful noises, and we were all put under deck, so that we could not see how they managed the vessel. But this disappointment was the least of my sorrow. The stench of the hold while we were on the coast was so intolerably <u>loathsome</u>, that it was dangerous to remain there for any time, and some of us had been permitted to stay on the deck for the fresh air; but now that the whole ship's cargo were confined together, it became absolutely <u>pestilential.</u> The closeness of the place, and the heat of the climate, added to the number in the ship, which was so crowded that each had scarcely room to turn himself, almost suffocated us. This produced <u>copious</u> perspirations, so that the air soon became unfit for respiration, from a variety of loathsome smells, and brought on a sickness among the slaves, of which many died—thus falling victims to the <u>improvident avarice</u>, as I may call it, of their purchasers. This wretched situation was again aggravated by the galling of the chains, now become insupportable, and the filth of the necessary tubs, into which the children often fell, and were almost suffocated. The shrieks of the women, and the groans of the dying, rendered the whole a scene of horror almost inconceivable. Happily perhaps, for myself, I was soon reduced so low here that it was thought necessary to keep me almost always on deck; and from my extreme youth I was not put in fetters.[1] In this situation I expected every hour to share the fate of my companions, some of whom

---

Vocabulary Development: **loathsome** (LOHTH suhm) *adj.* hateful; detestable
pestilential (pes tuh LEN shuhl) *adj.* likely to cause disease
copious (KOH pee uhs) *adj.* plentiful; abundant
improvident (im PRAHV uh duhnt) *adj.* short-sighted; failing to provide for the future
avarice (AV uhr is) *n.* greed for riches

---

1. **fetters** (FET uhrz) *n.* chains

TAKE NOTES

Activate Prior Knowledge

It is almost impossible to imagine the horror that Equiano describes in this **slave narrative**, or true story of his own life. How can horrifying experiences change the way someone looks at the world?

_____

_____

_____

_____

_____

Reading Strategy

Reread the two bracketed sentences. Briefly **summarize** the two sentences, or restate them in your own words.

_____

_____

_____

_____

Reading Check

Why is the narrator, or storyteller, not put in chains?

_____

_____

_____

_____

_____

_____

Circle three phrases on this page that contribute to the **emotional appeal** of this selection.

Summarize, or rewrite briefly in your own words, the incident in the bracketed sentence on this page.

_____

_____

_____

_____

_____

_____

_____

In the middle of these horrors, the narrator stops to notice flying fishes and a quadrant. What does that tell you about what kind of person he is?

_____

_____

_____

_____

_____

_____

were almost daily brought upon deck at the point of death, which I began to hope would soon put an end to my miseries. Often did I think many of the inhabitants of the deep much more happy than myself. I envied them the freedom they enjoyed, and as often wished I could change my condition for theirs. Every circumstance I met with, served only to render my state more painful, and heightened my apprehensions, and my opinion of the cruelty of the whites.

One day they had taken a number of fishes; and when they had killed and satisfied themselves with as many as they thought fit, to our astonishment who were on deck, rather than give any of them to us to eat, as we expected, they tossed the remaining fish into the sea again, although we begged and prayed for some as well as we could, but in vain; and some of my countrymen, being pressed by hunger, took an opportunity, when they thought no one saw them, of trying to get a little privately; but they were discovered, and the attempt procured them some very severe floggings. One day, when we had a smooth sea and moderate wind, two of my wearied countrymen who were chained together (I was near them at the time), preferring death to such a life of misery, somehow made through the nettings and jumped into the sea; immediately, another quite dejected fellow, who, on account of his illness, was suffered to be out of irons, also followed their example; and I believe many more would very soon have done the same, if they had not been prevented by the ship's crew, who were instantly alarmed. Those of us that were the most active, were in a moment put down under the deck; and there was such a noise and confusion amongst the people of the ship as I never heard before, to stop her, and get the boat out to go after the slaves. However, two of the wretches were drowned, but they got the other, and afterwards flogged him unmercifully, for thus attempting to prefer death to slavery. In this manner we continued to undergo more hardships than I can now relate, hardships which are inseparable from this accursed trade. Many a time we were near suffocation from the want of fresh air, which we were often without for whole days together. This, and the stench of the necessary tubs, carried off many.

During our passage, I first saw flying fishes, which surprised me very much; they used frequently to fly across the ship, and many of them fell on the deck. I also now first saw the use of the quadrant;[2] I had often with astonishment seen the mariners make observations with it, and I could not think what it meant. They at last took notice of my surprise; and one of them, willing to increase it, as well as to gratify my curiosity, made me one day look through it. The clouds appeared to me to be land, which disappeared as they

2. **quadrant** (KWAH druhnt) _n._ an instrument used by navigators to determine the position of a ship.

passed along. This heightened my wonder; and I was now more persuaded than ever, that I was in another world, and that every thing about me was magic. At last, we came in sight of the island of Barbados, at which the whites on board gave a great shout, and made many signs of joy to us. We did not know what to think of this; but as the vessel drew nearer, we plainly saw the harbor, and other ships of different kinds and sizes, and we soon anchored amongst them, off Bridgetown.[3] Many merchants and planters now came on board, though it was in the evening. They put us in separate parcels,[4] and examined us attentively. They also made us jump, and pointed to the land, signifying we were to go there. We thought by this, we should be eaten by these ugly men, as they appeared to us; and, when soon after we were all put down under the deck again, there was much dread and trembling among us, and nothing but bitter cries to be heard all the night from these apprehensions, insomuch, that at last the white people got some old slaves from the land to <u>pacify</u> us. They told us we were not to be eaten, but to work, and were soon to go on land, where we should see many of our country people. This report eased us much. And sure enough, soon after we were landed, there came to us Africans of all languages.

We were conducted immediately to the merchant's yard, where we were all pent up together, like so many sheep in a fold, without regard to sex or age. . . . We were not many days in the merchant's custody, before we were sold after their usual manner, which is this: On a signal given (as the beat of a drum), the buyers rush at once into the yard where the slaves are confined, and make choice of that parcel they like best. . . .

Vocabulary Development: pacify (PAS uh fy) *v.* calm; soothe

---

3. **Bridgetown** *n.* the capital of Barbados.
4. **parcels** (PAHR suhlz) *n.* groups.

Reader's Response: List two or more adjectives to describe the slave traders.

_____

_____

Thinking About the Skill: How did **summarizing** sentences from this selection help you to understand it better?

_____

_____

TAKE NOTES

Literary Analysis

This selection represents a literary form called a **slave narrative,** or a story based on life as a slave. List three reasons why you think this selection qualifies as a slave narrative.

1. _____

_____

2. _____

_____

3. _____

_____

Reading Check

What happens to the slaves at the end of their journey?

_____

_____

_____

_____

from The Interesting Narrative of the Life of Olaudah Equiano

1. **Draw Conclusions:** What does the treatment of the slaves reveal about the captors' attitudes toward human life?

   _____

   _____

2. **Literary Analysis:** According to Equiano's **slave narrative**, what was the slaves' attitude toward their situation on the ship?

   _____

   _____

3. **Literary Analysis:** Use the following chart to list three **emotional appeals** in Equiano's narrative, and then tell the effect of each.

Emotional Appeal			
	↓	↓	↓
Effect on Reader			

4. **Reading Strategy:** Name three main ideas from Equiano's narrative.

   _____

   _____

   _____

5. **Reading Strategy:** **Summarize** what happened after the ship reached Barbados.

   _____

   _____

   _____

   _____

The Declaration of Independence • *from* The Crisis, Number 1

LITERARY ANALYSIS

Writers and speakers use **persuasion** to convince their audience to think or act in a certain way. A persuasive writer or speaker

- appeals to the audience's emotions and reason
- offers opinions, as well as facts, about a subject
- gives evidence to support the argument
- suggests a course of action or solution to a problem

Thomas Jefferson and Thomas Paine use persuasion in their writing to support the Revolutionary cause. Both writers appeal to the colonists' emotions. Jefferson and Paine also offer logical arguments to appeal to their audience's sense of reason.

READING STRATEGY

Charged words are often found in persuasive writing and speeches. These words produce a strong emotional response. For example, the word *tyranny* means "unfair power." This word has negative **connotations**, which means that it suggests negative ideas.

- When you identify charged words, look for support that backs up those words. Take care not to be convinced by charged words. If there is no supporting evidence, reject the argument.
- Use this chart to list charged words in the selections. Write the words' connotations, or the ideas that they suggest. Then identify the emotions caused by those words.

Selection	Word	Connotation	Emotion
The Declaration of Independence			
from The Crisis, Number 1			

The Declaration of Independence

Thomas Jefferson

Summary Thomas Jefferson explains that it is important to explain why America is separating from Britain. He claims certain basic rights for the colonists and says that the English king abuses those rights. Based on this abuse, the colonies are independent of Britain and the colonists pledge their support of this declaration.

Note-taking Guide

Use this diagram to list Jefferson's main reasons for going to war with the British.

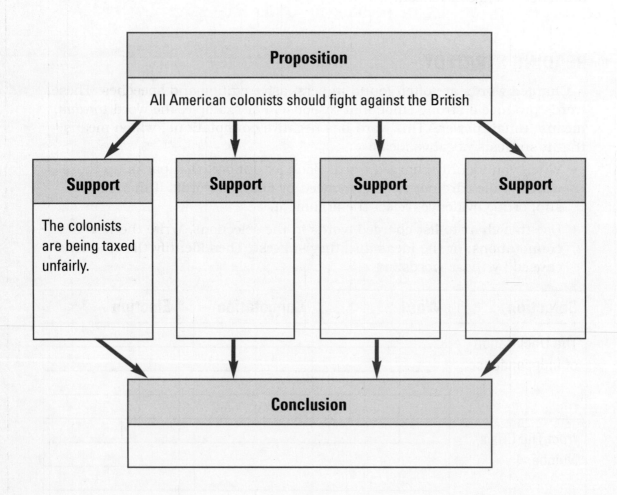

Proposition

All American colonists should fight against the British

Support

The colonists are being taxed unfairly.

Support

Support

Support

Conclusion

from The Crisis, Number 1

Thomas Paine

Summary Thomas Paine writes his essay to the American colonists. He wants to encourage them to fight against the British. Paine writes that God supports the American cause. He also argues that a good father will fight. If the fathers fight, their children may live in peace. Paine then asks Americans in every state to unite.

Note-taking Guide

Paine wants the colonists to agree that they should go to war. Use this chart to list evidence that Paine uses in his argument.

Evidence

Americans have already tried to avoid war in every way.

Activate Prior Knowledge

Think of speeches you have heard as part of political campaigns. Also think of editorials you have read that take a strong position on an issue. Then, as you read, notice the ways that Paine persuades his audience. Think about how his techniques compare to those of speeches and editorials today.

Literary Analysis

This selection is an example of **persuasion,** which is writing that tries to convince people to think or behave in a certain way. Reread the bracketed sentence. Paine persuades by saying that only summer soldiers or sunshine patriots would avoid serving their country now. Why would a reader not want to be called a summer soldier or a sunshine patriot?

_____

_____

_____

Reading Strategy

To persuade his readers, Paine uses **charged words.** These are words with strong connotations, or associations that the words create in addition to their dictionary definitions. Charged words produce an emotional response. One example is *tyranny*, a word that makes Paine's point that Britain is oppressing the colonists. Circle two more **charged words** on this page and write them below.

_____

_____

_____

from The Crisis, Number 1
Thomas Paine

Thomas Paine was inspired by Benjamin Franklin to emigrate from Britain to the American colonies. Once there, he enlisted in the American army and became one of the strongest voices supporting the war against the British.

These are the times that try men's souls. The summer soldier and the sunshine patriot will in this crisis, shrink from the service of his country; but he that stands it NOW, deserves the love and thanks of man and woman. Tyranny, like hell, is not easily conquered; yet we have this consolation with us, that the harder the conflict, the more glorious the triumph. What we obtain too cheap, we esteem too lightly; 'tis dearness only that gives everything its value. Heaven knows how to put a proper price upon its goods; and it would be strange indeed, if so celestial an article as FREEDOM should not be highly rated. Britain, with an army to enforce her tyranny, has declared that she has a right (*not only* to TAX) but "to BIND *us in* ALL CASES WHATSOEVER," and if being *bound in that manner,* is not slavery, then is there not such a thing as slavery upon earth. Even the expression is impious, for so unlimited a power can belong only to God . . .

I have as little superstition in me as any man living, but my secret opinion has ever been, and still is, that God Almighty will not give up a people to military destruction, or leave them unsupportedly to perish, who have so earnestly and so repeatedly sought to avoid the calamities of war, by every decent method which wisdom could invent. Neither have I so much of the infidel in me, as to suppose that he has relinquished the government of the world, and given us up to the care of devils; and as I do not, I cannot see on what grounds the king of Britain can look up to heaven for help against us: a common murderer, a highwayman, or a housebreaker, has as good a pretense as he . . .

I once felt all that kind of anger, which a man ought to feel, against the mean[1] principles that are held by the Tories:[2] a noted one, who kept a tavern at Amboy, was standing at his door, with as pretty a child in his hand,

Vocabulary Development:	impious (IM pee uhs) *adj.* lacking reverence for God
	infidel (IN fuh duhl) *n.* a person who holds no religious belief

---

1. **mean** *adj.* here, small-minded.
2. **Tories** colonists who remained loyal to Great Britain.

about eight or nine years old, as I ever saw, and after speaking his mind as freely as he thought was prudent, finished with this unfatherly expression, *"Well! give me peace in my day."* Not a man lives on the continent but fully believes that a separation must some time or other finally take place, and a generous parent should have said, *"If there must be trouble let it be in my day, that my child may have peace"*; and this single reflection, well applied, is sufficient to awaken every man to duty. Not a place upon earth might be so happy as America. Her situation is remote from all the wrangling world, and she has nothing to do but to trade with them. A man can distinguish himself between temper and principle, and I am as confident, as I am that God governs the world, that America will never be happy till she gets clear of foreign dominion. Wars, without ceasing, will break out till that period arrives, and the continent must in the end be conqueror; for though the flame of liberty may sometimes cease to shine, the coal can never expire . . .

I turn with the warm ardor of a friend to those who have nobly stood, and are yet determined to stand the matter out: I call not upon a few, but upon all; not on *this* state or *that* state, but on *every* state; up and help us; lay your shoulders to the wheel; better have too much force than too little, when so great an object is at stake. Let it be told to the future world, that in the depth of winter, when nothing but hope and virtue could survive, that the city and the country, alarmed at one common danger, came forth to meet and to repulse it. Say not that thousands are gone, turn out your tens of thousands; throw not the burden of the day upon Providence, but *"show your faith by your works,"* that God may bless you. It matters not where you live, or what rank of life you hold, the evil or the blessing will reach you all. The far and the near, the home counties and the back, the rich and the poor, will suffer or rejoice alike. The heart that feels not now, is dead: the blood of his children will curse his cowardice, who shrinks back at a time when a little might have saved the whole, and made *them* happy. (I love the man that can smile at trouble; that can gather strength from distress, and grow brave by reflection.) 'Tis the business of little minds to shrink; but he whose heart is firm, and whose conscience approves his conduct, will pursue his principles unto death. My own line of reasoning is to myself as straight and clear as a ray of light. Not all the treasures of the world, so far as I believe, could have induced me to support an offensive war, for I think it murder; but if a thief breaks into my house, burns and destroys my property, and kills or threatens to kill me, or those that are in it, and to *"bind me in all cases whatsoever,"* to his absolute will, am I to suffer it? What signifies it to me, whether he who does it is a king

© Pearson Education, Inc., publishing as Pearson Prentice Hall.

from The Crisis, Number 1 **63**

TAKE NOTES

Literary Analysis

Reread the bracketed sentences carefully. Paine is using strong words and images here to **persuade** his readers. Summarize his argument in this section by rewriting each sentence in your own words.

_____

_____

_____

_____

_____

_____

_____

Reading Strategy

Paine uses **parallelism** to emphasize the importance of his ideas and to create rhythm. **Parallelism** is the repeated use of phrases, clauses, or sentences that are alike in structure or in meaning. Find one example of parallelism on this page and circle it.

Reading Check

How far does Paine say that a man of conscience should pursue his principles?

_____

_____

_____

_____

_____

Reading Check

Why does Paine compare the king to a thief?

_____

_____

_____

_____

_____

_____

or a common man: my countryman, or not my countryman; whether it be done by an individual villain or an army of them? If we reason to the root of things we shall find no difference; neither can any just cause be assigned why we should punish in the one case and pardon in the other.

Reader's Response: Paine wants all Americans to join forces against the British. What makes his arguments persuasive to you?

_____

_____

Thinking About the Skill: How will recognizing **charged words** help you evaluate arguments in other persuasive pieces you read?

_____

_____

The Declaration of Independence • *from* The Crisis, Number 1

1. **Evaluate:** Is Thomas Jefferson's argument effective? _____ Why or why not?

   _____

   _____

2. **Literary Analysis**: Why does Jefferson present a long list of grievances, or complaints, as part of his **persuasive** writing?

   _____

   _____

3. **Literary Analysis:** Paine uses **aphorisms**, brief statements that express wise observations. Use this chart to identify three aphorisms in Paine's essay. Analyze how each one contributes to his persuasive message.

Aphorism	Meaning	Purpose

4. **Reading Strategy:** Jefferson and Paine use **charged words** to stir readers' emotions. What emotional responses are associated with the words *liberty, justice, honor,* and *barbarous*?

   _____

   _____

5. **Reading Strategy:** Paine uses the word *thief* to refer to the colonists' British rulers. Would Paine have created a different response if he had used the word *supporters* instead? Explain.

   _____

   _____

An Hymn to the Evening • To His Excellency, General Washington

LITERARY ANALYSIS

Personification is a figure of speech that gives human qualities to something that is not human. For example, notice the way Phillis Wheatley describes the ocean in these lines:

> *Enwrapp'd in tempest and a night of storms;*
> *Astonish'd ocean feels the wild uproar . . .*

The poet personifies the sea by giving it human emotions. In both poems, notice how Wheatley uses personification to describe her subjects in human terms.

READING STRATEGY

When reading poetry, you may need to **clarify the meaning** of passages that at first seem unclear. In these poems, Wheatley often reverses the usual order of sentences by placing a verb before its subject. Clarify meaning by rephrasing unusual word order and checking the definitions of unfamiliar words. Use this chart to aid your understanding.

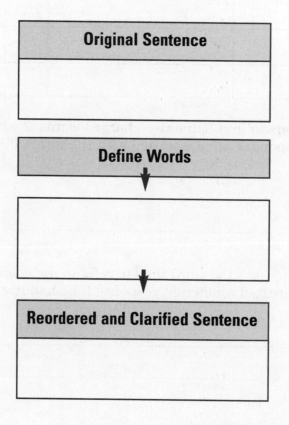

Original Sentence

Define Words

Reordered and Clarified Sentence

An Hymn to the Evening •
To His Excellency, General Washington

Phillis Wheatley

Summaries In "An Hymn to the Evening," the speaker sees a higher power in the beauty of the sunset. She hopes that virtue as bright as the sunset and peaceful sleep will cause people to wake up to the next day pure and safe from sin. "To His Excellency, General Washington" praises the revolutionary cause by personifying America as the goddess Columbia. The poem also praises George Washington for his bravery and leadership.

Note-taking Guide

Use this diagram to compare and contrast the two poems.

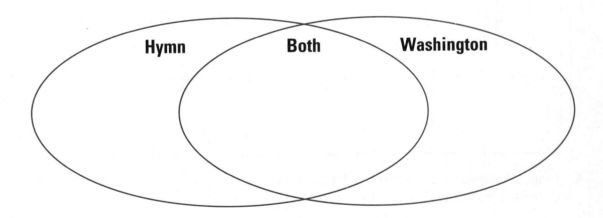

Hymn   **Both**   **Washington**

An Hymn to the Evening • To His Excellency, General Washington

1. **Compare and Contrast:** In "An Hymn to the Evening," what mood or feeling does the poet connect with each time of day?

   _____

   _____

2. **Relate:** If you were going to write a poem of praise, how would you **personify** the spirit of the United States today?

   _____

   _____

3. **Literary Analysis:** Use this chart to analyze two examples of **personification** in "An Hymn to the Evening."

Object/Idea	Human Qualities		Poet's Meaning
		→	

4. **Literary Analysis:** Reread lines 9-12 of "To His Excellency, General Washington." What details does Wheatley use to describe the way Columbia looks?

   _____

   _____

5. **Reading Strategy:** Clarify lines 11-14 of "To His Excellency, General Washington" by defining *unnumber'd* and *graces* and reordering the sentence parts.

   _____

   _____

Press Releases

ABOUT PRESS RELEASES

A **press release,** or **news release** is a document that is used to give information to news organizations. A press release might announce
- an upcoming lecture, conference, or performance
- a newly published book
- the results of a scientific study
- the winners of awards or honors
- a change in leadership at an organization or a company

The purpose of a press release is to encourage the media to report on the event. Press releases are also written to influence the way writers cover an event.

READING STRATEGY

Distinguishing Between Fact and Opinion

Journalists need to **distinguish between fact and opinion** when reading press releases.
- A fact is a statement that can be proved true.
- An **opinion** is a judgment or viewpoint that can be supported by facts and well-reasoned arguments, but not proved.

You should be able to tell the difference between facts and opinions when reading a press release or any other public statement.

Use the information in the chart to help you distinguish between facts and opinions as you read a press release.

Identifying Facts and Opinions
Facts
• can be proved true • can be verified through proof or experiment, or confirmed by an authority **Example:** "Professor Gates is coeditor . . . of the encyclopedia *Encarta Africana*." **Example:**
Opinions

• cannot be proved true or false
• are judgments or viewpoints
• may be supported by facts, arguments, or persuasive emotional appeals
    Example: Gates is a "relentless and outspoken champion for tolerance through understanding."
    Example:

NEWS RELEASE

The Echo Foundation *Voices Against Indifference Initiative*

The Henry Louis Gates, Jr. Project • November 11, 2003 • Charlotte, NC

THE ECHO FOUNDATION BRINGS HENRY LOUIS GATES, JR. TO CHARLOTTE;
Noted Scholar, Literary Critic To Hold Public Lecture, Student Dialogue Nov. 11th

September 26, 2003 (Charlotte, NC) - Henry Louis (Skip) Gates, Jr., chair of Harvard's African and Afro-American Studies department and director of the W.E.B. Du Bois Institute, will be in Charlotte, **Tues., Nov. 11th** for a public lecture, student dialogue and an adult leadership forum as part of The Echo Foundation's "*Voices Against Indifference Initiative.*" Nobel Laureate for literature Wole Soyinka will introduce Gates' lecture, "*W.E.B. Du Bois and the Encyclopedia Africana,*" at **7 p.m.** at Spirit Square's McGlohon Theatre, 345 N. College St. **Call 704.372.1000 for reserved seats: individual ($20) and student groups ($5). Call 704.347.3844 for patron tickets ($65)**, which include a pre-event reception with Gates and Soyinka at the Noel Gallery, 401 N. Tryon St.

The "*Voices Against Indifference Initiative*" is an Echo Foundation program that brings speakers to Charlotte whose personal experience illuminates the power of the individual to have a positive impact on humanity through moral courage, action, and words.

Gates will share his story in several community venues on Nov. 11th. Some 400 students and teachers from Charlotte area private and public high schools are studying curriculum materials to prepare for the Gates dialogue at Providence Day School from 11:15 - 12:30 p.m. Plans are also underway for an adult leadership forum with Gates about social capital issues, and he will be the featured guest on "*Charlotte Talks*" with Mike Collins at 9 a.m. on WFAE Radio (90.7 FM).

A relentless and outspoken champion for tolerance through understanding, Gates has earned numerous awards and accolades for broadening the discourse on African American literature and cultural tradition in his various roles as an educator, scholar, literary critic and writer. One recent accomplishment, the completion of *Encarta Africana*, is the result of his 25-year quest to realize the dream of W.E.B. Du Bois. The renowned early 20th century black intellectual and civil rights leader envisioned a comprehensive encyclopedia about the entire black world that could be used as an instrument to fight racism by building greater awareness and understanding of the African culture. The 2.25 billion-word encyclopedia project, co-edited by Gates and Princeton professor K. Anthony Appiah, and published in hardbound print and CD-ROM format, was dedicated in memory of Du Bois and in honor of Nelson Mandela on Martin Luther King's birthday, Jan. 19, 1999.

###

NOTE TO THE EDITORS: The following page includes more detailed information about Gates and The Echo Foundation. Photos are available through The Echo Foundation.

The Echo Foundation
1125E. Morehead Street • Suite 106 • Charlotte, NC 28204 •
Tel 704.347.3844 • Fax 704.347.3845
www.echofoundation.org Charlotteechoes@aol.com

TAKE NOTES

Reading Strategy

Readers of a press release must **distinguish between fact and opinion**. List two words that show a statement of opinion in the paragraph before NOTE TO THE EDITORS.

Reading Check

Henry Louis Gates, Jr. will be speaking at a program. Underline the purpose of the program.

ABOUT HENRY LOUIS GATES, JR.

W.E.B. Du Bois Professor of the Humanities, Harvard University, Chair of Afro-American Studies
Director of the W.E.B. Du Bois Institute for Afro-American Research

Professor Gates is co-editor with K. Anthony Appiah of the encyclopedia *Encarta Africana* published on CD-ROM by Microsoft (1999), and in book form by Basic Civitas Books under the title *Africana: The Encyclopedia of the African and African American Experience* (1999). He is the author of *Wonders of the African World* (1999), the book companion to the six-hour BBC/PBS television series of the same name.

Professor Gates is the author of several works of literary criticism, including *Figures in Black: Words, Signs and the 'Racial' Self* (Oxford University Press, 1987); *The Signifying Monkey: A Theory of Afro-American Literary Criticism* (Oxford, 1988), 1989 winner of the American Book Award; and *Loose Canons: Notes on the Culture Wars* (Oxford, 1992.) He has also authored *Colored People: A Memoir* (Knopf, 1994), which traces his childhood experiences in a small West Virginia town in the 1950s and 1960s; *The Future of the Race* (Knopf, 1996), co-authored with Cornel West; and *Thirteen Ways of Looking at a Black Man* (Random House, 1997). Professor Gates has edited several anthologies, including *The Norton Anthology of African American Literature* (W. W. Norton, 1996); and *The Oxford-Schomburg Library of Nineteenth Century Black Women Writers* (Oxford, 1991). In addition, Professor Gates is co-editor of *Transition* magazine. An influential cultural critic, Professor Gates's publications include a 1994 cover story for *Time* magazine on the new black Renaissance in art, as well as numerous articles for *The New Yorker*.

Professor Gates earned his M.A. and Ph.D. in English Literature from Clare College at the University of Cambridge. He received a B.A. *summa cum laude* from Yale University in 1973 in English Language and Literature. Before joining the faculty of Harvard in 1991, he taught at Yale, Cornell, and Duke Universities. His honors and grants include a MacArthur Foundation "genius grant" (1981), the George Polk Award for Social Commentary (1993), Chicago Tribune Heartland Award (1994), the Golden Plate Achievement Award (1995), *Time* magazine's "25 Most Influential Americans" list (1997), a National Humanities Medal (1998), and election to the American Academy of Arts and Letters (1999).

ABOUT THE ECHO FOUNDATION

The Echo Foundation was founded in 1997 to carry on the message that Nobel Peace Prize winner Elie Wiesel brought to Charlotte that year—a call to action for human dignity, justice and moral courage. Its mission is "to sponsor and facilitate those voices which speak of human dignity, justice and moral courage in a way that will lead to positive action for humankind."

The Echo Foundation
1125E. Morehead Street • Suite 106 • Charlotte, NC 28204 •
Tel 704.347.3844 • Fax 704.347.3845
www.echofoundation.org Charlotteechoes@aol.com

Reading Check

The article includes information on accomplishments and education. Underline the sentences that tell about Gates's education.

THINKING ABOUT THE PRESS RELEASE

1. What is the topic of Henry Louis Gates's public lecture?

_____

2. Based on information in the **press release,** why do you think Gates is speaking on this topic?

_____

_____

READING STRATEGY

3. Find two facts in the press release that support this opinion: Gates is an influential cultural critic.

_____

_____

4. Why do you think the Echo Foundation invited Gates to speak? Use at least two facts and one opinion from the press release in your response. Be sure to **distinguish between facts and opinion in your response.**

_____

_____

_____

TIMED WRITING: EVALUATION (30 minutes)

Write a newspaper article that reports the event announced in this press release. Be sure to include the facts.
Answer these questions to get started.

- Who? _____
- What? _____
- When? _____
- Where? _____
- Why? _____

Speech in the Virginia Convention • Speech in the Convention

LITERARY ANALYSIS

Speeches are written works that are then spoken to an audience. Effective speakers and writers both use persuasive techniques like these to emphasize their points:

- *Restatement*: repeating an idea in a variety of ways
- *Repetition*: restating an idea using the same words
- *Parallelism*: repeating similar grammatical structures
- *Rhetorical questions*: asking a question whose answer is obvious

You will find examples of these techniques in the speeches by Patrick Henry and Benjamin Franklin.

READING STRATEGY

Speakers often appeal to people's emotions in order to make an impact. **Evaluating persuasive appeals** can help you when you read or hear a persuasive speech.

- Think about the speaker's reasons for stirring up the emotions of the audience.
- Identify the speaker's arguments and the evidence used to support those arguments.
- Decide if the arguments and emotional appeals are appropriate for the occasion.
- Use this diagram to record the persuasive appeals made by each speaker.

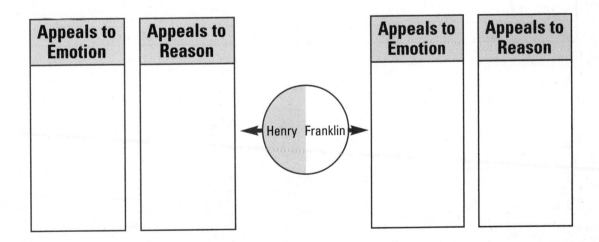

Speech in the Virginia Convention

Patrick Henry

Summary In this speech, Patrick Henry says that he respectfully disagrees with the previous speeches. He believes that the actions of the British mean that they are preparing for war. The colonists have tried to discuss the problem, but continue to be ignored. Henry claims that the war has already begun. The only choices, he believes, are to fight or to become slaves.

Note-taking Guide

Use this chart to compare the arguments for and against going to war.

Against	For
The colonists are too weak.	The colonists are as strong as they will ever be.

Speech in the Virginia Convention
Patrick Henry

The last line of this speech is one of the most famous lines in American history: "… give me liberty or give me death!" Remember that all of the colonists were risking their lives by planning a revolution. As colonists of England, rebellious Americans could be accused of treason and executed.

Mr. President: No man thinks more highly than I do of the patriotism, as well as abilities, of the very worthy gentlemen who have just addressed the house. But different men often see the same subject in different lights; and, therefore, I hope it will not be thought disrespectful to those gentlemen, if, entertaining, as I do, opinions of a character very opposite to theirs, I shall speak forth my sentiments freely and without reserve. This is no time for ceremony. The question before the house is one of awful moment[1] to this country. For my own part, I consider it as nothing less than a question of freedom or slavery. And in proportion to the magnitude of the subject ought to be the freedom of the debate. It is only in this way that we can hope to arrive at truth, and fulfill the great responsibility which we hold to God and our country. Should I keep back my opinions at such a time, through fear of giving offense, I should consider myself as guilty of treason toward my country, and of an act of disloyalty toward the Majesty of Heaven, which I revere above all earthly kings.

Mr. President, it is natural to man to indulge in the illusions of hope. We are apt to shut our eyes against a painful truth, and listen to the song of that siren till she transforms us into beasts.[2] Is this the part of wise men, engaged in a great and <u>arduous</u> struggle for liberty? Are we disposed to be of the number of those who having eyes see not, and having ears hear not,[3] the things which so nearly concern their temporal salvation? For my part, whatever anguish of spirit it may cost, I am willing to know the whole truth; to know the worst and to provide for it.

I have but one lamp by which my feet are guided, and that is the lamp of experience. I know of no way of judging of the

---

Vocabulary Development: arduous (AHR joo wuhs) *adj.* difficult

---

1. **moment** importance.
2. **listen . . . beasts** In Homer's *Odyssey*, the enchantress Circe transforms men into swine after charming them with her singing.
3. **having eyes . . . hear not** In Ezekiel 12:2, those "who have eyes to see, but see not, who have ears to hear, but hear not" are addressed.

TAKE NOTES

Activate Prior Knowledge

Ads on television and radio try to persuade you to spend your money. Think about the techniques of persuasion that these ads use. Then be alert for any of the same techniques as you read this selection.

_____

_____

_____

Literary Analysis

This selection is a **speech**, or a talk given to an audience. One effective way to begin a speech is to make the audience feel comfortable. How does Henry do that at the beginning of this speech?

_____

_____

_____

Reading Strategy

Diction is a speaker's choice of words, part of the speaker's style. Henry's diction is formal and eloquent, with long sentences and difficult vocabulary. Read slowly, use the footnotes, and determine the meaning of each sentence before you go on to the next one. For example, write the meaning of the bracketed sentences below.

_____

_____

_____

_____

Persuasive appeals can be to the emotions, ethics, or to the intellect. **Evaluate** the **persuasive appeal** in the bracketed paragraph. How can you tell that Henry is appealing to his audience's intellect?

_____

_____

_____

_____

Why does Henry say we should not try argument with the British?

_____

_____

_____

_____

_____

An effective technique in a **speech** is to use **parallelism,** or repeated grammatical structures like adjectives or clauses. Reread the underlined sentence, noticing the repeated subject/verb pattern. Circle one more example of parallelism on this page.

future but by the past. And judging by the past, I wish to know what there has been in the conduct of the British ministry for the last ten years to justify those hopes with which gentlemen have been pleased to solace themselves and the house? Is it that <u>insidious</u> smile with which our petition has been lately received? Trust it not, sir; it will prove a snare to your feet. Suffer not yourselves to be betrayed with a kiss.[4] Ask yourselves how this gracious reception of our petition comports with those warlike preparations which cover our waters and darken our land. Are fleets and armies necessary to a work of love and reconciliation? Have we shown ourselves so unwilling to be reconciled that force must be called in to win back our love? Let us not deceive ourselves, sir. These are the implements of war and <u>subjugation</u>—the last arguments to which kings resort.

I ask gentlemen, sir, what means this martial array, if its purpose be not to force us to submission? Can gentlemen assign any other possible motive for it? Has Great Britain any enemy in this quarter of the world, to call for all this accumulation of navies and armies? No, sir, she has none. They are meant for us: they can be meant for no other. They are sent over to bind and rivet upon us those chains which the British ministry have been so long forging.

And what have we to oppose to them? Shall we try argument? Sir, we have been trying that for the last ten years. Have we anything new to offer upon the subject? Nothing. We have held the subject up in every light of which it is capable; but it has been all in vain. Shall we resort to entreaty and humble supplication? What terms shall we find which have not been already exhausted? Let us not, I beseech you, sir, deceive ourselves longer. Sir, we have done everything that could be done to avert the storm which is now coming on. <u>We have petitioned; we have remonstrated; we have supplicated; we have prostrated ourselves before the throne, and have implored its interposition[5] to arrest the tyrannical hands of the ministry and Parliament.</u> Our petitions have been slighted; our remonstrances have produced additional violence and insult; our supplications have been disregarded; and we have been spurned with contempt from the foot of the throne! In vain, after these

---

Vocabulary Development: **insidious** (in SID ee uhs) *adj.* deceitful; treacherous
subjugation (sub juh GAY shuhn) *n.* the act of conquering

---

4. **betrayed with a kiss** In Luke 22:47-48, Jesus is betrayed with a kiss.
5. **interposition** intervention.

things, may we indulge the fond[6] hope of peace and reconciliation. There is no longer any room for hope. If we wish to be free, if we mean to preserve inviolate those inestimable privileges for which we have been so long contending, if we mean not basely to abandon the noble struggle in which we have been so long engaged, and which we have pledged ourselves never to abandon until the glorious object of our contest shall be obtained—we must fight! I repeat it, sir, we must fight! An appeal to arms and to the God of Hosts is all that is left us!

They tell us, sir, that we are weak—unable to cope with so formidable an adversary. But when shall we be stronger? Will it be the next week, or the next year? Will it be when we are totally disarmed, and when a British guard shall be stationed in every house? Shall we gather strength by irresolution and inaction? Shall we acquire the means of effectual resistance by lying supinely on our backs and hugging the delusive phantom of hope until our enemies shall have bound us hand and foot? Sir, we are not weak, if we make a proper use of those means which the God of nature hath placed in our power. Three millions of people, armed in the holy cause of liberty, and in such a country as that which we possess, are invincible by any force which our enemy can send against us. Besides, sir, we shall not fight our battles alone. There is a just God who presides over the destinies of nations and who will raise up friends to fight our battles for us. The battle, sir, is not to the strong alone;[7] it is to the <u>vigilant</u>, the active, the brave. Besides, sir, we have no election;[8] if we were base enough to desire it, it is now too late to retire from the contest. There is no retreat but in submission and slavery! Our chains are forged! Their clanging may be heard on the plains of Boston! The war is inevitable—and let it come! I repeat it, sir, let it come!

It is in vain, sir, to extenuate the matter. Gentlemen may cry, "Peace, peace"—but there is no peace. The war is actually begun! The next gale that sweeps from the north[9] will bring to our ears the clash of resounding arms! Our brethren are already in the field! Why stand we here idle?

TAKE NOTES

Reading Check

What is Henry's response to those who say the colonists are too weak to fight the British?

_____

_____

_____

_____

_____

Vocabulary Development: vigilant (VIJ uh luhnt) *adj.* alert to danger

---

6. **fond** foolish.
7. **The battle...alone** "The race is not to the swift, nor the battle to the strong" (Ecclesiastes 9:11).
8. **election** choice.

Evaluate the **persuasive appeal** of the end of this speech (see the bracketed section on this page and page 79). How can you tell that Henry is now appealing to his audience's emotions?

_____

_____

_____

_____

_____

_____

_____

What is it that gentlemen wish? What would they have? Is life so dear, or peace so sweet, as to be purchased at the price of chains and slavery? Forbid it, Almighty God! I know not what course others may take; but as for me, give me liberty or give me death!

_____

9. **The next gale…north** In Massachusetts, some colonists had already shown open resistance to the British.

Reader's Response: What is your response to the combination of emotional and intellectual persuasive arguments that Henry uses? Which type is more appealing to you?

_____

_____

_____

Thinking About the Skill: How will **evaluating the persuasive appeal** help you make judgments about speeches that you read or hear?

_____

_____

_____

Speech in the Convention

Benjamin Franklin

Summary Benjamin Franklin expresses his doubts about the Constitution, but still approves of the document. He gives several reasons to support his opinions. Franklin thinks that this Constitution is the best document that imperfect men can offer. He also thinks that it is important to show unified support for the Constitution.

Note-taking Guide

Franklin suggests that a perfect Constitution will never be created. Use this chart to list his reasons that delegates should support the Constitution, even though it is not perfect.

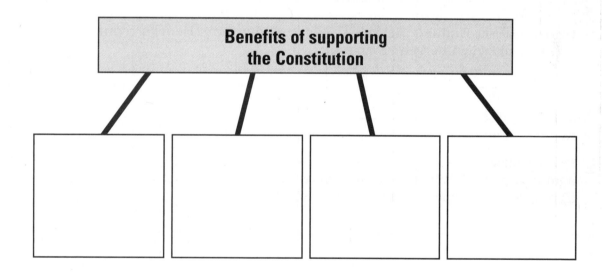

Speech in the Virginia Convention • Speech in the Convention

1. **Compare and Contrast:** Compare and contrast the endings of Henry's and Franklin's speeches. Which ending do you think will make the biggest impact on the audience? Explain.

   _____

   _____

2. **Literary Analysis:** Use this chart to identify the persuasive techniques used in each one of these **speeches**.

	Example	Effect
Restatement		
Repetition		
Parallelism		

3. **Literary Analysis:** Evaluate Henry's speech. Do you think Henry's reputation as a great speaker is deserved? Explain.

   _____

   _____

4. **Reading Strategy:** The purpose of Henry's speech is to urge the colonists to revolt against England. Why are **persuasive appeals** to both emotions and reasons appropriate in a speech with this purpose?

   _____

   _____

Letter to Her Daughter From the New White House • *from* Letters From an American Farmer

LITERARY ANALYSIS

Personal, **private letters** usually have an informal style that sounds like conversation. You might write private letters to close friends or family members. The writer of a private letter believes that the person to whom the letter is addressed is the only one who will read it. In her letter to her daughter, for example, Abigail Adams reminds her daughter to keep all the information to herself.

Public letters, often called **epistles**, are essays written in the form of a letter. These letters are written for a wider audience. The writer can use an informal tone while writing about public ideas.

READING STRATEGY

When **distinguishing between fact and opinion**, remember

- A **fact** is information that can be proved.
- An **opinion** is a personal belief. Opinions can be supported but not proved.
- Phrases such as "I think" and "it seems" often signal opinions.

Use this chart to keep track of facts and opinions in these letters.

Statement	Fact or Opinion?	Words Showing a Judgment If It Is an Opinion	How It can Be Proved If It Is a Fact
The American ought therefore to love his country much better.	Opinion	ought	

Letter to Her Daughter From the New White House

Abigail Adams

Summary First Lady Abigail Adams describes her journey to the new city of Washington, D.C. The new White House is huge and filled with servants. The building and city, however, lack conveniences. Adams asks her daughter to tell others that the house and city are beautiful. Adams also mentions that she has been invited to visit the homes of many famous people.

Note-taking Guide

Adams presents two different views of Washington, D.C. In one, she describes the enjoyable parts of living there. In the other, she talks about the inconveniences. Use this chart to keep track of her remarks and decide whether Adams likes or dislikes her new surroundings.

What Adams likes	What Adams wants
a river view	firewood

Letter to Her Daughter From the New White House

Abigail Adams

Abigail Adams, like Barbara Bush, had the unusual experience of being the wife of one president, John Adams, and the mother of a later president, John Quincy Adams. Her husband spent years away from home during and after the American Revolution, and her letters to him and to her family provide unique insights into the period in which she lived.

Washington, 21 November, 1800

My Dear Child:

I arrived here on Sunday last, and without meeting with any accident worth noticing, except losing ourselves when we left Baltimore and going eight or nine miles on the Frederick road, by which means we were obliged to go the other eight through woods, where we wandered two hours without finding a guide or the path. Fortunately, a straggling black came up with us, and we engaged him as a guide to <u>extricate</u> us out of our difficulty; but woods are all you see from Baltimore until you reach the *city*, which is only so in name. Here and there is a small cot, without a glass window, interspersed amongst the forests, through which you travel miles without seeing any human being. In the city there are buildings enough, if they were compact and finished, to accommodate Congress and those attached to it; but as they are, and scattered as they are, I see no great comfort for them. The river, which runs up to Alexandria,[1] is in full view of my window, and I see the vessels as they pass and repass. The house is upon a grand and superb scale, requiring about thirty servants to attend and keep the apartments in proper order, and perform the ordinary business of the house and stables; an establishment very well proportioned to the President's salary. The lighting of the apartments, from the kitchen to parlors and chambers, is a tax indeed; and the fires we are obliged to keep to secure us from daily

---

Vocabulary Development: extricate (EKS truh kayt) *v.* set free

---

1. **Alexandria** city in northeastern Virginia.

TAKE NOTES

Activate Prior Knowledge

Think about what it must be like to move to a new home, especially if it is not quite finished. You can be excited about the new home and miss the previous home at the same time—and it is really difficult to avoid comparing the two. Notice how Abigail Adams struggles to stay positive in spite of the challenges of her new home.

Reading Strategy

As you read nonfiction, it is important to know the difference between **facts**—statements that can be proven—and **opinions**—personal beliefs that cannot be proven. Reread the bracketed sentences. Write the section that is an opinion below.

_____

_____

_____

_____

_____

Literary Analysis

This selection is a **private letter** written by a mother to her daughter. Private letters are written in a conversational style and are intended to be read only by the person to whom they are addressed. Circle two phrases on this page that Adams may not have used if she had thought her letter would become public.

Reading Check

Why is it so difficult to get fire-wood?

_____

_____

_____

Literary Analysis

Reread the underlined sentence. How does this sentence make it clear that this selection is a **private letter**?

_____

_____

_____

_____

_____

Reading Strategy

Reread the bracketed sentence. Distinguish the **facts** from the **opinions** in this sentence and write them below.

Fact:

_____

_____

_____

_____

Opinion:

_____

_____

_____

_____

agues is another very cheering comfort. To assist us in this great castle, and render less attendance necessary, bells are wholly wanting, not one single one being hung through the whole house, and promises are all you can obtain. This is so great an inconvenience, that I know not what to do, or how to do. The ladies from Georgetown[2] and in the city have many of them visited me. Yesterday I returned fifteen visits—but such a place as Georgetown appears—why, our Milton is beautiful.

But no comparisons—if they will put me up some bells and let me have wood enough to keep fires, I design to be pleased. I could content myself almost anywhere three months; but, surrounded with forests, can you believe that wood is not to be had because people cannot be found to cut and cart it? Briesler entered into a contract with a man to supply him with wood. A small part, a few cords only, has he been able to get. Most of that was expended to dry the walls of the house before we came in, and yesterday the man told him it was impossible for him to procure it to be cut and carted. He has had recourse to coals; but we cannot get grates made and set. We have, indeed, come into a *new country*.

You must keep all this to yourself, and, when asked how I like it, say that I write you the situation is beautiful, which is true. The house is made habitable, but there is not a single apartment finished, and all withinside, except the plastering, has been done since Briesler came. We have not the least fence, yard, or other convenience without and the great unfinished audience room I make a drying-room of, to hang up the clothes in. The principal stairs are not up, and will not be this winter. Six chambers are made comfortable; two are occupied by the President and Mr. Shaw; two lower rooms, one for a common parlor, and one for a levee room. Upstairs there is the oval room, which is designed for the drawing room, and has the crimson furniture in it. It is a very handsome room now; but, when completed, it will be beautiful. If the twelve years, in which this place has been considered as the future seat of government had been improved, as they would have been if in New England, very many of the present inconveniences would have been removed. It is a beautiful spot, capable of every improvement, and, the more I view it, the more I am

---

Vocabulary Development: agues (AY gyooz) *n.* fits of shivering

---

2. **Georgetown** section of Washington, D.C.

delighted with it.

Since I sat down to write, I have been called down to a servant from Mount Vernon,[3] with a billet[4] from Major Custis, and a haunch of venison, and a kind, congratulatory letter from Mrs. Lewis, upon my arrival in the city, with Mrs. Washington's love, inviting me to Mount Vernon, where, health permitting, I will go before I leave this place.

Affectionately, your mother,
Abigail Adams

3. **Mount Vernon** home of George Washington, located in northern Virginia.
4. **billet** (bil′ it) *n.* brief letter.

Reader's Response: What questions would you like to ask Abigail Adams after reading her letter?

_____

_____

_____

_____

Thinking About the Skill: How will **distinguishing between fact and opinion** help you evaluate the nonfiction accounts that you read?

_____

_____

_____

_____

from Letters From an American Farmer

Michel-Guillaume Jean de Crèvecoeur

Summary Crèvecoeur describes the situation of many American immigrants. In Europe, these people are starving and out of work. In America, laws protect them and help them succeed. As a result, people come to America from many different places. They come to start new lives where they can work for themselves and be free.

Note-taking Guide
Coming to America gives many immigrants things that they did not have in their old country. Use this chart to list the benefits that Crèvecoeur mentions.

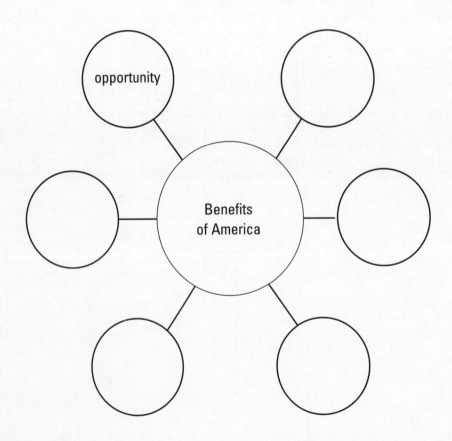

from Letters From an American Farmer

Michel-Guillaume Jean de Crèvecoeur

Although Crèvecoeur did do some farming, he was also a statesman, an explorer, and a soldier. In this letter he assumes the identity of an American farmer to speak glowingly of the opportunities available in America.

In this great American <u>asylum</u>, the poor of Europe have by some means met together, and in consequence of various causes; to what purpose should they ask one another what countrymen they are? Alas, two thirds of them had no country. Can a wretch who wanders about, who works and starves, whose life is a continual scene of sore affliction or pinching <u>penury</u>, can that man call England or any other kingdom his country? A country that had no bread for him, whose fields procured him no harvest, who met with nothing but the frowns of the rich, the severity of the laws, with jails and punishments; who owned not a single foot of the extensive surface of this planet? No! Urged by a variety of motives, here they came. Everything has tended to regenerate them; new laws, a new mode of living, a new social system; here they are become men: in Europe they were as so many useless plants, wanting vegetative mold[1] and refreshing showers; they withered, and were mowed down by want, hunger, and war; but now by the power of transplantation, like all other plants they have taken root and flourished!

Formerly they were not numbered in any civil lists[2] of their country, except in those of the poor; here they rank as citizens. By what invisible power has this surprising metamorphosis been performed? By that of the laws and that of their industry. The laws, the indulgent laws, protect them as they arrive, stamping on them the symbol of adoption; they receive ample rewards for their labors; these accumulated rewards procure them lands; those lands confer on them the title of freemen, and to that title every benefit is affixed which men can possibly require. This is the great operation daily performed by our laws. From whence proceed these laws? From our government. Whence the government? It is derived from the original genius and strong desire of the people ratified and confirmed by the crown. . . .

| **Vocabulary Development:** | **asylum** (uh SY luhm) *n.* place of refuge |
| | **penury** (PEN yuh ree) *n.* lack of money, property, or necessities |

---

1. **vegetative mold** enriched soil.
2. **civil lists** lists of distinguished persons.

TAKE NOTES

Activate Prior Knowledge

Now and then you will see what is called an *Open Letter* in a newspaper or a magazine—often to a public figure. Think about why someone would write a letter to an individual and then make the letter public on purpose.

Reading Strategy

As you read nonfiction, it is important to distinguish between **facts**—statements that can be proven—and **opinions**—personal beliefs that cannot be proven. Reread the first paragraph. Which part of the paragraph is fact and which is opinion?

_____

_____

_____

_____

_____

Literary Analysis

This selection is an **epistle,** or a public letter written for a wide audience. How would you describe the intended audience for Crèvecoeur's letter?

_____

_____

_____

_____

_____

_____

Letters, speeches, essays, and other documents written by people who actually participated in historical events are called **primary source documents.** Crèvecoeur's letter is such a document. How does knowing that Crèvecoeur was alive during the period of history he is writing about affect your response to his letter?

_____

_____

_____

_____

Reading Check

Why does Crèvecoeur say that Americans should love this country more than the countries from which they have come?

_____

_____

_____

_____

_____

_____

What attachment can a poor European emigrant have for a country where he had nothing? The knowledge of the language, the love of a few kindred as poor as himself, were the only cords that tied him: his country is now that which gives him land, bread, protection, and consequence: *Ubi panis ibi patria*[3] is the motto of all emigrants. What then is the American, this new man? He is either a European, or the descendant of a European, hence that strange mixture of blood, which you will find in no other country. I could point out to you a family whose grandfather was an Englishman, whose wife was Dutch, whose son married a French woman, and whose present four sons have now four wives of different nations. *He* is an American, who, leaving behind him all his ancient prejudices and manners, receives new ones from the new mode of life he has embraced, the new government he obeys, and the new rank he holds. He becomes an American by being received in the broad lap of our great *Alma Mater.*[4] Here individuals of all nations are melted into a new race of men, whose labors and posterity will one day cause great changes in the world. Americans are the western pilgrims, who are carrying along with them that great mass of arts, sciences, vigor, and industry which began long since in the east; they will finish the great circle. The Americans were once scattered all over Europe: here they are incorporated into one of the finest systems of population which has ever appeared, and which will hereafter become distinct by the power of the different climates they inhabit. The American ought therefore to love this country much better than that wherein either he or his forefathers were born. Here the rewards of his industry follow with equal steps the progress of his labor; his labor is founded on the basis of nature, *self-interest*; can it want a stronger allurement? Wives and children, who before in vain demanded of him a morsel of bread, now, fat and frolicsome, gladly help their father to clear those fields whence exuberant crops are to arise to feed and to clothe them all; without any part being claimed, either by a <u>despotic</u> prince, a rich abbot,[5] or a mighty lord. Here religion demands but little of him; a small voluntary

---

Vocabulary Development: despotic (de SPAHT ik) *adj.* harsh; cruel; unjust

---

3. ***Ubi…patria*** (U bee pah nis IB ee PAH tree uh) "Where there is bread, there is one's fatherland" (Latin).
4. ***Alma Mater*** (AHL muh MAH tuhr) "Fostering mother." Here, referring to America; usually used in reference to a school or college (Latin).
5. **abbot** *n.* the head of a monastery.

salary to the minister, and gratitude to God; can he refuse these? The American is a new man, who acts upon new principles; he must therefore entertain new ideas, and form new opinions. From involuntary idleness, servile dependence, penury, and useless labor, he has passed to toils of a very different nature, rewarded by ample <u>subsistence</u>—This is an American.

Reading Check

How is the American a new man?

_____

_____

_____

_____

_____

Vocabulary Development: **subsistence** (suhb SIS tuhns) *n.* means of support

---

Reader's Response: How does this letter make you feel about being an American?

_____

_____

_____

Thinking About the Skill: How will **distinguishing between fact and opinion** help you evaluate the nonfiction accounts that you read?

_____

_____

_____

Letter to Her Daughter From the New White House •
from Letters From an American Farmer

1. **Analyze:** Does Crèvecoeur present a realistic or an idealized view of America? Explain.

_____

_____

2. **Literary Analysis:** Use this chart to list words that show Adam's **private letter** is not meant for a public audience. Revise them for a public audience.

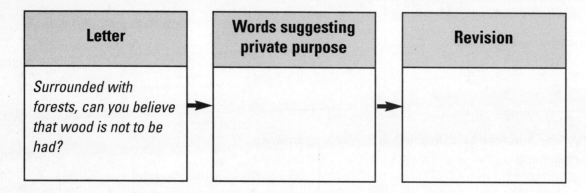

Letter	Words suggesting private purpose	Revision
Surrounded with forests, can you believe that wood is not to be had?		

3. **Literary Analysis:** What kinds of information would be appropriate in a private letter from Crèvecoeur to a friend, but not appropriate in an **epistle?**

_____

_____

4. **Reading Strategy:** Distinguish between the facts and opinions in this statement:

"Upstairs there is the oval room, which is designed for the drawing room, and has the crimson furniture in it. It is a very handsome room now; but, when completed, it will be beautiful."

What are the facts?

_____

_____

What are the opinions?

_____

_____

The Devil and Tom Walker

LITERARY ANALYSIS

When an author creates a story with an **omniscient point of view**, he or she uses an all-knowing narrator who tells the events of the story. Stories that use an omniscient point of view have the following features:

- A narrator who is not part of the action
- Details about the thoughts and feelings of each character
- Commentary from the narrator about events in the story

As you read "The Devil and Tom Walker," notice how an all-knowing narrator presents information that a character from the story would not know.

READING STRATEGY

A story can reveal **cultural attitudes** about people. Authors do this by using the following elements:

- Descriptive details
- Narrator's comments
- Characters' dialogue

Authors then let the readers **make inferences** based on this information. In "The Devil and Tom Walker," the reference to Native Americans as "savages" reveals cultural attitudes. Use the following chart to track examples of cultural attitudes presented in the story.

Detail	Cultural Attitude

The Devil and Tom Walker

Washington Irving

Summary Tom Walker meets the Devil ("Old Scratch") in a swamp. The Devil offers the pirate Captain Kidd's treasure to Tom on certain conditions. Tom's wife encourages him to accept, but Tom refuses. She leaves to find the Devil and make her own bargain. After her second try, she doesn't come back. Later, Tom finds her apron with a heart and liver in it. He assumes that the Devil has killed her. Almost grateful, Tom looks for the Devil again. This time, he makes a deal. Tom will get Captain Kidd's treasure if he becomes a moneylender. Later, Tom regrets his deal and starts going to church often. But the Devil returns and sends Tom off on horseback into a storm. Tom never comes back, though his troubled spirit appears on stormy nights.

Note-taking Guide

Use this sequence chart to keep track of events in the story.

Event 1: Tom Walker takes a shortcut throught the swamp and finds a skull.
Event 2:
Event 3:
Event 4:
Event 5:
Event 6:
Event 7:
Event 8:
Event 9:
Event 10:

The Devil and Tom Walker
Washington Irving

This short story is Washington Irving's version of an ancient legend. The legend tells the story of Faust, who sells his soul to the Devil to receive knowledge and power on Earth. In Irving's version, Tom Walker sells his soul not for knowledge and power, but for money.

A few miles from Boston in Massachusetts, there is a deep inlet, winding several miles into the interior of the country from Charles Bay, and terminating in a thickly wooded swamp or morass. On one side of this inlet is a beautiful dark grove; on the opposite side the land rises abruptly from the water's edge into a high ridge, on which grow a few scattered oaks of great age and immense size. Under one of these gigantic trees, according to old stories, there was a great amount of treasure buried by Kidd the pirate.[1] The inlet allowed a facility to bring the money in a boat secretly and at night to the very foot of the hill; the elevation of the place permitted a good look-out to be kept that no one was at hand; while the remarkable trees formed good landmarks by which the place might easily be found again. The old stories add, moreover, that the Devil presided at the hiding of the money, and took it under his guardianship; but this it is well known he always does with buried treasure, particularly when it has been ill-gotten.

Be that as it may, Kidd never returned to recover his wealth; being shortly after seized at Boston, sent out to England, and there hanged for a pirate.

About the year 1727, just at the time that earthquakes were prevalent in New England, and shook many tall sinners down upon their knees, there lived near this place a meager, miserly fellow, of the name of Tom Walker. He had a wife as miserly as himself: they were so miserly that they even conspired to cheat each other. Whatever the woman could lay hands on, she hid away; a hen could not cackle but she was on the alert to secure the new-laid egg. Her husband was continually prying about to detect her secret hoards, and many and fierce were the conflicts that took place about what ought to have been common property. They lived in a forlorn-looking house that stood alone, and had an air of starvation. A few straggling savin trees, emblems of sterility, grew near it; no smoke ever curled from its chimney; no traveler stopped at its door. A miserable horse, whose ribs were as articulate as the bars of a gridiron, stalked about a field, where a thin carpet of moss, scarcely covering the ragged beds of puddingstone, tantalized and balked his hunger; and

---

1. **Kidd the pirate** Captain William Kidd (1645–1701).

© Pearson Education, Inc., publishing as Pearson Prentice Hall.

The Devil and Tom Walker **95**

TAKE NOTES

Activate Prior Knowledge

This story is set in the 1700s. Think about what you have learned in your social studies classes about Puritan New England at that time. What do you think eighteenth-century New Englanders believed about the Devil?

_____

_____

_____

Reading Check

Read this story slowly and carefully. Stop at the end of each paragraph and check your understanding. Summarize what you have read and ask yourself questions. For example, according to an old story, what is buried under one of the big oak trees?

_____

_____

_____

Literary Analysis

This story is told by an **omniscient narrator,** a storyteller who stands outside the story and knows the thoughts and feelings as well as the actions of all the characters. The omniscient, or all-knowing, narrator of this story knows about conflicts between Tom Walker and his wife. Why are the two always fighting?

_____

_____

_____

Reread the underlined sentence. What can you **infer**, or figure out, from the comment about Tom's face?

_____

_____

_____

_____

Washington Irving is known as a master of the **short story**. In this story, his vivid descriptions of the **setting** make the events come alive. Reread the bracketed paragraph. To what animals does Irving compare the trunks of the trees?

_____

_____

_____

_____

Where does Tom Walker stop to rest?

_____

_____

_____

_____

sometimes he would lean his head over the fence, look piteously at the passerby, and seem to petition deliverance from this land of famine.

The house and its inmates had altogether a bad name. Tom's wife was a tall termagant,[2] fierce of temper, loud of tongue, and strong of arm. Her voice was often heard in wordy warfare with her husband; and his face sometimes showed signs that their conflicts were not confined to words. No one ventured, however, to interfere between them. The lonely wayfarer shrunk within himself at the horrid clamor and clapperclawing;[3] eyed the den of discord askance; and hurried on his way, rejoicing, if a bachelor, in his celibacy.

One day that Tom Walker had been to a distant part of the neighborhood, he took what he considered a shortcut homeward, through the swamp. Like most shortcuts, it was an ill-chosen route. The swamp was thickly grown with great gloomy pines and hemlocks, some of them ninety feet high, which made it dark at noonday, and a retreat for all the owls of the neighborhood.

It was full of pits and quagmires, partly covered with weeds and mosses, where the green surface often betrayed the traveler into a gulf of black, smothering mud; there were also dark and stagnant pools, the abodes of the tadpole, the bullfrog, and the watersnake; where the trunks of pines and hemlocks lay half-drowned, half-rotting, looking like alligators sleeping in the mire.

Tom had long been picking his way cautiously through this treacherous forest; stepping from tuft to tuft of rushes and roots, which afforded precarious footholds among deep sloughs; or pacing carefully, like a cat, along the prostrate trunks of trees; startled now and then by the sudden screaming of the bittern, or the quacking of a wild duck, rising on the wing from some solitary pool. At length he arrived at a piece of firm ground, which ran out like a peninsula into the deep bosom of the swamp. It had been one of the strongholds of the Indians during their wars with the first colonists. Here they had thrown up a kind of fort, which they had looked upon as almost impregnable, and had used as a place of refuge for their squaws and children. Nothing remained of the old Indian fort but a few embankments, gradually sinking to the level of the surrounding earth, and already overgrown in part by oaks and other forest trees, the foliage of which formed a contrast to the dark pines and hemlocks of the swamp.

It was late in the dusk of evening when Tom Walker reached the old fort, and he paused there awhile to rest himself. Anyone but he would have felt unwilling to linger in

2. **termagant** (TER muh guhnt) *n.* quarrelsome woman.
3. **clapperclawing** (KLAP er KLAW ing) *n.* clawing or scratching.

this lonely, melancholy place, for the common people had a bad opinion of it, from the stories handed down from the time of the Indian wars; when it was asserted that the savages held incantations here, and made sacrifices to the evil spirit.

Tom Walker, however, was not a man to be troubled with any fears of the kind. He reposed himself for some time on the trunk of a fallen hemlock, listening to the boding cry of the tree toad, and delving with his walking staff into a mound of black mold at his feet. As he turned up the soil unconsciously, his staff struck against something hard. He raked it out of the vegetable mold, and lo! a cloven skull, with an Indian tomahawk buried deep in it, lay before him. The rust on the weapon showed the time that had elapsed since this deathblow had been given. It was a dreary memento of the fierce struggle that had taken place in this last foothold of the Indian warriors.

"Humph!" said Tom Walker, as he gave it a kick to shake the dirt from it.

"Let that skull alone!" said a gruff voice. Tom lifted up his eyes, and beheld a great black man seated directly opposite him, on the stump of a tree. He was exceedingly surprised, having neither heard nor seen anyone approach; and he was still more perplexed on observing, as well as the gathering gloom would permit, that the stranger was neither Negro nor Indian. It is true he was dressed in a rude half-Indian garb, and had a red belt or sash swathed round his body; but his face was neither black nor copper color, but swarthy and dingy, and begrimed with soot, as if he had been accustomed to toil among fires and forges. He had a shock of coarse black hair, that stood out from his head in all directions, and bore an ax on his shoulder.

He scowled for a moment at Tom with a pair of great red eyes.

"What are you doing on my grounds?" said the black man, with a hoarse growling voice.

"Your grounds!" said Tom with a sneer, "no more your grounds than mine; they belong to Deacon Peabody."

"Deacon Peabody be d—d," said the stranger, "as I flatter myself he will be, if he does not look more to his own sins and less to those of his neighbors. Look yonder, and see how Deacon Peabody is faring."

Tom looked in the direction that the stranger pointed, and beheld one of the great trees, fair and flourishing without, but rotten at the core, and saw that it had been nearly hewn through, so that the first high wind was likely to blow it down. On the bark of the tree was scored the name of Deacon Peabody, an eminent man, who had waxed wealthy by driving shrewd bargains with the Indians. He now looked round, and found most of the tall trees marked

Literary Analysis

Reread the underlined sentence. How does this sentence suggest that the story is being told by an **omniscient**, or all-knowing, **narrator**?

_____

_____

_____

Reading Strategy

Reread the bracketed paragraph. Keeping in mind the title of this story, what can you **infer** about this stranger? Write your inference below. Then circle the sections of the paragraph that help you **draw** this **conclusion**.

_____

_____

_____

_____

_____

Reading Check

What does the stranger have to say about Deacon Peabody?

_____

_____

_____

_____

Reread the underlined passage. What can you **infer** about the **cultural attitudes** of New Englanders during this period from this comment about Crowninshield?

_____

_____

_____

_____

At what point do you know for sure that the stranger is the Devil?

_____

_____

_____

_____

Reread the bracketed paragraph. How does this paragraph make it clear that the story is being told by an **omniscient,** or all-knowing, **narrator**?

_____

_____

_____

_____

_____

with the name of some great man of the colony, and all more or less scored by the ax. The one on which he had been seated, and which had evidently just been hewn down, bore the name of Crowninshield: and he recollected a mighty rich man of that name, who made a vulgar display of wealth, which it was whispered he had acquired by buccaneering.

"He's just ready for burning!" said the black man, with a growl of triumph. "You see I am likely to have a good stock of firewood for winter."

"But what right have you," said Tom, "to cut down Deacon Peabody's timber?"

"The right of a prior claim," said the other. "This woodland belonged to me long before one of your white-faced race put foot upon the soil."

"And pray, who are you, if I may be so bold?" said Tom.

"Oh, I go by various names. I am the wild huntsman in some countries; the black miner in others. In this neighborhood I am known by the name of the black woodsman. I am he to whom the red men consecrated this spot, and in honor of whom they now and then roasted a white man, by way of sweet-smelling sacrifice. Since the red men have been exterminated by you white savages, I amuse myself by presiding at the persecutions of Quakers and Anabaptists;[4] I am the great patron and prompter of slave dealers, and the grandmaster of the Salem witches."

"The upshot of all which is, that, if I mistake not," said Tom, sturdily, "you are he commonly called Old Scratch."

"The same, at your service!" replied the black man, with a half-civil nod.

Such was the opening of this interview, according to the old story; though it has almost too familiar an air to be credited. One would think that to meet with such a singular personage, in this wild, lonely place, would have shaken any man's nerves; but Tom was a hard-minded fellow, not easily daunted, and he had lived so long with a termagant wife, that he did not even fear the Devil.

It is said that after this commencement they had a long and earnest conversation together, as Tom returned homeward. The black man told him of great sums of money buried by Kidd the pirate, under the oak trees on the high ridge, not far from the morass. All these were under his command, and protected by his power, so that none could find them but such as propitiated his favor. These he offered to place within Tom Walker's reach, having conceived an especial kindness for him; but they were to be had only on certain conditions. What these conditions were may easily

---

4. **Quakers and Anabaptists** two religious groups that were persecuted for their beliefs.

be surmised, though Tom never disclosed them publicly. They must have been very hard, for he required time to think of them, and he was not a man to stick at trifles where money was in view. When they had reached the edge of the swamp, the stranger paused— "What proof have I that all you have been telling me is true?" said Tom. "There is my signature," said the black man, pressing his finger on Tom's forehead. So saying, he turned off among the thickets of the swamp, and seemed, as Tom said, to go down, down, down, into the earth, until nothing but his head and shoulders could be seen, and so on, until he totally disappeared.

When Tom reached home, he found the black print of a finger, burnt, as it were, into his forehead, which nothing could obliterate.

The first news his wife had to tell him was the sudden death of Absalom Crowninshield, the rich buccaneer. It was announced in the papers with the usual flourish, that "A great man had fallen in Israel."[5]

Tom recollected the tree which his black friend had just hewn down, and which was ready for burning, "Let the freebooter roast," said Tom, "who cares!" He now felt convinced that all he had heard and seen was no illusion.

He was not prone to let his wife into his confidence; but as this was an uneasy secret, he willingly shared it with her. All her avarice was awakened at the mention of hidden gold, and she urged her husband to comply with the black man's terms and secure what would make them wealthy for life. However Tom might have felt disposed to sell himself to the Devil, he was determined not to do so to oblige his wife; so he flatly refused, out of the mere spirit of contradiction. Many and bitter were the quarrels they had on the subject, but the more she talked, the more resolute was Tom not to be damned to please her.

At length she determined to drive the bargain on her own account, and if she succeeded, to keep all the gain to herself. Being of the same fearless temper as her husband, she set off for the old Indian fort towards the close of a summer's day. She was many hours absent. When she came back, she was reserved and sullen in her replies. She spoke something of a black man, whom she had met about twilight, hewing at the root of a tall tree. He was sulky, however, and would not come to terms: she was to go again with a propitiatory offering, but what it was she forbore to say.

Vocabulary Development: avarice (AV uh ris) *n.* greed

---

5. **A . . . Israel** a reference to II Samuel 3:38 in the Bible. The Puritans often called New England "Israel."

The Devil and Tom Walker **99**

TAKE NOTES

Reading Check

Tom's wife gives him some news when he gets home. (1) What is the news? (2) How does the news convince him that he has really met the Devil?

1. _____

_____

_____

_____

2. _____

_____

_____

_____

Reading Strategy

Reread the underlined sentence. What phrase in this sentence makes it clear that the story is being told by an **omniscient,** or all-knowing, **narrator**?

_____

_____

_____

Reading Strategy

How successful is Tom's wife in her first meeting with the Devil?

_____

_____

_____

_____

Circle two of the theories that historians have about what happened to Tom's wife. What can you **infer** about the **cultural attitudes** of New Englanders during this period from the various theories they have about Tom's wife's disappearance?

_____

_____

_____

_____

Why do you think Tom is more worried about his property than he is about his wife? Do you know anyone who is that greedy?

_____

_____

_____

_____

_____

What does Tom find wrapped up in his wife's checked apron?

_____

_____

_____

The next evening she set off again for the swamp, with her apron heavily laden. Tom waited and waited for her, but in vain; midnight came, but she did not make her appearance: morning, noon, night returned, but still she did not come. Tom now grew uneasy for her safety, especially as he found she had carried off in her apron the silver teapot and spoons, and every portable article of value. Another night elapsed, another morning came; but no wife. In a word, she was never heard of more.

What was her real fate nobody knows, in consequence of so many pretending to know. It is one of those facts which have become confounded by a variety of historians. Some asserted that she lost her way among the tangled mazes of the swamp, and sank into some pit or slough; others, more uncharitable, hinted that she had eloped with the household booty, and made off to some other province; while others surmised that the tempter had decoyed her into a dismal quagmire, on the top of which her hat was found lying. In confirmation of this, it was said a great black man, with an ax on his shoulder, was seen late that very evening coming out of the swamp, carrying a bundle tied in a checked apron, with an air of surly triumph.

The most current and probable story, however, observes that Tom Walker grew so anxious about the fate of his wife and his property, that he set out at length to seek them both at the Indian fort. During a long summer's afternoon he searched about the gloomy place, but no wife was to be seen. He called her name repeatedly, but she was nowhere to be heard. The bittern alone responded to his voice, as he flew screaming by; or the bullfrog croaked dolefully from a neighboring pool. At length, it is said, just in the brown hour of twilight, when the owls began to hoot, and the bats to flit about, his attention was attracted by the clamor of carrion crows hovering about a cypress tree. He looked up, and beheld a bundle tied in a checked apron, and hanging in the branches of the tree, with a great vulture perched hard by, as if keeping watch upon it. He leaped with joy; for he recognized his wife's apron, and supposed it to contain the household valuables.

"Let us get hold of the property," said he, consolingly to himself, "and we will endeavor to do without the woman."

As he scrambled up the tree, the vulture spread its wide wings, and sailed off screaming into the deep shadows of the forest. Tom seized the checked apron, but woeful sight! found nothing but a heart and liver tied up in it!

Such, according to the most authentic old story, was all that was to be found of Tom's wife. She had probably attempted to deal with the black man as she had been accustomed to deal with her husband; but though a female scold is generally considered a match for the Devil, yet in this instance she appears to have had the worst of it. She must have died game, however; for it is said Tom noticed many prints of cloven feet deeply stamped about the tree, and found handfuls of hair, that looked as if they had been plucked from the coarse black shock of the woodsman. Tom knew his wife's prowess by experience. He shrugged his shoulders, as he looked at the signs of a fierce clapperclawing. "Egad," said he to himself, "Old Scratch must have had a tough time of it!"

Tom consoled himself for the loss of his property, with the loss of his wife, for he was a man of fortitude. He even felt something like gratitude towards the black woodsman, who, he considered, had done him a kindness. He sought, therefore, to cultivate a further acquaintance with him, but for some time without success; the old blacklegs played shy, for whatever people may think, he is not always to be had for calling for: he knows how to play his cards when pretty sure of his game.

At length, it is said, when delay had whetted Tom's eagerness to the quick, and prepared him to agree to anything rather than not gain the promised treasure, he met the black man one evening in his usual woods-man's dress, with his ax on his shoulder, sauntering along the swamp, and humming a tune. He affected to receive Tom's advances with great indifference, made brief replies, and went on humming his tune.

By degrees, however, Tom brought him to business, and they began to haggle about the terms on which the former was to have the pirate's treasure. There was one condition which need not be mentioned, being generally understood in all cases where the Devil grants favors; but there were others about which, though of less importance, he was inflexibly obstinate. He insisted that the money found through his means should be employed in his service. He proposed, therefore, that Tom should employ it in the black traffic; that is to say, that he should fit out a slave ship. This, however, Tom resolutely refused: he was bad enough in all conscience, but the Devil himself could not tempt him to turn slave-trader.

Finding Tom so squeamish on this point, he did not insist upon it, but proposed, instead, that he should turn usurer; the Devil being extremely anxious for the increase of usurers, looking upon them as his peculiar[6] people.

Vocabulary Development: usurers (YOO zhuhr uhrz) *n.*
moneylenders who charge very high interest

---

6. **peculiar** particular;

The Devil and Tom Walker **101**

TAKE NOTES

Literary Analysis

Reread the underlined sentence. How does this sentence suggest that the story is being told by an **omniscient,** or all-knowing, **narrator?**

_____

_____

_____

_____

Reading Strategy

Reread the bracketed paragraph. What can you **infer** about the one condition of the Devil's agreement with Tom that "need not be mentioned"?

_____

_____

_____

Reading Strategy

In the bracketed paragraph, the Devil suggests that Tom use Captain Kidd's treasure to set himself up in the slave trade. What can you **infer** about the **cultural attitudes** of Puritan New England—or at least of Washington Irving—by Tom's refusal?

_____

_____

_____

_____

What business does Tom open up in Boston?

_____

_____

_____

_____

The bracketed paragraph describes the economic problems at this time. Use **inference** to write down the reasons why this is a good time for Tom to start his moneylending business. What **prediction** can you make about the success of Tom's business?

_____

_____

_____

_____

The **omniscient,** or all-knowing, **narrator** describes difficult economic problems in the bracketed paragraph. What does the narrator compare the speculation to?

_____

_____

_____

_____

To this no objections were made, for it was just to Tom's taste.

"You shall open a broker's shop in Boston next month," said the black man.

"I'll do it tomorrow, if you wish," said Tom Walker.

"You shall lend money at two per cent a month."

"Egad, I'll charge four!" replied Tom Walker.

"You shall <u>extort</u> bonds, foreclose mortgages, drive the merchant to bankruptcy—"

"I'll drive him to the D—l," cried Tom Walker.

"You are the usurer for my money!" said the blacklegs with delight. "When will you want the rhino?"[7]

"This very night."

"Done!" said the Devil.

"Done!" said Tom Walker. So they shook hands and struck a bargain.

A few days' time saw Tom Walker seated behind his desk in a countinghouse in Boston.

His reputation for a ready-moneyed man, who would lend money out for a good consideration, soon spread abroad. Everybody remembers the time of Governor Belcher,[8] when money was particularly scarce. It was a time of paper credit. The country had been deluged with government bills; the famous Land Bank[9] had been established; there had been a rage for speculating; the people had run mad with schemes for new settlements, for building cities in the wilderness; land jobbers[10] went about with maps of grants, and townships, and El Dorados,[11] lying nobody knew where, but which everybody was ready to purchase. In a word, the great speculating fever which breaks out every now and then in the country, had raged to an alarming degree, and everybody was dreaming of making sudden fortunes from nothing. As usual the fever had subsided; the dream had gone off, and the imaginary fortunes with it; the patients were left in doleful plight, and the whole country resounded with the consequent cry of "hard times."

At this propitious time of public distress did Tom Walker set up as usurer in Boston. His door was soon thronged by customers. The needy and adventurous, the gambling

---

Vocabulary Development: extort (eks TAWRT) *v.* to obtain by threat or violence

---

7. **rhino** (RY noh) *n.* slang term for money.
8. **Governor Belcher** Jonathan Belcher, the governor of Massachusetts Bay Colony from 1730 through 1741.
9. **Land Bank** a bank that financed transactions in real estate.
10. **land jobbers** people who bought and sold undeveloped land.
11. **El Dorados** (el doh RAH dohz) *n.* places that are rich in gold or opportunity. El Dorado was a legendary country in South America sought by early Spanish explorers for its gold and precious stones.

speculator, the dreaming land jobber, the thriftless tradesman, the merchant with cracked credit, in short, everyone driven to raise money by desperate means and desperate sacrifices, hurried to Tom Walker.

Thus Tom was the universal friend of the needy, and acted like a "friend in need"; that is to say, he always exacted good pay and good security. In proportion to the distress of the applicant was the hardness of his terms. He accumulated bonds and mortgages; gradually squeezed his customers closer and closer, and sent them at length, dry as a sponge, from his door.

In this way he made money hand over hand, became a rich and mighty man, and exalted his cocked hat upon 'Change.[12] He built himself, as usual, a vast house, out of ostentation; but left the greater part of it unfinished and unfurnished, out of parsimony. He even set up a carriage in the fullness of his vainglory, though he nearly starved the horses which drew it; and as the ungreased wheels groaned and screeched on the axletrees, you would have thought you heard the souls of the poor debtors he was squeezing.

As Tom waxed old, however, he grew thoughtful. Having secured the good things of this world, he began to feel anxious about those of the next. He thought with regret on the bargain he had made with his black friend, and set his wits to work to cheat him out of the conditions. He became, therefore, all of a sudden, a violent churchgoer. He prayed loudly and strenuously, as if heaven were to be taken by force of lungs. Indeed, one might always tell when he had sinned most during the week, by the clamor of his Sunday devotion. The quiet Christians who had been modestly and steadfastly traveling Zionward,[13] were struck with self-reproach at seeing themselves so suddenly outstripped in their career by this new-made convert. Tom was as rigid in religious as in money matters; he was a stern supervisor and censurer of his neighbors, and seemed to think every sin entered up to their account became a credit on his own side of the page. He even talked of the expediency of reviving the persecution of Quakers and Anabaptists. In a word, Tom's zeal became as notorious as his riches.

Still, in spite of all this strenuous attention to forms, Tom had a lurking dread that the Devil, after all, would have his due. That he might not be taken unawares, therefore, it is

---

Vocabulary Development: ostentation (AH sten TAY shuhn) *n.* boastful display

parsimony (PAHR suh MOH nee) *n.* stinginess

---

12. **'Change** exchange where bankers and merchants did business.
13. **Zionward** (ZY uhn werd) toward heaven.

TAKE NOTES

Reading Strategy

What can you **infer** from the underlined sentence about the kind of moneylender Tom becomes?

_____

_____

_____

Literary Analysis

Reread the bracketed sentences. How do these sentences make it clear that the story is being told by an **omniscient,** or all-knowing, narrator?

_____

_____

_____

Reading Check

Why does Tom suddenly become a churchgoer?

_____

_____

_____

What does Tom do that makes people think he is becoming crazy as he ages?

_____

_____

_____

_____

_____

The Devil is soon to claim Tom Walker. Circle two facts that the **omniscient**, or all-knowing, **narrator** mentions in the bracketed paragraph that make you suspect that the time is coming soon.

_____

_____

_____

_____

Why is it important that Tom has no Bible with him when he answers the three knocks on his door?

_____

_____

_____

_____

said he always carried a small Bible in his coat pocket. He had also a great folio Bible on his countinghouse desk, and would frequently be found reading it when people called on business; on such occasions he would lay his green spectacles in the book, to mark the place, while he turned round to drive some usurious bargain.

Some say that Tom grew a little crackbrained in his old days, and that fancying his end approaching, he had his horse newly shod, saddled and bridled, and buried with his feet uppermost; because he supposed that at the last day the world would be turned upside down, in which case he should find his horse standing ready for mounting, and he was determined at the worst to give his old friend a run for it. This, however, is probably a mere old wives' fable. If he really did take such a precaution, it was totally superfluous; at least so says the authentic old legend, which closes his story in the following manner.

One hot summer afternoon in the dog days, just as a terrible black thunder-gust was coming up, Tom sat in his countinghouse in his white linen cap and India silk morning gown. He was on the point of foreclosing a mortgage, by which he would complete the ruin of an unlucky land speculator for whom he had professed the greatest friendship. The poor land jobber begged him to grant a few months' indulgence. Tom had grown testy and irritated, and refused another day.

"My family will be ruined and brought upon the parish," said the land jobber. "Charity begins at home," replied Tom; "I must take care of myself in these hard times."

"You have made so much money out of me," said the speculator.

Tom lost his patience and his piety—"The Devil take me," said he, "if I have made a farthing!"

Just then there were three loud knocks at the street door. He stepped out to see who was there. A black man was holding a black horse, which neighed and stamped with impatience.

"Tom, you're come for," said the black fellow, gruffly. Tom shrunk back, but too late. He had left his little Bible at the bottom of his coat pocket, and his big Bible on the desk buried under the mortgage he was about to foreclose: never was sinner taken more unawares. The black man whisked him like a child into the saddle, gave the horse the lash, and away he galloped, with Tom on his back, in the midst of the thunderstorm. The clerks stuck their pens behind their ears, and stared after him from the windows. Away went Tom Walker, dashing down the streets, his white cap bobbing up and down, his morning gown fluttering in the wind, and his steed striking fire out of the pavement at every bound. When the clerks turned to look for the black man he had disappeared.

Tom Walker never returned to foreclose the mortgage. A countryman who lived on the border of the swamp, reported that in the height of the thunder-gust he had heard a great clattering of hoofs and a howling along the road, and running to the window caught sight of a figure, such as I have described, on a horse that galloped like mad across the fields, over the hills and down into the black hemlock swamp towards the old Indian fort; and that shortly after a thunderbolt falling in that direction seemed to set the whole forest in a blaze.

The good people of Boston shook their heads and shrugged their shoulders, but had been so much accustomed to witches and goblins and tricks of the Devil, in all kind of shapes from the first settlement of the colony, that they were not so much horror struck as might have been expected. Trustees were appointed to take charge of Tom's effects. There was nothing, however, to administer upon.

On searching his coffers all his bonds and mortgages were found reduced to cinders. In place of gold and silver his iron chest was filled with chips and shavings; two skeletons lay in his stable instead of his half-starved horses, and the very next day his great house took fire and was burned to the ground.

Such was the end of Tom Walker and his ill-gotten wealth. Let all griping money brokers lay this story to heart. The truth of it is not to be doubted. The very hole under the oak trees, whence he dug Kidd's money, is to be seen to this day; and the neighboring swamp and old Indian fort are often haunted in stormy nights by a figure on horseback, in morning gown and white cap, which is doubtless the troubled spirit of the usurer. In fact, the story has resolved itself into a proverb, and is the origin of that popular saying, so prevalent throughout New England, of "The Devil and Tom Walker."

Reader's Response: Why do people enjoy scary stories? What about this story reminds you of other scary stories you know?

_____

_____

_____

Thinking About the Skill: How did **inferring cultural attitudes** help you to understand this legend? How will it help you read similar selections in the future?

_____

_____

_____

TAKE NOTES

Reading Strategy

Reread the bracketed paragraph. What can you **infer** about the **cultural attitudes** of the people of Boston at this time from the fact that they are not horrified at Tom's disappearance?

_____

_____

_____

_____

_____

Stop to Reflect

This story is a **legend**, or a traditional story that reflects cultural values. Legends often deal with a particular person—a hero, a saint, or a national leader. Tom Walker is not any of those things. How would you describe him? How is Tom similar to or different from other legendary characters you have read about or seen on television or in the movies?

_____

_____

_____

_____

_____

Reading Check

When and where is Tom's spirit seen again?

_____

_____

The Devil and Tom Walker **105**

The Devil and Tom Walker

1. **Evaluate:** What kind of people do you think Tom Walker and his wife are? Explain.

   _____

   _____

2. **Literary Analysis:** Using the diagram shown, give two examples of what the **omniscient point of view** narrator reveals about the thoughts and feelings of each character.

   ```
   ┌──────────┐                              ┌──────────┐
   │          │                              │          │
   └──────────┘                              └──────────┘
         ┌────────────┐  ┌──────────────┐  ┌────────────┐
         │ Tom Walker │──│  Omniscient  │──│ Mrs. Walker│
         └────────────┘  │   Narrator   │  └────────────┘
   ┌──────────┐          └──────────────┘          ┌──────────┐
   │          │         ┌────────────┐             │          │
   └──────────┘         │ The Devil  │             └──────────┘
                        └────────────┘
   ```

3. **Reading Strategy:** Based on Irving's story, what **inference** can you make about New Englanders' **cultural attitudes** toward religion in the 1720s?

   _____

   _____

   _____

4. **Reading Strategy:** Based on Irving's story, what inference can you make about New Englanders' cultural attitudes toward moneylenders in the 1720s.

   _____

   _____

   _____

The Tide Rises, The Tide Falls • Thanatopsis • Old Ironsides • *from* Snowbound

LITERARY ANALYSIS

In poetry, syllables are arranged in patterns called **meter.** Some syllables are stressed and some are unstressed. The meter is the arrangement of these stressed and unstressed syllables.

- The basic unit of meter is called the *foot.* The type and number of feet in a line of poetry determines the poem's meter.
- A foot usually has one stressed and one or more unstressed syllables.
- One type of foot is called the *iamb.* An iamb is one unstressed syllable followed by a stressed syllable.
- One pattern of iambs is *iambic tetrameter* which has four iambs per line. The following line from *Snowbound* is in iambic tetrameter. Count the four iambs. The stressed syllables are capitalized.

  The SUN that BRIEF DeCEMber DAY

READING STRATEGY

Summarizing helps you to check your understanding of what you have read. To summarize:

- Accurately state the main ideas and supporting details of a work or section of a work.
- Use your own words.

Summarize each poem using the following chart.

Poem	Main Idea	Supporting Details
The Tide Rises, The Tide Falls		
Thanatoposis		
Old Ironsides		
from Snowbound		

The Tide Rises, The Tide Falls

Henry Wadsworth Longfellow

Thanatopsis

William Cullen Bryant

Old Ironsides

Oliver Wendell Holmes

from Snowbound

John Greenleaf Whittier

Summaries The subjects of these poems connect to life in New England. Longfellow's **"The Tide Rises, The Tide Falls"** compares the cycle of tides in the ocean to the cycle of life and death. In **"Thanatopsis,"** Bryant also explores the theme of death through images from nature, such as the earth and ocean. Holmes celebrates a ship's history at sea in **"Old Ironsides."** Finally, Whittier describes the beauty of a world covered in snow in an excerpt from *Snowbound.*

Note-taking Guide

Use the chart below to record images of nature found in each of these poems.

The Tide Rises, The Tide Falls	Thanatoposis	Old Ironsides	*from* Snowbound

The Tide Rises, The Tide Falls • Thanatopsis •
Old Ironsides • *from* Snowbound

1. **Assess:** Choose one of these poems. In what ways has life changed since the poem was written in the mid-1860s?

   Name of Poem _____

   _____

   _____

2. **Literary Analysis:** A poem's **meter** is the rhythm of stressed and unstressed syllables in a line. Read these lines from "Thanatopsis." Then, mark the stressed (/) and unstressed (˘) syllables of the meter.

   > So shalt thou rest, and what if thou withdraw
   > In silence from the living, and no friend.

3. **Literary Analysis:** An **iamb** is a type of foot that has one unstressed syllable followed by a stressed syllable. Read the second stanza of "Old Ironsides." Which lines are in iambic tetrameter (four iambs)?

   _____

Key Details	Summary
Stanza 1	
Stanza 2	

4. **Reading Strategy: Summarize** the main idea of "Thanatopsis." Write the summary as though it is a guide for someone unfamiliar with the poem.

   _____

   _____

   _____

   _____

MEMORANDUMS

About Memorandums

A **memorandum** is a business document that tells employees about upcoming events, policy changes, or other business matters. In today's workplace, the average memorandum is brief and informal. It usually contains a heading that indicates the sender, recipient, date, and subject. The body explains the subject in detail.

Historic memorandums are often more formal and detailed. Look for these qualities in this historic memorandum in which Thomas Jefferson assigned Meriwether Lewis the task of exploring the Missouri River in 1803.

Reading Strategy

Analyzing Text Structures: Patterns of Organization

Informative writing can follow several different **patterns of organization**. Three patterns are described in the chart below.

Pattern of Organization	Structure	Type of Writing in Which It Is Found
Chronological Order	Step-by-step details are presented in time order.	Do-it-yourself instructions
Order of Importance	Ideas flow from most to least important or from least to most important.	Persuasive writing
Enumeration	Supportive details are provided in list form.	Brochure or sales documents

BUILD UNDERSTANDING

Knowing these words will help you read this historic memorandum.

commerce (KAHM ers) *n.* the buying and selling of goods

latitude and longitude east/west and north/south geographic lines that are used to pinpoint any location on Earth's surface

portage (POR tij) *n.* an area of land across which boats must be carried in order to reach the next stretch of open water

Commission of Meriwether Lewis

Thomas Jefferson

June 20, 1803

To Meriwether Lewis, esquire, captain of the first regiment of infantry of the United States of America: Your situation as secretary of the president of the United States, has made you acquainted with the objects of my confidential message of January 18, 1803, to the legislature; you have seen the act they passed, which, though expressed in general terms, was meant to sanction those objects, and you are appointed to carry them into execution.

. . .

The object of your mission is to explore the Missouri river, and such principal streams of it, as, by its course and communication[1] with the waters of the Pacific ocean, whether the Columbia, Oregan [sic], Colorado, or any other river, may offer the most direct and practicable[2] water-communication across the continent, for the purposes of commerce.

Beginning at the mouth of the Missouri, you will take observations of latitude and longitude, at all remarkable points on the river, and especially at the mouths of rivers, at rapids, at islands, and other places and objects distinguished by such natural marks and characters, of a durable kind, as that they may with certainty be recognized hereafter. The courses of the river between these points of observation may be supplied

---

TAKE NOTES

Reading Memorandums

Historic **memorandums** differ in format but contain the same information as modern memos. Circle the name of the person who received this memorandum. Underline the sender and the date.

Reading Check

Read the bracketed passage. Then, **summarize** what you have read by filling in the blanks with your own words.

Lewis's task was to

_____

in order to_____

_____.

List three things that Jefferson wants Lewis to observe.

1. _____

2. _____

3. _____

Why would Lewis's observations be important for future travel and trade?

_____

_____

_____

_____

What does Jefferson suggest that Lewis do when he has leisure time during the journey?

_____

_____

by the compass, the log-line, and by time, corrected by the observations themselves. The variations of the needle, too, in different places, should be noticed.

The interesting points of the portage between the heads of the Missouri,[3] and of the water offering the best communication with the Pacific Ocean, should also be fixed by observation;[4] and the course of that water to the ocean, in the same manner as that of the Missouri.

Your observations are to be taken with great pains and accuracy; to be entered distinctly and intelligibly for others as well as yourself; to comprehend all the elements necessary, with the aid of the usual tables, to fix the latitude and longitude of the places at which they were taken; and are to be rendered to the war-office, for the purpose of having the calculations made concurrently by proper persons within the United States. Several copies of these, as well as of your other notes, should be made at leisure times, and put into the care of the most trustworthy of your attendants to guard, by multiplying them against the accidental losses to which they will be exposed. A further guard would be, that one of these copies be on the cuticular membranes of the paper-birch, as less liable to injury from damp than common paper.

The commerce which may be carried on with the people inhabiting the line you will pursue, renders a knowledge of those people important. You will therefore endeavor to make yourself acquainted, as far as a diligent pursuit of your journey shall admit, with the names of the nations and their numbers;

---

3. **heads of the Missouri** the sources of the Missouri River.
4. **fixed by observation** established the position of a place based on measurements or surroundings.

The extent and limits of their possessions;

Their relations with other tribes or nations;

Their language, traditions, monuments;

Their ordinary occupations in agriculture, fishing, hunting, war, arts, and the implements for these;

Their food, clothing, and domestic accommodations;

The diseases prevalent among them, and the remedies they use;

Moral and physical circumstances which distinguish them from the tribes we know;

Peculiarities in their laws, customs, and dispositions[5];

And articles of commerce they may need or furnish, and to what extent.

And, considering the interest which every nation has in extending and strengthening the authority of reason and justice among the people around them, it will be useful to acquire what knowledge you can of the state of morality, religion, and information among them; as it may better enable those who may endeavor to civilize and instruct them, to adapt their measures to the existing notions and practices of those on whom they are to operate. . . .

In all your [dealings] with the natives, treat them in the most friendly and conciliatory manner which their own conduct will admit; allay all jealousies as to the object of your journey; satisfy them of its innocence; make them acquainted with the position, extent, character, peaceable and commercial dispositions of the United States; of our wish to be neighborly, friendly, and useful to them, and of our dispositions to a commercial [relationship] with them; confer with them on the points most convenient as mutual emporiums,[6] and the articles of most desirable interchange for them and us. If a few of their influential chiefs, within practicable

5. **dispositions** (DIS puh ZI shunz) *n.* leanings.
6. **emporiums** (em POR ee ums) *n.* trading centers.

TAKE NOTES

Reading Strategy

Circle the letter of the **pattern of organization** that Jefferson uses in the bracketed section.

a. chronological

b. order of importance

c. enumeration

Explain your answer.

_____

_____

_____

_____

Stop to Reflect

In the bracketed section, Jefferson says Lewis should become familiar with the beliefs and values of native people, so later settlers can "civilize and instruct them." What is Jefferson assuming about native people?

_____

_____

_____

Stop to Reflect

What advantages could Lewis gain from being friendly toward the native people?

_____

_____

_____

A **memorandum** is often written using the *imperative*, or command, form. On this page, underline three commands that Jefferson gives Lewis. Circle the verb in each example.

distance, wish to visit us, arrange such a visit with them, and furnish them with authority to call on our officers on their entering the United States, to have them conveyed to this place at the public expense. If any of them should wish to have some of their young people brought up with us, and taught such arts as may be useful to them, we will receive, instruct, and take care of them. Such a mission, whether of influential chiefs, or of young people, would give some security to your own party. Carry with you some matter of the kine-pox; inform those of them with whom you may be of its efficacy as a preservative from the small-pox, and instruct and encourage them in the use of it. This may be especially done wherever you winter.

As it is impossible for us to foresee in what manner you will be received by those people, whether with hospitality or hostility, so is it impossible to prescribe the exact degree of perseverance with which you are to pursue your journey. We value too much the lives of citizens to offer them to probable destruction. Your numbers will be sufficient to secure you against the unauthorized opposition of individuals, or of small parties; but if a superior force, authorized, or not authorized, by a nation, should be arrayed against your further passage, and inflexibly determined to arrest it, you must decline its further pursuit and return. In the loss of yourselves we should lose also the information you will have acquired. By returning safely with that, you may enable us to renew the essay with better calculated means. To your own discretion, therefore, must be left the degree of danger you may risk, and the point at which you should decline, only saying, we wish you to err on the side of your safety, and to bring back your party safe, even if it be with less information. . . .

THINKING ABOUT MEMORANDUMS

1. Why does Jefferson want Lewis to copy his observations multiple times?

_____

_____

2. What instructions does Jefferson give Lewis on how to treat the Native Americans he meets?

_____

_____

READING STRATEGY

3. Why do you think Jefferson starts his **memorandum** by stating Meriwether Lewis's mission?

_____

_____

4. What is the overall pattern of organization in this memorandum? Explain.

_____

_____

TIMED WRITING: PERSUASION (25 minutes)

Identify one topic in Jefferson's memorandum. Write a brief summary of the topic. Remember to focus on key points. Answer the questions below to help you organize your writing.

• What is the topic? _____

• What details explain the topic? _____

_____

• Which pattern of organization—chronological order, order of importance, or enumeration—works best to present this information?

_____

Crossing the Great Divide •
The Most Sublime Spectacle on Earth

LITERARY ANALYSIS

Description in writing captures the sensations of sight, sound, smell, taste, and touch. Consider this example from Powell's journal:

> But form and color do not exhaust all the divine qualities of the Grand Canyon. It is the land of music. The river thunders in perpetual roar . . .

Look for other examples of descriptive language that bring scenes to life. Use the chart shown to record descriptive details.

Descriptions	
Sight	
Sound	
Taste	
Touch	

READING STRATEGY

Noting spatial relationships as you read can help to clarify the size, distance, and location of features in a text. Using this information will help you form an accurate mental picture of the subject. Look for spatial relationships in these selections to gain a better understanding of the features they describe.

Crossing the Great Divide

Meriwether Lewis

Summary Lewis reports on his early exploration of the American West. He speaks about the Native Americans he meets and how they helped him. He tells a positive story of American movement westward. Lewis tells the Native Americans that the United States government wishes to be friendly toward them. He also explains how new trade routes will help them.

Note-taking Guide

Use this diagram to record the main idea in Lewis's report. Then, list three details that support or illustrate this idea.

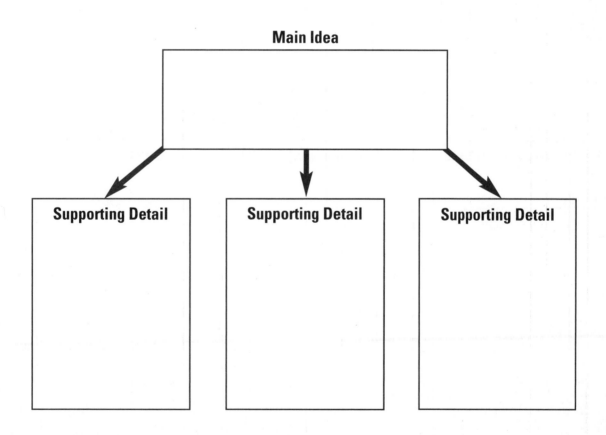

Main Idea

Supporting Detail

Supporting Detail

Supporting Detail

The Most Sublime Spectacle on Earth

John Wesley Powell

Summary Powell speaks of the beauty of the Grand Canyon. He explains that rain and rivers formed the canyon over many centuries. He describes the complexity and depth of the canyon's history and beauty. Rather than speaking about himself, Powell focuses entirely on the magnificence of the Grand Canyon.

Note-taking Guide

Use this diagram to record the main idea in Powell's report. Then, list three details that support or illustrate this idea.

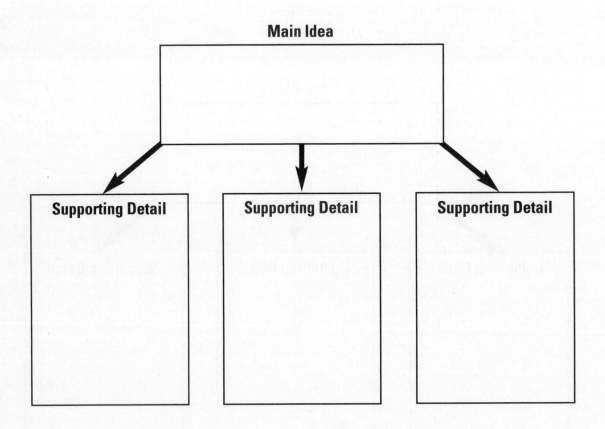

Main Idea

Supporting Detail

Supporting Detail

Supporting Detail

Crossing the Great Divide • The Most Sublime Spectacle on Earth

1. **Compare and Contrast:** What might a painting of a scene from the American West show that these two written descriptions cannot?

   _____

   _____

2. **Literary Analysis:** Find two sentences that contain **description** in "The Most Sublime Spectacle on Earth" and write them on the lines.

   _____

   _____

3. **Literary Analysis:** Explain what makes the sentences you identified above effective.

   _____

   _____

4. **Reading Strategy: Noting spatial relationships** of space and size as Powell describes them, explain which is greater: the erosion of the canyons or the erosion of the region?

   _____

   _____

5. **Reading Strategy:** In the chart shown, list details that indicate size and spatial relationships of the Grand Canyon. Then, describe these relationships in your own words.

Description	Spatial Relationships	In My Own Words

The Fall of the House of Usher • The Raven

LITERARY ANALYSIS

Edgar Allan Poe argued that a short story should be constructed to achieve a **single effect.** Poe believed that every character, event, and detail should contribute to this single effect. As you read, consider the ways in which Poe writes to produce a single effect.

Both "The Fall of the House of Usher" and "The Raven" are examples of **Gothic literature.** The Gothic style uses the following elements:

- bleak or remote settings
- gruesome or violent plot incidents
- tormented and disturbed characters
- supernatural or otherworldly events

As you read, pay attention to how Poe uses different Gothic elements.

READING STRATEGY

Long, complex sentences can challenge your understanding. A good strategy is to **break down long sentences** into logical parts. First, look for the sentence's subject and verb. Then, look for other clues, such as punctuation, conjunctions, and modifying words. Use this chart to break down some of Poe's lengthy sentences into manageable parts.

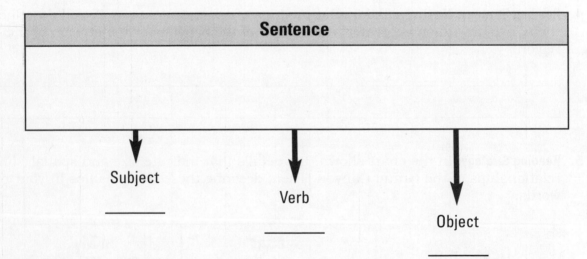

Sentence

Subject _____

Verb _____

Object _____

The Fall of the House of Usher

Edgar Allan Poe

Summary Roderick Usher has asked the narrator to stay with him while he is ill. The narrator answers his old friend's request and travels to Usher's gloomy mansion. There, he learns that Usher is not well physically or mentally. The narrator also finds out that Usher's twin sister, Madeline, is ill. One evening, Usher tells the narrator that his sister has died. Usher and the narrator take her coffin to a vault within the mansion. After they seal her inside, strange things begin to happen.

Note-taking Guide

Complete the following timeline with events from the story.

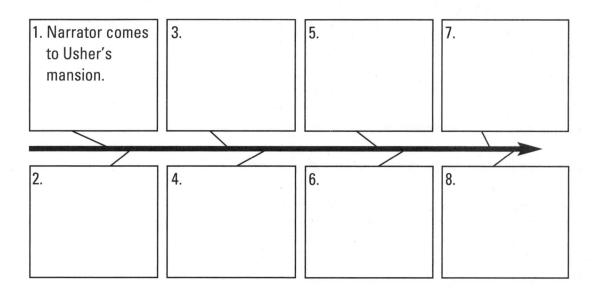

1. Narrator comes to Usher's mansion.
2.
3.
4.
5.
6.
7.
8.

The Raven

Edgar Allan Poe

Summary The speaker in this poem sits alone reading at night. A mysterious raven comes knocking at his door. The speaker has been grieving for his lost love, Lenore. He begins to ask the raven questions, but the raven only has one response. Through the man's conversation with the raven, Poe explores a mind falling into madness.

Note-taking Guide

Complete the following chart by telling how the raven responds to the speaker.

What the speaker of the poem says	What the speaker hears the raven answer
• Excuse me, I was napping. ⟶	
• Lenore! ⟶	
• Tell me your name. ⟶	
• The bird will leave me tomorrow, as others have. ⟶	
• I need respite from my grief over Lenore. ⟶	
• "Is there balm in Gilead?" ⟶	
• Will I hold Lenore again? ⟶	

The Raven
Edgar Allan Poe

Edgar Allan Poe is well known for short stories and poems about mysterious and frightening events. He also writes frequently about the sometimes terrifying power of the imagination. As you read this poem, try to separate what is really happening from what the speaker is imagining.

Once upon a midnight dreary, while I pondered, weak
    and weary,
Over many a quaint and curious volume of forgotten
    lore—
While I nodded, nearly napping, suddenly there came
    a tapping,
As of some one gently rapping, rapping at my
    chamber door.
5 "'Tis some visitor," I muttered, "tapping at my
    chamber door—
                Only this, and nothing more."

Ah, distinctly I remember it was in the bleak December;
And each separate dying ember wrought its ghost
    upon the floor.
Eagerly I wished the morrow;—vainly I had sought
    to borrow
10 From my books surcease[1] of sorrow—sorrow for the
    lost Lenore—
For the rare and radiant maiden whom the angels
    name Lenore—
             Nameless *here* for evermore.

And the silken, sad, uncertain rustling of each purple
    curtain
Thrilled me—filled me with fantastic terrors never felt
    before;
15 So that now, to still the beating of my heart, I stood
    repeating
"'Tis some visitor entreating entrance at my chamber
    door—
Some late visitor entreating entrance at my chamber
    door;—
           This it is and nothing more."

Presently my soul grew stronger; hesitating then
    no longer,
20 "Sir," said I, "or Madam, truly your forgiveness
    I implore;
But the fact is I was napping, and so gently you
    came rapping,

---

1. **surcease** (ser SEES) end.

© Pearson Education, Inc., publishing as Pearson Prentice Hall.

© Pearson Education, Inc., publishing as Pearson Prentice Hall.

What does the speaker find when he opens his door the first time?

_____

_____

Reread the underlined sentence. **Break this long sentence down** as you read. Look for the core of the sentence. Then, rewrite the sentence in your own words.

_____

_____

_____

Gothic writing influenced Poe greatly. Gothic novels usually take place in old, gloomy castles where frightening supernatural events happen. What gothic elements have you noticed so far in this poem?

_____

_____

_____

What happens when the speaker opens his door a second time?

_____

_____

_____

And so faintly you came tapping, tapping at my
    chamber door,
That I scarce was sure I heard you"—here I opened
    wide the door;—
              Darkness there and nothing more.

25 Deep into that darkness peering, long I stood there
    wondering, fearing,
Doubting, dreaming dreams no mortal ever dared to
    dream before;
But the silence was unbroken, and the stillness gave
    no token,
And the only word there spoken was the whispered
    word, "Lenore?"
This I whispered, and an echo murmured back the
    word, "Lenore!"
30   Merely this and nothing more.

Back then into the chamber turning, all my soul
    within me burning,
Soon again I heard a tapping somewhat louder
    than before.
"Surely," said I, "surely that is something at my
    window lattice;
Let me see, then, what thereat is, and this mystery
    explore—
35 Let my heart be still a moment and this mystery
    explore;—
             'Tis the wind and nothing more!"

Open here I flung the shutter, when, with many a
    flirt and flutter,
In there stepped a stately Raven of the saintly days
    of yore;
Not the least obeisance made he; not a minute
    stopped or stayed he;
40 But, with mien of lord or lady, perched above my
    chamber door—
Perched upon a bust of Pallas[2] just above my
chamber door—
            Perched, and sat, and nothing more.

Then this ebony bird beguiling[3] my sad fancy into
smiling,

Vocabulary Development: obeisance (oh BAY suhns) *n.* gesture
of respect

---

2. **Pallas** (PAL us) Pallas Athena, the ancient Greek goddess of wisdom.
3. **beguiling** (bi GYL ing) charming.

By the grave and stern decorum of the countenance[4]
    it wore,
45 "Though thy crest be shorn and shaven, thou," I said,
    "art sure no <u>craven</u>,
Ghastly grim and ancient Raven wandering from the
    Nightly shore—
Tell me what thy lordly name is on the Night's
    Plutonian[5] shore!"
                  Quoth the Raven, "Nevermore."

Much I marveled this ungainly fowl to hear discourse
    so plainly,
50 Though its answer little meaning—little relevancy
    bore;
For we cannot help agreeing that no living human
    being
Ever yet was blessed with seeing bird above his
    chamber door—
Bird or beast upon the sculptured bust above his
    chamber door,
           With such name as "Nevermore."

55 But the Raven, sitting lonely on the placid bust,
    spoke only
That one word, as if his soul in that one word he did
    outpour.
Nothing farther than he uttered—not a feather then
    he fluttered—
Till I scarcely more than muttered, "Other friends
    have flown before—
On the morrow he will leave me, as my Hopes have
    flown before."
60   Then the bird said, "Nevermore."

Startled at the stillness broken by reply so aptly
    spoken,
"Doubtless," said I, "what it utters is its only stock
    and store
Caught from some unhappy master whom unmerciful
    Disaster
Followed fast and followed faster till his songs one
    burden bore—
65 Till the dirges of his Hope that melancholy burden
    bore
           Of 'Never—nevermore.'"

Vocabulary Development: craven (KRAY vuhn) *adj.* very
                      cowardly

---

4. **countenance** (KOWN tuh nuhns) *n.* facial expression.
5. **Plutonian** (ploo TOH nee uhn) *adj.* like the underworld or infernal regions.
   Refers to Pluto, Roman god of the underworld.

TAKE NOTES

Reading Check

The speaker asks the raven what his name is. What does the raven reply?

_____

_____

Literary Analysis

In **gothic** writing, frightening supernatural events often happen. What gothic elements have you noticed on this page of the poem?

_____

_____

_____

Literary Analysis

With every character, detail, and incident in this poem, Poe tries to achieve **a single effect**. What is the single effect that Poe is trying to achieve in the bracketed section?

_____

_____

_____

Stop to Reflect

Has anyone ever told you that your imagination was running away with you? The speaker of this poem is letting his imagination run away with him. What clues do you have that he is?

_____

_____

_____

Reread the underlined sentence. **Break down this long sentence** as you read. Circle the subject and the predicate. Then, rewrite the sentence in your own words on the lines below.

_____

_____

_____

_____

Reread the bracketed stanzas. The speaker is angry with the raven here. What is the **single effect** that Poe is trying to achieve in these stanzas?

_____

_____

_____

_____

The speaker asks the raven when he will forget Lenore. What does the raven reply?

_____

_____

_____

_____

But the Raven still beguiling my sad fancy into
    smiling,
Straight I wheeled a cushioned seat in front of bird,
    and bust and door;
Then, upon the velvet sinking, I betook myself to
    linking
70 Fancy unto fancy, thinking what this ominous[6] bird
    of yore—
What this grim, ungainly, ghastly, gaunt, and
    ominous bird of yore
               Meant in croaking "Nevermore."

This I sat engaged in guessing, but no syllable
    expressing
To the fowl whose fiery eyes now burned into my
    bosom's core;
75 This and more I sat divining, with my head at ease
    reclining
On the cushion's velvet lining that the lamp-light
    gloated o'er,
But whose velvet-violet lining with the lamp-light
    gloating o'er,
               She shall press, ah, nevermore!

Then, methought, the air grew denser, perfumed
    from an unseen censer
80 Swung by seraphim whose foot-falls tinkled on the
    tufted floor.
"Wretch," I cried, "thy God hath lent thee—by these
    angels he hath sent thee
Respite—respite and nepenthe[7] from thy memories
    of Lenore;
Quaff, oh quaff this kind nepenthe and forget this
    lost Lenore!"
               Quoth the Raven, "Nevermore."

85 "Prophet!" said I, "thing of evil!—prophet still, if bird
    or devil!—
Whether Tempter sent, or whether tempest tossed
    thee here ashore,
Desolate yet all undaunted, on this desert land
    enchanted—
On this home by Horror haunted—tell me truly,
    I implore—
Is there—is there balm in Gilead?[8]—tell me—tell me,
    I implore!"
90   Quoth the Raven, "Nevermore."

---

6. **ominous** (AHM uh nuhs) *adj.* threatening; sinister.
7. **nepenthe** (ni PEN thee) *n.* drug that the ancient Greeks believed could relieve sorrow.
8. **balm in Gilead** (GIL ee uhd) in the Bible, a healing ointment made in Gilead, a region of ancient Palestine.

"Prophet!" said I, "thing of evil!—prophet still, if bird
    or devil!
By that Heaven that bends above us—by that God
    we both adore—
Tell this soul with sorrow laden if, within the distant
    Aidenn,[9]
It shall clasp a sainted maiden whom the angels
    name Lenore—
95 Clasp a rare and radiant maiden whom the angels
    name Lenore."
              Quoth the Raven, "Nevermore."

"Be that word our sign of parting, bird or fiend!"
    I shrieked, upstarting—
"Get thee back into the tempest and the Night's
    Plutonian shore!
Leave no black plume as a token of that lie thy soul
    hath spoken!
100 Leave my loneliness unbroken!—quit the bust
    above my door!
Take thy beak from out my heart, and take thy form
    from off my door!"
              Quoth the Raven, "Nevermore."

And the Raven, never flitting, still is sitting, still is
    sitting
On the pallid bust of Pallas just above my chamber
    door;
105 And his eyes have all the seeming of a demon's
    that is dreaming;
And the lamp-light o'er him streaming throws his
    shadow on the floor;
And my soul from out that shadow that lies floating
    on the floor
              Shall be lifted—nevermore!

---

9. **Aidenn** (AY den) arabic for Eden or heaven.

Reader's Response: Try reading the poem aloud or listening to
a taped version. Notice the repeated words and sounds.
What is your reaction to the sounds of this poem?

_____

_____

Thinking About the Skill: How did breaking long sentences
down help you to understand this poem? How will this
technique help you read other poems in the future?

_____

_____

TAKE NOTES

Literary Analysis

The raven answers "Nevermore" to
three different questions in the last
three stanzas of this poem. What is
the **single effect** that Poe is trying
to achieve by repeating
"Nevermore"?

_____

_____

_____

_____

_____

Reading Strategy

The last stanza of this poem is one
long sentence. **Break this long
sentence down** into several shorter
sentences as you read the stanza.
Then, rewrite the sentence in your
own words on the lines below.

_____

_____

_____

_____

_____

_____

_____

The Fall of the House of Usher • The Raven

1. **Connect:** In what ways is the appearance of the interior of Usher's house related to the condition of Usher's mind?

   _____

   _____

2. **Analyze:** By the end of the poem, what does the Raven come to represent?

   _____

   _____

3. **Literary Analysis:** How does the storm contribute to the **single effect** of a growing sense of terror in "The Fall of the House of Usher"?

   _____

   _____

4. **Literary Analysis:** Use this chart to compare the **Gothic** elements in the story and poem.

Gothic Element	House of Usher	Raven
Setting		
Violence		
Characterization		
The Supernatural		

5. **Reading Strategy:** Break down this **sentence** and rewrite it in your own words.

   At times, again, I was obliged to resolve all into the mere inexplicable vagaries of madness, for I beheld him gazing upon vacancy for long hours, in an attitude of the profoundest attention, as if listening to some imaginary sound.

   _____

   _____

   _____

The Minister's Black Veil

LITERARY ANALYSIS

A **parable** is a simple, usually brief, story that teaches a moral lesson. Unlike a fable, which features animal characters, a parable features human beings. A parable is a type of **allegory**—a story with both a literal and a symbolic meaning. In subtitling this story "A Parable," Hawthorne indicates that the story conveys an important moral message. As you read, think about the lesson Hawthorne wants his story to communicate.

The veil that Mr. Hooper vows never to remove is a **symbol**—something that has meaning in itself while also standing for something greater. To discover the veil's symbolic meaning, notice Hawthorne's descriptions of the veil and its effects on the characters in the story.

READING STRATEGY

When the message of a work of fiction is conveyed indirectly, as it is in this symbolic story, the reader must **draw inferences,** or conclusions, by looking closely at details, especially description and dialogue. Use this chart to draw inferences about the story's characters and events.

Description/Dialogue

↓

Inference

The Minister's Black Veil

Nathaniel Hawthorne

Summary The parson, Mr. Hooper, arrives at church wearing a black veil over his face. He wears the veil without explanation through his sermon, through the following sermon, and then through a funeral and a wedding. The congregation whispers among themselves. They fear the veil. Only Mr. Hooper's fiancée has the courage to ask him why he wears the veil. She does not understand the answer and leaves him. Mr. Hooper wears the veil for the rest of his life. In fact, he offers no other explanation for it until his death.

Note-taking Guide

Use this character wheel to record information about Reverend Hooper.

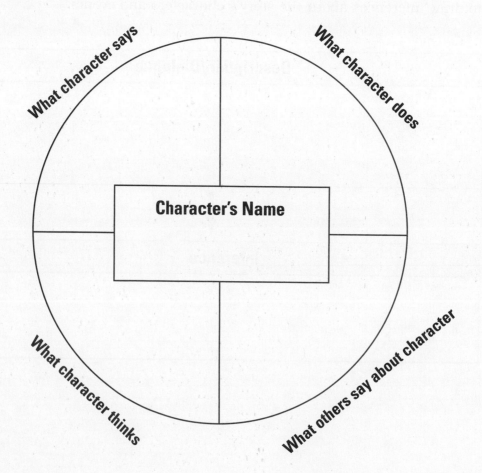

What character says

What character does

Character's Name

What character thinks

What others say about character

The Minister's Black Veil

1. **Analyze:** In what way does the veil affect Mr. Hooper's relationship with his congregation?

   _____

   _____

2. **Literary Analysis:** In what ways does this **parable** convey the message that people possess the potential to be both good and evil?

   _____

   _____

3. **Literary Analysis:** A **symbol** is something that has meaning in itself but also represents something else. Record three descriptions of the veil in this chart. Analyze the emotional associations and symbolic meaning of each description.

Descriptive Detail	Emotional Associations	Symbolic Meaning

4. **Reading Strategy:** Draw **inferences** about Hawthorne's views of human nature based on the villagers' reactions to Mr. Hooper.

   _____

   _____

5. **Reading Strategy:** "What can you **infer** about the author's attitude toward the Puritans from this story? Explain.

   _____

   _____

from Moby-Dick

LITERARY ANALYSIS

A **symbol** is a person, place, or thing that has its own meaning and also represents something else. Writers often use symbols that appear in the literature of many different cultures. Such symbols are called **archetypes.** For example, Melville's whale is like the whale that swallows Jonah in the Bible. However, Moby-Dick is an extremely complex symbol. To understand Moby-Dick's meaning, examine every aspect of the whale's behavior and appearance.

- Moby-Dick is massive, threatening, and awe-inspiring yet beautiful.
- Moby-Dick seems unpredictable but is controlled by natural laws.
- Moby-Dick seems immortal and indifferent to human suffering.

Analyzed in this way, Moby-Dick seems to symbolize all that is mysterious and uncontrollable in life.

READING STRATEGY

To **recognize symbols,** look for characters, places, or objects that are mentioned repeatedly or linked to larger concepts. For example, Ahab's description of Moby-Dick gives the whale symbolic meaning:

> I see him in outrageous strength, with an inscrutable malice sinewing it. That inscrutable malice is chiefly what I hate . . .

From this description, you might guess that Moby-Dick symbolizes nature's destructive power. Use this chart to record and interpret other symbols.

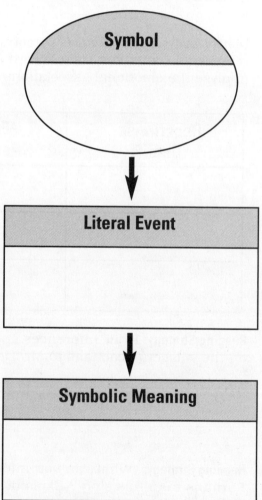

from Moby-Dick

Herman Melville

Summary Captain Ahab has led the crew of the *Pequod* on a whale hunt. In the first excerpt from *Moby-Dick*, Ahab explains that they are not hunting for business. Instead, Ahab is looking for revenge. He wants to hunt and kill the great white whale called Moby-Dick. He blames the whale for the loss of his leg. The second excerpt from *Moby-Dick* is the final chapter. Here, the narrator tells what happens when Ahab and his crew finally catch up with the whale.

Note-taking Guide

Put the events in order according to when they happen in the story. Write the letter for each event in the chart.

A Moby-Dick is harpooned and attacks the ship.

B Ahab tells the crew that they will hunt Moby-Dick.

C Ahab's ship is destroyed and Ahab is lost at sea.

D Ahab sets off in a whale boat to chase Moby-Dick.

E Ahab paces the deck.

F The ship's crew drinks together and swears to kill the whale.

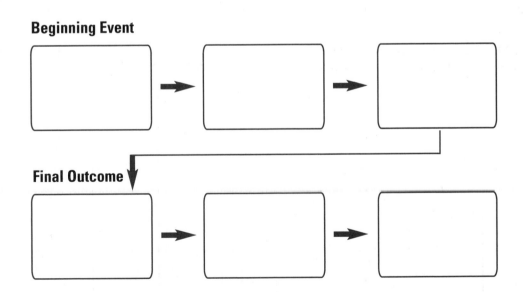

Beginning Event

Final Outcome

from **Moby-Dick**

1. **Compare and Contrast:** What does Moby-Dick's reaction to the ship reveal about the real whale versus the whale in Ahab's imagination?

   _____

   _____

2. **Literary Analysis:** Use this chart to identify the meaning of some of the **symbols** in this excerpt from *Moby-Dick*.

Symbol	Meaning
the color white	
the crew of the *Pequod*	
Moby-Dick	
the voyage of the *Pequod*	

3. **Reading Strategy:** What events, dialogue, or descriptions lead you to **recognize** Moby-Dick as a **symbol** of nature's power?

   _____

   _____

4. **Reading Strategy:** This novel has been called a symbolic "voyage of the soul." Would you agree or disagree with that assessment? Explain.

   _____

   _____

   _____

from Nature • from Self-Reliance • Concord Hymn • The Snowstorm

LITERARY ANALYSIS

Transcendentalism was an intellectual movement founded by Emerson. These are the cornerstones of Transcendentalist beliefs:

- Human senses are limited. Human senses convey knowledge of the physical world, but deeper truths can be grasped only through intuition.
- The observation of nature illuminates the nature of human beings.
- God, nature, and humanity are united in a shared universal soul, or Over-Soul.

These beliefs pervade all of Emerson's work.

READING STRATEGY

When you read a work that presents an argument, do not simply accept the ideas—challenge them. To **challenge a text,** question the author's assertions and reasoning. Compare the evidence the author offers with your personal experience or other reading. Then, decide whether you agree. Use this chart to record your thoughts about the selections.

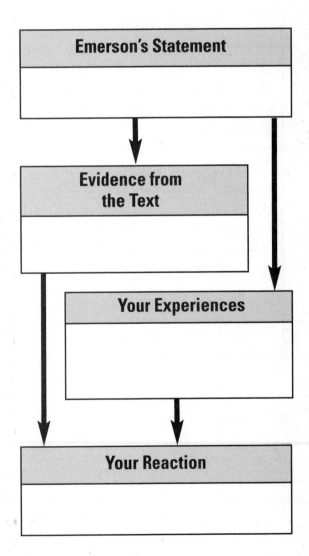

PREVIEW

from Nature

Ralph Waldo Emerson

Summary In this selection, Emerson writes about the harmony between himself and nature. He believes all living things are connected and reflect each other. Emerson describes how beauty, peace, and spirituality can be found in the natural world.

Note-taking Guide

Read the selection. Using the chart, rewrite complicated or long sentences in your own words.

from Nature:	In your own words:
"In the woods, too, a man casts off his years, as the snake his slough, and at what period soever of life is always a child."	
"I become a transparent eyeball; I am nothing; I see all; the currents of the Universal Being circulate through me; I am part or parcel of God."	

from Self-Reliance

Ralph Waldo Emerson

Summary In this excerpt, Emerson speaks to the individual. He urges readers to avoid conforming to the standards of society. Instead, Emerson urges readers to think and act independently.

Note-taking Guide

Read the selection. Using the chart, rewrite complicated or long sentences in your own words.

from Self-Reliance:	In your own words:
"Trust thyself; every heart vibrates to that string"	
"Nothing is at last sacred but the integrity of your own mind. Absolve you to yourself, and you shall have the suffrage of the world . . ."	

Concord Hymn • The Snowstorm

Ralph Waldo Emerson

Summaries In these two poems, Emerson celebrates country and nature. "Concord Hymn" honors the Minutemen who fought at Lexington and Concord during the American Revolution. The poem suggests that those who make great sacrifices for others should not be forgotten. "The Snowstorm" wonders at the power of nature to create amazing beauty.

Note-taking Guide

Read each selection. Using the chart, rewrite complicated or long sentences in your own words.

Concord Hymn:	In your own words:
"On this green bank, by this soft stream, / We set today a votive stone; / That memory may their deed redeem, / When, like our sires, our sons are gone."	

The Snowstorm:	In your own words:
"Come see the north wind's masonry."	

from Nature • from Self-Reliance • Concord Hymn • The Snowstorm

1. **Infer:** In what way does "Concord Hymn" reflect Emerson's belief in an Over-Soul?

_____

_____

2. **Literary Analysis:** What does "Nature" reveal about the **Transcendentalist** attitude toward nature? Explain.

_____

_____

_____

3. **Literary Analysis:** Use this chart to compare and contrast Emerson's descriptions of the bonds between people and society and the bonds between people and nature.

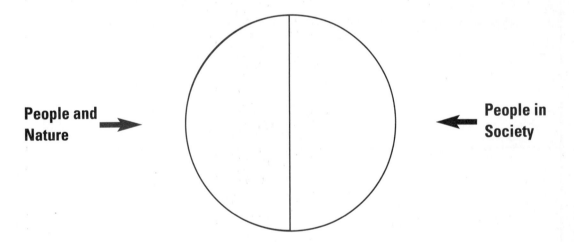

People and Nature →   ← People in Society

4. **Reading Strategy:** Emerson makes this claim in "Self-Reliance": "A foolish consistency is the hobgoblin of little minds." **Challenge the text** by identifying evidence Emerson uses to support this position.

_____

_____

_____

from **Walden** • *from* **Civil Disobedience**

LITERARY ANALYSIS

Style refers to the manner in which a writer puts his or her thoughts into words. Thoreau constructs paragraphs so that the sentences build to a climax. Thoreau also repeats his main ideas to reinforce his message. As you read, watch for these signposts of Thoreau's style.

Thoreau often uses **metaphors**—figures of speech that compare two unlike things without using the words *like* or *as.* As you read, notice the metaphors that Thoreau uses.

READING STRATEGY

As a reader, you are not bound to accept everything you see in print. In fact, when reading essays written about ideas, you should **evaluate the writer's philosophy.** To do this, pay attention to the support the writer provides to back up his or her outlook. As you read Thoreau's works, compare his ideas and supporting details with your own experiences. Use this chart to organize your comparison.

Thoreau's Ideas	Your Experiences	Your Reaction

from Walden

Henry David Thoreau

Summary For two years, Henry David Thoreau lived alone in a small cabin. He had built the cabin above Walden Pond. Seven years after he left the cabin, he used his journal to write *Walden.* In these selections, Thoreau shares his Transcendentalist vision. He believes human society has become too complex. He encourages people to simplify their lives, to slow down and do less, and to enjoy more.

Note-taking Guide

Use this table to keep track of Thoreau's statements and the details that support or clarify them.

Thoreau's Statement	Details
"The Holowell Farm has real attractions."	1. far from village 2. located on river

Activate Prior Knowledge

This selection is filled with quotable phrases and sentences that express Thoreau's **philosophy** of life, or the beliefs that guide his life and his actions. Do you have a philosophy of life? Can you express this philosophy in one sentence?

_____

_____

_____

Reading Strategy

In this selection, Thoreau uses long sentences and an old-fashioned style to **state his philosophy** of life. Read the selection slowly, sentence by sentence. Break down each sentence as you read it. Then, try to summarize the sentence in your own words. For example, reread the sentence in brackets. Using the footnote to help you, write a summary of the sentence below.

_____

_____

_____

Literary Analysis

The way a writer puts thoughts into words is called that writer's **style**. Thoreau wants his readers to look closely at the way they live, so he builds to a climax, or high point of interest, at the end of each paragraph. Reread the first paragraph of this selection. How is the underlined part of the sentence the climax of this paragraph?

_____

_____

_____

from Walden
Henry David Thoreau

Thoreau has become a hero to environmentalists because of his commitment to nature. Walden Pond in Concord, Massachusetts, has been designated a National Historical and Literary Landmark. The site of the cabin where Thoreau lived in the woods is a popular tourist attraction.

from Where I Lived, and What I Lived For

At a certain season of our life we are accustomed to consider every spot as the possible site of a house. I have thus surveyed the country on every side within a dozen miles of where I live. In imagination I have bought all the farms in succession, for all were to be bought, and I knew their price. I walked over each farmer's premises, tasted his wild apples, discoursed on husbandry[1] with him, took his farm at his price, at any price, mortgaging it to him in my mind; even put a higher price on it—took everything but a deed of it—took his word for his deed, for I dearly love to talk—cultivated it, and him too to some extent, I trust, and withdrew when I had enjoyed it long enough, leaving him to carry it on. This experience entitled me to be regarded as a sort of real-estate broker by my friends. Wherever I sat, there I might live, and the landscape radiated from me accordingly. What is a house but a sedes, a seat?—better if a country seat. I discovered many a site for a house not likely to be soon improved, which some might have thought too far from the village, but to my eyes the village was too far from it. Well, there might I live, I said; and there I did live, for an hour, a summer and a winter life; saw how I could let the years run off, buffet the winter through, and see the spring come in. The future inhabitants of this region, wherever they may place their houses, may be sure that they have been anticipated. An afternoon sufficed to lay out the land into orchard woodlot and pasture, and to decide what fine oaks or pines should be left to stand before the door, and whence each blasted tree could be seen to the best advantage; and then I let it lie, fallow[2] perchance, for a man is rich in proportion to the number of things which he can afford to let alone.

My imagination carried me so far that I even had the refusal of several farms—the refusal was all I wanted—but I never got my fingers burned by actual possession. The nearest that I came to actual possession was when I bought the Hollowell Place, and had begun to sort my seeds, and collected materials with which to make a wheelbarrow to

---

1. **husbandry** (HUZ buhn dree) *n.* farming.
2. **fallow** (FAL oh) *adj.* left uncultivated or unplanted.

carry it on or off with; but before the owner gave me a deed of it, his wife—every man has such a wife—changed her mind and wished to keep it, and he offered me ten dollars to release him. Now, to speak the truth, I had but ten cents in the world, and it surpassed my arithmetic to tell, if I was that man who had ten cents, or who had a farm, or ten dollars, or all together. However, I let him keep the ten dollars and the farm too, for I had carried it far enough; or rather, to be generous, I sold him the farm for just what I gave for it, and, as he was not a rich man, made him a present of ten dollars, and still had my ten cents, and seeds, and materials for a wheel-barrow left. I found thus that I had been a rich man without any damage to my poverty. But I retained the landscape, and I have since annually carried off what it yielded without a wheelbarrow. With respect to landscapes:

> "I am monarch of all I survey,
> My right there is none to dispute."[3]

I have frequently seen a poet withdraw, having enjoyed the most valuable part of a farm, while the crusty farmer supposed that he had got a few wild apples only. <u>Why, the owner does not know it for many years when a poet has put his farm in rhyme, the most admirable kind of invisible fence, has fairly impounded it, milked it, skimmed it, and got all the cream, and left the farmer only the skimmed milk.</u>

The real attractions of the Hollowell farm, to me, were: its complete retirement, being about two miles from the village, half a mile from the nearest neighbor, and separated from the highway by a broad field; its bounding on the river, which the owner said protected it by its fogs from frosts in the spring, though that was nothing to me; the gray color and ruinous state of the house and barn, and the <u>dilapidated</u> fences, which put such an interval between me and the last occupant; the hollow and lichen-covered apple trees, gnawed by rabbits, showing what kind of neighbors I should have; but above all, the recollection I had of it from my earliest voyages up the river, when the house was concealed behind a dense grove of red maples, through which I heard the house-dog bark. I was in haste to buy it, before the proprietor finished getting out some rocks, cutting down the hollow apple trees, and grubbing up some young birches which had sprung up in the pasture, or, in short, had made any more of his improvements. To enjoy these advantages I was ready to carry it on; like Atlas,[4] to take the world on my

---

Vocabulary Development: dilapidated (di LAP uh day tid) *adj.*
in disrepair

---

3. **"I . . . dispute"** from William Cowper's *Verses Supposed to Be Written by Alexander Selkirk.*
4. **Atlas** (AT luhs) from Greek mythology, a Titan who supported the heavens on his shoulders.

TAKE NOTES

Literary Analysis

A figure of speech that refers to one thing as if it were something else (without using the words "like" or "as") is called a **metaphor**. In the underlined sentence, Thoreau uses a metaphor to compare writing a poem about a farm to milking a cow. Circle the words in the sentence that refer to milking a cow.

_____

_____

_____

_____

Reading Strategy

Thoreau's description of the attractions of Hollowell farm gives you an opportunity to **evaluate the writer's philosophy**—that is, to form your own opinion of the writer's beliefs and values. List below three things that Thoreau likes about Hollowell's farm. Then, write what these things tell you about his philosophy, or his beliefs and values.

1. _____

_____

2. _____

_____

3. _____

_____

_____

_____

Consider the underlined sentence and **evaluate the writer's philosophy.** What does Thoreau mean? Do you agree or disagree? Why?

_____

_____

_____

Think carefully about what you have learned so far about this **writer's philosophy** of life. Then, reread the bracketed section. How does Thoreau's description of the house compare with Thoreau's philosophy? How would you feel about living in such a house?

_____

_____

_____

_____

When does Thoreau begin living in the woods?

_____

_____

_____

_____

shoulders—I never heard what compensation he received for that—and do all those things which had no other motive or excuse but that I might pay for it and be unmolested in my possession of it; for I knew all the while that it would yield the most abundant crop of the kind I wanted if I could only afford to let it alone. But it turned out as I have said.

All that I could say, then, with respect to farming on a large scale (I have always cultivated a garden) was that I had had my seeds ready. Many think that seeds improve with age. I have no doubt that time discriminates between the good and the bad; and when at last I shall plant, I shall be less likely to be disappointed. But I would say to my fellows, once for all, As long as possible live free and uncommitted. It makes but little difference whether you are committed to a farm or the county jail.

Old Cato,[5] whose "De Re Rustica" is my "Cultivator," says, and the only translation I have seen makes sheer nonsense of the passage, "When you think of getting a farm, turn it thus in your mind, not to buy greedily; nor spare your pains to look at it, and do not think it enough to go round it once. The oftener you go there the more it will please you, if it is good." I think I shall not buy greedily, but go round and round it as long as I live, and be buried in it first, that it may please me the more at last. . . .

I do not propose to write an ode to dejection, but to brag as lustily as chanticleer[6] in the morning, standing on his roost, if only to wake my neighbors up.

When first I took up my abode in the woods, that is, began to spend my nights as well as days there, which, by accident, was on Independence Day, or the fourth of July, 1845, my house was not finished for winter, but was merely a defense against the rain, without plastering or chimney, the walls being of rough weatherstained boards, with wide chinks, which made it cool at night. The upright white hewn studs and freshly planed door and window casings gave it a clean and airy look, especially in the morning, when its timbers were saturated with dew, so that I fancied that by noon some sweet gum would exude from them. To my imagination it retained throughout the day more or less of this auroral[7] character, reminding me of a certain house on a mountain which I had visited the year before. This was an airy and unplastered cabin, fit to entertain a traveling god, and where a goddess might trail her garments. The winds which passed over my dwelling were such as sweep over the ridges of

---

5. **Old Cato** Roman statesman (234–149 B.C.). "De Re Rustica" is Latin for "Of Things Rustic."
6. **chanticleer** (CHAN tuh kleer) *n.* rooster.
7. **auroral** (uh ROHR ul) *adj.* resembling the dawn.

over my dwelling were such as sweep over the ridges of mountains, bearing the broken strains, or celestial parts only, of terrestrial music. The morning wind forever blows, the poem of creation is uninterrupted; but few are the ears that hear it. Olympus[8] is but the outside of the earth everywhere. . . .

I went to the woods because I wished to live deliberately, to front only the essential facts of life, and see if I could not learn what it had to teach, and not, when I came to die, discover that I had not lived. I did not wish to live what was not life, living is so dear; nor did I wish to practice resignation, unless it was quite necessary. I wanted to live deep and suck out all the marrow of life, to live so sturdily and Spartanlike[9] as to put to rout all that was not life, to cut a broad swath and shave close, to drive life into a corner, and reduce it to its lowest terms, and, if it proved to be mean, why then to get the whole and genuine meanness of it, and publish its meanness to the world; or if it were <u>sublime</u>, to know it by experience, and be able to give a true account of it in my next excursion. For most men, it appears to me, are in a strange uncertainty about it, whether it is of the devil or of God, and have somewhat hastily concluded that it is the chief end of man here to "glorify God and enjoy him forever."[10]

Still we live meanly, like ants; though the fable tells us that we were long ago changed into men; like pygmies we fight with cranes:[11] it is error upon error, and clout upon clout, and our best virtue has for its occasion a <u>superfluous</u> and <u>evitable</u> wretchedness. <u>Our life is frittered away by detail.</u> An honest man has hardly need to count more than his ten fingers, or in extreme cases he may add his ten toes, and lump the rest. Simplicity, simplicity, simplicity! I say, let your affairs be as two or three, and not a hundred or a thousand; instead of a million count half a dozen, and keep your accounts on your thumbnail. In the midst of this chopping sea of civilized life, such are the clouds and storms and quicksands and thousand-and-one items to be allowed for, that a man has to live, if he would not founder and go to the

---

Vocabulary Development: **sublime** (suh BLYM) *adj.* noble; majestic

superfluous (soo PUR floo us) *adj.* excessive; not necessary

evitable (EV uh tuh buhl) *adj.* avoidable

---

8. **Olympus** (oh LIM pus) in Greek mythology, the home of the gods.
9. **Spartanlike** like the people of Sparta, an ancient Greek state whose citizens were known to be hardy, stoical, simple, and highly disciplined.
10. **"glorify . . . forever"** the answer to the question "What is the chief end of man?" in the Westminster catechism.
11. **like . . . cranes** in the Iliad, the Trojans are compared to cranes fighting against pygmies.

TAKE NOTES

Reading Check

Why does Thoreau go to live in the woods?

_____

_____

_____

_____

_____

Reading Strategy

Consider the underlined sentence and **evaluate the writer's philosophy.** What does Thoreau mean? Do you agree or disagree? Why?

_____

_____

_____

_____

Literary Analysis

Consider the sentence "Simplicity, simplicity, simplicity!" Why does Thoreau use this **style** of writing—repeating a word three times and ending with an exclamation point—at this point in the paragraph? Before you answer, look again at the other sentences in the paragraph.

_____

_____

_____

_____

Thoreau says that the nation lives too fast. We are living even faster now than people were when Thoreau was alive. What are the advantages and disadvantages of living life as fast as we do?

_____

_____

_____

_____

Literary Analysis

Reread the underlined sentence, noticing that a stream is a **metaphor** for time. Read the next few sentences and explain the metaphor in your own words below.

_____

_____

_____

_____

_____

Reading Check

Why does Thoreau think that all his best faculties are concentrated in his head?

_____

_____

_____

_____

_____

bottom and not make his port at all, by dead reckoning,[12] and he must be a great calculator indeed who succeeds. Simplify, simplify. Instead of three meals a day, if it be necessary eat but one; instead of a hundred dishes, five; and reduce other things in proportion. Our life is like a German Confederacy,[13] made up of petty states, with its boundary forever fluctuating, so that even a German cannot tell you how it is bounded at any moment. The nation itself, with all its so-called internal improvements, which, by the way, are all external and superficial, is just such an unwieldy and overgrown establishment, cluttered with furniture and tripped up by its own traps, ruined by luxury and heedless expense, by want of calculation and a worthy aim, as the million households in the land; and the only cure for it as for them is in a rigid economy, a stern and more than Spartan simplicity of life and elevation of purpose. It lives too fast. Men think that it is essential that the Nation have commerce, and export ice, and talk through a telegraph, and ride thirty miles an hour, without a doubt, whether they do or not; but whether we should live like baboons or like men, is a little uncertain. If we do not get out sleepers,[14] and forge rails, and devote days and nights to the work, but go to tinkering upon our lives to improve them, who will build railroads? And if railroads are not built, how shall we get to heaven in season? But if we stay at home and mind our business, who will want railroads? We do not ride on the railroad; it rides upon us. . . .

Time is but the stream I go a-fishing in. I drink at it; but while I drink I see the sandy bottom and detect how shallow it is. Its thin current slides away, but eternity remains. I would drink deeper; fish in the sky, whose bottom is pebbly with stars. I cannot count one. I know not the first letter of the alphabet. I have always been regretting that I was not as wise as the day I was born. The intellect is a cleaver; it discerns and rifts its way into the secret of things. I do not wish to be any more busy with my hands than is necessary. My head is hands and feet. I feel all my best faculties concentrated in it. My instinct tells me that my head is an organ for burrowing, as some creatures use their snout and forepaws, and with it I would mine and burrow my way through these hills. I think that the richest vein is somewhere hereabouts; so by the divining rod[15] and thin rising vapors I judge; and here I will begin to mine. . . .

12. **dead reckoning** navigating without the assistance of stars.
13. **German Confederacy** at the time, Germany was a loose union of thirty-eight independent states, with no common government.
14. **sleepers (SLEE perz)** _n._ ties supporting railroad tracks.
15. **divining rod** a forked branch or stick thought to reveal underground water or minerals

from The Conclusion

I left the woods for as good a reason as I went there. Perhaps it seemed to me that I had several more lives to live, and could not spare any more time for that one. It is remarkable how easily and insensibly we fall into a particular route, and make a beaten track for ourselves. I had not lived there a week before my feet wore a path from my door to the pondside; and though it is five or six years since I trod it, it is still quite distinct. It is true, I fear that others may have fallen into it, and so helped to keep it open. The surface of the earth is soft and impressible by the feet of men; and so with the paths which the mind travels. How worn and dusty, then, must be the highways of the world, how deep the ruts of tradition and conformity! I did not wish to take a cabin passage, but rather to go before the mast and on the deck of the world, for there I could best see the moon-light amid the mountains. I do not wish to go below now.

I learned this, at least, by my experiment; that if one advances confidently in the direction of his dreams, and endeavors to live the life which he has imagined, he will meet with a success unexpected in common hours. He will put some things behind, will pass an invisible boundary; new, universal, and more liberal laws will begin to establish themselves around and within him; or the old laws be expanded, and interpreted in his favor in a more liberal sense, and he will live with the license of a higher order of beings. In proportion as he simplifies his life, the laws of the universe will appear less complex, and solitude will not be solitude, nor poverty poverty, nor weakness weakness. If you have built castles in the air, your work need not be lost; that is where they should be. Now put the foundations under them. . . .

Why should we be in such desperate haste to succeed, and in such desperate enterprises? If a man does not keep pace with his companions, perhaps it is because he hears a different drummer. Let him step to the music which he hears, however measured or far away. It is not important that he should mature as soon as an apple tree or an oak. Shall he turn his spring into summer? If the condition of things which we were made for is not yet, what were any reality which we can substitute? We will not be shipwrecked on a vain reality. Shall we with pains erect a heaven of blue glass over ourselves, though when it is done we shall be sure to gaze still at the true ethereal heaven far above, as if the former were not? . . .

However mean your life is, meet it and live it; do not shun it and call it hard names. It is not so bad as you are. It looks poorest when you are richest. The faultfinder will find faults even in paradise. Love your life, poor as it is. You may perhaps have some pleasant, thrilling, glorious hours, even in a poorhouse. The setting sun is reflected from the windows

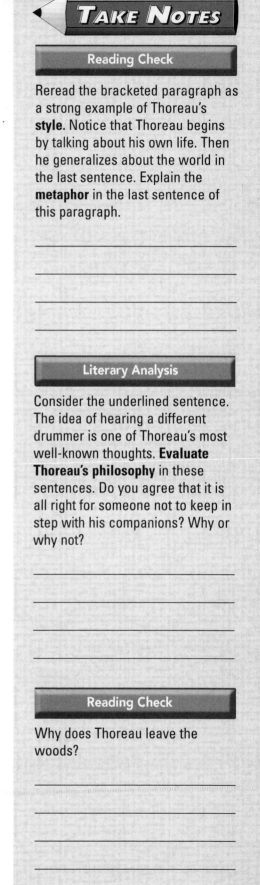

TAKE NOTES

Reading Check

Reread the bracketed paragraph as a strong example of Thoreau's **style**. Notice that Thoreau begins by talking about his own life. Then he generalizes about the world in the last sentence. Explain the **metaphor** in the last sentence of this paragraph.

_____

_____

_____

_____

Literary Analysis

Consider the underlined sentence. The idea of hearing a different drummer is one of Thoreau's most well-known thoughts. **Evaluate Thoreau's philosophy** in these sentences. Do you agree that it is all right for someone not to keep in step with his companions? Why or why not?

_____

_____

_____

_____

Reading Check

Why does Thoreau leave the woods?

_____

_____

_____

_____

Stop to Reflect

Thoreau encourages his readers to love their lives even if they are poor. He even says that the poor in his town live the most independent lives. What questions would you like to ask Thoreau about his view of poverty?

_____

_____

_____

Reading Strategy

Consider the underlined sentence. **Evaluate Thoreau's philosophy** in this sentence. Do you agree that you do not need money for things that are necessary for the soul? Why or why not?

_____

_____

_____

_____

Literary Analysis

Thoreau's **style** includes many striking thoughts that make interesting individual quotations. Circle your favorite phrase or sentence on this page.

_____

_____

_____

_____

of the almshouse[16] as brightly as from the rich man's abode; the snow melts before its door as early in the spring. I do not see but a quiet mind may live as contentedly there, and have as cheering thoughts, as in a palace. The town's poor seem to me often to live the most independent lives of any. Maybe they are simply great enough to receive without misgiving. Most think that they are above being supported by the town; but it oftener happens that they are not above supporting themselves by dishonest means, which should be more disreputable. Cultivate poverty like a garden herb, like sage. Do not trouble yourself much to get new things, whether clothes or friends. Turn the old; return to them. Things do not change; we change. Sell your clothes and keep your thoughts. God will see that you do not want society. If I were confined to a corner of a garret[17] all my days, like a spider, the world would be just as large to me while I had my thoughts about me. The philosopher said: "From an army of three divisions one can take away its general, and put it in disorder; from the man the most abject and vulgar one cannot take away his thought." Do not seek so anxiously to be developed, to subject yourself to many influences to be played on; it is all dissipation. Humility like darkness reveals the heavenly lights. The shadows of poverty and meanness gather around us, "and lo! creation widens to our view."[18] We are often reminded that if there were bestowed on us the wealth of Croesus,[19] our aims must still be the same, and our means essentially the same. Moreover, if you are restricted in your range by poverty, if you cannot buy books and newspapers, for instance, you are but confined to the most significant and vital experiences; you are compelled to deal with the material which yields the most sugar and the most starch. It is life near the bone where it is sweetest. You are defended from being a trifler. No man loses ever on a lower level by magnanimity on a higher. Superfluous wealth can buy superfluities only. Money is not required to buy one necessary of the soul. . . .

The life in us is like the water in the river. It may rise this year higher than man has ever known it, and flood the parched uplands; even this may be the eventful year, which will drown out all our muskrats. It was not always dry land where we dwell. I see far inland the banks which the stream

---

Vocabulary Development: magnanimity (MAG nuh nim uh tee)
n. generosity

---

16. **almshouse** *n.* home for people too poor to support themselves.
17. **garret** (GAYR it) *n.* attic.
18. **"and . . . view"** from the sonnet "To Night" by British poet Joseph Blanco White (1775–1841).
19. **Croesus** (KREE sus) king of Lydia (d. 546 B.C.), believed to be the wealthiest person of his time.

anciently washed, before science began to record its freshets. Everyone has heard the story which has gone the rounds of New England, of a strong and beautiful bug which came out of the dry leaf of an old table of apple-tree wood, which had stood in a farmer's kitchen for sixty years, first in Connecticut, and afterward in Massachusetts—from an egg deposited in the living tree many years earlier still, as appeared by counting the annual layers beyond it; which was heard gnawing out for several weeks, hatched perchance by the heat of an urn. Who does not feel his faith in a resurrection and immortality strengthened by hearing of this? Who knows what beautiful and winged life, whose egg has been buried for ages under many concentric layers of woodenness in the dead dry life of society, deposited at first in the alburnum[20] of the green and living tree, which has been gradually converted into the semblance of its well-seasoned tomb—heard perchance gnawing out now for years by the astonished family of man, as they sat round the festive board—may unexpectedly come forth from amidst society's most trivial and handselled furniture, to enjoy its perfect summer life at last!

I do not say that John or Jonathan[21] will realize all this; but such is the character of that morrow which mere lapse of time can never make to dawn. The light which puts out our eyes is darkness to us. Only that day dawns to which we are awake. There is more day to dawn. The sun is but a morning star.

---

20. **alburnum** (al BER nuhm) *n.* soft wood between the bark and the heartwood, where water is conducted.
21. **John or Jonathan** average person.

TAKE NOTES

Literary Analysis

One characteristic of Thoreau's **style** is to tell a story to illustrate the point he wants to make. Retell the story of the "strong and beautiful bug" in your own words. What is the point of this story?

_____

_____

_____

_____

_____

Reading Check

What do you think Thoreau means when he says, "Only that day dawns to which we are awake"?

_____

_____

_____

_____

_____

_____

Reader's Response: Do you want to read more writings by Thoreau? Why or why not?

_____

_____

_____

Thinking About the Skill: How has **evaluating the writer's philosophy** helped you understand Thoreau? How will it help you understand other selections in the future?

_____

_____

_____

from Civil Disobedience

Henry David Thoreau

Summary In 1846, Henry David Thoreau spent a night in jail. He had refused to pay his taxes because he believed the tax money would support the war against Mexico. He opposed the war. After he was released, he wrote "Civil Disobedience." In this essay, Thoreau argues that people should oppose laws that violate their principles. In this excerpt, he explains his views on government.

Note-taking Guide

Use this chart to keep track of Thoreau's comments about the government.

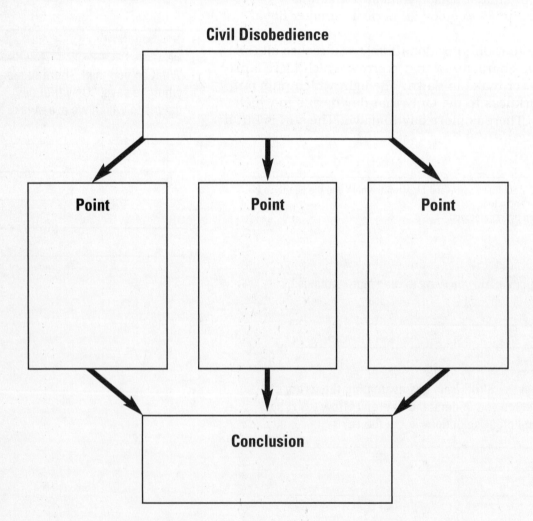

Civil Disobedience

Point

Point

Point

Conclusion

from Walden • *from* Civil Disobedience

1. **Deduce:** What did Thoreau hope to achieve by living at Walden Pond?

_____

_____

2. **Literary Analysis:** Thoreau's writing **style** uses sentences that build to a climax. Reread the paragraph in Walden that begins "Still we live meanly." Explain how this paragraph is an example of Thoreau's style.

_____

_____

3. **Literary Analysis: Metaphors** are figures of speech that compare two unlike things without using *like* or *as.* Use this chart to identify three of Thoreau's metaphors and interpret their meaning.

Metaphor	Things Compared	Meaning

4. **Reading Strategy:** Thoreau claims that the "government is best which governs not at all." **Evaluate the writer's philosophy** by explaining what evidence Thoreau uses to support his claim.

_____

_____

5. **Reading Strategy:** Evaluate Thoreau's philosophy that people should simplify their lives. Do you agree? Explain.

_____

_____

Emily Dickinson's Poetry

LITERARY ANALYSIS

Poets use rhyme to create pleasant musical sounds and to unify groups of lines. **Exact rhyme** occurs when two words have identical sounds in their final accented syllables. In **slant rhyme,** the final sounds are similar but not identical.

Exact rhyme: glove/above

Slant rhyme: glove/prove

Dickinson used both types of rhyme in her poetry. As you read her poems, look for her uses of rhyme and consider the effects they create.

READING STRATEGY

Poets often link concepts such as love and death to images, or word pictures. It is helpful to **analyze images** to clarify the poet's message. As you read Dickinson's poems, use the chart below to connect images with abstract ideas.

Image	Abstract Idea

Emily Dickinson's Poetry

Summaries In "**Because I could not stop for Death,**" the poet imagines that a carriage takes her to her grave after she dies. The poet also writes about her own death in "**I heard a fly buzz—when I died.**" "**There's a certain slant of light**" tells about the sad afternoon light of winter. In "**My life closed twice before its close,**" the poet thinks about enduring a terrible event. The poet speaks of the soul's tendency to prefer one person over all others in "**The Soul selects her own Society.**" "**The Brain—is wider than the sky—**" is a poem that claims that all of nature and even God can be contained in the mind. In "**There is a solitude of space,**" the soul offers more solitude than any earthly place. The poet suggests that things can only be known through their opposites in "**Water, is taught by thirst.**"

Note-taking Guide

Record references to nature found in Dickinson's poems in the diagram below.

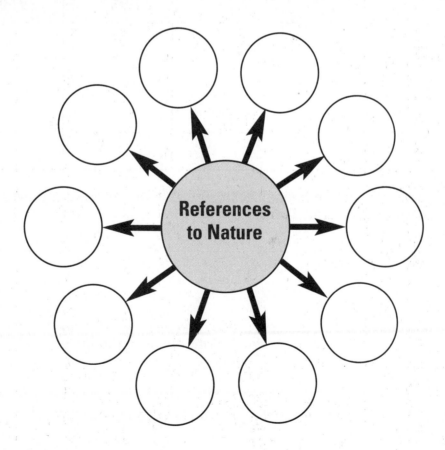

Emily Dickinson's Poetry

1. **Analyze:** In which poems does Dickinson write about the limitless nature of human consciousness?

_____

_____

2. **Literary Analysis:** Identify the three words that create **slant rhymes** for the words *Immortality, Civility,* and *Eternity* in "Because I could not stop for Death."

_____

_____

3. **Literary Analysis:** The chart below shows the *abc* system of representing rhyme scheme. Use the chart to describe the pattern of rhyme in "There's a certain slant of light.

	Stanza One	Two	Three	Four
Line 1	a			
Line 2	b			
Line 3	c			
Line 4	b			

4. **Reading Strategy: Analyze** the **image** Dickinson uses to represent a gravesite in "Because I could not stop for Death."

_____

_____

5. **Reading Strategy:** Identify two images in "The Brain—is wider than the Sky" and two images in "Water, is Taught by thirst." Write them on the lines.

_____

_____

Walt Whitman's Poetry

LITERARY ANALYSIS

Many poets write poems that have a fixed meter and line length. Others write **free verse,** or poetry that has an irregular meter and line length. One goal of free verse is to imitate the flow of everyday speech. Thus, Whitman varies his rhythms and line lengths to fit his message:

> Do I contradict myself?
> Very well then I contradict myself . . .

Whitman did not invent free verse, but he was the first American poet to use it. It proved to be the perfect form to let him express himself without formal restraints.

Along with his use of free verse, Whitman's **diction**—word choice and arrangement—also plays a key role in his voice. Whitman's diction is characterized by the use of two main techniques:

- The use of catalogs, or long lists
- The use of **parallelism**—the repetition of phrases or sentences with similar structures or meanings.

READING STRATEGY

You can **infer a poet's attitude** toward a subject by looking at his or her choice of words and details. Consider this passage from Whitman's "Song of Myself":

> I jump from the crossbeams and seize the clover and timothy,
> And roll head over heels . . .

Use the following chart to note key words and images in Whitman's poems and to identify the attitude each shows.

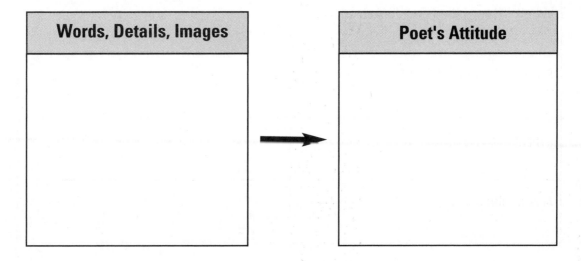

Words, Details, Images	Poet's Attitude

PREVIEW

Walt Whitman's Poetry

Summaries In the Preface to the 1855
Edition of *Leaves of Grass*, the speaker
says the United States is a great poem.
In "Song of Myself," he describes himself. Then, he considers the grass as a
symbol of immortality. The speaker
leaves a lecture on the stars to view the
heavens in "perfect silence" in "When I
Heard the Learn'd Astronomer." "By the
Bivouac's Fitful Flame" is a poem that
considers the army, life, and death.
The speaker tells about carpenters,
masons, and other workers in "I Hear
America Singing." In "A Noiseless
Patient Spider," the speaker compares a
spider's work to that of a soul trying to become attached to something.

Note-taking Guide

Write the main idea of each poem in this chart.

Poem	Main Idea
from Preface to the 1855 Edition of Leaves of Grass	
from Song of Myself	
When I Heard the Learn'd Astronomer	
By the Bivouac's Fitful Frame	
I Hear America Singing	
A Noiseless Patient Spider	

APPLY THE SKILLS

Walt Whitman's Poetry

1. **Synthesize:** Whitman believed that the world of nature mirrors the human spirit. What aspects of "A Noiseless Patient Spider" reflect this belief?

_____

_____

_____

_____

2. **Literary Analysis:** In what way does the use of **free verse** in "Song of Myself" allow the speaker to share his ideas more freely?

_____

_____

_____

_____

3. **Literary Analysis:** Whitman uses catalogs, or lists, in his poems. Analyze the catalogs Whitman uses in "By the Bivouac's Fitful Flame" and "When I Heard the Learn'd Astronomer." Use this chart to record what you find.

Poem	Cataloging	What the Details Share	Effect

4. **Reading Strategy:** In Section 14, lines 11–14, of "Song of Myself," what can you infer about the speaker's attitude toward people who work outdoors?

_____

_____

Walt Whitman's Poetry (cont'd)

5. **Reading Strategy:** Give examples of the language in "When I Heard the Learn'd Astronomer" that helps you **infer the speaker's attitude** toward astronomy.

_____

_____

_____

_____

_____

An Episode of War •
Willie Has Gone to the War

LITERARY ANALYSIS

In reaction to Romanticism—a movement that emphasized emotion, imagination, and nature—two literary movements emerged during the mid- to late-nineteenth century: **Realism** and **Naturalism**.

• Realism sought to portray life as faithfully and accurately as possible, focusing on ordinary people suffering the harsh realities of everyday life.
• Naturalism also sought to portray ordinary people's lives, but suggested that environment, heredity, and chance, or forces they could neither understand nor control, determined people's fate.

As you read, look for elements related to these two literary movements.

READING SKILL

The social and political climate surrounding these Civil War snapshots form part of their setting and context. When you **recognize historical details,** you determine how the attitudes of both writers and characters reflect the ideas of their day. As you read, use this chart to record events that suggest historical context.

Event	Historical Context
Battles	
Medical Practices	
Political Situations	
Social Attitudes	

An Episode of War • Willie Has Gone to the War **159**

An Episode of War

Stephen Crane

Summary A soldier fighting in the Civil War prepares the day's portions of coffee for his squad. As he measures the coffee, a bullet strikes him in the arm and changes his life. This story follows the soldier as he confronts the tragedy of war

Note-taking Guide

Use this chart to record what happens to the lieutenant.

Beginning Event

> A lieutentant is shot in the arm while measuring coffee for his squad.

↓

>

↓

>

↓

>

Final Outcome

>

An Episode of War

Stephen Crane

Writers before Stephen Crane often described war as a noble and glorious adventure. They left out the grim details and the reality of war. Crane writes compellingly about just those details, even though he himself did not fight in the Civil War.

The lieutenant's rubber blanket lay on the ground, and upon it he had poured the company's supply of coffee. Corporals and other representatives of the grimy and hot-throated men who lined the breast-work[1] had come for each squad's portion.

The lieutenant was frowning and serious at this task of division. His lips pursed as he drew with his sword various crevices in the heap, until brown squares of coffee, astoundingly equal in size, appeared on the blanket. He was on the verge of a great triumph in mathematics, and the corporals were thronging forward, each to reap a little square, when suddenly the lieutenant cried out and looked quickly at a man near him as if he suspected it was a case of personal assault. The others cried out also when they saw blood upon the lieutenant's sleeve.

He had winced like a man stung, swayed dangerously, and then straightened. The sound of his hoarse breathing was plainly audible. He looked sadly, mystically, over the breast-work at the green face of a wood, where now were many little puffs of white smoke. During this moment the men about him gazed statuelike and silent, astonished and awed by this catastrophe which happened when catastrophes were not expected—when they had leisure to observe it.

As the lieutenant stared at the wood, they too swung their heads, so that for another instant all hands, still silent, contemplated the distant forest as if their minds were fixed upon the mystery of a bullet's journey.

The officer had, of course, been compelled to take his sword into his left hand. He did not hold it by the hilt. He gripped it at the middle of the blade, awkwardly. Turning his eyes from the hostile wood, he looked at the sword as he held it there, and seemed puzzled as to what to do with it, where to put it. In short, this weapon had of a sudden become a strange thing to him. He looked at it in a kind of

---

1. breast-work low wall put up quickly as a defense in battle.

TAKE NOTES

Activate Prior Knowledge

Think of an unexpected event that happened to you. In what ways did that event change everything that happened afterward?

_____

_____

_____

_____

Reading Strategy

What **details** about the shooting of the lieutenant make his wound so unexpected?

_____

_____

_____

_____

Reading Check

Realism is a literary movement that focused on ordinary people and tried to portray real life as accurately as possible. How is the beginning of this story realistic?

_____

_____

_____

_____

Why do the lieutenant and the other soldiers stare into the woods after the shooting?

_____

_____

_____

_____

_____

Why does the lieutenant have so much trouble sheathing his sword?

_____

_____

_____

_____

_____

_____

Another literary movement related to **realism** is **naturalism.** Characters in naturalistic writing are ordinary people who are controlled by forces they do not understand. Reread the bracketed paragraph. Then circle the sentence that indicates that this story is an example of naturalism.

stupefaction, as if he had been endowed with a trident, a sceptre,[2] or a spade.

Finally he tried to sheathe it. To sheathe a sword held by the left hand, at the middle of the blade, in a scabbard hung at the left hip, is a feat worthy of a sawdust ring.[3] This wounded officer engaged in a desperate struggle with the sword and the wobbling scabbard, and during the time of it breathed like a wrestler.

But at this instant the men, the spectators, awoke from their stone-like poses and crowded forward sympathetically. The orderly-sergeant took the sword and tenderly placed it in the scabbard. At the time, he leaned nervously backward, and did not allow even his finger to brush the body of the lieutenant. A wound gives strange dignity to him who bears it. Well men shy from his new and terrible majesty. It is as if the wounded man's hand is upon the curtain which hangs before the revelations of all existence—the meaning of ants, potentates,[4] wars, cities, sunshine, snow, a feather dropped from a bird's wing; and the power of it sheds radiance upon a bloody form, and makes the other men understand sometimes that they are little. His comrades look at him with large eyes thoughtfully. Moreover, they fear vaguely that the weight of a finger upon him might send him headlong, precipitate the tragedy, hurl him at once into the dim, grey unknown. And so the orderly-sergeant, while sheathing the sword, leaned nervously backward.

There were others who proffered assistance. One timidly presented his shoulder and asked the lieutenant if he cared to lean upon it, but the latter waved him away mournfully. He wore the look of one who knows he is the victim of a terrible disease and understands his helplessness. He again stared over the breast-work at the forest, and then, turning, went slowly rearward. He held his right wrist tenderly in his left hand as if the wounded arm was made of very brittle glass.

And the men in silence stared at the wood, then at the departing lieutenant; then at the wood, then at the lieutenant.

Vocabulary Development: precipitate (pree SIP uh tayt) *v.* cause to happen before expected or desired

---

2. **a trident, a sceptre** (TRYD uhnt; SEP ter) three-pronged spear; decorated ornamental rod or staff symbolizing royal authority.
3. **sawdust ring** ring in which circus acts are performed.
4. **potentates** (POHT uhn tayts) *n.* rulers; powerful people.

As the wounded officer passed from the line of battle, he was enabled to see many things which as a participant in the fight were unknown to him. He saw a general on a black horse gazing over the lines of blue infantry at the green woods which veiled his problems. An aide galloped furiously, dragged his horse suddenly to a halt, saluted, and presented a paper. It was, for a wonder, precisely like a historical painting.

To the rear of the general and his staff a group, composed of a bugler, two or three orderlies, and the bearer of the corps standard,[5] all upon maniacal horses, were working like slaves to hold their ground, preserve their respectful interval, while the shells boomed in the air about them, and caused their chargers to make furious quivering leaps.

A battery, a tumultuous and shining mass, was swirling toward the right. The wild thud of hoofs, the cries of the riders shouting blame and praise, menace and encouragement, and, last, the roar of the wheels, the slant of the glistening guns, brought the lieutenant to an intent pause. The battery swept in curves that stirred the heart; it made halts as dramatic as the crash of a wave on the rocks, and when it fled onward this aggregation of wheels, levers, motors had a beautiful unity, as if it were a missile. The sound of it was a war-chorus that reached into the depths of man's emotion.

The lieutenant, still holding his arm as if it were of glass, stood watching this battery until all detail of it was lost, save the figures of the riders, which rose and fell and waved lashes over the black mass.

Later, he turned his eyes toward the battle, where the shooting sometimes crackled like bush-fires, sometimes sputtered with exasperating irregularity, and sometimes reverberated like the thunder. He saw the smoke rolling upward and saw crowds of men who ran and cheered, or stood and blazed away at the inscrutable distance.

He came upon some stragglers, and they told him how to find the field hospital. They described its exact location. In fact, these men, no longer having part in the

---

> **Vocabulary Development: aggregation** (ag gruh GAY shuhn) *n.* group or mass of distinct objects or individuals
> **inscrutable** (in SKROOT uh buhl) *adj.* impossible to see; completely obscure or mysterious

---

5. **corps** (KOHR) **standard** flag or banner representing a military unit.

TAKE NOTES

Reading Strategy

Historical details, or details that are specific to a particular period of history, help you to understand the setting of a story. Reread the underlined sentences. On the lines below, write the **historical details** in this sentence—that is, those details that are particular to the period of the Civil War.

_____

_____

_____

_____

_____

Stop to Reflect

Have you ever had the feeling that everything has slowed down or that things are happening in slow motion? Sometimes an injury or a shock makes people feel this way. Consider how closely the lieutenant is watching the battery and the battle, when you would expect him to hurry to the field hospital. Why do you think the lieutenant focuses on the battery and the battle instead of on treatment for his injury?

_____

_____

_____

_____

How does the lieutenant locate the field hospital?

_____

_____

_____

_____

After the first description of the lieutenant's wound, when he winces, there is no mention of the pain of the wound. What **detail** in the underlined sentence tells you that the lieutenant is in pain as he looks for the field hospital?

_____

_____

_____

_____

_____

What **historical details** in the bracketed paragraph signal that the events of this story take place during the Civil War, not today?

_____

_____

_____

_____

battle, knew more of it than others. They told the performance of every corps, every division, the opinion of every general. The lieutenant, carrying his wounded arm rearward, looked upon them with wonder.

At the roadside a brigade was making coffee and buzzing with talk like a girls' boarding-school. Several officers came out to him and inquired concerning things of which he knew nothing. One, seeing his arm, began to scold. "Why, man, that's no way to do. You want to fix that thing." He appropriated the lieutenant and the lieutenant's wound. He cut the sleeve and laid bare the arm, every nerve of which softly fluttered under his touch. He bound his handkerchief over the wound, scolding away in the meantime. His tone allowed one to think that he was in the habit of being wounded every day. The lieutenant hung his head, feeling, in this presence, that he did not know how to be correctly wounded.

The low white tents of the hospital were grouped around an old schoolhouse. There was here a singular commotion. In the foreground two ambulances interlocked wheels in the deep mud. The drivers were tossing the blame of it back and forth, gesticulating and berating, while from the ambulances, both crammed with wounded, there came an occasional groan. An interminable crowd of bandaged men were coming and going. Great numbers sat under the trees nursing heads or arms or legs. There was a dispute of some kind raging on the steps of the schoolhouse. Sitting with his back against a tree a man with a face as grey as a new army blanket was serenely smoking a corncob pipe. The lieutenant wished to rush forward and inform him that he was dying.

A busy surgeon was passing near the lieutenant. "Good-morning," he said, with a friendly smile. Then he caught sight of the lieutenant's arm, and his face at once changed. "Well, let's have a look at it." He seemed possessed suddenly of a great contempt for the lieutenant. This wound evidently placed the latter on a very low social plane. The doctor cried out impatiently, "What mutton-head had tied it up that way anyhow?" The lieutenant answered, "Oh, a man."

When the wound was disclosed the doctor fingered it disdainfully. "Humph," he said. "You come along with me and I'll 'tend to you." His voice contained the same scorn as if he were saying: "You will have to go to jail."

Vocabulary Development: disdainfully (dis DAYN fuhl ee) *adv.*
showing scorn or contempt

The lieutenant had been very meek, but now his face flushed, and he looked into the doctor's eyes. "I guess I won't have it amputated," he said.

"Nonsense, man! Nonsense! Nonsense!" cried the doctor. "Come along, now. I won't amputate it. Come along. Don't be a baby."

"Let go of me," said the lieutenant, holding back wrathfully, his glance fixed upon the door of the old schoolhouse, as sinister to him as the portals of death.

And this is the story of how the lieutenant lost his arm. When he reached home, his sisters, his mother, his wife, sobbed for a long time at the sight of the flat sleeve. "Oh, well," he said, standing shamefaced amid these tears, "I don't suppose it matters so much as all that."

Literary Analysis

Naturalism in literature describes characters who endure with strength and dignity, even though their fate is determined by chance. How is the lieutenant's conversation with the doctor an example of naturalism?

_____

_____

_____

_____

Reading Check

What is the reaction of the lieutenant's family when they see his flat sleeve?

_____

_____

_____

_____

Reader's Response: What was your reaction when you found out that the doctor had amputated the lieutenant's arm? How do you feel about the doctor's promise?

_____

_____

Thinking About the Skill: How did recognizing **historical details** help you to appreciate this short story? How will this skill help you as you read stories in the future?

_____

_____

_____

Willie Has Gone to the War

George Cooper

Summary These song lyrics show another side to the Civil War. The speaker of the poem is a woman who waits by a brook. That is where she last saw the man she loves before he went to fight in the war. Her words speak of her sadness and how she misses him.

Note-taking Guide

Use this character wheel to record what you learn about Willie.

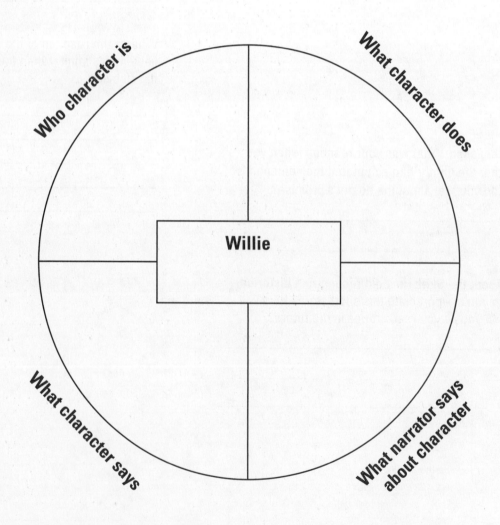

An Episode of War • Willie Has Gone to the War

1. **Apply:** According to the Naturalists, humans are weak beings subject to mysterious forces. How might this idea apply to "An Episode of War"?

   _____

   _____

2. **Literary Analysis:** List two details from "Willie Has Gone to the War" that show that it is more romantic than realistic.

   _____

   _____

3. **Literary Analysis:** Use this chart to record an example of **Realism** and an example of **Naturalism** from the story.

Realism	Naturalism

4. **Reading Skill: Recognize historical details** that describe medical practices during the Civil War. Think about what you know about Civil War medical practices. Why does the doctor promises the lieutenant that he will not amputate?

   _____

   _____

5. **Reading Skill:** Reread the paragraphs that describe the wounded lieutenant's walk to find the hospital. List two details about battle during the Civil War era that you learn.

   _____

   _____

Swing Low, Sweet Chariot • Go Down, Moses

LITERARY ANALYSIS

If you are searching for the meaning of a song or poem, you will often find it in the **refrain**. A refrain is a word, phrase, line, or group of lines that appears regularly throughout the work. Refrains serve these key functions:

- They emphasize the most important ideas.
- They help establish the rhythm of the song.

Most spirituals contain at least one refrain. For example, the line "Coming for to carry me home" appears throughout "Swing Low, Sweet Chariot." As you read these songs, think about the message each refrain conveys.

READING STRATEGY

People create songs for the ear and not the eye. **Listening** is an especially important skill for appreciating lyrics.

- Read each spiritual aloud, listening to its rhythm.
- Notice rhymes and other repeated sounds. For example, the opening line in "Go Down, Moses" contains three stressed syllables in a row.

Often, the rhythms and sounds of a song suggest a specific mood. As you read these spirituals, think about the different moods and effects that the sounds of the songs create. Use this chart to record some of the effects.

Song Text
Go down Moses, /Way down in Egypt land /Tell old Pharoah /To let my people go.

Mood Conveyed

Swing Low, Sweet Chariot • Go Down, Moses

Summaries In the spiritual **"Swing Low, Sweet Chariot,"** the chorus describes a chariot coming to take the singer home to heaven. The singer also describes crossing the river Jordan with a band of angels. If listeners get to heaven first, they are encouraged to tell everyone that the singer is on the way. In **"Go Down, Moses,"** the singer tells the story of Moses following God's command to free the Israelites from Egypt. Moses tells the Pharaoh to "let my people go!" or God will punish the Egyptians.

Note-taking Guide

Write down the **symbols** that you see in these spirituals. Symbols are words that stand for something else. Write a brief phrase that explains what you think the symbol stands for. Use your prior knowledge of slavery in the American South.

Symbols	Possible Meaning
chariot	way to escape from slavery; Underground Railroad

Swing Low, Sweet Chariot • Go Down, Moses

1. **Interpret:** Spirituals were often used as "code" songs for escape. What hidden message do you see in "Swing Low, Sweet Chariot"?

_____

_____

2. **Literary Analysis:** A **refrain** can be a line or a group of lines, called a stanza. What refrains are used in "Swing Low, Sweet Chariot"?

_____

_____

3. **Reading Strategy:** Read each spiritual aloud and **listen** to the words. Explain how each of the songs uses rhythm, rhyme, and repetition to reinforce meaning.

_____

_____

_____

4. **Reading Strategy:** Rhythm, rhyme, and repetition are called sound elements. Use this diagram to compare the sound elements in the two spirituals.

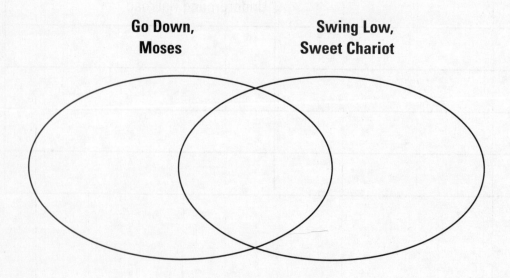

Go Down, Moses   **Swing Low, Sweet Chariot**

from My Bondage and My Freedom

LITERARY ANALYSIS

An **autobiography** is a person's written account of his or her life. It focuses on the events the author considers most important. Usually, writers of auto-biographies believe that their lives are interesting or important and can in some way help others. Frederick Douglass wrote his autobiography because he believed that his life proved that blacks were no less intelligent or capable than whites, as he states directly in these lines:

> "I could talk and sing; I could laugh and weep; I could reason and remember . . ."

As you read about Douglass's experiences, notice how they might serve as examples for others.

READING SKILL

Establish a purpose for reading so that you have an idea or concept on which to focus. For example, as you read from Douglass's autobiography, establish the purpose of learning about his special qualities. Also, read to expand your understanding of what it was like to be a slave. Use this chart to record details that support your purpose for reading.

Douglass's Character Traits	Details about Slavery

from My Bondage and My Freedom

Frederick Douglass

Summary Frederick Douglass learns to read from his mistress. As he reads, he learns that he has the same abilities and the same rights to freedom as white children. Soon, his mistress begins to act differently toward Douglass. The change in his mistress teaches Douglass that slavery makes both slaves and slave-owners less human. His autobiography tells about his struggle to gain knowledge and freedom.

Note-taking Guide

As you read, use this diagram to keep track of the events that occur in this section of Douglass's autobiography.

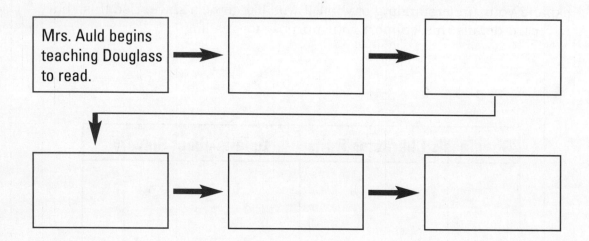

Mrs. Auld begins teaching Douglass to read.

from My Bondage and My Freedom
Frederick Douglass

People who are determined have a firm purpose and work towards it. Those who persist refuse to give up—they keep going firmly and steadily even when problems come up. Frederick Douglass was both determined and persistent. Despite the fact that he was born a slave, he learned to read, escaped to freedom, and became famous as a writer and a lecturer.

I lived in the family of Master Hugh, at Baltimore, seven years, during which time—as the almanac makers say of the weather—my condition was variable. The most interesting feature of my history here, was my learning to read and write, under somewhat marked disadvantages. In attaining this knowledge, I was compelled to resort to indirections by no means <u>congenial</u> to my nature, and which were really humiliating to me. My mistress—who had begun to teach me—was suddenly checked in her <u>benevolent</u> design, by the strong advice of her husband. In faithful compliance with this advice, the good lady had not only ceased to instruct me, herself, but had set her face as a flint against my learning to read by any means. It is due, however, to my mistress to say, that she did not adopt this course in all its <u>stringency</u> at the first. She either thought it unnecessary, or she lacked the <u>depravity</u> indispensable to shutting me up in mental darkness. It was, at least, necessary for her to have some training, and some hardening, in the exercise of the slaveholder's prerogative, to make her equal to forgetting my human nature and character, and to treating me as a thing destitute of a moral or an intellectual nature. Mrs. Auld—my mistress—was, as I have said, a most kind and tenderhearted woman; and, in the humanity of her heart, and the simplicity of her mind, she set out, when I first went to live with her, to treat me as she supposed one human being ought to treat another.

It is easy to see, that, in entering upon the duties of a slaveholder, some little experience is needed. Nature has done almost nothing to prepare men and women to be either slaves or slaveholders. Nothing but rigid training,

---

Vocabulary Development: **congenial** (kuhn JEEN yuhl) *adj.* agreeable
benevolent (buh NEV uh lent) *adj.* kindly; charitable
stringency (STRIN juhn see) *n.* strictness; severity
depravity (di PRAYV uh tee) *n.* corruption; wickedness

Activate Prior Knowledge

Make a list of three or more things you do every day that require reading. What would your life be like if you could not read at all?.

1. _____
2. _____
3. _____

Reading Strategy

Before you begin to read, you should **establish a purpose,** or decide on a reason for your reading. Knowing your purpose will help you to focus on the most important ideas. One purpose you probably have for reading this selection is to find out more about Frederick Douglass. What other purpose do you have for reading this selection?

_____

Literary Analysis

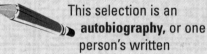

This selection is an **autobiography,** or one person's written account of his or her own life. It is almost always written in the first person, which means it uses the pronouns "I," "me," and "my" frequently. Reread the first paragraph of this selection. Circle all occurrences of "I," "me," or "my" in that paragraph. What is the effect of all these personal pronouns in one paragraph?

_____

long persisted in, can perfect the character of the one or the other. One cannot easily forget to love freedom; and it is as hard to cease to respect that natural love in our fellow creatures. On entering upon the career of a slaveholding mistress, Mrs. Auld was singularly deficient; nature, which fits nobody for such an office, had done less for her than any lady I had known. It was no easy matter to induce her to think and to feel that the curly-headed boy, who stood by her side, and even leaned on her lap; who was loved by little Tommy, and who loved little Tommy in turn; sustained to her only the relation of a chattel. I was *more* than that, and she felt me to be more than that. I could talk and sing; I could laugh and weep; I could reason and remember; I could love and hate. I was human, and she, dear lady, knew and felt me to be so. How could she, then, treat me as a brute, without a mighty struggle with all the noble powers of her own soul. That struggle came, and the will and power of the husband was victorious. Her noble soul was overthrown; but, he that overthrew it did not, himself, escape the consequences. He, not less than the other parties, was injured in his domestic peace by the fall.

When I went into their family, it was the abode of happiness and contentment. The mistress of the house was a model of affection and tenderness. Her fervent piety and watchful uprightness made it impossible to see her without thinking and feeling—"that woman is a Christian." There was no sorrow nor suffering for which she had not a tear, and there was no innocent joy for which she did not have a smile. She had bread for the hungry, clothes for the naked, and comfort for every mourner that came within her reach. Slavery soon proved its ability to divest her of these excellent qualities, and her home of its early happiness. Conscience cannot stand much violence. Once thoroughly broken down, *who* is he that can repair the damage? It may be broken toward the slave, on Sunday, and toward the master on Monday. It cannot endure such shocks. It must stand entire, or it does not stand at all. If my condition waxed bad, that of the family waxed not better. The first step, in the wrong direction, was the violence done to nature and to conscience, in arresting the benevolence that would have enlightened my young mind. In ceasing to instruct me, she must begin to justify herself *to* herself; and, once consenting to take sides in such a debate, she was riveted to her position. One needs very little knowledge of moral philosophy, to see *where* my mistress now landed. She finally became even more violent in her opposition to my learning to read, than was her husband himself. She was not satisfied with simply doing as *well* as her husband had commanded her, but seemed resolved to better his instruction. Nothing appeared to make my poor mistress—after her turning

---

Reading Strategy

Try **establishing a purpose** for reading each paragraph of this selection. For example, reread the bracketed paragraph. What is the purpose of your reading so much about Mrs. Auld when this is the autobiography of Frederick Douglass?

_____

_____

_____

_____

_____

Stop to Reflect

One of the points that Douglass makes as he talks about the change in Mrs. Auld is that slavery hurts the slave owner as well as the slave. How is Mrs. Auld hurt by slavery?

_____

_____

toward the downward path—more angry, than seeing me, seated in some nook or corner, quietly reading a book or a newspaper. I have had her rush at me, with the utmost fury, and snatch from my hand such newspaper or book, with something of the wrath and <u>consternation</u> which a traitor might be supposed to feel on being discovered in a plot by some dangerous spy.

Mrs. Auld was an apt woman, and the advice of her husband, and her own experience, soon demonstrated, to her entire satisfaction, that education and slavery are incompatible with each other. When this conviction was thoroughly established, I was most narrowly watched in all my movements. If I remained in a separate room from the family for any considerable length of time, I was sure to be suspected of having a book, and was at once called upon to give an account of myself. All this, however, was entirely *too late*. The first, and never to be retraced, step had been taken. In teaching me the alphabet, in the days of her simplicity and kindness, my mistress had given me the "inch," and now, no ordinary precaution could prevent me from taking the "ell."[1]

Seized with a determination to learn to read, at any cost, I hit upon many expedients to accomplish the desired end. The plea which I mainly adopted, and the one by which I was most successful, was that of using my young white playmates, with whom I met in the street, as teachers. I used to carry, almost constantly, a copy of Webster's spelling book in my pocket; and, when sent on errands, or when play time was allowed me, I would step, with my young friends, aside, and take a lesson in spelling. I generally paid my *tuition fee* to the boys, with bread, which I also carried in my pocket. For a single biscuit, any of my hungry little comrades would give me a lesson more valuable to me than bread. Not everyone, however, demanded this consideration, for there were those who took pleasure in teaching me, whenever I had a chance to be taught by them. I am strongly tempted to give the names of two or three of those little boys, as a slight testimonial of the gratitude and affection I bear them, but prudence forbids; not that it would injure me, but it might, possibly, embarrass them; for it is almost an unpardonable offense to do anything, directly or indirectly, to promote a slave's

---

Vocabulary Development:	**consternation** (kahn ster NAY shuhn) *n.* great fear or shock that makes one feel helpless or bewildered

---

1. **ell** *n.* former English measure of length, equal to forty-five inches.

TAKE NOTES

Reading Check

What does Mrs. Auld now do when she finds Douglass reading?

_____

_____

_____

_____

_____

Reading Strategy

Once you know that Mrs. Auld has stopped teaching Douglass to read, **establish a purpose** for reading more of this selection.

_____

_____

_____

_____

Literary Analysis

Because this selection is an **autobiography,** Douglass provides a great deal of information about himself. What does Douglass do when Mrs. Auld stops teaching him? What does this reaction tell you about Douglass?

_____

_____

_____

_____

Why doesn't Douglass give the names of the boys who help him learn to read?

_____

_____

_____

_____

Read the underlined sentence carefully. What does this sentence mean? Summarize it in your own words on the lines below. Then, **establish a purpose** for reading the rest of this paragraph. Write your purpose below.

Summary_____

_____

_____

Purpose_____

_____

_____

In this section of his **autobiography,** Douglass talks about a book that changes his life. What is the book? How is Douglass changed by what he learns from the book?

_____

_____

_____

_____

freedom, in a slave state. It is enough to say, of my warm-hearted little play fellows, that they lived on Philpot Street, very near Durgin & Bailey's shipyard.

Although slavery was a delicate subject, and very cautiously talked about among grownup people in Maryland, I frequently talked about it—and that very freely—with the white boys. I would, sometimes, say to them, while seated on a curbstone or a cellar door, "I wish I could be free, as you will be when you get to be men." "You will be free, you know, as soon as you are twenty-one, and can go where you like, but I am a slave for life. Have I not as good a right to be free as you have?" Words like these, I observed, always troubled them; and I had no small satisfaction in wringing from the boys, occasionally, that fresh and bitter condemnation of slavery, that springs from nature, unsearcd and unperverted.[2] Of all consciences let me have those to deal with which have not been bewildered by the cares of life. I do not remember ever to have met with a *boy*, while I was in slavery, who defended the slave system; but I have often had boys to console me, with the hope that something would yet occur, by which I might be made free. Over and over again, they have told me, that "they believed *I* had as good a right to be free as *they* had"; and that "they did not believe God ever made anyone to be a slave." The reader will easily see, that such little conversations with my play fellows, had no tendency to weaken my love of liberty, nor to render me contented with my condition as a slave.

When I was about thirteen years old, and had succeeded in learning to read, every increase of knowledge, especially respecting the free states, added something to the almost intolerable burden of the thought—"I am a slave for life." To my bondage I saw no end. It was a terrible reality, and I shall never be able to tell how sadly that thought chafed my young spirit. Fortunately, or unfortunately, about this time in my life, I had made enough money to buy what was then a very popular schoolbook, the *Columbian Orator*. I bought this addition to my library, of Mr. Knight, on Thames street, Fell's Point, Baltimore, and paid him fifty cents for it. I was first led to buy this book, by hearing some little boys say they were going to learn some little pieces out of it for the exhibition. This volume was, indeed, a rich treasure, and every opportunity afforded me, for a time, was spent in diligently perusing it . . . The dialogue and the speeches were all redolent of the principles of liberty,

> **Vocabulary Development: redolent** (RED uhl ent) *adj.*
> suggestive

_____

2. **unperverted** (un per VERT id) *adj.* uncorrupted; pure.

and poured floods of light on the nature and character of slavery. As I read, behold! the very discontent so graphically predicted by Master Hugh, had already come upon me. I was no longer the light-hearted, gleesome boy, full of mirth and play, as when I landed first at Baltimore. Knowledge had come . . . This knowledge opened my eyes to the horrible pit, and revealed the teeth of the frightful dragon that was ready to pounce upon me, but it opened no way for my escape. I have often wished myself a beast, or a bird—anything, rather than a slave. I was wretched and gloomy, beyond my ability to describe. I was too thoughtful to be happy. It was this everlasting thinking which distressed and tormented me; and yet there was no getting rid of the subject of my thoughts. All nature was redolent of it. Once awakened by the silver trump[3] of knowledge, my spirit was roused to eternal wakefulness. Liberty! the inestimable birthright of every man, had, for me, converted every object into an asserter of this great right. It was heard in every sound, and beheld in every object. It was ever present, to torment me with a sense of my wretched condition. The more beautiful and charming were the smiles of nature, the more horrible and desolate was my condition. I saw nothing without seeing it, and I heard nothing without hearing it. I do not exaggerate, when I say, that it looked from every star, smiled in every calm, breathed in every wind, and moved in every storm.

I have no doubt that my state of mind had something to do with the change in the treatment adopted, by my once kind mistress toward me. I can easily believe, that my leaden, downcast, and discontented look, was very offensive to her. Poor lady! She did not know my trouble, and I dared not tell her. Could I have freely made her acquainted with the real state of my mind, and given her the reasons therefor, it might have been well for both of us. Her abuse of me fell upon me like the blows of the false prophet upon his ass; she did not know that an *angel* stood in the way;[4] and—such is the relation of master and slave—I could not tell her. Nature had made us *friends*; slavery made us *enemies*. My interests were in a direction opposite to hers, and we both had our private thoughts and plans. She aimed to keep me ignorant; and I resolved to know, although knowledge only increased my discontent. My feelings were not the result of any marked cruelty in the treatment I received; they sprung from the consideration of my being a slave at all. It was

---

3. **trump** trumpet.
4. **blows . . . the way** allusion to a biblical story (Numbers 22:21–35) about an ass that cannot move, though she is beaten by her master, because her path is blocked by an angel.

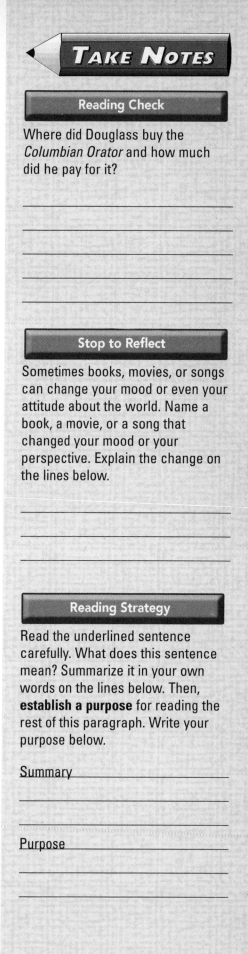

TAKE NOTES

Reading Check

Where did Douglass buy the *Columbian Orator* and how much did he pay for it?

_____

_____

_____

_____

Stop to Reflect

Sometimes books, movies, or songs can change your mood or even your attitude about the world. Name a book, a movie, or a song that changed your mood or your perspective. Explain the change on the lines below.

_____

_____

_____

Reading Strategy

Read the underlined sentence carefully. What does this sentence mean? Summarize it in your own words on the lines below. Then, **establish a purpose** for reading the rest of this paragraph. Write your purpose below.

Summary_____

_____

_____

Purpose_____

_____

_____

from My Bondage and My Freedom **177**

In this **autobiography,** Douglass speaks of his feelings about slavery. How does slavery affect his relationship with Mrs. Auld?

_____

_____

_____

_____

_____

Why does Douglass say that Mrs. Auld cannot censure him for what he says?

_____

_____

_____

_____

_____

slavery—not its mere _incidents_—that I hated. I had been cheated. I saw through the attempt to keep me in ignorance . . . The feeding and clothing me well, could not atone for taking my liberty from me. The smiles of my mistress could not remove the deep sorrow that dwelt in my young bosom. Indeed, these, in time, came only to deepen my sorrow. She had changed; and the reader will see that I had changed, too. We were both victims to the same overshadowing evil—_she_, as mistress, _I_, as slave. I will not censure her harshly; she cannot censure me, for she knows I speak but the truth, and have acted in my opposition to slavery, just as she herself would have acted, in a reverse of circumstances.

Reader's Response: Douglass says in several ways that slavery itself—as an institution—creates evil in otherwise good people. Do you agree or disagree? Why?

_____

_____

Thinking About the Skill: How did **setting a purpose** as you read each paragraph help your understanding of this selection? How will it help you read other **autobiographies** in the future?

_____

_____

from My Bondage and My Freedom

1. **Connect:** How does gaining knowledge change Douglass's attitude?

   _____

   _____

   _____

2. **Literary Analysis:** How does Douglass use his **autobiography** to make a case against slavery?

   _____

   _____

   _____

3. **Literary Analysis:** An autobiography is shaped by the author's own feelings, beliefs, and experiences. In what ways would the selection be different if it were Mrs. Auld's autobiography?

   _____

   _____

   _____

4. **Reading Strategy:** After **establishing a purpose** to learn more about slavery, tell what you learned from Douglass's autobiography. Use this chart.

Douglass's Account	Effects of Slavery
_____ →	_____

An Occurrence at Owl Creek Bridge

LITERARY ANALYSIS

In this story, Bierce uses his main character's warped sense of time to twist the reader's sense of reality. The way that you understand time in a story may depend on the **point of view** from which it is told.

- In stories told from an *omniscient point of view,* the narrator is an "all-knowing" observer.

- In stories told from a *limited third-person point of view*, the narrator relates the inner thoughts and feelings of a single character.

As the point of view in this story shifts from omniscient to limited third-person, the emotional tone and sense of time change as well.

READING STRATEGY

In Bierce's story, the action moves back and forth in time. To see the true sequence of events, a reader must place them in **chronological order**. Use this chart to write the order of events in this story.

Event

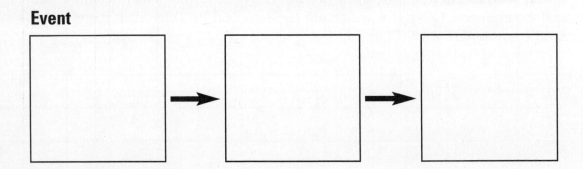

An Occurrence at Owl Creek Bridge

Ambrose Bierce

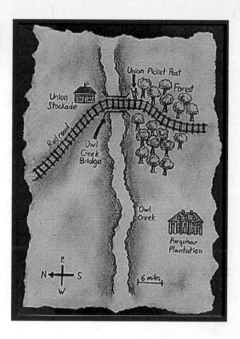

Summary A southern plantation owner is about to be hanged. He stands at the edge of the Owl Creek Bridge. Union soldiers prepare to put him to death for trying to burn down the bridge. A sergeant releases the plank that supports the plantation owner, and the author describes what happens as the man falls.

Note-taking Guide

Make a story map by completing the chart below. Record your responses in the second column.

Setting	
Characters	
Main Events	
High Point of Story	
Conclusion	

An Occurrence at Owl Creek Bridge

1. **Extend:** What does this story suggest about the mind of a person facing a life or death situation?

_____

_____

2. **Literary Analysis:** Analyze the story to identify two different **points of view** and the effects created by each one. Write your responses in a chart like this one.

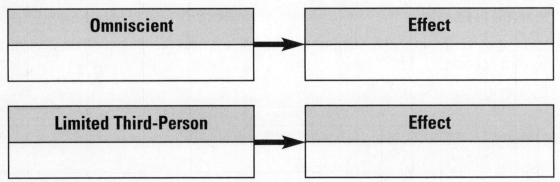

3. **Literary Analysis:** The point of view shifts in the last paragraph of the story. What effect does that shift have on you?

_____

4. **Reading Skill:** Identify the **chronological order** in the story by deciding which happened first: Farquhar's encounter with the Federal scout or his preoccupation with his ticking watch.

_____

5. **Reading Skill:** How much real time probably passes between the opening scene of the story and the last scene of the story? Explain your answer.

_____

_____

The Gettysburg Address • Second Inaugural Address • Letter to His Son

LITERARY ANALYSIS

Diction is a writer's choice and arrangement of words. Diction gives a piece of writing its unique quality. Whether formal or informal, concrete or abstract, the words a writer chooses express feelings beyond the ideas alone. Look at these examples of formal and informal diction from the selections:

Lincoln: "Four score and seven years ago our fathers brought forth . . ."

Lee: ". . . I must try and be patient and await the end . . ."

As you read, contrast the ways in which each writer's diction reflects the different audiences, purposes, and occasions for writing.

READING STRATEGY

It is helpful to know background information about a historical event when reading a historical document. Use **background knowledge** of the Civil War to analyze ideas, actions, and decisions in historical context. Use this chart to organize your ideas.

	Concept in the Text	Background Knowledge	What Text Means
The Gettysburg Address			
Second Inaugural Address			
Letter to His Son			

The Gettysburg Address •
Second Inaugural Address
Abraham Lincoln

Letter to His Son
Robert E. Lee

Summaries Abraham Lincoln delivers a brief speech to honor those who died at the battle of Gettysburg, Pennsylvania. In **"The Gettysburg Address"** he calls on people to continue fighting to save the Union.

Lincoln delivers his **"Second Inaugural Address"** while the Civil War continues. He recalls the beginning of the war. Lincoln does not predict how the war will end. Instead, he urges citizens to work for peace.

Robert E. Lee writes this **"Letter to His Son"** before the Civil War starts. He notes that four states have seceded from, or left, the Union. He worries that more will follow. Lee discusses the conflict he feels over his belief in the Union and his commitment to his home state of Virginia.

Note-taking Guide

Use this chart to write down the main points from the selections.

	The Gettysburg Address	Second Inaugural Address	Letter to His Son
Point 1	The nation was formed around the idea that all men are created equal.	The Civil War began because the nation was divided on the issue of slavery.	Washington would be sad to see what happened to the nation he fought hard to form.
Point 2			
Point 3			
Point 4			

The Gettysburg Address • Second Inaugural Address • Letter to His Son

1. **Apply:** In what ways are Lincoln's addresses similar to and different from modern presidential speeches?

   _____

   _____

2. **Literary Analysis:** Analyze the **diction** of Lincoln and Lee. Use the chart to provide examples. Then, explain why each writer's diction is appropriate for his audience and purpose.

	Examples of Diction	Audience	Purpose
Lincoln			
Lee			

3. **Reading Strategy: Use background knowledge** to explain why Lincoln's speech at Gettysburg is so short.

   _____

   _____

   _____

4. **Reading Strategy:** Using information you already know about Lee, explain why he was so opposed to states seceding from the Union.

   _____

   _____

PUBLIC DOCUMENTS

About Public Documents

A **public document** is an official government paper. A law is an example of a public document. All citizens have the right to read, analyze, and discuss public documents.

This public document is the text of an official announcement. President Lincoln signed this announcement on January 1, 1863. The announcement says that "all persons held as slaves" in those states in rebellion against the Union are freed. Many historians believe that this document changed the course of the Civil War.

Reading Strategy

Some public documents are **objective**. This means that they present factual information and do not support a point of view or an opinion. Other public documents are **subjective**. These documents include opinions and express a particular point of view.

Read subjective public documents critically to **analyze an author's beliefs**. To analyze an author's beliefs, you must find the author's opinions. Then, you should look at the beliefs and assumptions the author uses to support his or her opinions. Assumptions are claims that must be true if the opinion or belief is true.

As you read, keep these points in mind:
- Writers can state their assumptions *explicitly*. This means that an author tells you exactly what he or she thinks.
- Often, writers state their assumptions *implicitly*. This means that an author does not tell you his or her assumptions directly. They are implied in the author's arguments.

Step One	Step Two	Step Three
Look for opinion phrases such as *I think, I believe,* or *in my opinion*. These phrases signal explicit beliefs.	Look for words that suggest opinions. These words might be adjectives that have clear opposites. For example, one writer might say that an action is *just;* another might say that it is *unfair*.	Look for details that suggest a specific point of view. Read the document sentence by sentence. Think about whether each sentence is factual or whether someone can make an argument against it.

By the President of the United States of America:

A Proclamation.

Whereas, on the twenty-second day of September, in the year of our Lord one thousand eight hundred and sixty-two, a proclamation was issued by the President of the United States, containing, among other things, the following, to wit:

"That on the first day of January, in the year of our Lord one thousand eight hundred and sixty-three, all persons held as slaves within any State or designated part of a State, the people whereof shall then be in rebellion against the United States, shall be then, thenceforward, and forever free; and the Executive Government of the United States, including the military and naval authority thereof, will recognize and maintain the freedom of such persons, and will do no act or acts to repress such persons, or any of them, in any efforts they may make for their actual freedom"

"That the Executive will, on the first day of January aforesaid, by proclamation, designate the States and parts of States, if any, in which the people thereof, respectively, shall then be in rebellion against the United States; and the fact that any State, or the people thereof, shall on that day be, in good faith, represented in the Congress of the United States by members chosen thereto at elections wherein a majority of the qualified voters of such State shall have participated, shall, in the absence of strong countervailing testimony, be deemed conclusive evidence that such State, and the people thereof, are not then in rebellion against the United States."

TAKE NOTES

Reading Strategy

The source and type of a **public document** is usually presented clearly. Who is the source of this document?

_____

What type of document is it?

_____

Read Fluently

Many public documents are written in language that provides a great amount of detail. Read the bracketed paragraph aloud. Then, find three details in the paragraph to answer the following questions:

1. Whom does this proclamation affect?

_____

2. How will these people be affected?

_____

_____

3. Who must recognize the effect of the proclamation?

_____

TAKE NOTES

Reading Strategy

One way to **analyze an author's beliefs** is to look for words that suggest an opinion. Look at the underlined passage. What belief about war do Lincoln's words express?

_____

_____

_____

Stop to Reflect

Proclamations often contain legal and formal language. Underline three examples of such language in the bracketed paragraph. Why do you think such language is used?

_____

_____

_____

Now, therefore I, Abraham Lincoln, President of the United States, by virtue of the power in me vested as Commander-in-Chief, of the Army and Navy of the United States in time of actual armed rebellion against the authority and government of the United States, and as a <u>fit and necessary war measure for suppressing said rebellion</u>, do, on this first day of January, in the year of our Lord one thousand eight hundred and sixty-three, and in accordance with my purpose so to do publicly proclaimed for the full period of one hundred days, from the day first above mentioned, order and designate as the States and parts of States wherein the people thereof respectively, are this day in rebellion against the United States, the following, to wit:

Arkansas, Texas, Louisiana, (except the Parishes of St. Bernard, Plaquemines, Jefferson, St. John, St. Charles, St. James Ascension, Assumption, Terrebonne, Lafourche, St. Mary, St. Martin, and Orleans, including the City of New Orleans) Mississippi, Alabama, Florida, Georgia, South Carolina, North Carolina, and Virginia, (except the forty-eight counties designated as West Virginia, and also the counties of Berkley, Accomac, Northampton, Elizabeth City, York, Princess Ann, and Norfolk, including the cities of Norfolk and Portsmouth[)], and which excepted parts, are for the present, left precisely as if this proclamation were not issued.

And by virtue of the power, and for the purpose aforesaid, I do order and declare that all persons held as slaves within said designated States, and parts of States, are, and henceforward shall be free; and that the Executive government of the United States, including the military and naval authorities thereof, will recognize and maintain the freedom of said persons.

188 Reader's Notebook

© Pearson Education, Inc., publishing as Pearson Prentice Hall.

And I hereby enjoin upon the people so declared to be free to abstain from all violence, unless in necessary self-defence; and I recommend to them that, in all cases when allowed, they labor faithfully for reasonable wages.

And I further declare and make known, that such persons of suitable condition, will be received into the armed service of the United States to garrison forts, positions, stations, and other places, and to man vessels of all sorts in said service.

And upon this act, sincerely believed to be an act of justice, warranted by the Constitution, upon military necessity, I invoke the considerate judgment of mankind, and the gracious favor of Almighty God.

In witness whereof, I have hereunto set my hand and caused the seal of the United States to be affixed.

Done at the City of Washington, this first day of January, in the year of our Lord one thousand eight hundred and sixty three, and of the Independence of the United States of America the eighty-seventh.

By the President: *Abraham Lincoln*
Secretary of State. *William H. Seward*

Reading Strategy

What **belief** is explicitly stated by Lincoln in the bracketed paragraph?

_____

_____

_____

Reading Informational Materials

Place and date are key elements of a **public document**. When and where was the Emancipation Proclamation signed?

_____

_____

Why do you think this information is important?

_____

_____

Thinking About Public Documents

1. Why does Lincoln decide to issue the Emancipation Proclamation?

_____

_____

2. Which parts of the United States are not included in the proclamation?

_____

Reading Strategy: Analyzing an Author's Beliefs

3. Think about the implicit and explicit beliefs expressed by Lincoln in the Emancipation Proclamation. What does Lincoln believe about the Constitution's authority, or power?

_____

_____

_____

4. What does Lincoln believe about the need for emancipation?

_____

_____

Timed Writing: Proclamation (25 minutes)

Write a public document to announce a new national holiday or tradition.

Select an important event, person, or cause to honor.

_____

List two reasons why you think your event, person, or cause is important.

_____

Choose a date for your new holiday or tradition. Be sure to tell about the manner in which people will celebrate.

_____

Use your notes to write your proclamation.

Civil War Diaries, Journals, and Letters

LITERARY ANALYSIS

Diaries, journals, and **letters** are personal records of events, thoughts, feelings, and observations. These literary forms allow people to record immediate responses to their day-to-day experiences.

Diaries and journals are usually for personal use. They are most often written in an informal style. They capture the writers' ideas and emotions.

Personal letters are not written for general publication. However, because they are addressed to another person, the writing is not entirely private.

As you read, use this chart to analyze the information each selection provides and to determine what those details reveal about the writer.

Title	Statement From Writer	What it Reveals
Civil War	There may be a chance for peace, after all.	Chestnut doesn't want the country to fight a civil war.

READING STRATEGY

A *fact* is a statement that can be proved to be true. An *opinion* is a judgment that cannot be proved to be true. As you read, **distinguish fact from opinion** by determining whether a statement can be proved or merely supported.

Civil War Diaries, Journals, and Letters

Summaries The writers of these selections describe their personal experiences during the Civil War. In **"Civil War,"** Mary Chestnut writes about the tension and excitement in the days before the bombing of Fort Sumter in South Carolina. In **"Recollections of a Private,"** Warren Lee Goss describes the excitement and nervousness he feels when he enlists in the Union army. **"A Confederate Account of the Battle of Gettysburg"** is Randolph McKim's description of the South's costly defeat at the Battle of Gettysburg. In **"An Account of the Battle of Bull Run,"** Stonewall Jackson writes to his wife about his role in the South's first victory. In **"Reaction to the Emancipation Proclamation,"** Reverend Henry M. Turner records the excitement that surrounds the first issuance of the proclamation in September 1862. Finally, in **"An Account of an Experience With Discrimination,"** Sojourner Truth tells about the discrimination she experiences six months after the end of the Civil War.

Note-taking Guide

Use this table to record the main idea of each selection.

Title	Main Idea

Civil War Diaries, Journals, and Letters

1. **Compare and Contrast:** What can you learn from reading these diaries, journals, and letters that you cannot learn from reading a textbook account of the Civil War?

   _____

   _____

2. **Literary Analysis:** Identify one detail from Mary Chesnut's **diary** that shows her dislike of war.

   _____

   _____

3. **Literary Analysis:** What do details in Sojourner Truth's **letter** tell you about her personality?

   _____

   _____

4. **Reading Skill:** Underline the **facts** and draw a circle around the **opinions** in the following passage.

   The forage cap was an ungainly bag with pasteboard top and leather visor; the blouse was the only part which seemed decent; while the overcoat made me feel like a little nubbin of corn in a large preponderance of husk.

5. **Reading Skill:** Record one fact and one opinion from Stonewall Jackson's account in the following chart.

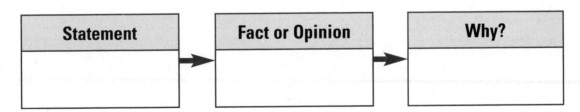

Statement	Fact or Opinion	Why?

The Boys' Ambition *from* Life on the Mississippi • The Notorious Jumping Frog of Calaveras County

LITERARY ANALYSIS

Humor is writing that is meant to make readers laugh. Humorists use many different techniques to make their work amusing. Many western humorists of the 1800s perfected these comic techniques:

- Exaggerating to build comedy
- Using a narrator or storyteller who takes a serious tone

These writers then add humor by suggesting that the story teller is unaware of the story's ridiculous qualities.

As you read, notice details in these selections that make the stories humorous.

READING STRATEGY

Much of the humor in Twain's writing comes from his colorful uses of language. Twain was a master at re-creating **regional dialect**. This is language specific to a particular area of the country. Reading aloud will help you recognize regional pronunciations of words you already know. Use this chart to translate dialect into modern Standard English.

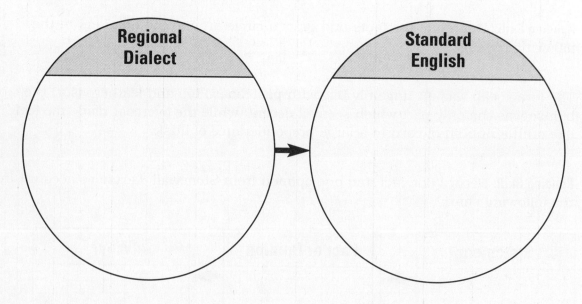

PREVIEW

The Boys' Ambition *from* Life on the Mississippi • The Notorious Jumping Frog of Calaveras County

Mark Twain

Summaries In "The Boys' Ambition," a boy dreams of becoming a steamboat captain. This selection comes from the book *Life on the Mississippi*. In that book, Mark Twain shares the thoughts of a young boy who grows up along the Mississippi River. Twain uses humor to describe the boy, who longs for adventure.

In "The Notorious Jumping Frog of Calaveras County," Twain uses an amusing narrator. This storyteller shares a humorous tale about a betting man and his frog. The characters engage in an unlikely event meant to make readers laugh.

Note-taking Guide

Use this chart to explore Twain's purposes, or reasons, for writing each piece.

The Boys' Ambition

Author's Purpose	Examples From Text
To inform	
To entertain	
To persuade	
To reflect	

The Notorious Jumping Frog of Calaveras County

Author's Purpose	Examples From Text
To inform	
To entertain	
To persuade	
To reflect	

Some people watch horse races because they love horses. Others watch because they want to see which horse will win. What contests featuring animals have you seen? Were you more interested in the animals or in who would win?

_____

_____

_____

_____

Reading Strategy

Read the first paragraph of this story slowly and carefully. Use the Vocabulary Development notes to help you. Break each sentence down and then, in your own words, **summarize** the paragraph on the lines below.

_____

_____

_____

_____

_____

Reading Check

What does Simon Wheeler look like?

_____

_____

_____

_____

The Notorious Jumping Frog of Calaveras County

Mark Twain

In most families or neighborhoods, one relative or friend loves to tell stories—long, complicated stories. These stories can be funny even when the storyteller doesn't intend them to be, especially when the storyteller exaggerates. This story by Mark Twain features just such a storyteller. Be alert for the humor in his exaggerations.

In compliance with the request of a friend of mine, who wrote me from the East, I called on good-natured, garrulous old Simon Wheeler, and inquired after my friend's friend, Leonidas W. Smiley, as requested to do, and I hereunto append the result. I have a lurking suspicion that *Leonidas W.* Smiley is a myth; that my friend never knew such a personage: and that he only conjectured that if I asked old Wheeler about him, it would remind him of his infamous *Jim* Smiley, and he would go to work and bore me to death with some exasperating reminiscence of him as long and as tedious as it should be useless to me. If that was the design, it succeeded.

I found Simon Wheeler dozing comfortably by the barroom stove of the dilapidated tavern in the decayed mining camp of Angel's, and I noticed that he was fat and baldheaded, and had an expression of winning gentleness and simplicity upon his tranquil countenance. He roused up, and gave me good day. I told him a friend of mine had commissioned me to make some inquiries about a cherished companion of his boyhood named *Leonidas W.* Smiley—Rev. *Leonidas W.* Smiley, a young minister of the Gospel, who he had heard was at one time a resident of Angel's Camp. I added that if Mr. Wheeler could tell me anything about this Rev. Leonidas W. Smiley, I would feel under many obligations to him.

Simon Wheeler backed me into a corner and blockaded me there with his chair, and then sat down and reeled off the monotonous narrative which follows this paragraph. He never smiled, he never frowned, he never changed his voice from the gentle-flowing key to which he tuned his initial sentence, he never betrayed the slightest suspicion of enthusiasm; but all through the interminable narrative

Vocabulary Development:	**garrulous** (GAR uh lus) *adj.* talking too much
	conjectured (kuhn JEK churd) *v.* guessed
	monotonous (muh NAHT uh nus) *adj.* tiresome because unvarying
	interminable (in TUR mi nuh buhl) *adj.* seeming to last forever

there ran a vein of impressive earnestness and sincerity, which showed me plainly that, so far from his imagining that there was anything ridiculous or funny about his story, he regarded it as a really important matter, and admired its two heroes as men of transcendent genius in *finesse.* I let him go on in his own way, and never interrupted him once.

"Rev. Leonidas W. H'm, Reverend Le— well, there was a feller here once by the name of *Jim Smiley*, in the winter of '49—or maybe it was the spring of '50—I don't recollect exactly, somehow, though what makes me think it was one or the other is because I remember the big flume[1] warn't finished when he first come to the camp; but anyway, he was the curiousest man about always betting on anything that turned up you ever see, if he could get anybody to bet on the other side; and if he couldn't he'd change sides. Any way that suited the other man would suit *him*—any way just so's he got a bet, *he* was satisfied. But still he was lucky, uncommon lucky; he most always come out winner. He was always ready and laying for a chance; there couldn't be no solit'ry thing mentioned but that feller'd offer to bet on it, and take ary side you please, as I was just telling you. If there was a horse race, you'd find him flush or you'd find him busted at the end of it; if there was a dogfight, he'd bet on it; if there was a cat fight, he'd bet on it; if there was a chicken fight, he'd bet on it; why, if there was two birds setting on a fence, he would bet you which one would fly first; or if there was a camp meeting,[2] he would be there reg'lar to bet on Parson Walker, which he judged to be the best exhorter about here and so he was too, and a good man. If he even see a straddle bug[3] start to go anywheres, he would bet you how long it would take him to get to—to wherever he was going to, and if you took him up, he would foller that straddle bug to Mexico but what he would find out where he was bound for and how long he was on the road. Lots of the boys here has seen that Smiley, and can tell you about him. Why, it never made no difference to *him*—he'd bet on any thing—the dangdest feller. Parson Walker's wife laid very sick once, for a good while, and it seemed as if they warn't going to save her; but one morning he come in, and Smiley up and asked him how she was, and he said she was considable better—thank the Lord for his inf'nite mercy—and coming on so smart that with the blessing of Prov'dence she'd get well yet; and Smiley, before he thought, says, 'Well, I'll resk two-and-a-half she don't anyway.'

---

1. **flume** (FLOOM) *n.* artificial channel for carrying water to provide power and transport objects.
2. **camp meeting** religious gathering at the mining camp.
3. **straddle bug** insect with long legs.

TAKE NOTES

Reading Strategy

When Simon Wheeler begins to tell his story, he uses **regional dialect**, or language that is specific to a particular region of the country. Reading regional dialect may seem like translating a foreign language, but try saying unfamiliar words or phrases aloud to yourself. As you sound the words out, you will usually recognize words that you know. For example, four words are underlined in blue on this page. Write what each word means on the lines below.

1. _____
2. _____
3. _____
4. _____

Literary Analysis

Writing that intends to make you laugh is called **humor**. Simon Wheeler is telling his story with a straight face, but what he is saying is so ridiculous that it is funny. Circle two examples of humor on this page.

Reading Check

Underline the sentence in which Simon Wheeler offers proof that what he says about Jim Smiley is true.

Simon Wheeler continues to use **regional dialect** throughout his story. Circle two examples of regional dialect on this page. On the lines below, write what the dialect means.

_____

_____

_____

_____

Write two things about the dog Andrew Jackson that contribute to the **humor** of this story. Explain why you think they are humorous.

_____

_____

_____

_____

_____

Thish-yer Smiley had a mare—the boys called her the fifteen-minute nag, but that was only in fun, you know, because of course she was faster than that—and he used to win money on that horse, for all she was so slow and always had the asthma, or the distemper, or the consumption, or something of that kind. They used to give her two or three hundred yards start, and then pass her under way; but always at the fag end[4] of the race she'd get excited and desperate like, and come cavorting and straddling up, and scattering her legs around limber, sometimes in the air, and sometimes out to one side among the fences, and kicking up m-o-r-e dust and raising m-o-r-e racket with her coughing and sneezing and blowing her nose—and *always* fetch up at the stand just about a neck ahead, as near as you could cipher it down.

And he had a little small bull-pup, that to look at him you'd think he warn't worth a cent but to set around and look ornery and lay for a chance to steal something. But as soon as money was up on him he was a different dog; his under-jaw'd begin to stick out like the fo'castle[5] of a steamboat, and his teeth would uncover and shine like the furnaces. And a dog might tackle him and bullyrag him, and bite him, and throw him over his shoulder two or three times, and Andrew Jackson—which was the name of the pup—Andrew Jackson would never let on but what he was satisfied, and hadn't expected nothing else—and the bets being doubled and doubled on the other side all the time, till the money was all up; and then all of a sudden he would grab that other dog jest by the j'int of his hind leg and freeze to it—not chaw, you understand, but only just grip and hang on till they throwed up the sponge, if it was a year. Smiley always come out winner on that pup, till he harnessed a dog once that didn't have no hind legs, because they'd been sawed off in a circular saw, and when the thing had gone along far enough, and the money was all up, and he come to make a snatch for his pet holt,[6] he see in a minute how he'd been imposed on, and how the other dog had him in the door, so to speak, and he 'peared surprised, and then he looked sorter discouraged-like, and didn't try no more to win the fight, and so he got shucked out bad. He give Smiley a look, as much as to say his heart was broke, and it was his fault, for putting up a dog that hadn't no hind

---

Vocabulary Development: ornery (OHR nur ee) *adj.* having a mean disposition

---

4. **fag end** last part.
5. **fo'castle** (FOHK suhl) *n.* forecastle; the forward part of the upper deck.
6. **holt** hold.

legs for him to take holt of, which was his main dependence in a fight, and then he limped off a piece and laid down and died. It was a good pup, was that Andrew Jackson, and would have made a name for hisself if he'd lived, for the stuff was in him and he had genius—I know it, because he hadn't no opportunities to speak of, and it don't stand to reason that a dog could make such a fight as he could under them circumstances if he hadn't no talent. It always makes me feel sorry when I think of that last fight of his'n, and the way it turned out.

Well, thish-yer Smiley had rat terriers,[7] and chicken cocks,[8] and tomcats and all them kind of things, till you couldn't rest, and you couldn't fetch nothing for him to bet on but he'd match you. He ketched a frog one day, and took him home, and said he cal'lated to educate him; and so he never done nothing for three months but set in his back yard and learn that frog to jump. And you bet you he *did* learn him, too. He'd give him a little punch behind, and the next minute you'd see that frog whirling in the air like a doughnut—see him turn one summerset, or maybe a couple, if he got a good start, and come down flatfooted and all right, like a cat. He got him up so in the matter of ketching flies, and kep' him in practice so constant, that he'd nail a fly every time as fur as he could see him. Smiley said all a frog wanted was education, and he could do 'most anything—and I believe him. Why, I've seen him set Dan'l Webster down here on this floor—Dan'l Webster was the name of the frog—and sing out, "Flies, Dan'l, flies!" and quicker'n you could wink he'd spring straight up and snake a fly off'n the counter there, and flop down on the floor ag'in as solid as a gob of mud, and fall to scratching the side of his head with his hind foot as indifferent as if he hadn't no idea he'd been doin' any more'n any frog might do. You never see a frog so modest and straightfor'ard as he was, for all he was so gifted. And when it come to fair and square jumping on a dead level, he could get over more ground at one straddle than any animal of his breed you ever see. Jumping on a dead level was his strong suit, you understand; and when it come to that, Smiley would ante up money on him as long as he had a red.[9] Smiley was monstrous proud of his frog, and well he might be, for fellers that had traveled and been everywheres all said he laid over any frog that ever *they* see.

Well, Smiley kep' the beast in a little lattice box, and he used to fetch him downtown sometimes and lay for a bet. One day a feller—a stranger in the camp, he was—come acrost him with his box, and says:

---

7. **rat terriers** dogs skilled in catching rats.
8. **chicken cocks** roosters trained to fight.
9. **a red** red cent; colloquial expression for "any money at all."

TAKE NOTES

Reread the underlined sentence carefully. Rewrite the sentence on the lines below, changing the **regional dialect** to standard English. How does the effect of the sentence change when it is written in standard English?

_____

_____

_____

_____

_____

Circle two examples of **humor** in the bracketed paragraph. What makes them humorous?

_____

_____

_____

_____

What is Smiley's reaction when his frog loses the contest?

_____

_____

_____

_____

_____

'What might it be that you've got in the box?'

And Smiley says, sorter indifferent-like, 'It might be a parrot, or it might be a canary, maybe, but it ain't—it's only just a frog.'

And the feller took it, and looked at it careful, and turned it round this way and that, and says, 'H'm—so 'tis. Well, what's *he good* for?'

'Well,' Smiley says, easy and careless, 'he's good enough for *one* thing, I should judge—he can outjump any frog in Calaveras county.'

The feller took the box again, and took another long, particular look, and give it back to Smiley, and says, very deliberate, 'Well,' he says, 'I don't see no p'ints about that frog that's any better'n any other frog.'

'Maybe you don't,' Smiley says. 'Maybe you understand frogs and maybe you don't understand 'em; maybe you've had experience, and maybe you ain't only a amature, as it were. Anyways, I've got *my* opinion, and I'll resk forty dollars that he can outjump any frog in Calaveras county.'

And the feller studied a minute, and then says, kinder sad like, 'Well, I'm only a stranger here, and I ain't got no frog; but if I had a frog, I'd bet you.'

And then Smiley says, 'That's all right—that's all right—if you'll hold my box a minute, I'll go and get you a frog.' And so the feller took the box, and put up his forty dollars along with Smiley's, and set down to wait.

So he set there a good while thinking and thinking to hisself, and then he got the frog out and prized his mouth open and took a teaspoon and filled him full of quailshot[10]—filled him pretty near up to his chin—and set him on the floor. Smiley he went to the swamp and slopped around in the mud for a long time, and finally he ketched a frog, and fetched him in, and give him to this feller, and says:

'Now, if you're ready, set him alongside of Dan'l, with his forepaws just even with Dan'l's, and I'll give the word.' Then he says, 'One—two—three—*git!*' and him and the feller touched up the frogs from behind, and the new frog hopped off lively, but Dan'l give a heave, and hysted up his shoulders—so—like a Frenchman, but it warn't no use—he couldn't budge; he was planted as solid as a church, and he couldn't no more stir than if he was anchored out. Smiley was a good deal surprised, and he was disgusted too, but he didn't have no idea what the matter was, of course.

The feller took the money and started away; and when he was going out at the door, he sorter jerked his thumb over his shoulder—so—at Dan'l, and says again, very deliberate, 'Well,' he says, 'I don't see no p'ints about that frog that's any better'n any other frog.'

---

10. **quailshot** small lead pellets used for shooting quail.

Smiley he stood scratching his head and looking down at Dan'l a long time, and at last he says, 'I do wonder what in the nation that frog throw'd off for—I wonder if there ain't something the matter with him—he 'pears to look mighty baggy, somehow.' And he ketched Dan'l by the nap of the neck, and hefted him, and says, 'Why blame my cats if he don't weigh five pound!' and turned him upside down and he belched out a double handful of shot. And then he see how it was, and he was the maddest man—he set the frog down and took out after that feller, but he never ketched him. And—"

Here Simon Wheeler heard his name called from the front yard, and got up to see what was wanted. And turning to me as he moved away, he said: "Just set where you are, stranger, and rest easy—I ain't going to be gone a second."

But, by your leave, I did not think that a continuation of the history of the enterprising vagabond *Jim* Smiley would be likely to afford me much information concerning the *Rev. Leonidas W.* Smiley, and so I started away.

At the door I met the sociable Wheeler returning, and he buttonholed me and recommenced:

"Well, thish-yer Smiley had a yaller one-eyed cow that didn't have no tail, only just a short stump like a bannanner, and—"

However, lacking both time and inclination, I did not wait to hear about the afflicted cow, but took my leave.

Literary Analysis

There is **humor** in what Wheeler says even when he doesn't intend it. When someone calls him from the front yard, he tells the narrator that he'll only be gone a second. What is humorous about that remark?

_____

_____

_____

_____

_____

Reading Check

Circle the paragraph in which Wheeler begins to talk about Jim Smiley's cow.

Why doesn't the narrator wait to hear about the afflicted cow?

_____

_____

_____

_____

_____

_____

The Boys' Ambition *from* Life on the Mississippi • The Notorious Jumping Frog of Calaveras County

1. **Evaluate:** If Mark Twain were alive today, do you think he would make a good stand-up comic? Explain.

   _____

   _____

2. **Literary Analysis:** In "The Boys' Ambition," Twain uses the word "heavenly" to describe commonplace steamboat jobs such as shaking out a tablecloth or holding a rope. Why does Twain's use of language like "heavenly" create **humor** in the story?

   _____

   _____

3. **Literary Analysis:** Identify two examples of exaggeration in "The Notorious Jumping Frog of Calaveras County" and explain why each is amusing.

   _____

   _____

   _____

4. **Reading Strategy:** Read the examples of **regional dialect** given in the chart and write what each one means in Standard English.

Regional Dialect	St. Looey	reg'lar	warn't	thish-yer	feller
Standard English					

The Outcasts of Poker Flat

LITERARY ANALYSIS

Regionalism is a literary movement. Writers in this movement try to show the special qualities of a specific area and people.

Stories like "The Outcasts of Poker Flat" paint vivid pictures of what life was like in the far reaches of the country. As you read, notice how the author captures the characteristics of the region and the people who live there.

Local color highlights details that are unique to a specific area. Use this chart to record the elements of local color in the story.

Language	
Setting in Town	
Setting Outside Town	
Local Color	
Attitude Towards Vices	
Attitude Towards Religion	

READING SKILL

When you read literature, **question the text** to improve your involvement and understanding. Ask yourself questions like these:

- What is happening?
- What is the author's purpose, or reason, for writing?
- Why do the characters do the things they do?

As you read, look for answers to these questions.

The Outcasts of Poker Flat

Bret Harte

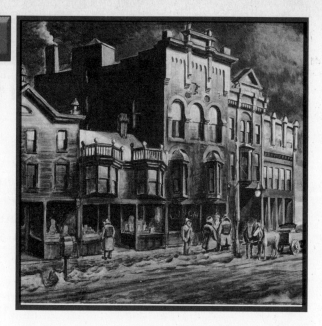

Summary The town of Poker Flat rids itself of four "undesirable characters": a gambler, two prostitutes, and a thief. The group travels into the foothills of the Sierra Nevada Mountains. There, they befriend two young travelers. As the story unfolds, the characters turn out to be more complex than the author originally presents them.

Note-taking Guide

In the chart, record an action taken by each of the characters that reveals some aspect of that character's personality.

Character	Action	What It Reveals
Mr. Oakhurst		
Duchess		
Mother Shipton		
Uncle Billy		
Tom Simson		
Piney Woods		

The Outcasts of Poker Flat

1. **Interpret:** What does the rescue party discover?

   _____

   What theme or message might this discovery—and the story—convey?

   _____

   _____

2. **Literary Analysis:** Identify three details that contribute to the **regionalism** of the story.

   _____

   _____

3. **Reading Strategy:** Harte's closing lines claim that Oakhurst "was at once the strongest and yet the weakest of the outcasts of Poker Flat." **Question the text** by asking what Harte means by those lines.

   _____

   _____

4. **Reading Strategy:** Find three passages from the story. Ask questions about those passages. Record your answers in a chart like the one shown.

Passage From Story	Question	Answer

Heading West • I Will Fight No More Forever

LITERARY ANALYSIS

Tone is a quality of language you encounter every day in speech. Two people might say the exact same words, but differences in tone reveal their individual emotions. In the same way, a writer's attitude emerges in his or her tone. Consider the optimistic, or positive, tone in this passage from Colt's diary:

> Full of hope, as we leave the smoking embers of our campfire this morning. Expect tonight to arrive at our new home.

The tone of a literary work is established by the writer's choice of descriptions and details. Use this chart to interpret the tone of these selections.

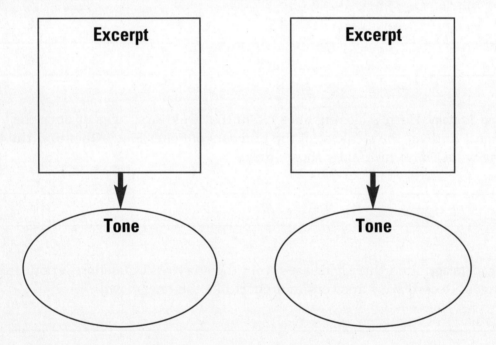

READING STRATEGY

The selections you are about to read describe life-changing events. Reading about life-changing events can produce strong emotions. As you read, take time to **respond** to the literature. Note the emotions you feel and the images each work brings to your mind.

Heading West

Miriam Davis Colt

Summary Miriam Davis Colt and her husband have decided to leave New York and settle in the Kansas Territory. They plan to join a community of vegetarians. Colt writes about her experiences as she journeys west. She is full of excitement and looks forward to beginning a new life in a new home.

Note-taking Guide

Colt uses vivid language to help the reader see what she experiences. Use this diagram to record the images Colt uses to describe what she sees and feels.

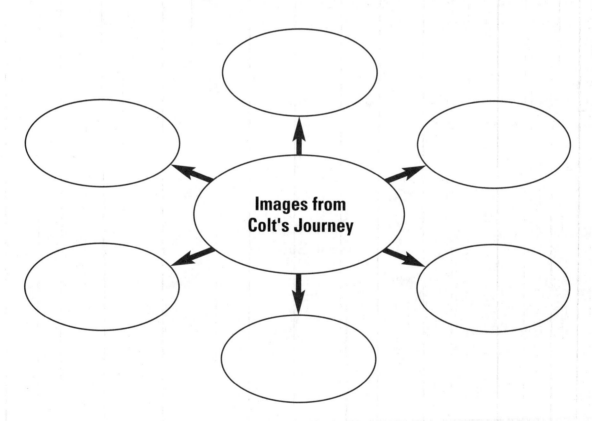

I Will Fight No More Forever

Chief Joseph

Summary Chief Joseph has decided to stop fighting. He grieves for his people who have died during their flight from the United States Army. Those who remain are cold and starving. Chief Joseph speaks beautifully and painfully of his sadness and of his decision to surrender.

Note-taking Guide

Chief Joseph uses vivid details to explain why he has decided to stop running from the United States Army. Use this diagram to record the reasons he lists.

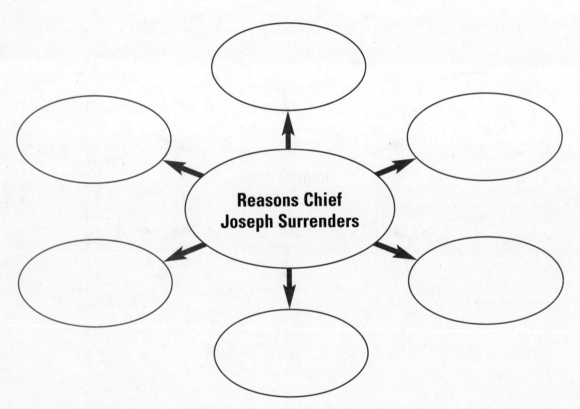

Reasons Chief Joseph Surrenders

Heading West • I Will Fight No More Forever

1. **Literary Analysis:** Miriam Davis Colt often uses a positive **tone** in her diary. Identify two examples of her upbeat tone.

   _____

   _____

2. **Literary Analysis:** Colt sometimes conveys a negative, downcast tone. Find an example of this discouraged tone.

   _____

   _____

3. **Literary Analysis:** What is Chief Joseph's overall tone as he offers his surrender?

   _____

   _____

4. **Compare and Contrast:** Octagon City does not turn out to be like Colt thought it would. Fill in the following chart to show the differences.

Colt's Expectations	
Reality	

5. **Reading Skill:** Identify a passage from Chief Joseph's speech that prompted you to **respond** in a powerful way. Explain your response.

   _____

   _____

To Build a Fire

LITERARY ANALYSIS

Conflict, the struggle between two opposing forces, can take two forms:
- **internal,** occurring within the mind of a character
- **external,** occurring between a character and society, nature, another person, God, or fate

A character's efforts to resolve conflict form the basis for the plot of a literary work. In "To Build a Fire," a man faces a deadly external conflict, struggling to survive in the bitter cold of the Alaskan wilderness.

READING STRATEGY

The main character in this story fails to recognize the seriousness of the conflict he faces until it is too late. A more alert person might have interpreted the signs of danger, guessed their outcome, and taken action. As a reader, you too can anticipate, or **predict**, what will happen by noting clues that hint at later events. Use this chart to identify clues and record your predictions.

Clues	Predictions

To Build a Fire

Jack London

Summary This story focuses on a man who has been searching for gold in the Yukon, a frozen wilderness in Alaska. The man and his dog are walking toward a camp. The man does not recognize the danger of his journey. He does not realize that the temperature is far too cold for him to be traveling alone. Then he builds his fire in the wrong place. The man's terrible mistakes turn out to be deadly.

Note-taking Guide

Writers use sensory language to help readers experience a story. Sensory language includes details that relate to the five senses—sight, sound, smell, taste, and touch. Use this diagram to show how London uses sensory language in "To Build a Fire."

Sights	Sounds	Smells	Tastes	Feelings

To Build a Fire

1. **Draw Conclusions:** What does this story suggest about human strength in the face of nature's power?

   _____

   _____

   _____

2. **Literary Analysis:** Analyze the details London uses to develop the central **external conflict**. Record two details in the chart.

The man versus nature	
Detail 1	
Detail 2	

3. **Literary Analysis:** Explain the **internal conflict** that develops as the plot of the story unfolds.

   _____

   _____

4. **Reading Strategy:** As you read the story, when did you make your first **prediction** that the man would die before he reached his friends?

   _____

   _____

5. **Reading Strategy:** What clues in the story helped you make your prediction about the man's fate?

   _____

   _____

The Story of an Hour

LITERARY ANALYSIS

Irony is a contradiction between appearance and reality, between expectation and outcome, or between meaning and intention. In literature, readers encounter three types of irony:

- **Verbal irony** occurs when someone says something that deliberately contradicts what that person actually means.
- **Situational irony** occurs when something happens that contradicts readers' expectations.
- **Dramatic irony** occurs when the reader is aware of something that a character does not know.

As you read, decide which type of irony best describes the events in this story.

READING STRATEGY

Readers need to **recognize ironic details** in order to understand irony. The details of a story often lead readers to have certain expectations. Readers recognize a sense of irony when events do not match their expectations. While reading "The Story of an Hour," use this chart to note how specific details imply certain feelings, circumstances, or events that may not, in fact, be what they appear. After reading the story, note whether or not your expectations were met.

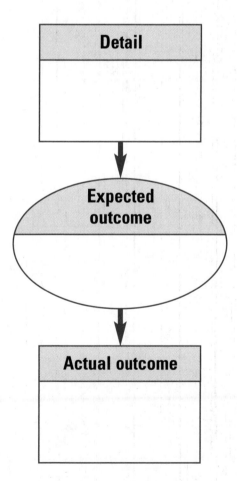

The Story of an Hour

Kate Chopin

Summary Mrs. Mallard has just learned that her husband has died in a train accident. She goes to her bedroom, sits in a comfortable armchair, and looks out her window. She feels something she does not understand. She grieves for her lost husband but she feels something else she has never felt before—freedom.

Note-taking Guide

Use this chart to make notes about the character of Mrs. Mallard.

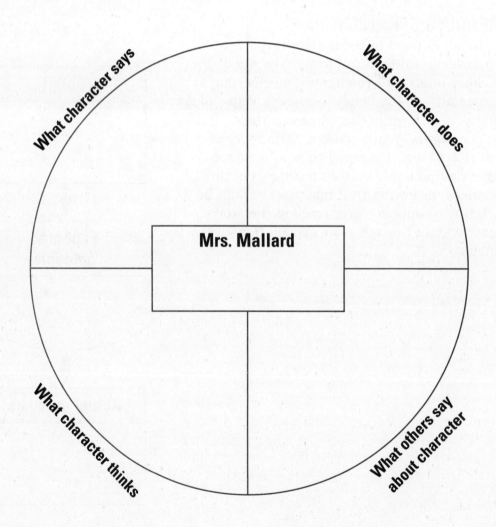

The Story of an Hour
Kate Chopin

Reactions to a sudden shock or a tragedy vary from person to person, but we expect people to react with sadness to death or with joy to winning the lottery. Sometimes, though, we are surprised by unexpected reactions, in ourselves or in others. As you read this short story, notice the ways that the writer surprises you by exploding your expectations.

Knowing that Mrs. Mallard was afflicted with a heart trouble, great care was taken to break to her as gently as possible the news of her husband's death.

It was her sister Josephine who told her, in broken sentences; veiled hints that revealed in half concealing. Her husband's friend Richards was there, too, near her. It was he who had been in the newspaper office when intelligence of the railroad disaster was received, with Brently Mallard's name leading the list of "killed." He had only taken the time to assure himself of its truth by a second telegram, and had hastened to <u>forestall</u> any less careful, less tender friend in bearing the sad message.

She did not hear the story as many women have heard the same, with a paralyzed inability to accept its significance. She wept at once, with sudden, wild abandonment, in her sister's arms. When the storm of grief had spent itself she went away to her room alone. She would have no one follow her.

There stood, facing the open window, a comfortable, roomy armchair. Into this she sank, pressed down by a physical exhaustion that haunted her body and seemed to reach into her soul.

She could see in the open square before her house the tops of trees that were all aquiver with the new spring life. The delicious breath of rain was in the air. In the street below a peddler was crying his wares. The notes of a distant song which someone was singing reached her faintly, and countless sparrows were twittering in the eaves.

There were patches of blue sky showing here and there through the clouds that had met and piled one above the other in the west facing her window.

She sat with her head thrown back upon the cushion of the chair, quite motionless, except when a sob came up into her throat and shook her, as a child who has cried itself to sleep continues to sob in its dreams.

Vocabulary Development: forestall (fohr STAHL) *v.* prevent by acting ahead of time

---

TAKE NOTES

Activate Prior Knowledge

Think about what you know about changes in the lives and roles women over the last hundred years. Kate Chopin wrote at the end of the 1800s. This was at a time when women could not vote and were usually completely financially dependent on fathers, brothers, or husbands. List several ways the lives of women have changed since then.

_____

_____

_____

_____

Reading Strategy

When the events of a story do not turn out the way we expect, it creates irony. The ability to **recognize ironic details** is an important reading skill. As you read this story, stop and note your expectation of what will happen next. For example, what do you expect after reading the first three paragraphs?

_____

_____

Literary Analysis

Irony is a contrast between what is stated and what is meant, or between what is expected to happen and what actually happens. Reread the bracketed paragraph carefully. What is ironic about this paragraph?

_____

_____

Reading Strategy

Mrs. Mallard feels something coming to her and waits for it. List below at least two **ironic details** that lead you to expect something terrible.

_____

_____

_____

_____

_____

Literary Analysis

Situational irony occurs when an outcome is different from what you expect. Circle the words on this page that indicate Mrs. Mallard's true reaction to her husband's death. How is this reaction an example of situational irony?

_____

_____

_____

_____

Reading Check

Does Mrs. Mallard love her husband?

_____

_____

_____

She was young, with a fair, calm face, whose lines bespoke repression and even a certain strength. But now there was a dull stare in her eyes, whose gaze was fixed away off yonder on one of those patches of blue sky. It was not a glance of reflection, but rather indicated a suspension of intelligent thought.

There was something coming to her and she was waiting for it, fearfully. What was it? She did not know; it was too subtle and elusive to name. But she felt it, creeping out of the sky, reaching toward her through the sounds, the scents, the color that filled the air.

Now her bosom rose and fell tumultuously. She was beginning to recognize this thing that was approaching to possess her, and she was striving to beat it back with her will—as powerless as her two white slender hands would have been.

When she abandoned herself, a little whispered word escaped her slightly parted lips. She said it over and over under her breath: "free, free, free!" The vacant stare and the look of terror that had followed it went from her eyes. They stayed keen and bright. Her pulses beat fast, and the coursing blood warmed and relaxed every inch of her body.

She did not stop to ask if it were or were not a monstrous joy that held her. A clear and exalted perception enabled her to dismiss the suggestion as trivial.

She knew that she would weep again when she saw the kind, tender hands folded in death; the face that had never looked save with love upon her, fixed and gray and dead. But she saw beyond that bitter moment a long procession of years to come that would belong to her absolutely. And she opened and spread her arms out to them in welcome.

There would be no one to live for her during those coming years; she would live for herself. There would be no powerful will bending hers in that blind persistence with which men and women believe they have a right to impose a private will upon a fellow creature. A kind intention or a cruel intention made the act seem no less a crime as she looked upon it in that brief moment of illumination.

And yet she had loved him—sometimes. Often she had not. What did it matter! What could love, the unsolved mystery, count for in face of this possession of self-assertion which she suddenly recognized as the strongest impulse of her being!

"Free! Body and soul free!" she kept whispering.

> **Vocabulary Development: repression** (ri PRESH uhn) *n.* restraint
> **elusive** (ee LOO siv) *adj.* hard to grasp
> **tumultuously** (too MUHL choo wuhs lee) *adv.* in an agitated way

Josephine was kneeling before the closed door with her lips to the keyhole, imploring for admission. "Louise, open the door! I beg; open the door—you will make yourself ill. What are you doing, Louise? For heaven's sake open the door."

"Go away. I am not making myself ill." No; she was drinking in a very elixir of life[1] through that open window.

Her fancy was running riot along those days ahead of her. Spring days, and summer days, and all sorts of days that would be her own. She breathed a quick prayer that life might be long. It was only yesterday she had thought with a shudder that life might be long.

She arose at length and opened the door to her sister's importunities. There was a feverish triumph in her eyes, and she carried herself unwittingly like a goddess of Victory. She clasped her sister's waist, and together they descended the stairs. Richards stood waiting for them at the bottom.

Someone was opening the front door with a latchkey. It was Brently Mallard who entered, a little travel-stained, composedly carrying his gripsack[2] and umbrella. He had been far from the scene of accident, and did not know there had been one. He stood amazed at Josephine's piercing cry; at Richards's quick motion to screen him from the view of his wife.

But Richards was too late.

When the doctors came they said she had died of heart disease—of joy that kills.

TAKE NOTES

Reading Check

Why is Mr. Mallard so amazed when Josephine cries out?

_____

_____

_____

Literary Analysis

The final irony of this story is an example of **dramatic irony**, which occurs when readers know something that the characters in the story do not know. The doctors say Mrs. Mallard dies of "joy that kills." What does she really die of?

_____

_____

_____

_____

_____

Reader's Response: What do you think of Mrs. Mallard's true reaction to the news of her husband's death?

_____

_____

Thinking About the Skill: How did it enrich your understanding of this story to **recognize ironic details**?

_____

_____

Vocabulary Development: importunities (im pohr TOON uh teez) *n.* persistent requests or demands

---

1. **elixir** (i LIK ser) **of life** imaginary substance believed in medieval times to prolong life indefinitely.
2. **gripsack** (GRIP sak) *n.* small bag for holding clothes.

The Story of an Hour

1. **Infer:** Mrs. Mallard whispers "free" over and over to herself as she sits in her room. What has she apparently resented about her marriage?

_____

_____

2. **Literary Analysis:** Explain why Mrs. Mallard's death is an example of **situational irony**.

_____

_____

3. **Literary Analysis:** Why is the diagnosis of Mrs. Mallard's cause of death an example of **dramatic irony**?

_____

_____

4. **Literary Analysis:** Identify ironic elements in descriptive passages in the story. Write your responses in this chart.

Passage	Ironic Elements

5. **Reading Strategy:** Which **detail** in the second paragraph do you **recognize** that makes Mr. Mallard's arrival at the end all the more ironic?

_____

_____

Douglass • We Wear the Mask

LITERARY ANALYSIS

Rhyme is the repetition of sounds in the accented syllables of two or more words appearing close together. Poets use rhyme in different ways:

- **Exact rhyme** occurs when the vowel sounds and any consonants appearing after them are exactly the same, as in *days* and *ways*.
- **Slant rhymes** occurs when words sound alike but do not rhyme exactly, as in *prove* and *love*.
- **End rhymes** occur at the ends of two or more poetic lines.
- **Internal rhymes** appear within a single line.

As you read the following poems, take note of Dunbar's use of rhyme.

READING STRATEGY

Poets often include many levels of meaning in their poems. For example, to **interpret** "We Wear the Mask," consider who *we* is and also consider the time and historical context in which the poem was written. Then, consider what the image of a mask suggests—what it reveals and what it hides. Use this chart to interpret these poems.

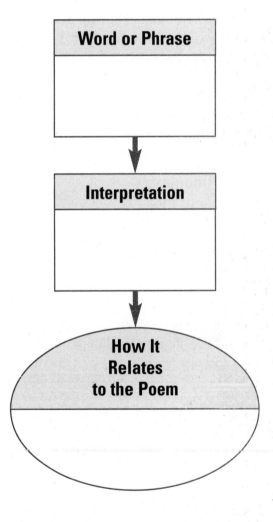

Word or Phrase

Interpretation

How It Relates to the Poem

PREVIEW

Douglass • We Wear the Mask

Paul Laurence Dunbar

Summaries In "Douglass," Dunbar appeals to Frederick Douglass. Douglass was a nineteenth-century abolitionist known for his strong speeches and writing. He worked to gain equal rights for African Americans. In his sonnet to Douglass, Dunbar writes that the fight for equality is not over.

In "We Wear the Mask," Dunbar describes the daily struggles of African Americans. He suggests that African Americans may appear content, but they are not. Dunbar describes how African Americans hide their despair from the eyes of white America.

Note-taking Guide

Use this chart to record the main ideas from each poem and the lines that support those ideas.

"Douglass" Main Idea	Lines that support the main idea

"We Wear the Mask" Main Idea	Lines that support the main idea

© Pearson Education, Inc., publishing as Pearson Prentice Hall.

Douglass • We Wear the Mask

1. **Compare and Contrast:** Which poem most closely reflects the poet's daily struggles and feelings?

   _____

   _____

2. **Analyze:** In "We Wear the Mask," Dunbar speaks for African Americans. What struggles do African Americans face?

   _____

   _____

3. **Literary Analysis:** List all the words in "We Wear the Mask" that are **exact rhymes** with *lies*.

   _____

   _____

4. **Literary Analysis:** In your opinion, what is the effect of rhyme in these poems?

   _____

   _____

5. **Reading Strategy:** Poets use symbolic language to explain feelings and ideas. Identify and **interpret** four examples of symbolic language that you find in the poems. Record your responses in the chart.

	Symbolic language	Interpretation
"Douglass"		
"We Wear the Mask"		

Luke Havergal • Richard Cory • Lucinda Matlock • Richard Bone

LITERARY ANALYSIS

The **speaker** is the voice that is speaking in a poem. Although the speaker may be the poet, it can also be a fictional character or a nonhuman entity. For example, the speakers of the poems in Masters's *Spoon River Anthology* are characters buried in a cemetery in the fictional town of Spoon River, as these lines from "Lucinda Matlock" demonstrate:

> At ninety-six I had lived enough, that is all,
> And passed to a sweet repose.

Instead of using a neutral speaker, Masters allows characters to speak for themselves. In this way, the poet can delve deeply into the minds and hearts of Spoon River's former citizens.

READING STRATEGY

The **attitudes** and beliefs of a poem's speaker contribute to the depiction of the characters, settings, and events. As you read a poem, determine who the speaker is, and look for clues to the speaker's attitudes. For example, in "Lucinda Matlock," the speaker believes that the younger generation is not as tough and hard-working as her generation was. Use this chart to help you recognize the speaker's attitudes in these poems.

Speaker's Attitude	Evidence

PREVIEW

Luke Havergal • Richard Cory

Edwin Arlington Robinson

Lucinda Matlock • Richard Bone

Edgar Lee Masters

Summaries The two poems by Robinson focus on the pain of loss. In "**Luke Havergal**," the speaker describes how Luke Havergal is grieving for his beloved. Havergal questions whether he can go on living. The speaker seems to suggest that Havergal can talk with her spirit until it is his time to die and meet her again in the afterlife. In contrast, "**Richard Cory**" describes a whole town in shock and grief over the suicide of wealthy man.

The two poems by Masters describe characters who have the ability to face life in a changing world. From the grave, both characters speak about their lives. "**Lucinda Matlock**" died when she was ninety-six after a hard but fulfilling life. She does not listen to the complaints of young people who she thinks do not embrace life. "**Richard Bone**" tells the story of the man who carves messages on tombstones.

Note-taking Guide

Use this chart to describe the title character in each of the four poems.

	What character does	Key character trait
Luke Havergal		
Richard Cory		prestige and charm
Lucinda Matlock		
Richard Bone	carves tombstones	

Luke Havergal • Richard Cory • Lucinda Matlock • Richard Bone

1. **Interpret:** In "Luke Havergal," the speaker has come from "out of the grave." What is the speaker's message?

   _____

   _____

2. **Infer:** Lucinda Matlock died at ninety-six. Why might she have thought she "lived enough"?

   _____

3. **Literary Analysis:** Masters writes poems in which the **speakers** are dead. Why would a dead speaker feel free to talk about his or her life?

   _____

   _____

4. **Reading Strategy:** Does the speaker in "Richard Cory" have an **attitude** about Richard Cory that differs from Cory's attitude toward himself? Explain.

   _____

   _____

5. **Reading Strategy:** Analyze Lucinda Matlock's outlook on life by filling in the chart.

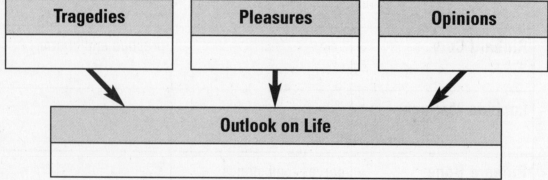

A Wagner Matinée

LITERARY ANALYSIS

A writer uses **characterization** to reveal a character's personality. Characterization is generally developed through one of the following methods:

- direct statements about the character
- descriptions of the character's appearance
- a character's actions, thoughts, and comments
- comments about the character made by other characters

As you read, note the methods of characterization the author uses to develop both Aunt Georgiana's and Clark's personalities.

READING STRATEGY

Cather's story is packed with details about its main character. To fully understand the character's action, **clarify** the details. This may involve reading a footnote or looking up a word in a dictionary. You may also need to reread a passage to refresh your memory about previous details or even read ahead to find details that clarify meaning.

Use this chart to clarify details from the text.

Difficult passage	Choose a strategy:	Reread	Use a dictionary	Use a footnote
	→			

A Wagner Matinée

Willa Cather

Summary Aunt Georgiana was a music teacher who lived in Boston. She met her husband and moved to the Nebraska Territory. She returns to Boston many years later. The narrator meets her at the train station. He remembers his early years with her in Nebraska. He wants to share something special with her, so he takes her to hear a performance of an opera by Wagner. The narrator is surprised by the effect the music has on his aunt.

Note-taking Guide

Use this chart to take notes about the two important places in this story.

Details about Boston	Details about Nebraska

A Wagner Matinée

1. **Interpret:** As a boy, Clark played music on the parlor organ in his aunt's house. Hearing him play, Aunt Georgiana told him: "Don't love it so well, Clark, or it may be taken from you." What does she mean by this statement?

_____

_____

_____

2. **Literary Analysis:** Cather uses several methods of **characterization** to show what Aunt Georgiana is like. Use the chart to write down examples of each method listed.

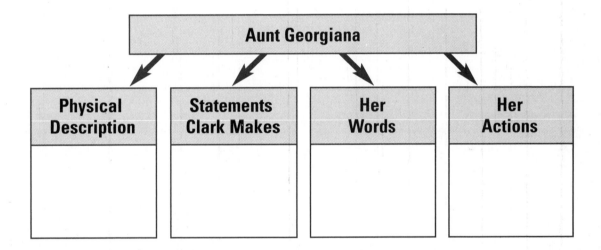

3. **Literary Analysis:** What does Aunt Georgiana's reaction to the opera show about her personality?

_____

_____

_____

A Wagner Matinée (cont'd)

4. **Reading Strategy:** Clarify your understanding of Aunt Georgiana's life. Find three details that describe the difficulties of her life in Nebraska.

_____

_____

_____

The Love Song of J. Alfred Prufrock

LITERARY ANALYSIS

J. Alfred Prufrock's "love song" is not really a love song. Instead, it is a reflection by a character named Prufrock on how love and life have passed him by. The poem takes the form of a dramatic monologue. A dramatic monologue is a poem or speech in which a character addresses a silent listener. A **dramatic monologue** lets you learn a great deal about that character. Use this chart to record Prufrock's thoughts about life and details of his personality. Also, write down details that show how he struggles with his own thoughts, desires, and feelings.

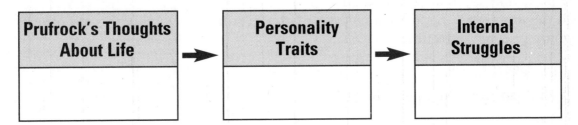

Prufrock's Thoughts About Life		Personality Traits		Internal Struggles
	→		→	

READING STRATEGY

This poem contains some of the most famous and haunting passages in literature. One reason the lines are so famous is that they have a musical quality. They contain repetition, rhyme, and other musical qualities. You must **listen** to the poem to fully appreciate it. Try reading the poem aloud, paying attention to the rhythms and repetitions. Consider how the music of the poem adds to its mood and meaning.

The Love Song of J. Alfred Prufrock

T. S. Eliot

Summary J. Alfred Prufrock invites someone to go for a walk in a city at evening.
The city he describes is gloomy and sad.
Then, Prufrock asks some questions
about himself: Could he have done more
with his life? Can he express love for a
woman? Is he able to do anything impor-
tant? Do the answers to his questions even matter? Prufrock sees himself and others
as drowning in a sea of troubles.

Note-taking Guide

Use this chart to record details about the poem.

Question	Your Answer	Detail from the Poem that Tells You
Who is speaker?		
At what time of the day does the poem take place?		
Where does the speaker go?		
What question does the speaker ask?		
What does the speaker seem to feel about himself?		

The Love Song of J. Alfred Prufrock

1. **Analyze:** In line 51, Prufrock says he has "measured out" his life with "coffee spoons." What does this say about how he has lived?

   _____

   _____

2. **Literary Analysis:** In this **dramatic monologue**, Prufrock does not come right out and say "I wish I were different than I am." What details tell you that he feels disappointment, or wishes he were different? Explain.

   _____

   _____

3. **Literary Analysis:** Prufrock makes many **allusions** to works of art. These allusions show how he sees himself. Use this chart to write down three allusions. Explain their meaning. Then, tell what they say about how Prufrock sees himself. One has been done for you.

Allusion	Meaning	How Prufrock Sees Himself
No! I am not Prince Hamlet . . .	Hamlet is the troubled hero in a play.	He does not think he can be a hero.

4. **Reading Strategy:** The speaker repeats the words "there will be time" in lines 23–34 and again in lines 37–48. Why might someone say such a phrase over and over?

   _____

   _____

Poems by Ezra Pound,
William Carlos Williams, and H.D.

LITERARY ANALYSIS

Imagist poems focus on creating emotion and sparking the imagination through the vivid presentation of a limited number of images. **Images** are words or phrases that appeal to the senses of sight, sound, taste, touch, or smell. The poem called "In a Station of the Metro" is an Imagist poem. It has only two lines and fourteen well-chosen words. Few poems have been written that convey so much meaning with such brevity.

READING STRATEGY

These poems are filled with vivid imagery. As you encounter each image, **engage your senses** by re-creating in your mind the sights, sounds, smells, tastes, and physical sensations associated with the image. Also, note that some images appeal to more than one sense. For example, you can see *and* feel the heaviness in the air as the speaker calls on the wind in "Heat":

Cut the heat—
plow through it,
turning it on either side

Use the chart below to write down what you see, smell, hear, taste, and feel as you read these poems. Provide at least one example for each sense.

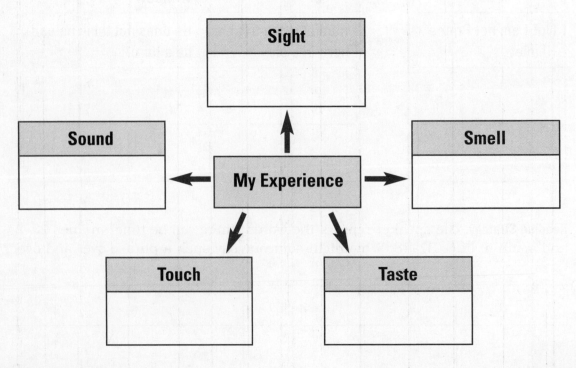

The Imagist Poets

Summaries In the essay "A Few Don'ts by an Imagiste," Ezra Pound talks about rules for writing Imagist poetry. He says it is important to use few words and to make sure they are strong and specific.

In "The River-Merchant's Wife: A Letter," a young Chinese woman writes to her husband, who is away. She longs for his return.

In "In a Station of the Metro," the speaker compares faces in a crowded subway station to flower petals on a tree branch.

In "The Red Wheelbarrow," the speaker describes a wheelbarrow and some chickens.

In "The Great Figure," the speaker describes a moving fire truck.

"This Is Just to Say" is in the style of a personal note. The speaker is sorry for eating plums someone left in the refrigerator.

In "Pear Tree," the speaker describes a tree in bloom.

In "Heat," the speaker talks to the wind. The speaker asks the wind to attack and break up the extreme heat.

Note-taking Guide

Use this chart to record the main image or images in each poem.

Poem	Main Image(s)
"In a Station of the Metro"	
"The Red Wheelbarrow"	
"The Great Figure"	
"This Is Just to Say"	
"Pear Tree"	
"Heat"	

The Imagist Poets

1. **Compare and Contrast:** In "The River-Merchant's Wife," the speaker's feelings for her husband change when she turns fifteen. Explain how her new feelings are similar to and different from her old feelings.

   _____

   _____

2. **Evaluate:** Which words in "The Red Wheelbarrow" and "This is Just to Say" show that the poet was interested in ordinary, everyday life? Explain your answer.

   _____

   _____

3. **Literary Analysis:** Color is often an important element in **Imagist poetry.** Use the chart below to state what the colors in poems by William Carlos Williams and H.D. make you see, think, and feel.

Poem	Main Image(s)	Feeling It Creates
The Red Wheelbarrow	a red wheel barrow	
	white chickens	
The Great Figure	figure 5 / in gold / on a red fire truck	
Pear Tree	Silver dust / lifted from the earth	
	a white leaf	
	purple hearts (of flowers)	

4. **Reading Skill:** Reread this line: "Petals on a wet, black bough." What **senses** other than sight could you **engage** to experience this image? Explain.

   _____

Winter Dreams

LITERARY ANALYSIS

Fitzgerald creates distinct personalities for his characters through **characterization**. Characterization can be direct or indirect.

- **Direct characterization**: The writer tells the readers what a character is like.
- **Indirect characterization**: The character's traits are shown through their words, actions, and thoughts, and by what other characters say to or about them.

An important part of characterization is a character's **motivations**—the reasons for acting as they do. A character's motivations may come from an internal source, such as feelings of loneliness, or an external source, such as danger. As you read, identify the characters' motivations for their actions.

READING STRATEGY

Fitzgerald lets the reader **draw conclusions about characters**. Readers do this by combining information from the story with their own experience. Read this example:

> Dexter stood perfectly still ... if he moved forward a step his stare would be in her line of vision—if he moved backward he would lose his full view of her face.

You can tell from this description that Dexter wants to look at Judy but does not want her to catch him staring.

Use this chart to draw conclusions about the characters in "Winter Dreams."

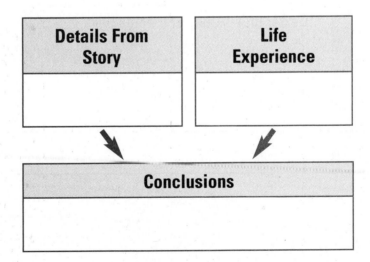

Winter Dreams

Summary Dexter Green is the son of a grocer in a small Minnesota town. He is in love with Judy Jones, the daughter of a wealthy local family. Dexter and Judy first meet at a country club when he is fourteen and she is eleven. He is attracted to her and quits his caddying job to avoid the humiliation of carrying her clubs. After college they meet again and begin a serious romance for one summer. Judy, however, does not want a commitment and dates other men. Dexter decides to marry the more sensible Irene Scheerer. On the eve of the engagement, Judy returns. She renews the relationship with Dexter, which causes Dexter to lose Irene. Judy then leaves Dexter once more. Years later, Dexter learns that Judy is now trapped in an unhappy marriage and has lost her beauty.

Note-taking Guide

Use this story map to record the main elements of the story.

Characters	
Setting	
Problem or Conflict	Dexter falls hopelessly in love with Judy, who is a big flirt.
Main Events	1. Dexter meets Judy and dates her. 2. 3. 4. 5.
Ending	

Winter Dreams

1. **Interpret:** At the beginning of Section II, Dexter says that he wants the glittering things of wealth. In what way does Judy represent Dexter's dreams?

_____

_____

_____

2. **Literary Analysis:** Use this chart to analyze Fitzgerald's **characterization** of Dexter.

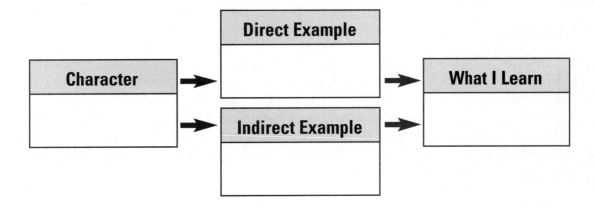

3. **Literary Analysis:** Success was very important to Dexter. What details in the story reveal Dexter's **motivation** to succeed?

_____

_____

4. **Reading Strategy:** Draw conclusions about the characters of Dexter and Judy. What does material wealth and social status mean to each of them?

_____

_____

_____

The Turtle *from* The Grapes of Wrath

LITERARY ANALYSIS

This narrative tells about a short episode in a turtle's life. The narrative presents an important **theme**, or insight into life. An author rarely states a theme directly. Instead, the author reveals theme in these ways:

- Through characters' comments and actions
- Through events in the plot
- Through the use of literary devices, such as **symbols**. A symbol is a person, place, or object that stand for something else.

Sometimes, small details can contribute to a theme, so consider all details as you read.

READING STRATEGY

You need to become a literary detective in order to interpret theme. Look carefully for **clues to the theme** in the writer's use of symbols, his or her choice of details, and characters' actions. For example, Steinbeck includes only slight descriptions of how two motorists react when they spot the turtle. These descriptions provide important clues to the theme. When you encounter such clues, consider the other meanings that they suggest. Gather clues in the following chart.

Clue	+	Clue	+	Clue	=	Theme

The Turtle *from* The Grapes of Wrath

John Steinbeck

Summary A turtle crawls over some grass toward a highway. As he moves, some wild oat seeds become attached to the turtle's legs. With great effort, the turtle gets onto the highway. One car nearly hits the turtle. Another vehicle does hit the turtle, and it rolls off the highway onto its shell. After some time, the turtle rolls itself over. As it rolls, the wild oat seeds fall onto the ground. As the turtle moves, it drags dirt over the seeds.

Note-taking Guide

Complete the following sequence chart.

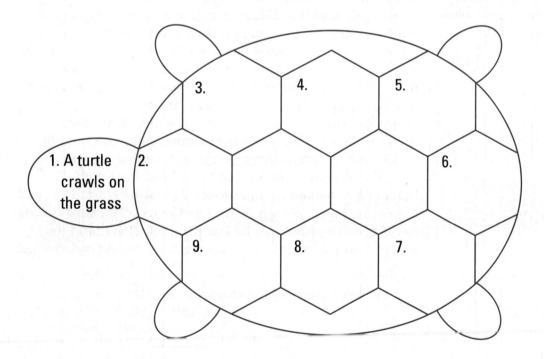

1. A turtle crawls on the grass
2.
3.
4.
5.
6.
7.
8.
9.

Activate Prior Knowledge

You have probably read about the Great Depression in your social studies classes. Your grandparents may also remember the Great Depression and talk about it with you. Write three things that you know about the Great Depression.

1. _____

_____

2. _____

_____

3. _____

_____

Literary Analysis

This story presents a **theme**, or an insight about life. As you read, look for **clues to the theme**. Circle three details from the second paragraph that are clues to the theme of this story.

The Turtle *from* The Grapes of Wrath
John Steinbeck

This selection is an excerpt from the opening of The Grapes of Wrath, *Steinbeck's award-winning novel about the Great Depression. The novel won both a Pulitzer Prize and a National Book Award. Steinbeck is well known as a writer who captures the reality of his characters' lives. As you read this selection, think about how you might compare the turtle's actions to the actions of human beings.*

The concrete highway was edged with a mat of tangled, broken, dry grass, and the grass heads were heavy with oat beards to catch on a dog's coat, and foxtails to tangle in a horse's fetlocks, and clover burrs to fasten in sheep's wool; sleeping life waiting to be spread and dispersed, every seed armed with an appliance of dispersal, twisting darts and parachutes for the wind, little spears and balls of tiny thorns, and all waiting for animals or the hem of a woman's skirt, all passive but armed with appliances of activity, still, but each possessed of the anlage[1] of movement.

The sun lay on the grass and warmed it, and in the shade under the grass the insects moved, ants and ant lions to set traps for them, grasshoppers to jump into the air and flick their yellow wings for a second, sow bugs like little armadillos, plodding restlessly on many tender feet. And over the grass at the roadside a land turtle crawled, turning aside for nothing, dragging his high-domed shell over the grass. His hard legs and yellow-nailed feet threshed slowly through the grass, not really walking, but boosting and dragging his shell along. The barley beards slid off his shell, and the clover burrs fell on him and rolled to the ground. His horny beak was partly opened, and his fierce, humorous eyes, under brows like fingernails, stared straight ahead. He came over the grass leaving a beaten trail behind him, and the hill, which was the highway <u>embankment</u>, reared up ahead of him. For a moment he stopped, his head held high. He blinked and looked up and down. At last he started to climb the embankment. Front clawed feet reached forward but did not touch. The hind feet kicked his shell along, and it scraped on the grass, and on the gravel. As the embankment

---

Vocabulary Development: embankment (em BANK´ ment) *n.* a mound of earth or stone built to hold back water or support a roadway

---

1. **anlage** (on LA guh) *n.* foundation; basis; the initial cell structure from which an embryonic part develops.

grew steeper and steeper, the more frantic were the efforts of the land turtle. Pushing hind legs strained and slipped, boosting the shell along, and the horny head <u>protruded</u> as far as the neck could stretch. Little by little the shell slid up the embankment until at last a parapet[2] cut straight across its line of march, the shoulder of the road, a concrete wall four inches high. As though they worked independently the hind legs pushed the shell against the wall. The head upraised and peered over the wall to the broad smooth plain of cement. Now the hands, braced on top of the wall, strained and lifted, and the shell came slowly up and rested its front end on the wall. For a moment the turtle rested. A red ant ran into the shell, into the soft skin inside the shell, and suddenly head and legs snapped in, and the armored tail clamped in sideways. The red ant was crushed between body and legs. And one head of wild oats was clamped into the shell by a front leg. For a long moment the turtle lay still, and then the neck crept out and the old humorous frowning eyes looked about and the legs and tail came out. The back legs went to work, straining like elephant legs, and the shell tipped to an angle so that the front legs could not reach the level cement plain. But higher and higher the hind legs boosted it, until at last the center of balance was reached, the front tipped down, the front legs scratched at the pavement, and it was up. But the head of wild oats was held by its stem around the front legs.

Now the going was easy, and all the legs worked, and the shell boosted along, waggling from side to side. A sedan driven by a forty-year-old woman approached. She saw the turtle and swung to the right, off the highway, the wheels screamed and a cloud of dust boiled up. Two wheels lifted for a moment and then settled. The car skidded back onto the road, and went on, but more slowly. The turtle had jerked into its shell, but now it hurried on, for the highway was burning hot.

And now a light truck approached, and as it came near, the driver saw the turtle and swerved to hit it. His front wheel struck the edge of the shell, flipped the turtle like a tiddly-wink, spun it like a coin, and rolled it off the highway. The truck went back to its course along the right side. Lying on its back, the turtle was tight in its shell for a long time.

Vocabulary Development: protruded (prō TROOD id) *v.* pushed or thrust outward

---

2. **parapet** (PAR uh pet) *n.* a low, protective wall or edge of a roof, balcony, or similar structure.

Reading Check

Why is the highway embankment a problem for the turtle?

_____

_____

_____

Reading Check

When the turtle pauses, what gets clamped into its shell by its front leg?

_____

_____

_____

_____

Reading Strategy

A **symbol** is anything that stands for something else.

1. What is the woman in the sedan a symbol of?

_____

_____

2. What is the man in the light truck a symbol of?

_____

_____

TAKE NOTES

What **theme**, or insight about life, does this story convey?

_____

_____

_____

_____

_____

But at last its legs waved in the air, reaching for something to pull it over. Its front foot caught a piece of quartz and little by little the shell pulled over and flopped upright. The wild oat head fell out and three of the spearhead seeds stuck in the ground. And as the turtle crawled on down the embankment, its shell dragged dirt over the seeds. The turtle entered a dust road and jerked itself along, drawing a wavy shallow trench in the dust with its shell. The old humorous eyes looked ahead, and the horny beak opened a little. His yellow toe nails slipped a fraction in the dust.

Reader's Response: What was your reaction to the turtle's commitment? Was there ever a time in your life when you kept going even when things were very difficult?

_____

_____

Thinking About the Skill: How did looking for **clues to the theme** help you to understand and appreciate this story?

_____

_____

The Turtle *from* The Grapes of Wrath

1. **Make a Judgment:** Name three obstacles the turtle encounters.

   _____

   Which is the most dangerous obstacle?

   _____

2. **Literary Analysis:** What parallels do you see between the experiences of the turtle and peoples' life experiences?

   _____

   _____

3. **Literary Analysis:** Use this chart to examine the turtle's actions and to understand what they **symbolize.**

	Obstacles	Turtle's Reactions	Symbolic Meaning
Climbs Embankment			
Crosses Road			

4. **Reading Strategy: Find clues to the theme** by examining the way that the author describes the turtle's actions. How do you think Steinbeck wants readers to respond to the turtle?

   _____

   _____

   _____

   _____

5. **Reading Strategy:** Which do you think Steinbeck feels is more important—nature or the modern world? Explain your answer.

   _____

   _____

old age sticks • anyone lived in a pretty how town • The Unknown Citizen

LITERARY ANALYSIS

Satire is writing that ridicules the faults of individuals, groups, institutions, or even people in general. Although satire is often humorous, its purpose is not simply to make readers laugh but also to point out the shortcomings of its subject. By poking fun at flaws, satirists hope to persuade readers to accept their point of view. As you read, think about the serious point each poet makes through satire.

Satirical writings vary in **tone**—a quality that reveals a writer's attitude toward his or her subject, characters, or audience. The tone of a satirical work may be humorous, bitter, or cruel. The tone of a literary work is shown through the writer's choice of words and details. For example, in naming his characters "anyone" and "noone," Cummings suggests the lack of personality that come with excessive obedience.

As you read these poems, compare each poet's tone, and identify the type of satire that results.

READING STRATEGY

You can often connect the ideas of poetry with the form the words take:

- **Structure** is the way a poem is put together in words, lines, and stanzas.
- **Meaning** is the central idea the poet wants to convey.

anyone lived in a pretty how town		old age sticks		The Unknown Citizen	
Structure	Meaning	Structure	Meaning	Structure	Meaning

In his poems, Cummings plays typographical games and breaks rules of grammar and syntax. His structure suits his theme: individual challenges to convention. Use this chart to link structure to meaning.

old age stick • anyone lived in a pretty how town • The Unknown Citizen

E. E. Cummings • W. H. Auden

Summaries In "old age sticks," the speaker says that the young ignore the warnings of the elderly. He suggests that although the young tear down warning "signs," one day they will be posting such "signs" themselves. In "anyone lived in a pretty how town," the speaker tells about an anonymous town in which people live routine and ordinary lives. The seasons pass with regular predictability as the main characters, "anyone" and "noone," do nothing special and are basically unnoticed by other people in the town. "The Unknown Citizen" honors a model citizen of his society. The speaker calls this man a saint because he served the Greater Community. However, no one knows anything about his true life experiences.

Note-taking Guide

As you read each poem, consider who is the subject of each poem and what happens. Use this chart to keep track of your information.

old age sticks
Who is the subject?
What happens?

anyone lived in a pretty how town
Who is the subject?
What happens?

The Unknown Citizen
Who is the subject?
What happens?

old age sticks • anyone lived in a pretty how town • The Unknown Citizen

1. **Interpret:** In the final stanza of "old age sticks," the poem says that youth is "growing old." What is ironic about this final stanza?

   _____

2. **Literary Analysis:** What small-town qualities and behaviors does Cummings **satirize** in "anyone lived in a pretty how town"?

   _____

   _____

3. **Literary Analysis:** Use this chart to name four groups that report on the unknown citizen's activities in "The Unknown Citizen." Then, tell what the concerns of these groups show about society.

   Society: _____

   _____

4. **Literary Analysis:** What is the **tone**, or attitude, of each poem?

   _____

5. **Reading Strategy:** Tell how Auden's style of capitalization affects the **meaning** and tone of his poem.

   _____

   _____

The Far and the Near

LITERARY ANALYSIS

The **climax** of a story is the high point of interest or suspense, the point when the conflict reaches its greatest intensity. Usually something decisive happens, showing how the conflict will end. When what happens is unexpectedly disappointing, ridiculous, or unimportant, it is called an **anticlimax**. Like a climax, an anticlimax is the key moment in the story. The reader, who has been expecting something important to occur, feels let down. When used effectively, an anticlimax can spark an emotion in the reader, such as sorrow or amusement.

To keep readers interested, writers must grab their interest early. Once a story's central conflict is introduced, the events leading up to the climax help build readers' anticipation. These events make up a story's **rising action**.

READING STRATEGY

This story about a train engineer's life is similar to a real train ride: Signposts guide the way to the final destination. These clues help you **predict** upcoming events and outcomes. Look for signals in the story's details that tell where the action is headed. Consider this passage from the story:

> Everyday, a few minutes after two o'clock in the afternoon, the limited express . . . passed this spot.

Because the writer tells you the place is important, you might predict that the story will involve "this spot" in some way. As you read, predict what is to come. Record the information in the following chart.

Story Detail	My Knowledge About This Detail	My Prediction

The Far and the Near

Thomas Wolfe

Summary The main character in this story is a train engineer. Every day for twenty years, he passes by a pleasant little cottage near the tracks. A woman and her daughter come out each time and wave to him as he passes. The woman, her daughter, and the house become symbols of happiness for him. At last, when he retires, he goes to visit the house. He soon discovers that the women are nothing like he expected.

Note-taking Guide Use this chart to keep track of the sequence of events in the story.

Sequence of Events					
1. For twenty years, a train engineer passes a white cottage with green blinds.	2.	3.	4.	5.	6.

The Far and the Near
Thomas Wolfe

Things—and people—seen from a distance can look different when you get closer to them. Sometimes they look better, but sometimes they look worse. Thomas Wolfe writes here of someone who tries to get close to a place and two people he has watched from a distance for years. As you read, be alert for clues. Will the place and the people look better or worse to him?

On the outskirts of a little town upon a rise of land that swept back from the railway there was a tidy little cottage of white boards, trimmed vividly with green blinds. To one side of the house there was a garden neatly patterned with plots of growing vegetables, and an arbor for the grapes which ripened late in August. Before the house there were three mighty oaks which sheltered it in their clean and massive shade in summer, and to the other side there was a border of gay flowers. The whole place had an air of tidiness, thrift, and modest comfort.

Every day, a few minutes after two o'clock in the afternoon, the limited express between two cities passed this spot. At that moment the great train, having halted for a breathing space at the town nearby, was beginning to lengthen evenly into its stroke, but it had not yet reached the full drive of its terrific speed. It swung into view deliberately, swept past with a powerful swaying motion of the engine, a low smooth rumble of its heavy cars upon pressed steel, and then it vanished in the cut. For a moment the progress of the engine could be marked by heavy bellowing puffs of smoke that burst at spaced intervals above the edges of the meadow grass, and finally nothing could be heard but the solid clacking <u>tempo</u> of the wheels receding into the drowsy stillness of the afternoon.

Every day for more than twenty years, as the train had approached this house, the engineer had blown on the whistle, and every day, as soon as she heard this signal, a woman had appeared on the back porch of the little house and waved to him. At first she had a small child clinging to her skirts, and now this child had grown to full womanhood, and every day she, too, came with her mother to the porch and waved.

The engineer had grown old and gray in service. He had driven his great train, loaded with its weight of lives, across the land ten thousand times. His own children had grown up and married, and four times he had seen before him on

---

Vocabulary Development: tempo (TEM poh) *n.* rate of activity of a sound or motion; pace

© Pearson Education, Inc., publishing as Pearson Prentice Hall.

Activate Prior Knowledge

Have you ever lived close to train tracks? When do trains usually whistle? Why do you think an engineer might blow the whistle at an unusual place?

_____

_____

_____

_____

_____

Reading Strategy

Reread the bracketed paragraph carefully. What do you **predict**, or foretell, will happen next in the story?

_____

_____

_____

Reading Check

What does the engineer do every day for more than twenty years?

_____

_____

TAKE NOTES

Reading Check

Give two examples of tragedies that the engineer has seen in his years on the train.

1. _____

_____

2. _____

_____

Literary Analysis

Events leading to the **climax**, or highest point of tension, in a story are called the rising action. Look carefully at the bracketed paragraphs. Why are these paragraphs part of the **rising action**?

_____

_____

_____

Reading Strategy

When he retires, the engineer goes to the town where the women live. What do you **predict** will happen when they all meet?

_____

_____

the tracks the ghastly dot of tragedy converging like a cannon ball to its eclipse of horror at the boiler head[1]—a light spring wagon filled with children, with its clustered row of small stunned faces; a cheap automobile stalled upon the tracks, set with the wooden figures of people paralyzed with fear; a battered hobo walking by the rail, too deaf and old to hear the whistle's warning; and a form flung past his window with a scream—all this the man had seen and known. He had known all the grief, the joy, the peril and the labor such a man could know; he had grown seamed and weathered in his loyal service, and now, schooled by the qualities of faith and courage and humbleness that attended his labor, he had grown old, and had the grandeur and the wisdom these men have.

But no matter what peril or tragedy he had known, the vision of the little house and the women waving to him with a brave free motion of the arm had become fixed in the mind of the engineer as something beautiful and enduring, something beyond all change and ruin, and something that would always be the same, no matter what mishap, grief or error might break the iron schedule of his days.

The sight of the little house and of these two women gave him the most extraordinary happiness he had ever known. He had seen them in a thousand lights, a hundred weathers. He had seen them through the harsh bare light of wintry gray across the brown and frosted stubble of the earth, and he had seen them again in the green luring sorcery of April.

He felt for them and for the little house in which they lived such tenderness as a man might feel for his own children, and at length the picture of their lives was carved so sharply in his heart that he felt that he knew their lives completely, to every hour and moment of the day, and he resolved that one day, when his years of service should be ended, he would go and find these people and speak at last with them whose lives had been so wrought into his own.

That day came. At last the engineer stepped from a train onto the station platform of the town where these two women lived. His years upon the rail had ended. He was a pensioned servant of his company, with no more work to do. The engineer walked slowly through the station and out into the streets of the town. Everything was as strange to him as if he had never seen this town before. As he walked on, his sense of bewilderment and confusion grew. Could this be the town he had passed ten thousand times? Were these the same houses he had seen so often from the high windows of his cab? It was all as unfamiliar, as disquieting as a city in a dream, and the perplexity of his spirit increased as he went on.

---

1. boiler head the front section of a steam locomotive.

Presently the houses thinned into the straggling outposts of the town, and the street faded into a country road—the one on which the women lived. And the man plodded on slowly in the heat and dust. At length he stood before the house he sought. He knew at once that he had found the proper place. He saw the lordly oaks before the house, the flower beds, the garden and the arbor, and farther off, the glint of rails.

Yes, this was the house he sought, the place he had passed so many times, the destination he had longed for with such happiness. But now that he had found it, now that he was here, why did his hand falter on the gate; why had the town, the road, the earth, the very entrance to this place he loved turned unfamiliar as the landscape of some ugly dream? Why did he now feel this sense of confusion, doubt and hopelessness?

At length he entered by the gate, walked slowly up the path and in a moment more had mounted three short steps that led up to the porch, and was knocking at the door. Presently he heard steps in the hall, the door was opened, and a woman stood facing him.

And instantly, with a sense of bitter loss and grief, he was sorry he had come. He knew at once that the woman who stood there looking at him with a mistrustful eye was the same woman who had waved to him so many thousand times. But her face was harsh and pinched and meager; the flesh sagged wearily in <u>sallow</u> folds, and the small eyes peered at him with timid suspicion and uneasy doubt. All the brave freedom, the warmth and the affection that he had read into her gesture, vanished in the moment that he saw her and heard her unfriendly tongue.

And now his own voice sounded unreal and ghastly to him as he tried to explain his presence, to tell her who he was and the reason he had come. But he faltered on, fighting stubbornly against the horror of regret, confusion, disbelief that surged up in his spirit, drowning all his former joy and making his act of hope and tenderness seem shameful to him.

At length the woman invited him almost unwillingly into the house, and called her daughter in a harsh shrill voice. Then, for a brief agony of time, the man sat in an ugly little parlor, and he tried to talk while the two women stared at him with a dull, bewildered hostility, a <u>sullen</u>, <u>timorous</u> restraint.

Vocabulary Development: sallow (SAL oh) *adj.* sickly; pale yellow
                   sullen (SUL un) *adj.* sulky; glum
                   timorous (TIM uhr uhs) *adj.* full of fear

Reading Strategy

Reread the bracketed paragraph.

1. Why does the engineer hesitate at the gate?

_____

_____

2. Why do you think he is suddenly confused?

_____

_____

_____

3. What do you predict will happen when he knocks on the door?

_____

_____

_____

Reading Check

Why is the engineer sorry he has come the minute the woman opens the door?

_____

_____

_____

Literary Analysis

The **climax** of a story is the moment when the conflict is resolved. But sometimes that moment is an **anticlimax** instead— a disappointing or trivial resolution. Identify the anticlimax in this story.

_____

_____

_____

Reading Check

Why does the engineer suddenly know that he is an old man?

_____

_____

_____

_____

And finally, stammering a crude farewell, he departed. He walked away down the path and then along the road toward town, and suddenly he knew that he was an old man. His heart, which had been brave and confident when it looked along the familiar vista of the rails, was now sick with doubt and horror as it saw the strange and unsuspected <u>visage</u> of an earth which had always been within a stone's throw of him, and which he had never seen or known. And he knew that all the magic of that bright lost way, the vista of that shining line, the imagined corner of that small good universe of hope's desire, was gone forever, could never be got back again.

Vocabulary Development: visage (VIZ iJ) *n.* appearance

Reader's Response: Are you sympathetic with the engineer's disappointment? Have you ever anticipated something for a long time and been disappointed when it finally happened?

_____

_____

_____

Thinking About the Skill: How did stopping to **predict** what would happen next keep you interested in the story?

_____

_____

_____

The Far and the Near

1. **Interpret:** Every day for twenty years, the engineer passes a cottage in a small town and a woman and her daughter wave at him. What does this tell you about the engineer's life?

   _____

   _____

2. **Literary Analysis:** What effect does the story's **anticlimax** have on both the engineer and the reader?

   _____

   _____

3. **Literary Analysis:** Use this chart to list three events in the **rising action** that lead to the moment of greatest tension.

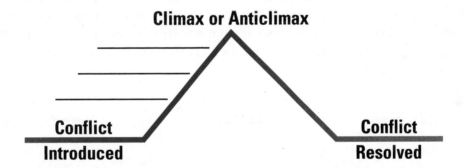

Climax or Anticlimax

Conflict Introduced

Conflict Resolved

4. **Reading Strategy:** When you read about the engineer's decision to visit the two women after retiring, what did you **predict** would happen?

   _____

   _____

5. **Reading Strategy:** Based on your own experience, did you predict that the engineer's view of the world would change when he stepped down from the "high windows of his cab"? Explain.

   _____

   _____

Of Modern Poetry • Anecdote of the Jar • Ars Poetica • Poetry

LITERARY ANALYSIS

A **simile** is a comparison between two seemingly different things. A connecting word such as *like* or *as* indicates the comparison. For example, the word *like* indicates the comparison in the following simile:

The sound of the explosion echoed through the air *like thunder*.

By comparing the sound of the explosion to thunder, the simile stresses its loud, jarring power.

Similes also help writers to create imagery. **Imagery** is language that uses **images**—words or phrases that relate to one or more of the five senses of sight, smell, touch, sound, or taste. As you read, notice the similes and imagery each poet uses.

READING STRATEGY

Poetry is written in verse and often contains unexpected words and images. For these reasons, it can be challenging to understand. One way to make sure that you grasp what you are reading is to **paraphrase**—to identify key ideas and restate them in your own words. Paraphrasing can remove barriers that make some poems seem too difficult. Use this chart to write paraphrases of difficult passages.

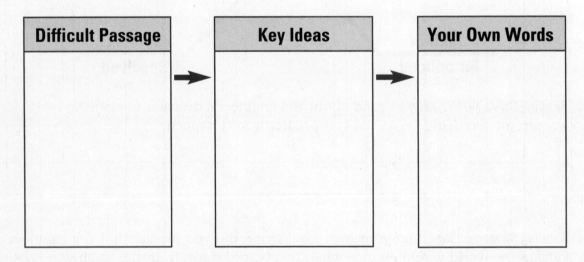

Difficult Passage	Key Ideas	Your Own Words

Of Modern Poetry • Anecdote of the Jar • Ars Poetica • Poetry

Wallace Stevens

Archibald MacLeish

Marianne Moore

Summaries All of these poems are about poems. Each poet says what he or she thinks a poem is or should be. They say what they like or do not like about poems. Sometimes, they say these things directly. Sometimes, they use images to give you a feeling about what they mean. In **"Of Modern Poetry,"** the speaker says that a poem must use the language of its own time. In **"Anecdote of the Jar,"** the presence of a jar on a hill gives order to the wilderness. The jar itself is "gray and bare." In **"Ars Poetica,"** the speaker compares a poem to several other things. He says that the image is the most important part of a poem. The meaning of the poem does not matter as much. In **"Poetry,"** the speaker feels sad for those who do not like poems. She thinks poems should be written so that readers can understand them.

Note-taking Guide

Use this chart to write down words and phrases from each poem that tell you what the poet likes about poetry or some poems. Write down words and phrases that tell you what the poet does not like about poetry or some poems.

Poem	Likes	Dislikes
Of Modern Poetry		
Anecdote of the Jar		
Ars Poetica		
Poetry		

Of Modern Poetry • Anecdote of the Jar • Ars Poetica • Poetry

1. **Speculate:** In "Ars Poetica," the speaker talks about **images** that show grief and love. Why do you think the poet chose to focus on these feelings?

   _____

2. **Synthesize:** In "Poetry," the speaker says "we do not admire what / we cannot understand." What qualities does the speaker think poems should have so that people will like them?

   _____

3. **Literary Analysis:** A **simile** uses the words *like* or *as* to compare two things. Find four similes in "Ars Poetica." Use this chart to explain what each simile means.

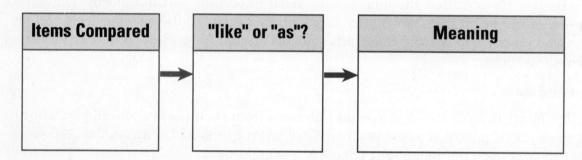

Items Compared	"like" or "as"?	Meaning

4. **Reading Strategy:** These are lines 6–9 from "Of Modern Poetry" with some words and phrases missing. Complete these lines with your own words. Keep the meaning of the original lines.

   It has to be _____, to learn the _____.

   It has to _____ the men _____ and to _____

   The women _____. It has to _____

   And it has to find what will _____...

5. **Reading Strategy:** Write out your **paraphrase** of lines 6-9 from "Of Modern Poetry."

   _____

   _____

In Another Country • The Corn Planting •
A Worn Path

LITERARY ANALYSIS

Point of view is the perspective from which a story is told.

- In the **first-person point of view,** the person telling the story takes part in the action, uses the pronoun *I,* and shares his or her own thoughts and feelings.

- In the **limited third-person point of view,** the narrator stands outside the action and does not use the pronoun *I.* However, this narrator sees the world through one character's eyes and shows only what that character is thinking and feeling.

As you read, use this chart to analyze the point of view in each story.

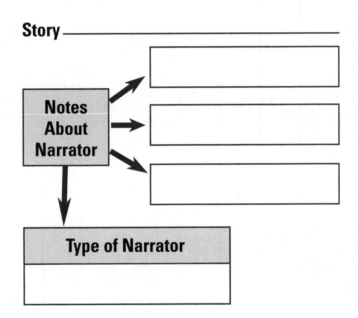

READING STRATEGY

When you **identify with characters**, you connect characters' thoughts and feelings with your own experiences. As you read, identify with characters by thinking of how you felt in similar situations.

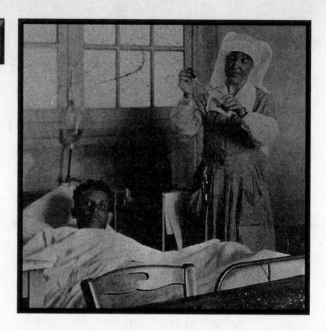

PREVIEW

In Another Country

Ernest Hemingway

Summary In "In Another Country," an American officer recovering from a war injury meets three young Italian officers and an older major. All of the men are wounded. The major helps the American with his Italian grammar, advises him not to marry, and mourns the death of his own wife.

Note-taking Guide

Use this chart to record information about Hemingway's story "In Another Country."

Setting	Characters	Problem	Resolution

In Another Country
Ernest Hemingway

For Ernest Hemingway, war is a powerful symbol of life and the world. He could not be a soldier himself because of a problem with his eye. But he was involved in World War I as an ambulance driver and in World War II as a journalist. He reflected what he saw and learned in those wars in much of his writing, for which he won both a Pulitzer Prize and a Nobel Prize.

In the fall the war[1] was always there, but we did not go to it any more. It was cold in the fall in Milan[2] and the dark came very early. Then the electric lights came on, and it was pleasant along the streets looking in the windows. There was much game hanging outside the shops, and the snow powdered in the fur of the foxes and the wind blew their tails. The deer hung stiff and heavy and empty, and small birds blew in the wind and the wind turned their feathers. It was a cold fall and the wind came down from the mountains.

We were all at the hospital every afternoon, and there were different ways of walking across the town through the dusk to the hospital. Two of the ways were alongside canals, but they were long. Always, though, you crossed a bridge across a canal to enter the hospital. There was a choice of three bridges. On one of them a woman sold roasted chestnuts. It was warm, standing in front of her charcoal fire, and the chestnuts were warm afterward in your pocket. The hospital was very old and very beautiful, and you entered through a gate and walked across a courtyard and out a gate on the other side. There were usually funerals starting from the courtyard. Beyond the old hospital were the new brick pavilions, and there we met every afternoon and were all very polite and interested in what was the matter, and sat in the machines that were to make so much difference.

The doctor came up to the machine where I was sitting and said: "What did you like best to do before the war? Did you practice a sport?"

I said: "Yes, football."

"Good," he said. "You will be able to play football again better than ever."

My knee did not bend and the leg dropped straight from the knee to the ankle without a calf, and the machine was to bend the knee and make it move as in riding a tricycle. But it did not bend yet, and instead the machine lurched when it came to the bending part. The doctor said: "That will all pass. You are a fortunate young man. You will play football again like a champion."

---

1. the war World War I (1914–1918).
2. Milan (mi LAHN) a city in northern Italy.

TAKE NOTES

Activate Prior Knowledge

The narrator, or the teller, of this story is "in another country" in several different ways. Have you ever felt separate or different from a group you see every day? Be alert as you read this story for evidence that the narrator feels separate from the other characters.

_____

_____

Reading Strategy

Reading is always more interesting if you can **identify with the characters** you are reading about. That means that you try to relate the experiences of the characters to your own experiences. Notice that the narrator says there are different ways to get to the hospital. Do you choose different ways to get to school each day? What are the advantages and disadvantages of each possible route?

_____

_____

Literary Analysis

The narrator of this story tells the story from the **first-person point of view**. That means that he tells what happens in his own words, using the first-person pronouns *I* and *we*. Circle three examples of the use of first-person pronouns on this page.

Describe the narrator's injury.

_____

_____

_____

Have you ever had an injury that required physical therapy after it healed? Or do you know anyone who has? It will help you to **identify with the characters** if you can imagine a similar experience. Did the therapy help the injury?

_____

_____

_____

Why does one of the wounded soldiers wear a black silk handkerchief across his face?

_____

_____

_____

Circle three or more examples of first-person pronouns on this page. The pronouns remind you that the **narrator** uses the **first-person point of view.**

In the next machine was a major who had a little hand like a baby's. He winked at me when the doctor examined his hand, which was between two leather straps that bounced up and down and flapped the stiff fingers, and said: "And will I too play football, captain-doctor?" He had been a very great fencer, and before the war the greatest fencer in Italy.

The doctor went to his office in a back room and brought a photograph which showed a hand that had been withered almost as small as the major's, before it had taken a machine course, and after was a little larger. The major held the photograph with his good hand and looked at it very carefully. "A wound?" he asked.

"An industrial accident," the doctor said.

"Very interesting, very interesting," the major said, and handed it back to the doctor.

"You have confidence?"

"No," said the major.

There were three boys who came each day who were about the same age I was. They were all three from Milan, and one of them was to be a lawyer, and one was to be a painter, and one had intended to be a soldier, and after we were finished with the machines, sometimes we walked back together to the Café Cova, which was next door to the Scala.[3] We walked the short way through the communist quarter because we were four together. The people hated us because we were officers, and from a wine-shop someone called out, "A basso gli ufficiali!"[4] as we passed. Another boy who walked with us sometimes and made us five wore a black silk handkerchief across his face because he had no nose then and his face was to be rebuilt. He had gone out to the front from the military academy and been wounded within an hour after he had gone into the front line for the first time. They rebuilt his face, but he came from a very old family and they could never get the nose exactly right. He went to South America and worked in a bank. But this was a long time ago, and then we did not any of us know how it was going to be afterward. We only knew then that there was always the war, but that we were not going to it any more.

We all had the same medals, except the boy with the black silk bandage across his face, and he had not been at the front long enough to get any medals. The tall boy with a very pale face who was to be a lawyer had been a lieutenant of Arditi[5] and had three medals of the sort we each had only one of. He had lived a very long time with death and was a little detached. We were all a little detached, and there was

---

3. **the Scala** (SHAH lah) an opera house in Milan.
4. **"A basso gli ufficiali!"** (A BA´ soh LYE oo fee CHAH´ lee) "Down with officers!" (Italian).
5. **Arditi** (ahr DEE tee) a select group of soldiers chosen specifically for dangerous campaigns.

nothing that held us together except that we met every afternoon at the hospital. Although, as we walked to the Cova through the tough part of town, walking in the dark, with light and singing coming out of the wine-shops, and sometimes having to walk into the street when the men and women would crowd together on the sidewalk so that we would have had to jostle them to get by, we felt held together by there being something that had happened that they, the people who disliked us, did not understand.

We ourselves all understood the Cova, where it was rich and warm and not too brightly lighted, and noisy and smoky at certain hours, and there were always girls at the tables and the illustrated papers on a rack on the wall. The girls at the Cova were very patriotic, and I found that the most patriotic people in Italy were the café girls—and I believe they are still patriotic.

The boys at first were very polite about my medals and asked me what I had done to get them. I showed them the papers, which were written in very beautiful language and full of *fratellanza* and *abnegazione*,[6] but which really said, with the adjectives removed, that I had been given the medals because I was an American. After that their manner changed a little toward me, although I was their friend against outsiders. I was a friend, but I was never really one of them after they had read the citations, because it had been different with them and they had done very different things to get their medals. I had been wounded, it was true; but we all knew that being wounded, after all, was really an accident. I was never ashamed of the ribbons, though, and sometimes, after the cocktail hour, I would imagine myself having done all the things they had done to get their medals; but walking home at night through the empty streets with the cold wind and all the shops closed, trying to keep near the street lights, I knew that I would never have done such things, and I was very much afraid to die, and often lay in bed at night by myself, afraid to die and wondering how I would be when I went back to the front again.

The three with the medals were like hunting-hawks; and I was not a hawk, although I might seem a hawk to those who had never hunted; they, the three, knew better and so we drifted apart. But I stayed good friends with the boy who had been wounded his first day at the front, because he would never know now how he would have turned out; so he could never be accepted either, and I liked him because I thought perhaps he would not have turned out to be a hawk either.

---

6. *fratellanza* (frah tayl AHN tsah) and *abnegazione* (AHB nay gah tzyoh nay) "brotherhood" and "self-denial" (Italian).

TAKE NOTES

Reading Check

The narrator shows the other boys his citations, or the papers that go with his medals. After that their manner changes.

1. Why did the narrator get his medals?

_____

_____

_____

2. How does the manner of the other boys change?

_____

_____

_____

Literary Analysis

The narrator's use of the **first person point of view** lets you into his mind to see his real feelings. How does the narrator feel when he thinks about going back to the front?

_____

_____

_____

Reading Strategy

Try to **identify with the main character** when he stops feeling accepted by the other boys. Underline the sentence that tells why the narrator does stay friends with one of the boys.

The major, who had been the great fencer, did not believe in bravery, and spent much time while we sat in the machines correcting my grammar. He had complimented me on how I spoke Italian, and we talked together very easily. One day I had said that Italian seemed such an easy language to me that I could not take a great interest in it; everything was so easy to say. "Ah yes," the major said. "Why, then, do you not take up the use of grammar?" So we took up the use of grammar, and soon Italian was such a difficult language that I was afraid to talk to him until I had the grammar straight in my mind.

The major came very regularly to the hospital. I do not think he ever missed a day, although I am sure he did not believe in the machines. There was a time when none of us believed in the machines, and one day the major said it was all nonsense. The machines were new then and it was we who were to prove them. It was an idiotic idea, he said, "a theory, like another." I had not learned my grammar, and he said I was a stupid impossible disgrace, and he was a fool to have bothered with me. He was a small man and he sat straight up in his chair with his right hand thrust into the machine and looked straight ahead at the wall while the straps thumped up and down with his fingers in them.

"What will you do when the war is over if it is over?" he asked me. "Speak grammatically!"

"I will go to the States."

"Are you married?"

"No, but I hope to be."

"The more of a fool you are," he said. He seemed very angry. "A man must not marry."

"Why, Signor Maggiore?"[7]

"Don't call me 'Signor Maggiore.'"

"Why must not a man marry?"

"He cannot marry. He cannot marry," he said angrily. "If he is to lose everything, he should not place himself in a position to lose that. He should not place himself in a position to lose. He should find things he cannot lose."

He spoke very angrily and bitterly, and looked straight ahead while he talked.

"But why should he necessarily lose it?"

"He'll lose it," the major said. He was looking at the wall. Then he looked down at the machine and jerked his little hand out from between the straps and slapped it hard against his thigh. "He'll lose it," he almost shouted. "Don't argue with me!" Then he called to the attendant who ran the machines. "Come and turn this damned thing off."

---

7. **Signor Maggiore** (seen YOHR mah JYOH ray) "Mr. Major" (Italian); a respectful way of addressing an officer.

He went back into the other room for the light treatment and the massage. Then I heard him ask the doctor if he might use his telephone and he shut the door. When he came back into the room, I was sitting in another machine. He was wearing his cape and had his cap on, and he came directly toward my machine and put his arm on my shoulder.

"I am so sorry," he said, and patted me on the shoulder with his good hand. "I would not be rude. My wife has just died. You must forgive me."

"Oh—" I said, feeling sick for him. "I am so sorry."

He stood there biting his lower lip. "It is very difficult," he said. "I cannot resign myself."

He looked straight past me and out through the window. Then he began to cry. "I am utterly unable to resign myself," he said and choked. And then crying, his head up looking at nothing, carrying himself straight and soldierly, with tears on both his cheeks and biting his lips, he walked past the machines and out the door.

The doctor told me that the major's wife, who was very young and whom he had not married until he was definitely <u>invalided</u> out of the war, had died of pneumonia. She had been sick only a few days. No one expected her to die. The major did not come to the hospital for three days. Then he came at the usual hour, wearing a black band on the sleeve of his uniform. When he came back, there were large framed photographs around the wall of all sorts of wounds before and after they had been cured by the machines. In front of the machine the major used were three photographs of hands like his that were completely restored. I do not know where the doctor got them. I always understood we were the first to use the machines. The photographs did not make much difference to the major because he only looked out of the window.

Vocabulary Development: invalided (IN vuh lid id) *v.* released because of illness or disability

---

Reading Strategy

Identify with the character of the major on this page as well. Why does he apologize to the narrator? How does he explain his behavior?

_____

_____

_____

Literary Analysis

In the last paragraph, the narrator uses the **first-person point of view** to tell you something about the character of the doctor. What do you learn about the doctor from this paragraph?

_____

_____

Reader's Response: Were you able to **identify with the characters** as you read this selection? Which character did you find it easiest to identify with?

_____

_____

Thinking About the Skill: How did it help you to be aware of the **first-person point of view** as you read this selection?

The Corn Planting

Sherwood Anderson

Summary In "The Corn Planting," an old farmer and his wife have two things they love—their farm and their son. One night, a telegram arrives telling of their son's death in a car accident. They spend the rest of that night planting corn as their way of dealing with grief.

Note-taking Guide

Use this diagram to record the message of the story "The Corn Planting." Then write story details that support the message of the story.

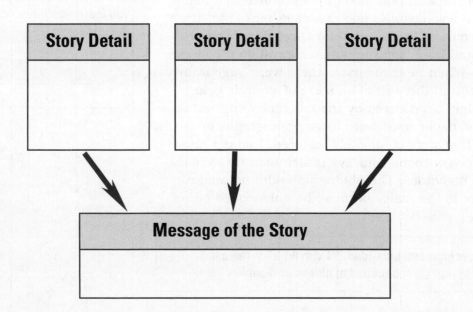

Story Detail	Story Detail	Story Detail

Message of the Story

A Worn Path

Eudora Welty

Summary In "A Worn Path," an old woman makes her way along a country path. Once in town, she goes to a doctor's office to get medicine for her grandson. She has been taking care of him since he swallowed lye some years before.

Note-taking Guide

Use this diagram to record information about Phoenix Jackson's journey in "A Worn Path."

Sequence of Events			
1.	**2.**	**3.**	**4.**
In December, Phoenix Jackson walks throgh the pine woods.			
5.	**6.**	**7.**	

How often do you walk long distances? Why would someone choose to walk a long distance instead of using some easier form of transportation?

_____

_____

Reading is more fun if you **identify with the characters**. That means that you look for ways to relate the character's experiences to your own. The main character of this story is an old woman. How can you identify with this character who is so different from you?

_____

_____

The narrator, or teller, of this story tells the story from the **limited third-person point of view.** That means that the narrator uses pronouns like *he, she,* and *they.* It also means that the narrator tells the thoughts of one character—in this case, Phoenix Jackson. Circle three examples of the use of third-person pronouns on this page.

What does Phoenix do when she hears noise in the thicket?

_____

_____

A Worn Path
Eudora Welty

Journeys in literature are often like the journey of life—they have ups and downs, easy times and hard times. Sometimes people are on their own and other times they get help from others. As you read this story, be alert for the reason that Phoenix Jackson takes her journey. Then ask yourself: Does her reason for the journey make the trip harder or easier?

It was December—a bright frozen day in the early morning. Far out in the country there was an old Negro woman with her head tied in a red rag, coming along a path through the pinewoods. Her name was Phoenix Jackson. She was very old and small and she walked slowly in the dark pine shadows, moving a little from side to side in her steps, with the balanced heaviness and lightness of a pendulum in a grandfather clock. She carried a thin, small cane made from an umbrella, and with this she kept tapping the frozen earth in front of her. This made a <u>grave</u> and persistent noise in the still air, that seemed meditative like the chirping of a solitary little bird.

She wore a dark striped dress reaching down to her shoe tops, and an equally long apron of bleached sugar sacks, with a full pocket all neat and tidy, but every time she took a step she might have fallen over her shoelaces, which dragged from her unlaced shoes. She looked straight ahead. Her eyes were blue with age. Her skin had a pattern all its own of numberless branching wrinkles and as though a whole little tree stood in the middle of her forehead, but a golden color ran underneath, and the two knobs of her cheeks were illumined by a yellow burning under the dark. Under the red rag her hair came down on her neck in the frailest of ringlets, still black, and with an odor like copper.

Now and then there was a quivering in the thicket. Old Phoenix said, "Out of my way, all you foxes, owls, beetles, jack rabbits, coons and wild animals! . . . Keep out from under these feet, little bobwhites[1]...Keep the big wildhogs out of my path. Don't let none of those come running my direction. I got a long way." Under her small black-freckled hand her cane, <u>limber</u> as a buggy whip, would switch at the brush as if to rouse up any hiding things.

Vocabulary Development: grave (GRAYV) *adj.* serious; solemn
limber (LIM buhr) *adj.* flexible

---

1. **bobwhites** *n.* partridges.

On she went. The woods were deep and still. The sun made the pine needles almost too bright to look at, up where the wind rocked. The cones dropped as light as feathers. Down in the hollow was the mourning dove—it was not too late for him.

The path ran up a hill. "Seem like there is chains about my feet, time I get this far," she said, in the voice of argument old people keep to use with themselves. "Something always take a hold of me on this hill—pleads I should stay."

After she got to the top she turned and gave a full, severe look behind her where she had come. "Up through pines," she said at length. "Now down through oaks."

Her eyes opened their widest, and she started down gently. But before she got to the bottom of the hill a bush caught her dress.

Her fingers were busy and intent, but her skirts were full and long, so that before she could pull them free in one place they were caught in another. It was not possible to allow the dress to tear. "I in the thorny bush," she said. "Thorns, you doing your appointed work. Never want to let folks pass, no sir. Old eyes thought you was a pretty little green bush."

Finally, trembling all over, she stood free, and after a moment dared to stoop for her cane.

"Sun so high!" she cried, leaning back and looking, while the thick tears went over her eyes. "The time getting all gone here."

At the foot of this hill was a place where a log was laid across the creek.

"Now comes the trial," said Phoenix.

Putting her right foot out, she mounted the log and shut her eyes. Lifting her skirt, leveling her cane fiercely before her, like a festival figure in some parade, she began to march across. Then she opened her eyes and she was safe on the other side.

"I wasn't as old as I thought," she said.

But she sat down to rest. She spread her skirts on the bank around her and folded her hands over her knees. Up above her was a tree in a pearly cloud of mistletoe. She did not dare to close her eyes, and when a little boy brought her a plate with a slice of marble cake on it she spoke to him. "That would be acceptable," she said. But when she went to take it there was just her own hand in the air.

So she left that tree, and had to go through a barbed-wire fence. There she had to creep and crawl, spreading her knees and stretching her fingers like a baby trying to climb the steps. But she talked loudly to herself: she could not let her dress be torn now, so late in the day, and she could not pay for having her arm or her leg sawed off if she got caught fast where she was.

TAKE NOTES

Literary Analysis

Circle one place on this page where the narrator's limited third-person point of view gives you information about what Phoenix is thinking.

Reading Strategy

Identify with the character of Phoenix as she catches her dress on thorns and crosses a creek on a log. Then reread the bracketed paragraph. Phoenix is so tired that she sees something that isn't there. What is it that she sees? How do you know it isn't really there?

_____

_____

_____

_____

Reading Check

Why is Phoenix so careful as she crawls through a barbed-wire fence?

_____

_____

Identify with the character of Phoenix as she sees a tall, black, skinny figure in front of her.

1. At first, what does she think the figure is?

_____

_____

2. What does the figure turn out to be?

_____

_____

Literary Analysis

Circle two places on this page where the **narrator's limited third-person point of view** gives you information about what Phoenix is thinking.

Reading Check

Why does Phoenix say "My senses is gone. I too old"?

_____

_____

_____

At last she was safe through the fence and risen up out in the clearing. Big dead trees, like black men with one arm, were standing in the purple stalks of the withered cotton field. There sat a buzzard.

"Who you watching?"

In the furrow she made her way along.

"Glad this not the season for bulls," she said, looking sideways, "and the good Lord made his snakes to curl up and sleep in the winter. A pleasure I don't see no two-headed snake coming around that tree, where it come once. It took a while to get by him, back in the summer."

She passed through the old cotton and went into a field of dead corn. It whispered and shook and was taller than her head. "Through the maze now," she said, for there was no path.

Then there was something tall, black, and skinny there, moving before her.

At first she took it for a man. It could have been a man dancing in the field. But she stood still and listened, and it did not make a sound. It was as silent as a ghost.

"Ghost," she said sharply, "who be you the ghost of? For I have heard of nary death close by."

But there was no answer—only the ragged dancing in the wind.

She shut her eyes, reached out her hand, and touched a sleeve. She found a coat and inside that an emptiness, cold as ice.

"You scarecrow," she said. Her face lighted. "I ought to be shut up for good," she said with laughter. "My senses is gone. I too old. I the oldest people I ever know. Dance, old scarecrow," she said, "while I dancing with you."

She kicked her foot over the furrow, and with mouth drawn down, shook her head once or twice in a little strutting way. Some husks blew down and whirled in streamers about her skirts.

Then she went on, parting her way from side to side with the cane, through the whispering field. At last she came to the end, to a wagon track where the silver grass blew between the red ruts. The quail were walking around like pullets, seeming all dainty and unseen.

"Walk pretty," she said. "This the easy place. This the easy going."

She followed the track, swaying through the quiet bare fields, through the little strings of trees silver in their dead leaves, past cabins silver from weather, with the doors and windows boarded shut, all like old women under a spell sitting there. "I walking in their sleep," she said, nodding her head vigorously.

In a ravine she went where a spring was silently flowing through a hollow log. Old Phoenix bent and drank. "Sweet gum² makes the water sweet," she said, and drank more. "Nobody know who made this well, for it was here when I was born."

The track crossed a swampy part where the moss hung as white as lace from every limb. "Sleep on, alligators, and blow your bubbles." Then the track went into the road.

Deep, deep the road went down between the high green-colored banks. Overhead the live-oaks met, and it was as dark as a cave.

A black dog with a lolling tongue came up out of the weeds by the ditch. She was meditating, and not ready, and when he came at her she only hit him a little with her cane. Over she went in the ditch, like a little puff of milkweed.³

Down there, her senses drifted away. A dream visited her, and she reached her hand up, but nothing reached down and gave her a pull. So she lay there and presently went to talking. "Old woman," she said to herself, "that black dog come up out of the weeds to stall you off, and now there he sitting on his fine tail, smiling at you."

A white man finally came along and found her—a hunter, a young man, with his dog on a chain.

"Well, Granny!" he laughed. "What are you doing there?"

"Lying on my back like a June bug waiting to be turned over, mister," she said, reaching up her hand.

He lifted her up, gave her a swing in the air, and set her down. "Anything broken, Granny?"

"No sir, them old dead weeds is springy enough," said Phoenix, when she had got her breath. "I thank you for your trouble."

"Where do you live, Granny?" he asked, while the two dogs were growling at each other.

"Away back yonder, sir, behind the ridge. You can't even see it from here."

"On your way home?"

"No sir, I going to town."

"Why, that's too far! That's as far as I walk when I come out myself, and I get something for my trouble." He patted the stuffed bag he carried, and there hung down a little closed claw. It was one of the bobwhites, with its beak hooked bitterly to show it was dead. "Now you go on home, Granny!"

"I bound to go to town, mister," said Phoenix. "The time come around."

He gave another laugh, filling the whole landscape. "I know you old colored people! Wouldn't miss going to town to see Santa Claus!"

---

2. **sweet gum** *n.* a tree that produces a fragrant juice.
3. **milkweed** *n.* a plant with pods that, when ripe, release feathery seeds.

Reading Check

What happens to Phoenix when the black dog comes up out of the weeds?

_____

_____

_____

_____

Reading Strategy

Try to **identify with the character** of Phoenix when she is lying in the ditch. How do you think she feels?

_____

_____

_____

_____

Literary Analysis

Using **limited third-person point of view,** the narrator describes the conversation that Phoenix has with the young hunter. Circle the sentence that tells how the hunter helps her.

Literary Analysis

The **limited third-person point of view** of the narrator shows how carefully Phoenix bends over to pick up the nickel. Why do you think she is so careful?

_____

_____

_____

Reading Check

When the hunter first points his gun at Phoenix, what do you think she is thinking?

_____

_____

_____

Reading Check

Circle the two smells that tell Phoenix that she has reached the town.

But something held old Phoenix very still. The deep lines in her face went into a fierce and different radiation. Without warning, she had seen with her own eyes a flashing nickel fall out of the man's pocket onto the ground.

"How old are you, Granny?" he was saying.

"There is no telling, mister," she said, "no telling."

Then she gave a little cry and clapped her hands and said, "Git on away from here, dog! Look! Look at that dog!" She laughed as if in admiration. "He ain't scared of nobody. He a big black dog." She whispered, "Sic him!"

"Watch me get rid of that cur," said the man. "Sic him, Pete! Sic him!"

Phoenix heard the dogs fighting, and heard the man running and throwing sticks. She even heard a gunshot. But she was slowly bending forward by that time, further and further forward, the lids stretched down over her eyes, as if she were doing this in her sleep. Her chin was lowered almost to her knees. The yellow palm of her hand came out from the fold of her apron. Her fingers slid down and along the ground under the piece of money with the grace and care they would have in lifting an egg from under a setting hen. Then she slowly straightened up, she stood erect, and the nickel was in her apron pocket. A bird flew by. Her lips moved. "God watching me the whole time. I come to stealing."

The man came back, and his own dog panted about them. "Well, I scared him off that time," he said, and then he laughed and lifted his gun and pointed it at Phoenix.

She stood straight and faced him.

"Doesn't the gun scare you?" he said, still pointing it.

"No, sir, I seen plenty go off closer by, in my day, and for less than what I done," she said, holding utterly still.

He smiled, and shouldered the gun. "Well, Granny," he said, "you must be a hundred years old, and scared of nothing. I'd give you a dime if I had any money with me. But you take my advice and stay home, and nothing will happen to you."

"I bound to go on my way, mister," said Phoenix. She inclined her head in the red rag. Then they went in different directions, but she could hear the gun shooting again and again over the hill.

She walked on. The shadows hung from the oak trees to the road like curtains. Then she smelled woodsmoke, and smelled the river, and she saw a steeple and the cabins on their steep steps. Dozens of little black children whirled around her. There ahead was Natchez[4] shining. Bells were ringing. She walked on.

4. **Natchez** (NACH iz) a town in southern Mississippi.

In the paved city it was Christmas time. There were red and green electric lights strung and criss-crossed everywhere, and all turned on in the daytime. Old Phoenix would have been lost if she had not distrusted her eyesight and depended on her feet to know where to take her.

She paused quietly on the sidewalk where people were passing by. A lady came along in the crowd, carrying an armful of red-, green- and silver-wrapped presents; she gave off perfume like the red roses in hot summer, and Phoenix stopped her.

"Please, missy, will you lace up my shoe?" She held up her foot.

"What do you want, Grandma?"

"See my shoe," said Phoenix. "Do all right for out in the country, but wouldn't look right to go in a big building."

"Stand still then, Grandma," said the lady. She put her packages down on the sidewalk beside her and laced and tied both shoes tightly.

"Can't lace em with a cane," said Phoenix. "Thank you, missy. I doesn't mind asking a nice lady to tie up my shoe, when I gets out on the street."

Moving slowly and from side to side, she went into the big building, and into a tower of steps, where she walked up and around and around until her feet knew to stop.

She entered a door, and there she saw nailed up on the wall the document that had been stamped with the gold seal and framed in the gold frame, which matched the dream that was hung up in her head.

"Here I be," she said. There was a fixed and ceremonial stiffness over her body.

"A charity case, I suppose," said an attendant who sat at the desk before her.

But Phoenix only looked above her head. There was sweat on her face, the wrinkles in her skin shone like a bright net.

"Speak up, Grandma," the woman said. "What's your name? We must have your history, you know. Have you been here before? What seems to be the trouble with you?"

Old Phoenix only gave a twitch to her face as if a fly were bothering her.

"Are you deaf?" cried the attendant.

But then the nurse came in.

"Oh, that's just old Aunt Phoenix," she said. "She doesn't come for herself—she has a little grandson. She makes these trips just as regular as clockwork. She lives away back off the Old Natchez Trace." She bent down. "Well, Aunt Phoenix, why don't you just take a seat? We won't keep you standing after your long trip." She pointed.

The old woman sat down, bolt upright in the chair.

"Now, how is the boy?" asked the nurse.

Old Phoenix did not speak.

© Pearson Education, Inc., publishing as Pearson Prentice Hall.

TAKE NOTES

Literary Analysis

Circle the reason that Phoenix asks a woman to lace up her shoe.

Literary Analysis

Reread the bracketed paragraph. How does this paragraph make it clear that the narrator is using **limited third-person point of view** to give the thoughts of Phoenix?

_____

_____

_____

Reading Check

What new information do you get about Phoenix from what the nurse says?

_____

_____

_____

Phoenix has a moment when her memory fails her.

1. What does she forget?

_____

_____

2. Why do you think she forgets?

_____

_____

The **narrator** gives a lot of information in this part of the story through **dialogue**, or conversation between the characters. What do you learn about Phoenix's grandson from her dialogue with the nurse?

_____

_____

_____

Identify with the character of the nurse, especially in the bracketed paragraph. Why is the nurse trying to hush Phoenix?

_____

_____

_____

"I said, how is the boy?"

But Phoenix only waited and stared straight ahead, her face very solemn and withdrawn into rigidity.

"Is his throat any better?" asked the nurse. "Aunt Phoenix, don't you hear me? Is your grandson's throat any better since the last time you came for the medicine?"

With her hands on her knees, the old woman waited, silent, erect and motionless, just as if she were in armor.

"You mustn't take up our time this way, Aunt Phoenix," the nurse said. "Tell us quickly about your grandson, and get it over. He isn't dead, is he?"

At last there came a flicker and then a flame of comprehension across her face, and she spoke.

"My grandson. It was my memory had left me. There I sat and forgot why I made my long trip."

"Forgot?" The nurse frowned. "After you came so far?"

Then Phoenix was like an old woman begging a dignified forgiveness for waking up frightened in the night. "I never did go to school. I was too old at the Surrender,[5] she said in a soft voice. "I'm an old woman without an education. It was my memory fail me. My little grandson, he is just the same, and I forgot it in the coming."

"Throat never heals, does it?" said the nurse, speaking in a loud, sure voice to old Phoenix. By now she had a card with something written on it, a little list. "Yes. Swallowed lye. When was it?—January—two-three years ago—"

Phoenix spoke unasked now. "No, missy, he not dead, he just the same. Every little while his throat begin to close up again, and he not able to swallow. He not get his breath. He not able to help himself. So the time come around, and I go on another trip for the soothing medicine."

"All right. The doctor said as long as you came to get it, you could have it," said the nurse. "But it's an <u>obstinate</u> case."

"My little grandson, he sit up there in the house all wrapped up, waiting by himself," Phoenix went on. "We is the only two left in the world. He suffer and it don't seem to put him back at all. He got a sweet look. He going to last. He wear a little patch quilt and peep out holding his mouth open like a little bird. I remembers so plain now. I not going to forget him again, no, the whole enduring time. I could tell him from all the others in creation."

"All right." The nurse was trying to hush her now. She brought her a bottle of medicine. "Charity," she said, making a check mark in a book.

Vocabulary Development: obstinate (AHB stuh nit) *adj.* stubborn

---

5. **the Surrender** the surrender of the Confederate army, which ended the Civil War.

Old Phoenix held the bottle close to her eyes, and then carefully put it into her pocket.

"I thank you," she said.

"It's Christmas time, Grandma," said the attendant. "Could I give you a few pennies out of my purse?"

"Five pennies is a nickel," said Phoenix stiffly.

"Here's a nickel," said the attendant.

Phoenix rose carefully and held out her hand. She received the nickel and then fished the other nickel out of her pocket and laid it beside the new one. She stared at her palm closely, with her head on one side.

Then she gave a tap with her cane on the floor.

"This is what come to me to do," she said. "I going to the store and buy my child a little windmill they sells, made out of paper. He going to find it hard to believe there such a thing in the world. I'll march myself back where he is waiting, holding it straight up in this hand."

She lifted her free hand, gave a little nod, turned around, and walked out of the doctor's office. Then her slow step began on the stairs, going down.

TAKE NOTES

Reading Check

What is Phoenix planning to do with her two nickels? What does her plan tell you about Phoenix?

_____

_____

_____

Reader's Response: Were you able **to identify with** Phoenix as you read this selection? Which of her characteristics did you find it easiest to identify with?

_____

_____

Thinking About the Skill: How did it help you to be aware of the **limited third-person point of view** as you read this selection?

_____

_____

In Another Country • The Corn Planting • A Worn Path

1. **Draw Conclusions:** Choose one of the three stories to explain the message about life that it reveals.

   _____

   _____

2. **Literary Analysis:** Identify three details that show Hemingway's story was written using a **first-person point of view.**

   _____

   _____

3. **Literary Analysis:** How would "A Worn Path" be different if Welty had told the story from Phoenix Jackson's first-person point of view?

   _____

   _____

4. **Reading Strategy:** From the three stories, choose the characters with whom you **identify** most and least. Provide reasons for your choices.

   _____

5. **Reading Strategy:** Using this diagram, list the personality traits, interests, or values that you share with a character in one of the stories. List these in the center. In the two separate circles, list differences.

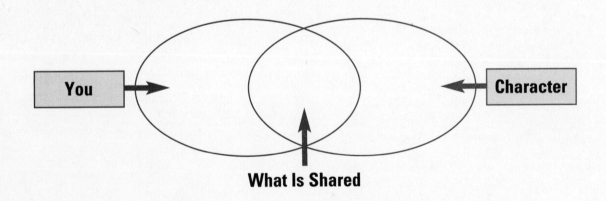

Chicago • Grass

LITERARY ANALYSIS

Apostrophe is a literary device in which a speaker directly addresses a thing, an abstract concept, or a person who is dead or absent. For example, in "Chicago," Carl Sandburg addresses the city as if it were a person:

> They tell me you are wicked and I believe them . . .
> And they tell me you are crooked and I answer: Yes . . .

As you read "Chicago," think about the effect of this technique, and identify the reasons Sandburg chose to speak directly to the city.

Both "Chicago" and "Grass" use **personification,** figurative language in which a non-human subject is given human qualities. Use the chart below to record the ways in which Sandburg uses personification in these two poems.

	Detail Expressing Human Trait
Chicago	
Grass	

READING STRATEGY

When you **respond** to a poem, you think about the message that the poet has conveyed. Then, you reflect on how you feel personally about the topic. You take the time to consider how the poet's message relates to your own life and to the world in which you live. You also think about how you can use or apply what you have learned from the poem. As you read these poems, connect your own experiences to the images and ideas Sandburg presents.

Chicago • Grass

Carl Sandburg

Summaries In "**Chicago**," Sandburg uses simple words to express his love and admiration for the city of Chicago. He challenges the reader to find a city with more life. In "**Grass**," the grass explains that there is only grass where once important battles between great armies took place. The calmness of nature hides the horror and senselessness of war.

Note-taking Guide:

Use the following chart to help you keep track of what each speaker talks about.

Chicago	
To whom is the speaker talking?	
What does the speaker talk about?	
What descriptions does the speaker use?	
Grass	
Who is the speaker	
What does the speaker talk about?	
What does the speaker claim to do?	

Chicago • Grass

1. **Interpret:** In the first stanza of "Chicago," the speaker calls the city by several names. What do these names tell you about the city's economy and atmosphere?

   _____

   _____

2. **Draw Conclusions:** In "Grass," what is Sandburg suggesting about the death and destruction of war?

   _____

   _____

3. **Literary Analysis:** Use this chart to contrast how Sandburg uses **apostrophe** to address the city of Chicago and another audience. Record the lines in which he addresses the city and the lines in which he addresses others. Note the imagery he uses when he addresses each audience.

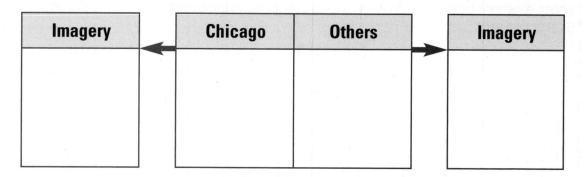

Imagery	Chicago	Others	Imagery

4. **Literary Analysis:** In "Grass," what words are examples of **personification?**

   _____

5. **Reading Strategy:** What is your **response** to the grass's message?

   _____

   _____

   _____

The Jilting of Granny Weatherall

LITERARY ANALYSIS

People's thoughts do not flow in neat patterns; they proceed in streams of insight, memory, and reflection. During the early 1900s, some writers began using a literary device called **stream of consciousness,** in which they tried to capture the natural flow of thoughts. These types of stories usually do the following:

- present sequences of thought as if they were coming straight from a character's mind
- leave out transitional words and phrases found in ordinary writing
- connect details only through a character's associations

Stream of consciousness stories often involve the use of **flashbacks.** These are interruptions in which an earlier event is described. A flashback may be a dream, a daydream, a memory, a story told by a character, or a switch by the narrator to a time in the past.

As you read, notice how Granny Weatherall's thoughts wander from topic to topic. Also, pay attention to the details that trigger Granny's flashbacks and decide how each flashback relates to events in the present. Use this chart to show how the events in Granny's past are connected to the events in the present.

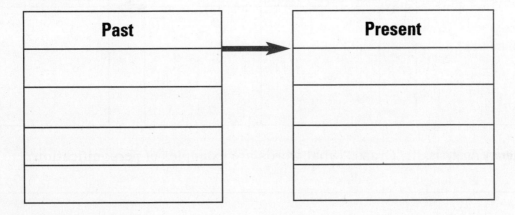

READING STRATEGY

This story evokes an array of different moments spanning eighty years as Granny Weatherall drifts in and out of reality. To stay oriented in this complex narrative, **clarify the sequence of events.** Watch for jumps in Granny's thinking, often signaled by a shift from present-moment dialogue to Granny's inner thoughts.

The Jilting of Granny Weatherall

Katherine Anne Porter

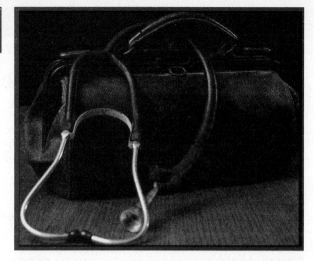

Summary Ellen Weatherall is on her deathbed. Her thoughts drift between moments in the present and memories of the past. She receives visits from her daughter, her doctor, and her priest. She recalls the people and events that filled her life. Her thoughts wander freely among the good and the bad memories.

Note-taking Guide:

Use this chart to put the events of Granny's life in order.

Event 1	Event 2	Event 3	Event 4	Event 5	Event 6
George leaves Ellen standing at the alter on their wedding day.					

The Jilting of Granny Weatherall

1. **Connect:** George left Granny standing at the altar sixty years ago. What is the connection between that experience and the final paragraph of the story?

_____

_____

2. **Literary Analysis: Stream-of-consciousness** writing tries to copy the natural flow of people's thoughts. Find three places in the story where Granny's thoughts drift from one topic to another topic that does not seem related. Explain your choices.

_____

_____

3. **Literary Analysis:** Fill in the chart with information about three **flashbacks** in the story.

Form	Trigger	What we learn

4. **Reading Strategy:** Clarify the sequence of events in this story by writing them down in the order in which they happened.

_____

_____

_____

A Rose for Emily •
Nobel Prize Acceptance Speech

LITERARY ANALYSIS

A **conflict** is a struggle between opposing forces. It is the element that drives most narrative and dramatic works. **Internal conflict** occurs within a character who is torn by competing values or needs. **External conflict** occurs between a character and an outside force, such as another person, society, nature, or fate. A conflict achieves **resolution** when the struggle ends and the outcome is revealed. Look beneath the surface of "A Rose for Emily" to find the hints of deeper struggles.

READING STRATEGY

Ambiguity occurs in a literary work when some element of the work can be interpreted in several different ways. To **clarify ambiguity** in fiction, recognize parts of the action, characterization, or description that the writer may have left purposely unclear. Then, look for details or clues in the writing that help you make a logical interpretation. In "A Rose for Emily," Faulkner uses these techniques to build questions for his readers:

- subtle hints or open-ended comments by the narrator

- limited information about the true order, or sequence, of events

- vague details about Emily's actions

As you read use this chart to note details that help you clarify ambiguities.

Ambiguous Event	Details
bad smell from the house	men sniff around cellar, spread lime in cellar, Emily watches, smell goes away
Emily buys poison	
Baptist minister visits Emily	

A Rose for Emily

William Faulkner

Summary Emily Grierson is a woman in a small Southern town. She lives under the watchful eyes of the community. Because she is secretive and private, the towns-people believe that she may be crazy. When Emily shows interest in a man from another town, people wonder whether she will marry him. When the man disappears from town, Emily begins keeping to herself again. After her death, people find something shocking in her bedroom.

Note-taking Guide

Faulkner tells this story in five sections. These sections do not occur in time order. To make sense of the story, analyze what happens in each section. Use the following chart to record your observations:

Section I What happens: Officials confront Emily about taxes.
Section II What happens: _____ _____
Section III What happens: _____ _____
Section IV What happens: _____ _____
Section V What happens: _____ _____

Nobel Prize Acceptance Speech

William Faulkner

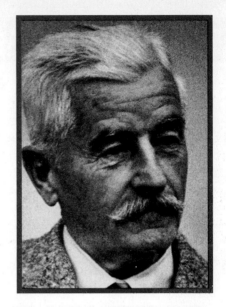

Summary William Faulkner received the Nobel Prize for literature in 1950. In his acceptance speech, Faulkner presents his opinions about world affairs. He also talks about the role of literature in helping people make sense of the world. Faulkner tells young writers to set aside their fear of world destruction and address the basic problems of love, honor, and caring for others. He explains that it is the writer's duty to help people carry on. Writers can do this by reminding people of the glory of their past.

Note-taking Guide

In the chart, record the main idea of each paragraph of Faulkner's speech.

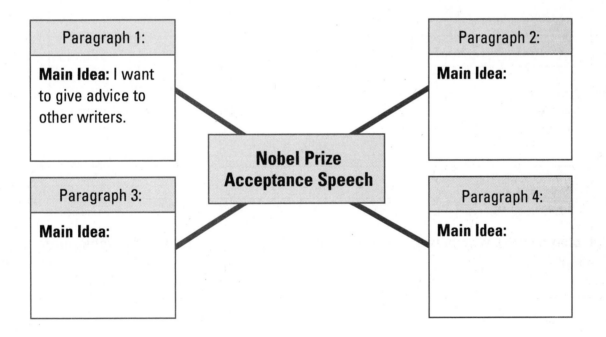

Paragraph 1:

Main Idea: I want to give advice to other writers.

Paragraph 2:

Main Idea:

Nobel Prize Acceptance Speech

Paragraph 3:

Main Idea:

Paragraph 4:

Main Idea:

A Rose for Emily • Nobel Prize Acceptance Speech

1. **Make a Judgment:** How well does "A Rose for Emily" demonstrate the qualities of literature that Faulkner describes in his Nobel Prize acceptance speech?

_____

_____

2. **Literary Analysis:** Use the following chart to analyze the **external** and **internal** conflicts that involve Emily. Then tell whether each has been resolved.

Conflict	Who vs. Who/What?	Resolution
nonpayment of taxes	Emily vs. town	

3. **Literary Analysis:** What do Emily's external conflicts with the people of Jefferson, Mississippi reveal about her?

_____

_____

4. **Reading Strategy:** Which event in "A Rose for Emily" did you find most **ambiguous**? Why?

_____

_____

5. **Reading Strategy:** How does the ambiguity add to the literary quality of "A Rose for Emily"?

_____

_____

Robert Frost's Poetry

LITERARY ANALYSIS

Many of Frost's poems do not contain rhyme, but their lines have a regular pattern of stressed and unstressed syllables, called *meter*.

- The basic unit of meter is a *foot*—usually one stressed syllable (´) and one or more unstressed syllables (˘).
- The most common foot is the *iamb*—one unstressed syllable followed by a stressed syllable (˘ ´).
- A line containing five iambs is written in *iambic pentameter*.
- Verse consisting of unrhymed lines of iambic pentameter is called **blank verse**.

As you read Frost's poems, use this chart to identify those that are written in blank verse.

READING STRATEGY

One way to appreciate blank verse is to **read it aloud in sentences** rather than silently. Avoid pausing at the end of each line. Instead, follow the punctuation as if you were reading prose. Pause briefly after commas and pause longer after periods. Notice how the flow of blank verse echoes the natural rhythms of speech.

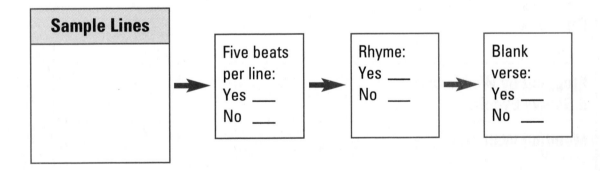

| Sample Lines | Five beats per line: Yes ___ No ___ | Rhyme: Yes ___ No ___ | Blank verse: Yes ___ No ___ |

Robert Frost's Poetry

Summaries: In "**Birches**," the speaker recalls the pleasure of swinging from birch trees as a child. "**Stopping by Woods on a Snowy Evening**" describes a man tempted to linger in the peaceful woods. In "**Mending Wall**," the speaker and his neighbor meet to repair breaks in the wall that separates their fields. The speaker wonders about the purpose of the wall and the forces of nature that continually pull it down. "**Out, Out—**" tells the harsh story of a young farm boy who loses control of his power saw while cutting wood. "**The Gift Outright**" examines the colonial spirit that struggled to tame a new land and form a nation. In "**Acquainted With the Night**," the speaker admits to moments of loneliness in his life.

Note-taking Guide:

Use this chart to record the main idea and an important detail from each of Frost's poems.

Poem	Main Idea	Important Detail
Birches		
Stopping by Woods on a Snowy Evening		
Mending Wall		
"Out, Out—"		
The Gift Outright		
Acquainted With the Night		

APPLY THE SKILLS

Robert Frost's Poetry

1. **Interpret:** The neighbor in "Mending Wall" repeats the statement, "Good fences make good neighbors." What does this saying mean?

_____

_____

2. **Generalize:** What picture of American history does Frost create in "The Gift Outright"?

_____

_____

3. **Literary Analysis:** Which two poems presented here are not written in **blank verse**? Explain your answer.

_____

_____

4. **Literary Analysis:** In "Birches," the speaker expresses conflicting feelings about life. Yet he adds "Earth's the right place for love." Use this chart to analyze his feelings.

Negative Ideas and Images		Positive Ideas and Images
	→ Life ←	

5. **Reading Strategy:** Rewrite the blank verse of "The Gift Outright" as five sentences. Then **read them aloud**.

_____

_____

_____

The Night the Ghost Got In • *from* Here Is New York

LITERARY ANALYSIS

"The Night the Ghost Got In" and "Here Is New York" are both **informal essays**. Informal essays are brief nonfiction pieces that have a relaxed, conversational style and structure. Informal essays usually address a narrow subject, are not well organized, and include digressions from the main point. Consider this example from "The Night the Ghost Got In":

> Glass tinkled into the bedroom occupied by a retired engraver named Bodwell and his wife. Bodwell had been for some years in rather a bad way and was subject to mild "attacks."

Informal essays give you a glimpse into a writer's personality. As you read each selection, consider what it suggests about its author. Use this chart to record your findings.

Informal Essays	Thurber	White
Writer's Style		
Writer's Purpose		
Writer's Personality		

Although the topics in these essays are completely different, both of the selections are meant to make the reader laugh. Thurber's **humor** focuses on an exaggerated account of a childhood experience. White's humor makes fun of New York City. Humorists often exaggerate details and facts to create a comic effect.

READING STRATEGY

These informal essays draw humor from **hyperbole**, or exaggerations and outrageous overstatements. Examples include bizarre events in Thurber's essay and the litany of probable disasters in White's essay. To **recognize hyperbole**, look for details that seem too absurd to be true.

The Night the Ghost Got In

James Thurber

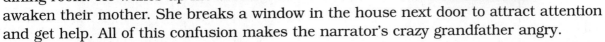

Summary One night, the narrator hears footsteps in the dining room. He wakes up his brother. The brothers then awaken their mother. She breaks a window in the house next door to attract attention and get help. All of this confusion makes the narrator's crazy grandfather angry.

Note-taking Guide:

As you read "the Night the Ghost Got In," use a chart like this one to identify the topic, or the main idea, of each paragraph. An example is provided below.

Paragraph	Topic/main Idea of the Paragraph
1	A ghost got into the house on November 17, 1915, and caused a great deal of confusion.
2	
3	
4	
5	
6	
7	
8	
9	
10	
11	
12	
13	
14	

from Here Is New York

E. B. White

Summary: New York City has a little bit of everything. This excerpt from "Here is New York" tells why New York is such a special city. Outsiders are often uncomfortable in the city because it seems so big. People who live there know that the city has thousands of tiny neighborhoods, where everybody knows everybody else.

Note-taking Guide:

White's essay shows that different people view the world in different ways. People who live in New York may appreciate different traits of the city than tourists and visitors. As you read, record the positive and negative traits as White presents them.

Positive Traits	Negative Traits

The Night the Ghost Got In • *from* Here Is New York

1. **Distinguish:** In what way does Thurber's portrayal of himself in "The Night the Ghost Got In" differ from his portrayal of the other characters?

   _____

   _____

2. **Compare and Contrast:** White describes New York's neighborhoods as small towns. In what way does he say the neighborhoods compare to small towns?

   _____

   _____

3. **Literary Analysis:** Cite language from "The Night the Ghost Got In" that shows the conversational style of an **informal essay**. Explain your choice.

   _____

   _____

4. **Literary Analysis:** White uses **humor** to show the city's many unique qualities. Use this chart to cite three humorous passages from the essay. Explain what each passage reveals about the city.

Humorous Passage	What It Reveals

5. **Literary Analysis:** Cite an example of **hyperbole** from each essay.

   _____

   _____

from Dust Tracks on the Road

LITERARY ANALYSIS

Autobiography is a nonfiction account of a writer's life told in his or her own words. Autobiographical writing tells the writer's feelings about key events and experiences. In addition to personal insights, autobiographies also reveal **social context**—the attitudes and customs of the culture in which the writer lived. The excerpt from Hurston's autobiography recalls an event from her childhood and provides a glimpse of life in her African American community in the South in the early 1900s.

Hurston helps her memories come to life through the use of **dialogue**, or the words people speak. The words people speak reflect their culture and reveal their personalities. As you read, notice how the dialogue adds to your understanding and enjoyment of Hurston's story.

READING STRATEGY

Hurston's **purpose**—to share her personal experience and show the vitality of the African American community—determines her choice of words, details, characters, and events. By linking her choices to her goals, you can analyze her success in achieving her purpose. As you read, use this chart to write down details, characters, and events that relate to Hurston's purpose.

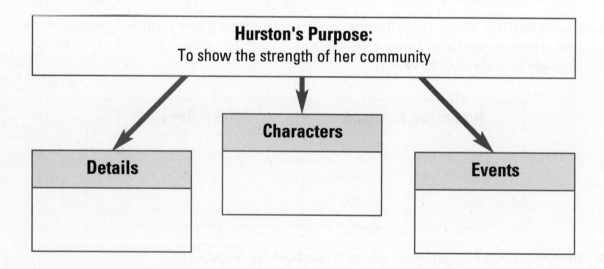

Hurston's Purpose:
To show the strength of her community

Characters

Details

Events

from Dust Tracks on a Road

Zora Neale Hurston

Summary This is a section from a longer work. The author describes events from her childhood in a small Florida town. She used to wait at the side of the road for white travelers to pass by. She would ask to go with them for a short distance. Hurston also talks about an experience that changed her life. Her school had visitors one day. These were two white women. Hurston read aloud and the women were impressed. They invited Hurston to visit them at their hotel. They gave her gifts. The gifts of books pleased Hurston more than the candy or pennies.

Note-taking Guide As you read this selection, write down details about the characters in the chart below.

Character	What the Character Wants	What the Character Does
Zora		
Grandmother		
Mrs. Calhoun		
Mrs. Johnstone and Miss Hurd		

from Dust Tracks on a Road

1   **Support:** Two white women visit Zora's school and ask to meet with her the next day. How can you tell that these two women make a strong impression on Zora? List three details from the text.

_____

_____

2.   **Literary Analysis:** What do you learn about the **social context** of Hurston's story from each of these details: (a) the schoolroom being cleaned for visitors, (b) Zora going to school barefoot?

_____

_____

3.   **Literary Analysis:** Hurston's **autobiography** contains many details that give you clues about the culture of her childhood. Use this chart to write down three details about the social context in this excerpt. Explain the attitude each detail reveals.

Detail of Social Context	Attitude It Reveals

4.   **Literary Analysis:** What do you learn about Hurston's personality from the **dialogue** she includes in the beginning of the selection?

_____

_____

5.   **Reading Strategy:** For what **purpose** do you think Hurston told this story about meeting the women from Minnesota?

_____

The Negro Speaks of Rivers • I, Too • Dream Variations • Refugee in America • The Tropics in New York

LITERARY ANALYSIS

The **speaker** is the voice of a poem. Often, the speaker is the poet. However, a speaker may also be an imaginary person, a group of people, an animal, or an inanimate object. In "The Tropics in New York," Claude McKay's speaker is a homesick adult who is probably the poet himself:

> A wave of longing through my body swept,
>
> And, hungry for the old, familiar ways
>
> I turned aside and bowed my head and wept.

As you read each poem, look for clues that reveal the identity of the speaker. Use this chart to record your observations.

	Clues in Poem	Identity of Speaker
The Negro Speaks of Rivers		
I, Too		
Dream Variations		
Refugee in America		
The Tropics in New York		

READING STRATEGY

Most often, writers do not reveal a poem's speaker directly. Instead, the reader must **draw inferences**, or reach conclusions, based on the speaker's choice of words and the details in the poem. Once you determine the speaker's identity, you can draw inferences about the speaker's attitudes, feelings, and experiences.

As you read these poems, look for clues about the speakers. Draw inferences about their personal qualities and their attitudes toward life.

The Negro Speaks of Rivers • I, • Too Dream Variations • Refugee in America

Langston Hughes

The Tropics in New York

Claude McKay

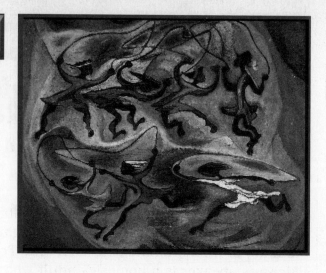

Summaries In "**The Negro Speaks of Rivers**," the speaker recalls the experience of his people along ancient rivers of the world. "**I, Too**" is Langston Hughes's response to a poem by Walt Whitman. Whitman's poem describes the variety that exists in America. The speaker in "**Dream Variations**" imagines a world in which he can play and rest freely and in which the blackness of his skin is accepted. "**Refugee in America**" challenges the reader to think more carefully about words such as *freedom* and *liberty*. In "**The Tropics in New York**," a window fruit display in New York takes the speaker back home to the tropics.

Note-taking Guide

Speakers in poems do not always directly say what they mean. As you read each poem, think about each speaker's message. Complete the chart below. Choose an example of what each speaker says and then explain what he means.

	What Does the Speaker Say?	**What Does the Speaker Mean?**
The Negro Speaks of Rivers		
I, Too		
Dream Variations		
Refugee in America		
The Tropics in New York		

The Negro Speaks of Rivers • I, Too • Dream Variations • Refugee in America • The Tropics in New York

1. **Interpret:** Based on lines 3 and 10 of "I, Too," what is it's theme, or main message?

   _____

   _____

2. **Literary Analysis:** Who is the **speaker** in "The Negro Speaks of Rivers"?

   _____

3. **Literary Analysis:** What common goal do the speakers in "Dream Variations" and "Refugee in America" share?

   _____

   _____

4. **Reading Strategy:** To **draw inferences** about the speaker, look closely at the speaker's choice of words and at details in the work. In three of these poems, find one line that reveals something about the speaker. Use this chart to record your inferences

Poem	Line	What It Reveals About the Speaker

From the Dark Tower • A Black Man Talks of Reaping • Storm Ending

LITERARY ANALYSIS

A **metaphor** is a comparison between two seemingly dissimilar things that does not use a connecting word such as *like* or as. A metaphor may be directly stated or implied. In these lines, Countee Cullen compares African American life to the toil of planting.

> We shall not always plant while others reap
> The golden increment of bursting fruit . . .

Although metaphors are usually brief, they may also be elaborate, lengthy comparisons. An **extended metaphor** is a comparison that is developed throughout several lines or an entire poem. As you read "Storm Ending," look for the extended metaphor Toomer develops.

Metaphors are often conveyed through the use of imagery—descriptive language that appeals to the senses. Use this chart to analyze each poem's imagery as you read

Poems	Metaphor	Image	Emotion/Ideas
From the Dark Tower	African Americans compared to farm workers	Silently working hard in fields of gold; weeping	Sorrow; anger
A Black Man Talks of Reaping			
Storm Ending			

READING STRATEGY

Many works of literature bear a direct relation to the time and place in which they were written. A reader must **connect** such works to their **historical contexts** in order to understand and appreciate them fully. To fully grasp the following poems—born in the cultural movement known as the Harlem Renaissance in the 1920s—review the information on pages 910–911 of your textbook.

From the Dark Tower • A Black Man Talks of Reaping • Storm Ending

Summaries In "**From the Dark Tower**," the speaker seems to say that better times are coming for those who plant "while others reap." He says the night is no less lovely because it is dark. He closes by referring to waiting in the dark, tending "our agonizing seeds." In "**A Black Man Talks of Reaping**," the speaker describes his careful planting of a large crop from which he reaped only a small harvest. While his brother's sons gather the crops, his own children eat bitter fruit gathered from fields they have not sown. In "**Storm Ending**," thunder and the storm are compared with huge, hollow flowers blossoming overhead. As the flowers bleed rain and drip like honey, the sweet earth flies from the storm.

Note-taking Guide

Use this diagram to record details from the three poems and the shared message the details suggest.

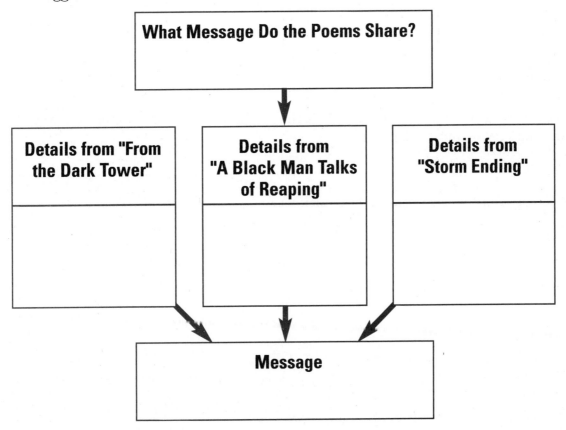

What Message Do the Poems Share?

Details from "From the Dark Tower"	Details from "A Black Man Talks of Reaping"	Details from "Storm Ending"

Message

From the Dark Tower • A Black Man Talks of Reaping
Storm Ending

1. **Infer:** In "A Black Man Talks of Reaping," who reaps what the speaker has sown?

   _____

2. **Literary Analysis:** Identify the metaphors that Countee Cullen uses in "From the Dark Tower."

   _____

   _____

3. **Literary Analysis:** Using this chart, identify and analyze the dominant image conveyed in two of the poems.

Poem	Image	Interpretation	Emotion

4. **Reading Strategy:** Identify a **historical** fact that enriches your reading of "A Black Man Talks of Reaping." Explain.

   _____

   _____

ABOUT PUBLIC RELATIONS DOCUMENTS

A **public relations document** shows the public face of a company or organization. Some familiar public relations documents are advertisements and press releases. Equally important are mission statements. These statements tell the mission, or purpose, of a business or organization by presenting three kinds of information:

1. "Who We Are"—a description of the purpose of the organization or business
2. "What We Do"—details that describe services or products
3. "Why We Do It"—a summary of an organization's goals and way of thinking

Read the mission statement and calendar of events from the Museum of Afro-American History. As you read, think about how the museum's mission is carried out through the events it holds.

READING STRATEGY

Inferences are assumptions or information that is not directly stated in a text. Good readers use their previous knowledge to fill in these gaps. As you read, make inferences and constantly test them by reading further. If reading further makes you doubt your inferences, change them or form new ones.

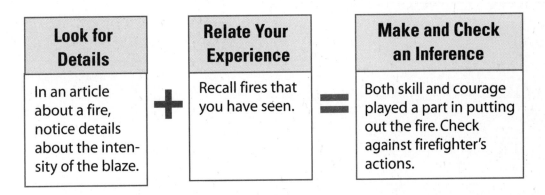

Look for Details		Relate Your Experience		Make and Check an Inference
In an article about a fire, notice details about the intensity of the blaze.	**+**	Recall fires that you have seen.	**=**	Both skill and courage played a part in putting out the fire. Check against firefighter's actions.

Build Understanding

Knowing this term will help you understand the information on this Web site.

artifacts (ART uh FAKTS) *n.* man-made objects that survive from earlier times.

TAKE NOTES

Read Public Relations Documents

A **mission statement** defines the limits of an organization. Based on the first paragraph, would the museum display the pen President Lincoln used to sign the Emancipation Proclamation (p. 223)? Why or why not?

_____

_____

Read Fluently

Read aloud the philosophy and goals of the museum contained in the bulleted list. In what way does the museum provide "A Foundation for the Future"?

_____

_____

_____

_____

Museum of Afro-American History
Boston and Nantucket

Mission Statement
A Foundation for the Future

The mission of the Museum of Afro-American History is to preserve, conserve and interpret the contributions of people of African descent and those who have found common cause with them in the struggle for liberty, dignity, and justice for all Americans. Therefore, we:

- collect and exhibit artifacts of distinction in this field and acquire and maintain physical structures and sites through the end of the 19th century;
- educate the public about the importance of the Afro-American historical legacy in general, its Boston and New England heritages, in particular;
- celebrate the enduring vitality[1] of African American culture;
- and advance on our own and in collaboration with others an appreciation of the past for the benefit of the custodians of the future.

---

1. vitality (vy TAL uh tee) *n.* power and endurance.

Museum of Afro-American History Boston

Calendar of Events

Events take place at 8 Smith Court, Beacon Hill, unless otherwise noted.

SATURDAY, FEB. 3, 7:30 P.M.

READING AND BOOK SIGNING

On Her Own Ground: The Life and Times of Madam C.J. Walker[2]

A'Lelia Bundles, former deputy bureau chief of ABC News in Washington and great-great granddaughter of Madam C.J. Walker, will discuss the writing of *On Her Own Ground*, the first historically accurate account of this legendary entrepreneur and social activist.

Sponsored by the Collection of African American Literature, a partnership between the Museum of Afro-American History, Suffolk University, and Boston African American Historic Site.

Refreshments and book sales following. FREE

TUESDAYS, 10:30–11:30 A.M.

Stories from African American Literature and Lore

Vibrant stories and activities presenting history for preschool aged children and parents. FREE

TAKE NOTES

Reading Strategy

Read the description of the first event. Do you think Ms. Bundles's portrayal of C.J. Walker would be positive?

_____

What clues from the text and from previous experience allow you to make that **inference**?

_____
_____
_____
_____

How could you check your inference?

_____
_____

2. Madame C.J. Walker (1867–1919) an African American woman who started her own beauty products company geared to the needs of African Americans. Praised as "the first black woman millionaire," Walker donated freely to charities and social causes.

TAKE NOTES

Jazz is a style of music that began in southern cities like New Orleans, then spread northward in the 1920s. Jazz rhythms have roots in West African music, and many famous jazz musicians have been African American. Early New Orleans jazz groups played at a variety of places, from house parties to funeral processions.

Reading Informational Materials

A **calendar of events** provides the public with basic information about upcoming events. Circle the dates, times, and admission fees for the Underground Railroad and jazz concert events.

FRIDAY, FEB. 16, 6 P.M.–9 A.M.

Museum Overnight: Underground Railroad[3]

Spend the night at the Museum exploring the Underground Railroad through the escape routes on Beacon Hill. Design and build your own safe house. Includes dinner, storytelling, activities, breakfast and a special "bundle" to take home.

GRADE 5-6. $30 NON-MEMBER $25 MEMBERS.

SUNDAY, MARCH 18, 3 P.M.

Marian Anderson/Roland Hayes Concert Series: A New Beginning

Makanda Ken McIntyre Jazz Quartet. Original jazz selections and standard favorites from this world-class composer and improviser.[4] McIntyre, a Boston native and NY resident, is a master of the alto sax, bass clarinet, oboe, flute, and bassoon. Reception immediately following.

Sponsored in part by the Office of Community Collaborations and Program Development at the New England Conservatory.

$10 NON-MEMBER; FREE MEMBER; GROUP RATES AVAILABLE.

---

3. Underground Railroad a system of safe houses set up by opponents of slavery before the Civil War. The "railroad" was established to help escaped slaves reach the Free States and Canada.

4. improviser (IM pruh VYZ er) *n.* a musician who composes music on the spot as he or she plays.

THINKING ABOUT A PUBLIC RELATIONS DOCUMENT

1. What is the main goal of the museum?

_____

_____

_____

_____

2. How does the museum work to achieve its mission and goals?

_____

_____

_____

_____

READING STRATEGY

3. Name one **inference** that you can make from reading the mission statement and the calendar of events.

_____

_____

_____

4. The program for preschool-aged children is free. What can you infer the museum wishes to encourage from this fact? Explain.

_____

_____

_____

TIMED WRITING: EVALUATION (25 minutes)

To help you write your mission statement, focus on writing for one of the following organizations:

- a museum devoted to a scientific or an artistic subject

- a magazine devoted to a sport or hobby

Before you write, consider what the organization does. Then, list the goals that the organization would have. Use these ideas to write your mission statement.

The Life You Save May Be Your Own

LITERARY ANALYSIS

In literature, the **grotesque character** is a character who has become bizarre or twisted, usually through some kind of obsession. Writers may express grotesque traits through a character's physical appearance. Grotesque traits may also be visible in a character's actions and emotions. In O'Connor's story, all the characters can be classified as grotesques. As you read, look for examples of bizarre behavior and distortions that combine to create images of the grotesque.

O'Connor reveals the personality of the characters through **characterization**. With **direct characterization**, a writer simply tells the reader what a character is like. With **indirect characterization**, characters' traits are revealed through

- the character's words, thoughts, and actions.
- descriptions of the character's appearance or background.
- what other characters say about him or her.
- the ways in which other characters react or respond.

READING STRATEGY

When you find yourself wondering how a series of events will unfold, pause and **predict** what will happen. Predict outcomes by looking back and thinking about what you have read. Pay attention to hints the author has dropped. Measure these hints against your own understanding of human behavior.

Shiftlet
Physical Appearance
One-armed
Words
Thoughts
Actions
What others say

The Life You Save May Be Your Own

Flannery O'Connor

Summary A one-armed man, Mr. Shiftlet, approaches a woman and her mentally challenged daughter, Lucynell. He agrees to fix up the old woman's property in exchange for food and a place to sleep. The woman wants him to marry her daughter. Eventually, he agrees. The woman gives him money to take a wedding trip. When Mr. Shiftlet and his new wife stop for food, he leaves her at the counter. He heads toward Mobile in the car. On the way, he picks up a hitchhiker. They argue and the boy jumps out of the car. Mr. Shiflet drives toward Mobile alone.

Note-taking Guide

Use the chart shown to record what each character does in the story.

Character	Actions
Lucynell (daughter)	Learned the word *bird* Fell asleep in the restaurant
Mrs. Crater	
Mr. Shiftlet	

The Life You Save May Be Your Own

1. **Make a Judgment:** Is Mrs. Crater's decision to marry Lucynell to Mr. Shiflet a good decision? Explain.

_____

_____

_____

2. **Literary Analysis:** Write two examples of physical description that make Mrs. Crater a grotesque.

_____

_____

3. **Literary Analysis:** Use this chart to examine Mr. Shiftlet. Identify his primary goal or obsession. Then, tell what actions he undertakes as a result of the obsession.

Character	Controlling Goal	Actions Undertaken

4. **Reading Strategy:** What **predictions** did you make about Mr. Shiftlet's actions concerning Mrs. Crater and Lucynell when he first appeared?

_____

_____

5. **Reading Strategy:** What predictions did you make when Mr. Shiftlet left with Lucynell after their wedding?

_____

_____

The First Seven Years

LITERARY ANALYSIS

In a traditional short story, the plot moves toward resolution, a point at which the conflict is untangled and the outcome of the action becomes clear. However, many twentieth-century writers turned away from such traditional plot structures. These writers constructed plots that move toward an **epiphany**, a moment when a character has a flash of insight that may alter the nature of the conflict without resolving it.

Conflict, a struggle between opposing forces, is the element around which most plots develop. There are two main types of conflict:

- An **internal conflict** takes place within a character and involves a person's struggle with his or her own ideas, beliefs, or attitudes.
- An **external conflict** takes place between a character and an outside force, such as society, nature, or an enemy.

In this story, the main character has an epiphany that forces him to re-think his assumptions. As you read, think about the conflicts each character in the story experiences. Use this chart to examine the conflicts of the main character, Feld.

READING STRATEGY

When you **identify with characters**, you connect their thoughts, feelings, circumstances, and actions to your own experience. Identifying with characters allows you to get more emotionally involved in your reading.

The First Seven Years

Bernard Malamud

Summary This story is about a shoe-maker named Feld who runs a shop. He has an assistant named Sobel. He also has a daughter named Miriam. Feld wants his daughter to have a better life than he and his wife have had. He asks a college student named Max to call on her. He hopes the two will get married. Sobel hears the conversation Feld has with Max and runs out of the shop. He does not come back. Feld struggles to manage the shop and find a new assistant. When Feld meets Sobel again, Feld learns something about love and happiness.

Note-taking Guide

This story is about differences between people in what they value or desire. As you read, write down details that show the things each character finds important (values) and the things each character wants (desires).

Character	Values	Desires
Field		
Miriam		
Max		
Sobel		

Fix-ups, blind dates, setups—people use different names for the same process. It's what happens when friends or family members are sure that they know someone that you would really like to go out with. Have you ever been on a blind date? How did it work out? Think about it as you read this story about a young woman whose father tries to fix her up.

_____

_____

Literary Analysis

In literature, a **conflict** is a struggle between opposing forces. Some conflicts are **internal**, or inside a character. Others are **external**, or between a character and an outside force, such as nature or another character. Name one conflict in the first paragraph. Then tell whether it is internal or external.

_____

_____

Reading Strategy

All reading is more interesting if you **identify with the characters**. That means that you connect their thoughts, feelings, and actions to your own life. On the issue of college, do you identify with Feld or with his daughter? Why?

_____

_____

_____

The First Seven Years
Bernard Malamud

Parents want the best for their children—particularly immigrant parents, who have made huge sacrifices so that their children will have a better life. But sometimes their ideas and their children's ideas don't match. This story explores an immigrant father's high hopes for his daughter—and the circumstances that show him how different his daughter's own dreams are.

Feld, the shoemaker, was annoyed that his helper, Sobel, was so insensitive to his reverie that he wouldn't for a minute cease his fanatic pounding at the other bench. He gave him a look, but Sobel's bald head was bent over the last[1] as he worked and he didn't notice. The shoemaker shrugged and continued to peer through the partly frosted window at the nearsighted haze of falling February snow. Neither the shifting white blur outside, nor the sudden deep remembrance of the snowy Polish village where he had wasted his youth could turn his thoughts from Max the college boy, (a constant visitor in the mind since early that morning when Feld saw him trudging through the snowdrifts on his way to school) whom he so much respected because of the sacrifices he had made throughout the years—in winter or direst heat—to further his education. An old wish returned to haunt the shoemaker: that he had had a son instead of a daughter, but this blew away in the snow for Feld, if anything, was a practical man. Yet he could not help but contrast the diligence of the boy, who was a peddler's son, with Miriam's unconcern for an education. True, she was always with a book in her hand, yet when the opportunity arose for a college education, she had said no she would rather find a job. He had begged her to go, pointing out how many fathers could not afford to send their children to college, but she said she wanted to be independent. As for education, what was it, she asked, but books, which Sobel, who diligently read the classics, would as usual advise her on. Her answer greatly grieved her father.

A figure emerged from the snow and the door opened. At the counter the man withdrew from a wet paper bag a pair of battered shoes for repair. Who he was the shoemaker for a moment had no idea, then his heart trembled as he realized,

---

Vocabulary Development:	**diligence** (DIL uh jens) _n._ constant, careful effort; perseverance

---

1. **last** _n._ block shaped like a person's foot, on which shoes are made or repaired.

before he had thoroughly discerned the face, that Max himself was standing there, embarrassedly explaining what he wanted done to his old shoes. Though Feld listened eagerly, he couldn't hear a word, for the opportunity that had burst upon him was deafening.

He couldn't exactly recall when the thought had occurred to him, because it was clear he had more than once considered suggesting to the boy that he go out with Miriam. But he had not dared speak, for if Max said no, how would he face him again? Or suppose Miriam, who harped so often on independence, blew up in anger and shouted at him for his meddling? Still, the chance was too good to let by: all it meant was an introduction. They might long ago have become friends had they happened to meet somewhere, therefore was it not his duty—an obligation—to bring them together, nothing more, a harmless <u>connivance</u> to replace an accidental encounter in the subway, let's say, or a mutual friend's introduction in the street? Just let him once see and talk to her and he would for sure be interested. As for Miriam, what possible harm for a working girl in an office, who met only loud-mouthed salesmen and <u>illiterate</u> shipping clerks, to make the acquaintance of a fine scholarly boy? Maybe he would awaken in her a desire to go to college; if not—the shoemaker's mind at last came to grips with the truth—let her marry an educated man and live a better life.

When Max finished describing what he wanted done to his shoes, Feld marked them, both with enormous holes in the soles which he pretended not to notice, with large white-chalk x's, and the rubber heels, thinned to the nails, he marked with o's, though it troubled him he might have mixed up the letters. Max inquired the price, and the shoemaker cleared his throat and asked the boy, above Sobel's insistent hammering, would he please step through the side door there into the hall. Though surprised, Max did as the shoemaker requested, and Feld went in after him. For a minute they were both silent, because Sobel had stopped banging, and it seemed they understood neither was to say anything until the noise began again. When it did, loudly, the shoemaker quickly told Max why he had asked to talk to him.

"Ever since you went to high school," he said, in the dimly-lit hallway, "I watched you in the morning go to the subway to school, and I said always to myself, this is a fine boy that he wants so much an education."

"Thanks," Max said, nervously alert. He was tall and grotesquely thin, with sharply cut features, particularly a

---

Vocabulary Development: connivance (kuh NY vuns) *n.* secret cooperation
illiterate (i LIT ur it) *adj.* unable to read or write

TAKE NOTES

Reading Check

Why is Feld so surprised to see Max in his store?

_____

_____

_____

_____

_____

_____

Literary Analysis

When a character suddenly has an insight about himself, about another character, or about life in general, the insight is called an **epiphany**. As Feld thinks that Max may motivate Miriam to think again about college, he has an epiphany. Circle it in the story.

Reading Strategy

Identify with the character of Max in the bracketed section. How do you think he feels when Feld asks him to step into the hall?

_____

_____

_____

_____

_____

1. What does Max look like?

_____

_____

_____

2. What is Max's first reaction when Feld asks him to meet Miriam?

_____

_____

_____

_____

Identify with the character of Feld as he and Max discuss the cost of repairing Max's shoes. Why does Feld hesitate and fumble when Max asks him the price?

_____

_____

_____

_____

_____

What does Sobel do after Feld's conversation with Max?

_____

_____

_____

_____

_____

beak-like nose. He was wearing a loose, long slushy overcoat that hung down to his ankles, looking like a rug draped over his bony shoulders, and a soggy, old brown hat, as battered as the shoes he had brought in.

"I am a business man," the shoemaker abruptly said to conceal his embarrassment, "so I will explain you right away why I talk to you. I have a girl, my daughter Miriam—she is nineteen—a very nice girl and also so pretty that everybody looks on her when she passes by in the street. She is smart, always with a book, and I thought to myself that a boy like you, an educated boy—I thought maybe you will be interested sometime to meet a girl like this." He laughed a bit when he had finished and was tempted to say more but had the good sense not to.

Max stared down like a hawk. For an uncomfortable second he was silent, then he asked, "Did you say nineteen?"

"Yes."

"Would it be all right to inquire if you have a picture of her?"

"Just a minute." The shoemaker went into the store and hastily returned with a snapshot that Max held up to the light.

"She's all right," he said. Feld waited.

"And is she sensible—not the flighty kind?"

"She is very sensible."

After another short pause, Max said it was okay with him if he met her.

"Here is my telephone," said the shoemaker, hurriedly handing him a slip of paper. "Call her up. She comes home from work six o'clock."

Max folded the paper and tucked it away into his worn leather wallet.

"About the shoes," he said. "How much did you say they will cost me?"

"Don't worry about the price."

"I just like to have an idea."

"A dollar—dollar fifty. A dollar fifty," the shoemaker said.

At once he felt bad, for he usually charged two twenty-five for this kind of job. Either he should have asked the regular price or done the work for nothing.

Later, as he entered the store, he was startled by a violent clanging and looked up to see Sobel pounding with all his might upon the naked last. It broke, the iron striking the floor and jumping with a thump against the wall, but before the enraged shoemaker could cry out, the assistant had torn his hat and coat from the hook and rushed out into the snow.

So Feld, who had looked forward to anticipating how it would go with his daughter and Max, instead had a great worry on his mind. Without his temperamental helper he was a lost man, especially since it was years now that he had carried the store alone. The shoemaker had for an age suffered from a heart condition that threatened collapse if he dared exert himself. Five years ago, after an attack, it had appeared as though he would have either to sacrifice his business upon the auction block and live on a pittance thereafter, or put himself at the mercy of some <u>unscrupulous</u> employee who would in the end probably ruin him. But just at the moment of his darkest despair, this Polish refugee, Sobel, appeared one night from the street and begged for work. He was a stocky man, poorly dressed, with a bald head that had once been blond, a severely plain face and soft blue eyes prone to tears over the sad books he read, a young man but old—no one would have guessed thirty. Though he confessed he knew nothing of shoemaking, he said he was apt and would work for a very little if Feld taught him the trade. Thinking that with, after all, a landsman,[2] he would have less to fear than from a complete stranger, Feld took him on and within six weeks the refugee rebuilt as good a shoe as he, and not long thereafter expertly ran the business for the thoroughly relieved shoemaker.

Feld could trust him with anything and did, frequently going home after an hour or two at the store, leaving all the money in the till, knowing Sobel would guard every cent of it. The amazing thing was that he demanded so little. His wants were few; in money he wasn't interested— in nothing but books, it seemed—which he one by one lent to Miriam, together with his profuse, queer written comments, manufactured during his lonely rooming house evenings, thick pads of commentary which the shoemaker peered at and twitched his shoulders over as his daughter, from her fourteenth year, read page by sanctified page, as if the word of God were inscribed on them. To protect Sobel, Feld himself had to see that he received more than he asked for. Yet his conscience bothered him for not insisting that the assistant accept a better wage than he was getting, though Feld had honestly told him he could earn a handsome salary if he worked elsewhere, or maybe opened a place of his own. But the assistant answered, somewhat ungraciously, that he was not interested in going elsewhere, and though Feld frequently asked himself what keeps him here? why does he stay? he finally answered it that the man, no doubt because of his terrible experiences as a refugee, was afraid of the world.

Vocabulary Development: unscrupulous (un SKROOP yuh lus) *adj.* not restrained by ideas of right and wrong

---

2. **landsman** *n.* fellow countryman.

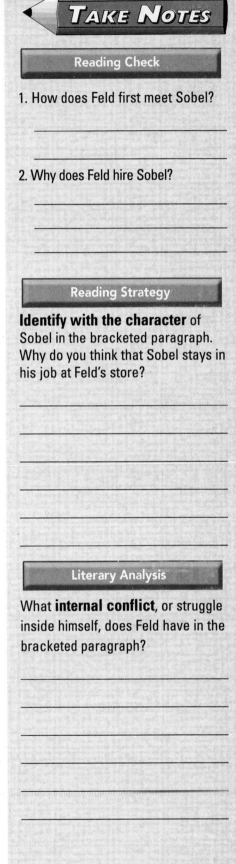

TAKE NOTES

Reading Check

1. How does Feld first meet Sobel?

_____

_____

2. Why does Feld hire Sobel?

_____

_____

_____

_____

Reading Strategy

Identify with the character of Sobel in the bracketed paragraph. Why do you think that Sobel stays in his job at Feld's store?

_____

_____

_____

_____

_____

_____

Literary Analysis

What **internal conflict**, or struggle inside himself, does Feld have in the bracketed paragraph?

_____

_____

_____

_____

_____

_____

1. Why is Feld sure that Sobel will come back to work if he asks him?

_____

_____

2. What happens when Feld goes to Sobel's rooming house?

_____

_____

3. What does Feld do about his store?

_____

_____

_____

_____

Identify with the character of Feld as he waits for Max and Miriam's date. Why do you think he has the date so much on his mind?

_____

_____

_____

_____

_____

_____

_____

_____

_____

After the incident with the broken last, angered by Sobel's behavior, the shoemaker decided to let him stew for a week in the rooming house, although his own strength was taxed dangerously and the business suffered. However, after several sharp nagging warnings from both his wife and daughter, he went finally in search of Sobel, as he had once before, quite recently, when over some fancied slight—Feld had merely asked him not to give Miriam so many books to read because her eyes were strained and red—the assistant had left the place in a huff, an incident which, as usual, came to nothing for he had returned after the shoemaker had talked to him, and taken his seat at the bench. But this time, after Feld had plodded through the snow to Sobel's house—he had thought of sending Miriam but the idea became <u>repugnant</u> to him—the burly landlady at the door informed him in a nasal voice that Sobel was not at home, and though Feld knew this was a nasty lie, for where had the refugee to go? still for some reason he was not completely sure of—it may have been the cold and his fatigue—he decided not to insist on seeing him. Instead he went home and hired a new helper.

Having settled the matter, though not entirely to his satisfaction, for he had much more to do than before, and so, for example, could no longer lie late in bed mornings because he had to get up to open the store for the new assistant, a speechless, dark man with an irritating rasp as he worked, whom he would not trust with the key as he had Sobel. Furthermore, this one, though able to do a fair repair job, knew nothing of grades of leather or prices, so Feld had to make his own purchases: and every night at closing time it was necessary to count the money in the till and lock up. However, he was not dissatisfied, for he lived much in his thoughts of Max and Miriam. The college boy had called her, and they had arranged a meeting for this coming Friday night. The shoemaker would personally have preferred Saturday, which he felt would make it a date of the first magnitude, but he learned Friday was Miriam's choice, so he said nothing. The day of the week did not matter. What mattered was the aftermath. Would they like each other and want to be friends? He sighed at all the time that would have to go by before he knew for sure. Often he was tempted to talk to Miriam about the boy, to ask whether she thought she would like his type—he had told her only that he considered Max a nice boy and had suggested he call her—but the one time he tried she snapped at him— justly—how should she know?

Vocabulary Development: repugnant (ri PUG nunt) *adj.*
offensive; disagreeable

At last Friday came. Feld was not feeling particularly well so he stayed in bed, and Mrs. Feld thought it better to remain in the bedroom with him when Max called. Miriam received the boy, and her parents could hear their voices, his throaty one, as they talked. Just before leaving, Miriam brought Max to the bedroom door and he stood there a minute, a tall, slightly hunched figure wearing a thick, droopy suit, and apparently at ease as he greeted the shoemaker and his wife, which was surely a good sign. And Miriam, although she had worked all day, looked fresh and pretty. She was a large-framed girl with a well-shaped body, and she had a fine open face and soft hair. They made, Feld thought, a first-class couple.

Miriam returned after 11:30. Her mother was already asleep, but the shoemaker got out of bed and after locating his bathrobe went into the kitchen, where Miriam, to his surprise, sat at the table, reading.

"So where did you go?" Feld asked pleasantly.

"For a walk," she said, not looking up.

"I advised him," Feld said, clearing his throat, "he shouldn't spend so much money."

"I didn't care."

The shoemaker boiled up some water for tea and sat down at the table with a cupful and a thick slice of lemon.

"So how," he sighed after a sip, "did you enjoy?"

"It was all right."

He was silent. She must have sensed his disappointment, for she added, "You can't really tell much the first time."

"You will see him again?"

Turning a page, she said that Max had asked for another date.

"For when?"

"Saturday."

"So what did you say?"

"What did I say?" she asked, delaying for a moment—"I said yes."

Afterwards she inquired about Sobel, and Feld, without exactly knowing why, said the assistant had got another job. Miriam said nothing more and began to read. The shoemaker's conscience did not trouble him; he was satisfied with the Saturday date.

During the week, by placing here and there a deft question, he managed to get from Miriam some information about Max. It surprised him to learn that the boy was not studying to be either a doctor or lawyer but was taking a business course leading to a degree in accountancy. Feld was a little disappointed because he thought of accountants as bookkeepers and would have preferred "a higher profession." However, it was not long before he had investigated the subject and discovered that Certified Public Accountants

TAKE NOTES

Reading Strategy

Identify with the character of Miriam in the conversation with her father after her date with Max. How do you think she feels as her father questions her about the date?

_____

_____

_____

_____

_____

_____

Reading Check

1. Why does Feld lie to Miriam about Sobel?

_____

_____

2. What does Feld find out about Max that disappoints him at first?

_____

_____

_____

_____

_____

were highly respected people, so he was thoroughly content as Saturday approached. But because Saturday was a busy day, he was much in the store and therefore did not see Max when he came to call for Miriam. From his wife he learned there had been nothing especially revealing about their meeting. Max had rung the bell and Miriam had got her coat and left with him—nothing more. Feld did not probe, for his wife was not particularly observant. Instead, he waited up for Miriam with a newspaper on his lap, which he scarcely looked at so lost was he in thinking of the future. He awoke to find her in the room with him, tiredly removing her hat. Greeting her, he was suddenly inexplicably afraid to ask anything about the evening. But since she volunteered nothing he was at last forced to inquire how she had enjoyed herself. Miriam began something noncommittal but apparently changed her mind, for she said after a minute, "I was bored."

When Feld had sufficiently recovered from his anguished disappointment to ask why, she answered without hesitation, "Because he's nothing more than a materialist."

"What means this word?"

"He has no soul. He's only interested in things."

He considered her statement for a long time but then asked, "Will you see him again?"

"He didn't ask."

"Suppose he will ask you?"

"I won't see him."

He did not argue: however, as the days went by he hoped increasingly she would change her mind. He wished the boy would telephone, because he was sure there was more to him than Miriam, with her inexperienced eye, could <u>discern</u>. But Max didn't call. As a matter of fact he took a different route to school, no longer passing the shoemaker's store, and Feld was deeply hurt.

Then one afternoon Max came in and asked for his shoes. The shoemaker took them down from the shelf where he had placed them, apart from the other pairs. He had done the work himself and the soles and heels were well built and firm. The shoes had been highly polished and somehow looked better than new. Max's Adam's apple went up once when he saw them, and his eyes had little lights in them.

"How much?" he asked, without directly looking at the shoemaker.

"Like I told you before," Feld answered sadly. "One dollar fifty cents."

Max handed him two crumpled bills and received in

Reading Check

When does Feld see Max again? Circle the sentence that gives you the answer.

Reading Strategy

Identify with the character of Max when he comes in to get his shoes. Why do you think that he doesn't mention Miriam?

_____

_____

_____

_____

_____

_____

Vocabulary Development: discern (di SURN) *v.* to perceive or recognize; make out clearly

return a newly-minted silver half dollar.

He left. Miriam had not been mentioned. That night the shoemaker discovered that his new assistant had been all the while stealing from him, and he suffered a heart attack.

Though the attack was very mild, he lay in bed for three weeks. Miriam spoke of going for Sobel, but sick as he was Feld rose in wrath against the idea. Yet in his heart he knew there was no other way, and the first weary day back in the shop thoroughly convinced him, so that night after supper he dragged himself to Sobel's rooming house.

He toiled up the stairs, though he knew it was bad for him, and at the top knocked at the door. Sobel opened it and the shoemaker entered. The room was a small, poor one, with a single window facing the street. It contained a narrow cot, a low table and several stacks of books piled haphazardly around on the floor along the wall, which made him think how queer Sobel was, to be uneducated and read so much. He had once asked him, Sobel, why you read so much? and the assistant could not answer him. Did you ever study in a college someplace? he had asked but Sobel shook his head. He read, he said, to know. But to know what, the shoemaker demanded, and to know, why? Sobel never explained, which proved he read much because he was queer.

Feld sat down to recover his breath. The assistant was resting on his bed with his heavy back to the wall. His shirt and trousers were clean, and his stubby fingers, away from the shoemaker's bench, were strangely pallid. His face was thin and pale, as if he had been shut in this room since the day he had bolted from the store.

"So when you will come back to work?" Feld asked him.

To his surprise, Sobel burst out, "Never."

Jumping up, he strode over to the window that looked out upon the miserable street. "Why should I come back?" he cried.

"I will raise your wages."

"Who cares for your wages!"

The shoemaker, knowing he didn't care, was at a loss what else to say.

"What do you want from me, Sobel?"

"Nothing."

"I always treated you like you was my son."

Sobel vehemently denied it. "So why you look for strange boys in the street they should go out with Miriam? Why you don't think of me?"

The shoemaker's hands and feet turned freezing cold. His voice became so hoarse he couldn't speak. At last he cleared his throat and croaked, "So what has my daughter got to do with a shoemaker thirty-five years old who works for me?"

"Why do you think I worked so long for you?" Sobel cried out. "For the stingy wages I sacrificed five years of my life

Why does Feld go back to Sobel's rooming house?

_____

_____

_____

_____

_____

_____

_____

Reading Strategy

Identify with the character of Sobel on this page. Why is he so angry at Feld? Would you be angry in his situation?

_____

_____

_____

_____

_____

_____

_____

Feld suddenly has an insight, or an **epiphany**, that Miriam knows that Sobel loves her. Circle the paragraph in which Feld has this epiphany.

Identify with the character of Feld in the bracketed paragraph. How does he feel about Sobel at this point in the story?

_____

_____

_____

Feld is himself a shoemaker like Sobel. Yet he calls the life Miriam will have with Sobel "ugly." Why do you think he feels this way when in many ways Miriam's life will be like his own?

_____

_____

_____

_____

so you could have to eat and drink and where to sleep?"

"Then for what?" shouted the shoemaker.

"For Miriam," he blurted—"for her."

The shoemaker, after a time, managed to say, "I pay wages in cash, Sobel," and lapsed into silence. Though he was seething with excitement, his mind was coldly clear, and he had to admit to himself he had sensed all along that Sobel felt this way. He had never so much as thought it consciously, but he had felt it and was afraid.

"Miriam knows?" he muttered hoarsely.

"She knows."

"You told her?"

"No."

"Then how does she know?"

"How does she know?" Sobel said, "because she knows. She knows who I am and what is in my heart."

Feld had a sudden insight. In some devious way, with his books and commentary, Sobel had given Miriam to understand that he loved her. The shoemaker felt a terrible anger at him for his deceit.

"Sobel, you are crazy," he said bitterly. "She will never marry a man so old and ugly like you."

Sobel turned black with rage. He cursed the shoemaker, but then, though he trembled to hold it in, his eyes filled with tears and he broke into deep sobs. With his back to Feld, he stood at the window, fists clenched, and his shoulders shook with his choked sobbing.

Watching him, the shoemaker's anger diminished. His teeth were on edge with pity for the man, and his eyes grew moist. How strange and sad that a refugee, a grown man, bald and old with his miseries, who had by the skin of his teeth escaped Hitler's incinerators,[3] should fall in love, when he had got to America, with a girl less than half his age. Day after day, for five years he had sat at his bench, cutting and hammering away, waiting for the girl to become a woman, unable to ease his heart with speech, knowing no protest but desperation.

"Ugly I didn't mean," he said half aloud.

Then he realized that what he had called ugly was not Sobel but Miriam's life if she married him. He felt for his daughter a strange and gripping sorrow, as if she were already Sobel's bride, the wife, after all, of a shoemaker, and had in her life no more than her mother had had. And all his dreams for her—why he had slaved and destroyed his heart with anxiety and labor—all these dreams of a better life were dead.

The room was quiet. Sobel was standing by the window

---

3. **Hitler's incinerators** During World War II, millions of Jews were murdered by the Nazis under the direction of German dictator Adolf Hitler (1889–1945).

reading, and it was curious that when he read he looked young.

"She is only nineteen," Feld said brokenly. "This is too young yet to get married. Don't ask her for two years more, till she is twenty-one, then you can talk to her."

Sobel didn't answer. Feld rose and left. He went slowly down the stairs but once outside, though it was an icy night and the crisp falling snow whitened the street, he walked with a stronger stride.

But the next morning, when the shoemaker arrived, heavy-hearted, to open the store, he saw he needn't have come, for his assistant was already seated at the last, pounding leather for his love.

Reader's Response: What did you think of Feld's actions in this story? If you were Miriam, how would you react to what Feld does?

_____

_____

_____

Thinking About the Skill: Were you able to **identify with the characters** of Feld, Sobel, or Miriam as you read this selection? Which character did you find it easiest to identify with? Why?

_____

_____

_____

What does the last paragraph tell you about the kind of man Sobel is?

_____

_____

_____

_____

_____

_____

The First Seven Years

1. **Interpret:** Max is a college student Feld sees as he walks to school. Why is Max so appealing to Feld?

   _____

   _____

2. **Literary Analysis:** One **epiphany** in this story happens when Feld visits Sobel. Feld learns something about Sobel and suddenly sees him in a new way. Use this chart to write down your ideas about this epiphany.

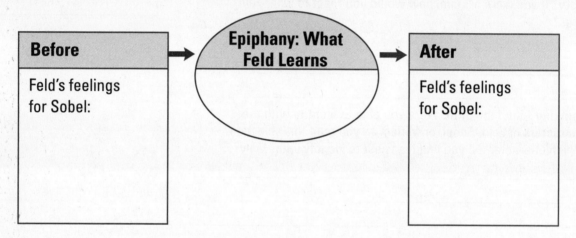

Before	Epiphany: What Feld Learns	After
Feld's feelings for Sobel:		Feld's feelings for Sobel:

3. **Literary Analysis:** What **external and internal conflicts** does Sobel have?

   _____

   _____

   _____

4. **Reading Strategy: Identify with a character** in this story. Choose a character and list ways in which his or her life reminds you of your own.

   _____

   _____

   _____

Aliceville

LITERARY ANALYSIS

The **tone** of a literary work is the writer's attitude toward his or her subject and audience. The tone may be serious or playful, analytical or emotional, sarcastic or sympathetic. Tone comes chiefly from a writer's word choice—through the emotional associations and images that the words create. Notice the simple but vivid words that set the scene and the tone for "Aliceville":

> This was in December, on one of those still evenings in the new part of winter when you cannot decide whether it is a good thing to inhale deeply, the air is so clean and sharp.

As you read "Aliceville," listen for the tone that Earley's narrator uses as he takes you further into his confidence.

READING STRATEGY

When you **visualize** a written text, you form a mental image of what you are reading—the scenes and actions described by the writer's words. Visualizing helps you enter the world of the story and follow the action. The narrator of "Aliceville" uses visual details to create word pictures of his family members, the town, nature, and the story's central experience. Look at this description of a flock of geese:

> The geese flew across the field and turned in a climbing curve against the wooded ridge on the other side of the creek, back the way they had come, toward Uncle Zeno and me.

You might be able to visualize this scene by imagining the "climbing curve" of the geese flying out one way and then turning back. As you read, record other especially vivid details in a chart like the one shown.

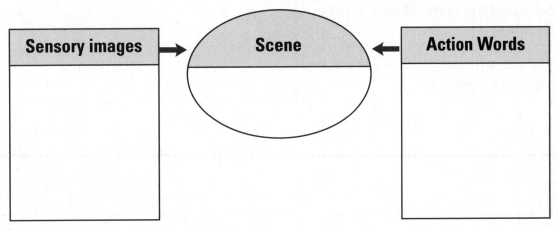

Sensory images → Scene ← Action Words

Aliceville

Tony Earley

Summary The narrator, Jim Glass, is a boy living with his mother and his uncle. One evening, Jim and his uncle are driving home. They see a flock of geese settling down for the night. Jim and his uncle form a plan to sneak out to hunt the geese. Jim is very excited. The next morning, Jim and his uncle sneak up on the geese. Something goes wrong, and the geese fly away.

Note-taking Guide

Using the chart, track Jim's emotions by recording his feelings after various events in the story.

Event	Jim's Emotions
Jim and his uncle see the geese for the first time.	He is amazed and a little frightened.
Jim keeps the secret of the hunt from his family.	
The geese fly away before Jim and his uncle can shoot.	

Aliceville

1. **Generalize:** What does Uncle Zeno's behavior during the expedition reveal about him as a person?

_____

_____

2. **Literary Analysis:** Choose one passage from the beginning of the story and one from the end of the story. Analyze the **tone** of each passage. Use the chart to identify each passage, list the details that create the tone, and determine the tone of each passage.

Passage	Words/Details Creating Tone		Tone
		→	

3. **Literary Analysis:** Select two passages from the story in which the tone clearly sounds like that of an adult. Write the passages on the lines.

_____

_____

_____

_____

4. **Reading Strategy:** Identify an action, a description, or a scene in the story that you can **visualize**. What makes the passage especially vivid?

_____

_____

_____

Gold Glade • The Light Comes Brighter • Traveling Through the Dark

LITERARY ANALYSIS

A writer's **style** is the manner in which he or she puts ideas into words. Style generally concerns *form* rather than *content*. In poetry, style is determined by a poet's use of these elements:

- Tone
- Sound devices
- Symbolism
- Rhythm
- The length and arrangement of lines
- Figurative language
- Punctuation and capitalization

Another important aspect of style is **diction**, or word choice. As you read these poems, note the ways in which each poet's style and diction reflect varying degrees of formality but also establish a unique voice—a distinctive way of "speaking" on the page.

READING STRATEGY

Some poems contain passages that are especially difficult to understand because of unusual vocabulary, complex sentences, or the ambiguities of poetic language. To improve your comprehension, **paraphrase**, or restate in your own words, any difficult passages you encounter. As you read these poems, use this chart to paraphrase difficult passages.

Passage from Poem	Paraphrase

Gold Glade • The Light Comes Brighter • Traveling Through the Dark

Robert Penn Warren, Theodore Roethke, William Stafford

Summaries In "Gold Glade," the speaker recalls an autumn walk through the woods. He remembers finding a beautiful hickory tree in the woods. He no longer remembers its location, but he knows that it still stands. In "The Light Comes Brighter," the speaker describes the arrival of spring. In "Traveling Through the Dark," the speaker finds a dead doe on the edge of the road. He hesitates before he pushes the animal into a river.

Note-taking Guide

Each of the speakers in these three poems sees something. What he sees has a powerful effect on him. Use this chart to record words from the poems that describe these experiences.

	What did the speaker see?	What words did the speaker use to describe what he saw?
"Gold Glade"	a glowing tree in a glade	"geometric," "circular," "gold"
"The Light Comes Brighter"		
"Traveling Through the Dark"		

Gold Glade • The Light Comes Brighter • Traveling Through the Dark

1. **Evaluate:** Which of these three poems made the strongest impression on you? Why?

_____

_____

2. **Literary Analysis:** Use this chart to analyze each poet's **diction**.

Poet	Formal or Informal	Plain or Ornate	Abstract or Concrete	Effect
Warren				
Roethke				
Stafford				

3. **Reading Strategy: Paraphrase** lines 16–20 of "Gold Glade."

_____

_____

_____

_____

4. **Reading Strategy:** Paraphrase lines 1–4 of "The Light Comes Brighter."

_____

_____

_____

_____

Average Waves in Unprotected Waters

LITERARY ANALYSIS

Foreshadowing is the use of details or clues that hint at what will occur later in a plot or suggest a certain outcome. It makes the reader wonder what will happen next, as this passage demonstrates:

> Maybe she felt to blame that he was going. But she'd done the best she could: babysat him all these years and only give up when he'd grown too strong and wild to manage.

As you read, notice how Tyler's use of foreshadowing keeps you guessing about the story's outcome.

Foreshadowing builds **suspense**. Suspense is a feeling of growing uncertainty about the outcome of events in a literary work. Writers create suspense by raising questions in readers' minds. Because most people are curious, they keep reading to find out what will happen next. As you read, notice how the suspense makes you anxious to learn the outcome.

READING STRATEGY

Most stories are written in chronological order—the order in which events happen in real time. Sometimes, however, the writer interrupts the sequence to present a flashback—a scene or event from an earlier time. As you read Tyler's story, **put the events in order** by noting the sequence in which they actually occurred. Use the chain-of-events diagram shown to record the events in order, from the earliest to the latest.

Order of Events

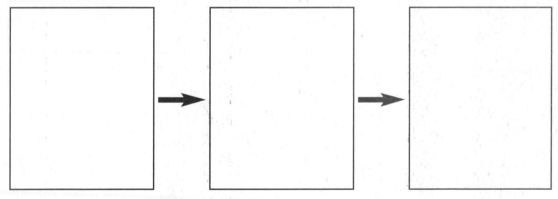

Average Waves in Unprotected Waters

Anne Tyler

Summary Bet feels that she can no longer care for her mentally challenged nine-year-old son, Arnold. She takes him to the state hospital. There, a nurse takes Arnold to a hallway lined with cots. The nurse tells Bet to wait six months before visiting Arnold. Bet's train home is late, but she distracts herself by listening to a speech by the Mayor.

Note-taking Guide

Use this chart to record Bet's regrets and struggles as they relate to members of her family.

Bet's family	Bet's Regrets and Struggles
parents	regrets marrying against their wishes; regrets their deaths
husband Avery	
son Arnold	

Average Waves in Unprotected Waters

1. **Infer:** Why does Bet insist that the cab driver wait for her outside the hospital?

   _____

   _____

2. **Literary Analysis:** In what way does Arnold's unwillingness to cooperate with his mother at the beginning of the story **foreshadow** the story's main event?

   _____

   _____

3. **Literary Analysis:** List two other examples of foreshadowing in this chart. Then, analyze their effects on the reader.

Foreshadowing	Effect on Reader

4. **Reading Strategy:** State the main events of the story in chronological **order**.

   _____

   _____

   _____

   _____

5. **Reading Strategy:** What flashback does Bet have?

   _____

   _____

from The Names • Mint Snowball • Suspended

LITERARY ANALYSIS

An **anecdote** is a short account of an amusing or interesting event. People tell anecdotes all the time, mostly for entertainment. Essayists tell anecdotes to make a point, make generalizations, or illustrate conclusions, as in this example from "Mint Snowball":

> Perhaps the clue to my entire personality connects to the lost Mint Snowball. I have always felt out-of-step with my environment, disjointed in the modern world.

Identify the anecdotes in these essays. Decide why the writer included each one, or what purpose it serves. Then, write down the generalizations or conclusions each one inspires. Use a chart like the one shown to help you.

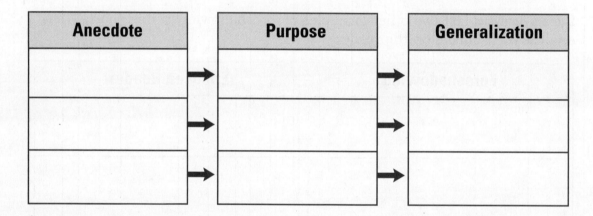

Anecdote	Purpose	Generalization

READING STRATEGY

Many common experiences know no cultural boundaries. If you have ever taken a journey, yearned for the past, or experienced an inner awakening, you can find a connection between your experiences and the ones expressed in these selections. **Relating to your own experiences** will increase your understanding and enjoyment of the essays.

PREVIEW

from The Names • Mint Snowball • Suspended

N. Scott Momaday • Naomi Shihab Nye • Joy Harjo

Summaries *The Names* is from a longer work. In this section, the author tells about the horse his parents gave him as a child. The horse's name was Pecos. The author still thinks about Pecos. In "Mint Snowball," the author recalls the drugstore that her great-grandfather used to own. She remembers an ice cream treat that he invented. After he died, nobody could ever make the treat the same way. In "Suspended," the author remembers a moment in her life before she could talk. She listened to jazz on the radio and realized music gave people a way to communicate.

Note-taking Guide

Each of these authors writes about something that affected his or her life. Use the chart below to collect important details about the subjects of each essay.

Essay	Subject	Details
from *The Names*		
Mint Snowball		
Suspended		

from The Names • Mint Snowball • Suspended

1. **Draw Conclusions:** Think about the important of horses in Kiowa culture. Why do you think Momaday's journey on horseback meant so much to him?

   _____

   _____

2. **Interpret:** Nye says she longs for "something she has never seen or tasted." What connections does she make between the lost recipe and her own life?

   _____

   _____

3. **Analyze:** How does Harjo feel about her father? Use two details from the essay in your answer.

   _____

   _____

4. **Literary Analysis:** Identify one **anecdote** from Momaday's essay and explain the idea it helps the author to share.

   _____

   _____

   _____

5. **Reading Strategy:** Relate your own experiences to those of the writers. Use this chart to write down connections you see between the experiences these writers describe and your own experiences.

Writer's Experience	My Experience	How They Relate

Everyday Use

LITERARY ANALYSIS

To truly know a character, you have to understand that character's **motivation**. Motivation is the reason or reasons behind a character's thoughts, actions, and speech. Characters may be motivated by their values, experiences, needs, or dreams. These lines of "Everyday Use" are clues to the narrator's motivation.

> Maggie will be nervous until her sister goes . . . She thinks her sister has held life always in the palm of one hand, that "no" is a word the world never learned to say to her.

This quotation suggests that the narrator is motivated by feelings of love and protectiveness for Maggie. As you read, ask yourself these questions:

- Why is this character doing or saying this?

- What need or goal does she hope to satisfy?

READING STRATEGY

As this story opens, you learn that two sisters and their life experiences are quite different. **Contrast the characters**, or identify the ways in which they differ. This will help you to uncover the major conflict in the story. Use this Venn diagram to note character traits that separate Dee from Maggie. These traits can include behavior, speech, and appearance. Also, consider the ways their experiences have shaped their differences.

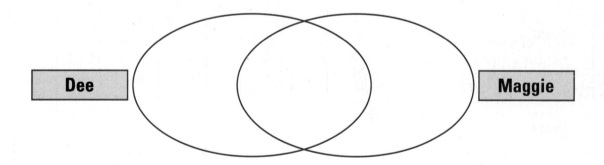

Everyday Use

Alice Walker

Summary The narrator and her daughter Maggie wait in the yard for the narrator's other daughter, Dee. The narrator is a hard-working woman from the Georgia countryside. Maggie is a shy young woman who was badly scarred during a house fire. Dee is an educated, confident woman. As a teenager, Dee abandoned her childhood home and culture. When Dee returns, she tries to take pieces of her heritage. Dee's visit helps Magggie and her mother discover their own pride and will.

Note-taking Guide

Use this plot diagram to keep track of the events in the story.

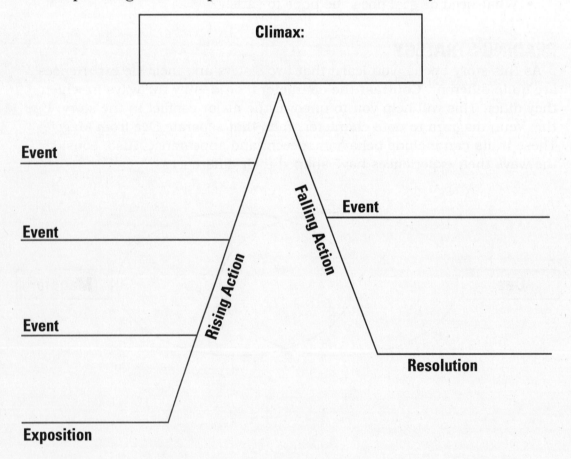

Everyday Use
Alice Walker

Members of a family can care about one another but not understand one another, especially as children grow up. In this story, Maggie and Dee are sisters, but they are very different. As you read this story, think about the ways in which you are like or unlike the other members of your family or your household. Ask yourself whether it is possible to have good relationships with family members who are very different from you.

I will wait for her in the yard that Maggie and I made so clean and wavy yesterday afternoon. A yard like this is more comfortable than most people know. It is not just a yard. It is like an extended living room. When the hard clay is swept clean as a floor and the fine sand around the edges lined with tiny, irregular grooves, anyone can come and sit and look up into the elm tree and wait for the breezes that never come inside the house.

Maggie will be nervous until after her sister goes: she will stand hopelessly in corners, homely and ashamed of the burn scars down her arms and legs, eyeing her sister with a mixture of envy and awe. She thinks her sister has held life always in the palm of one hand, that "no" is a word the world never learned to say to her.

You've no doubt seen those TV shows where the child who has "made it" is confronted, as a surprise, by her own mother and father, tottering in weakly from backstage. (A pleasant surprise, of course: What would they do if parent and child came on the show only to curse out and insult each other?) On TV mother and child embrace and smile into each other's faces. Sometimes the mother and father weep, the child wraps them in her arms and leans across the table to tell how she would not have made it without their help. I have seen these programs.

Sometimes I dream a dream in which Dee and I are suddenly brought together on a TV program of this sort. Out of a dark and soft-seated limousine I am ushered into a bright room filled with many people. There I meet a smiling, gray, sporty man like Johnny Carson who shakes my hand and tells me what a fine girl I have. Then we are on the stage and Dee is embracing me with tears in her eyes. She pins on my dress a large orchid, even though she has told me once that she thinks orchids are tacky flowers.

In real life I am a large, big-boned woman with rough, man-working hands. In the winter I wear flannel nightgowns to bed and overalls during the day. I can kill and clean a hog as mercilessly as a man. My fat keeps me hot in zero weather. I can work outside all day, breaking ice to get water for washing; I can eat pork liver cooked over the open fire

---

TAKE NOTES

Activate Prior Knowledge

Do you have special or valuable items in your home that have been passed down through your family? Do you use them every day, save them for special occasions, or display them without using them? If any of these items ever become yours, how will you use them?

_____

_____

_____

_____

Literary Analysis

The mother, who is the narrator of this story, tells the story from the **first-person point of view**. That means that she tells what happens in her own words, using the first-person pronouns *I* and *we*. Circle three examples of the use of first-person pronouns on this page.

Reading Strategy

Maggie and Dee, the two sisters in this story, are very different. By **contrasting characters,** or keeping track of the ways they are different, you can understand this story better. Start by writing two things that you learn about Maggie from the bracketed paragraph.

1. _____

_____

2. _____

_____

How are Dee and her mother different when they talk to white men?

_____

_____

_____

_____

_____

Reading Strategy

Contrast the characters of Maggie and Dee by keeping track of the ways they are different. Write two things that you learn about Dee from the bracketed paragraph.

_____

_____

_____

_____

_____

Literary Analysis

As you get to know a character in a story, you begin to understand the reasons for her thoughts, her words, and her actions. These are called the **character's motivation**. Reread the underlined sentences in the bracketed paragraph. Why do you think the narrator mentions Dee's hatred of the house?

_____

_____

_____

_____

_____

minutes after it comes steaming from the hog. One winter I knocked a bull calf straight in the brain between the eyes with a sledge hammer and had the meat hung up to chill before nightfall. But of course all of this does not show on television. I am the way my daughter would want me to be: a hundred pounds lighter, my skin like an uncooked barley pancake. My hair glistens in the hot bright lights. Johnny Carson has much to do to keep up with my quick and witty tongue.

But that is a mistake. I know even before I wake up. Who ever knew a Johnson with a quick tongue? Who can even imagine me looking a strange white man in the eye? It seems to me I have talked to them always with one foot raised in flight, with my head turned in whichever way is farthest from them. Dee, though. She would always look anyone in the eye. Hesitation was no part of her nature.

"How do I look, Mama?" Maggie says, showing just enough of her thin body enveloped in pink skirt and red blouse for me to know she's there, almost hidden by the door.

"Come out into the yard," I say.

Have you ever seen a lame animal, perhaps a dog run over by some careless person rich enough to own a car, sidle up to someone who is ignorant enough to be kind to him? That is the way my Maggie walks. She has been like this, chin on chest, eyes on ground, feet in shuffle, ever since the fire that burned the other house to the ground.

Dee is lighter than Maggie, with nicer hair and a fuller figure. She's a woman now, though sometimes I forget. How long ago was it that the other house burned? Ten, twelve years? Sometimes I can still hear the flames and feel Maggie's arms sticking to me, her hair smoking and her dress falling off her in little black papery flakes. Her eyes seemed stretched open, blazed open by the flames reflected in them. And Dee. I see her standing off under the sweet gum tree she used to dig gum out of; a look of concentration on her face as she watched the last dingy gray board of the house fall in toward the red-hot brick chimney. Why don't you do a dance around the ashes? I'd want to ask her. She had hated the house that much.

I used to think she hated Maggie, too. But that was before we raised the money, the church and me, to send her to Augusta to school. She used to read to us without pity; forcing words, lies, other folks' habits, whole lives upon us two, sitting trapped and ignorant underneath her voice. She washed us in a river of make-believe, burned us with a lot of knowledge we didn't necessarily need to know. Pressed us to her with the serious way she read, to shove us away at just the moment, like dimwits, we seemed about to understand.

Dee wanted nice things. A yellow organdy dress to wear to

her graduation from high school; black pumps to match a green suit she'd made from an old suit somebody gave me. She was determined to stare down any disaster in her efforts. Her eyelids would not flicker for minutes at a time. Often I fought off the temptation to shake her. At sixteen she had a style of her own, and knew what style was.

I never had an education myself. After second grade the school was closed down. Don't ask me why: in 1927 colored asked fewer questions than they do now. Sometimes Maggie reads to me. She stumbles along good-naturedly but can't see well. She knows she is not bright. Like good looks and money, quickness passed her by. She will marry John Thomas (who has mossy teeth in an earnest face) and then I'll be free to sit here and I guess just sing church songs to myself. Although I never was a good singer. Never could carry a tune. I was always better at a man's job. I used to love to milk till I was hooved in the side in '49. Cows are soothing and slow and don't bother you, unless you ty to milk them the wrong way.

I have deliberately turned my back on the house. It is three rooms, just like the one that burned, except the roof is tin; they don't make shingle roofs any more. There are no real windows, just some holes cut in the sides, like the portholes in a ship, but not round and not square, with rawhide holding the shutters up on the outside. This house is in a pasture, too, like the other one. No doubt when Dee sees it she will want to tear it down. She wrote me once that no matter where we "choose" to live, she will manage to come see us. But she will never bring her friends. Maggie and I thought about this and Maggie asked me, "Mama, when did Dee ever have any friends?"

She had a few. Furtive boys in pink shirts hanging about on washday after school. Nervous girls who never laughed. Impressed with her they worshiped the well-turned phrase, the cute shape, the scalding humor that erupted like bubbles in lye. She read to them.

When she was courting Jimmy T she didn't have much time to pay to us, but turned all her faultfinding power on him. He flew to marry a cheap city girl from a family of ignorant flashy people. She hardly had time to recompose herself.

When she comes I will meet—but there they are!

Maggie attempts to make a dash for the house, in her shuffling way, but I stay her with my hand. "Come back

---

Vocabulary Development: furtive (FUR tiv) *adj.* sneaky
lye (LY) *n.* strong alkaline solution used in cleaning and making soap

Literary Analysis

Understanding each **character's motivation** will help you understand this story. Look at the underlined sentence. Why do you think the narrator makes this comment about cows?

_____

_____

_____

_____

Reading Check

Reread the bracketed paragraph. Describe the house that Maggie and her mother live in.

_____

_____

_____

_____

Stop to Reflect

The narrator has said many things about both Maggie and Dee at this point. How do you think she feels about each of her daughters?

_____

_____

_____

_____

Literary Analysis

Think about the way the narrator describes Dee as she gets out of the car. Because the narrator uses **first-person point of view**, you see only what the narrator sees. How does the narrator feel about what Dee is wearing and how she looks?

_____

_____

_____

Reading Check

What does Maggie do when Dee's friend tries to hug her?

_____

_____

_____

Literary Analysis

Look at the bracketed paragraph. Dee takes a number of pictures of the house, her mother, and Maggie. What do you think is her **character's motivation,** or her reason, for taking the pictures?

_____

_____

_____

_____

here," I say. And she stops and tries to dig a well in the sand with her toe.

It is hard to see them clearly through the strong sun. But even the first glimpse of leg out of the car tells me it is Dee. Her feet were always neat-looking, as if God himself had shaped them with a certain style. From the other side of the car comes a short, stocky man. Hair is all over his head a foot long and hanging from his chin like a kinky mule tail. I hear Maggie suck in her breath. "Uhnnnh," is what it sounds like. Like when you see the wriggling end of a snake just in front of your foot on the road. "Uhnnnh."

Dee next. A dress down to the ground, in this hot weather. A dress so loud it hurts my eyes. There are yellows and oranges enough to throw back the light of the sun. I feel my whole face warming from the heat waves it throws out. Earrings gold, too, and hanging down to her shoulders. Bracelets dangling and making noises when she moves her arm up to shake the folds of the dress out of her armpits. The dress is loose and flows, and as she walks closer, I like it. I hear Maggie go "Uhnnnh" again. It is her sister's hair. It stands straight up like the wool on a sheep. It is black as night and around the edges are two long pigtails that rope about like small lizards disappearing behind her ears.

"Wa-su-zo-Tean-o!"[1] she says, coming on in that gliding way the dress makes her move. The short stocky fellow with the hair to his navel is all grinning and he follows up with "Asalamalakim,[2] my mother and sister!" He moves to hug Maggie but she falls back, right up against the back of my chair. I feel her trembling there and when I look up I see the perspiration falling off her chin.

"Don't get up," says Dee. Since I am stout it takes something of a push. You can see me trying to move a second or two before I make it. She turns, showing white heels through her sandals, and goes back to the car. Out she peeks next with a Polaroid. She stoops down quickly and lines up picture after picture of me sitting there in front of the house with Maggie cowering behind me. She never takes a shot without making sure the house is included. When a cow comes nibbling around the edge of the yard she snaps it and me and Maggie and the house. Then she puts the Polaroid in the back seat of the car, and comes up and kisses me on the forehead.

Meanwhile Asalamalakim is going through motions with Maggie's hand. Maggie's hand is as limp as a fish, and probably as cold, despite the sweat, and she keeps trying to pull it back. It looks like Asalamalakim wants to shake hands

1. **Wa-su-zo-Tean-o** (wah soo zoh TEN oh) African greeting.
2. **Asalamalakim** *Salaam aleikhim* (suh LAHM ah ly KEEM) Islamic greeting meaning "Peace be with you."

but wants to do it fancy. Or maybe he don't know how people shake hands. Anyhow, he soon gives up on Maggie.

"Well," I say. "Dee."

"No, Mama," she says. "Not 'Dee,' Wangero Leewanika Kemanjo!"

"What happened to 'Dee'?" I wanted to know.

"She's dead," Wangero said. "I couldn't bear it any longer, being named after the people who <u>oppress</u> me."

"You know as well as me you was named after your aunt Dicie," I said. Dicie is my sister. She named Dee. We called her "Big Dee" after Dee was born.

"But who was she named after?" asked Wangero.

"I guess after Grandma Dee," I said.

"And who was she named after?" asked Wangero.

"Her mother," I said, and saw Wangero was getting tired. "That's about as far back as I can trace it," I said. Though, in fact, I probably could have carried it back beyond the Civil War through the branches.

"Well," said Asalamalakim, "there you are."

"Uhnnnh," I heard Maggie say.

"There I was not," I said, "before 'Dicie' cropped up in our family, so why should I try to trace it that far back?"

He just stood there grinning, looking down on me like somebody inspecting a Model A car. Every once in a while he and Wangero sent eye signals over my head.

"How do you pronounce this name?" I asked.

"You don't have to call me by it if you don't want to," said Wangero.

"Why shouldn't I?" I asked. "If that's what you want us to call you, we'll call you."

"I know it might sound awkward at first," said Wangero.

"I'll get used to it," I said. "Ream it out again."

Well, soon we got the name out of the way. Asalamalakim had a name twice as long and three times as hard. After I tripped over it two or three times he told me to just call him Hakim-a-barber. I wanted to ask him was he a barber, but I didn't really think he was, so I didn't ask.

"You must belong to those beef-cattle people down the road," I said. They said "Asalamalakim" when they met you, too, but they didn't shake hands. Always too busy: feeding the cattle, fixing the fences, putting up salt-lick shelters, throwing down hay. When the white folks poisoned some of the herd the men stayed up all night with rifles in their hands. I walked a mile and a half just to see the sight.

Hakim-a-barber said, "I accept some of their <u>doctrines</u>,

---

TAKE NOTES

Reading Check

Dee has changed her name. Circle her new name. Then write the reason she gives for changing her name.

_____

_____

_____

Reading Strategy

The long conversation on this page gives you a chance to **contrast the characters** of Maggie and Dee. How is Maggie's participation in the conversation different from Dee's?

_____

_____

_____

_____

_____

| Vocabulary Development: | **oppress** (uh PRES) *v.* keep down by cruel or unjust use of power or authority |
| | **doctrines** (DAHK trinz) *n.* religious beliefs or principles |

Contrast the characters of Maggie and Dee (Wangero) in the bracketed section. What is different about what they remember about their past?

_____

_____

_____

_____

_____

_____

_____

_____

_____

Literary Analysis

When Dee finishes wrapping the dasher, the narrator takes it into her hands. What is her **character's motivation**, or reason, for doing that?

_____

_____

_____

_____

_____

_____

_____

_____

_____

but farming and raising cattle is not my style." (They didn't tell me, and I didn't ask, whether Wangero (Dee) had really gone and married him.)

We sat down to eat and right away he said he didn't eat collards[3] and pork was unclean. Wangero, though, went on through the chitlins[4] and corn bread, the greens and everything else. She talked a blue streak over the sweet potatoes. Everything delighted her. Even the fact that we still used the benches her daddy made for the table when we couldn't afford to buy chairs.

"Oh, Mama!" she cried. Then turned to Hakim-a-barber. "I never knew how lovely these benches are. You can feel the rump prints," she said, running her hands underneath her and along the bench. Then she gave a sigh and her hand closed over Grandma Dee's butter dish. "That's it!" she said. "I knew there was something I wanted to ask you if I could have." She jumped up from the table and went over in the corner where the churn stood, the milk in it clabber by now. She looked at the churn and looked at it.

"This churn top is what I need," she said. "Didn't Uncle Buddy whittle it out of a tree you all used to have?"

"Yes," I said.

"Uh huh," she said happily. "And I want the dasher, too."

"Uncle Buddy whittle that, too?" asked the barber.

Dee (Wangero) looked up at me.

"Aunt Dee's first husband whittled the dash, " said Maggie so low you almost couldn't hear her. "His name was Henry, but they called him Stash."

"Maggie's brain is like an elephant's," Wangero said, laughing. "I can use the churn top as a centerpiece for the alcove table," she said, sliding a plate over the churn, "and I'll think of something artistic to do with the dasher."

When she finished wrapping the dasher the handle stuck out. I took it for a moment in my hands. You didn't even have to look close to see where hands pushing the dasher up and down to make butter had left a kind of sink in the wood. In fact, there were a lot of small sinks; you could see where thumbs and fingers had sunk into the wood. It was beautiful light yellow wood, from a tree that grew in the yard where Big Dee and Stash had lived.

After dinner Dee (Wangero) went to the trunk at the foot of my bed and started rifling through it. Maggie hung back in the kitchen over the dishpan. Out came Wangero with two quilts. They had been pieced by Grandma Dee and then Big Dee and me had hung them on the quilt frames on the front

---

3. **collards** (KAHL urdz) _n._ leaves of the collard plant, often referred to as "collard greens."

4. **chitlins** (CHIT lunz) _n._ chitterlings, a pork dish popular among southern African Americans.

porch and quilted them. One was in the Lone Star pattern. The other was Walk Around the Mountain. In both of them were scraps of dresses Grandma Dee had worn fifty and more years ago. Bits and pieces of Grandpa Jarrell's Paisley shirts. And one teeny faded blue piece, about the size of a penny matchbox, that was from Great Grandpa Ezra's uniform that he wore in the Civil War.

"Mama," Wangero said sweet as a bird. "Can I have these old quilts?"

I heard something fall in the kitchen, and a minute later the kitchen door slammed.

"Why don't you take one or two of the others?" I asked. "These old things was just done by me and Big Dee from some tops your grandma pieced before she died."

"No," said Wangero. "I don't want those. They are stitched around the borders by machine."

"That'll make them last better," I said.

"That's not the point," said Wangero. "These are all pieces of dresses Grandma used to wear. She did all this stitching by hand. Imagine!" She held the quilts securely in her arms, stroking them.

"Some of the pieces, like those lavender ones, come from old clothes her mother handed down to her," I said, moving up to touch the quilts. Dee (Wangero) moved back just enough so that I couldn't reach the quilts. They already belonged to her.

"Imagine!" she breathed again, clutching them closely to her bosom.

"The truth is," I said, "I promised to give them quilts to Maggie, for when she marries John Thomas."

She gasped like a bee had stung her.

"Maggie can't appreciate these quilts!" she said. "She'd probably be backward enough to put them to everyday use."

"I reckon she would," I said. "God knows I been saving 'em for long enough with nobody using 'em. I hope she will!" I didn't want to bring up how I had offered Dee (Wangero) a quilt when she went away to college. Then she had told me they were old-fashioned, out of style.

"But they're *priceless*!" she was saying now, furiously; for she has a temper. "Maggie would put them on the bed and in five years they'd be in rags. Less than that!"

"She can always make some more," I said. "Maggie knows how to quilt."

Dee (Wangero) looked at me with hatred. "You just will not understand. The point is these quilts, *these quilts*!"

"Well," I said, stumped. "What would *you* do with them?"

"Hang them," she said. As if that was the only thing you *could* do with quilts.

Reading Check

Circle the short paragraph that shows Dee (Wangero) asking her mother for the quilts. Why is her voice as "sweet as a bird"?

_____

_____

_____

_____

Reading Strategy

You have been learning about Maggie and Dee throughout this story. In the bracketed paragraph, **contrast the two characters**. What is the difference in the way each thinks about the old quilts?

_____

_____

_____

_____

_____

_____

Reread the bracketed paragraph. **Contrast the characters** of Maggie and Dee. How is Maggie's reaction to the quilts different from Dee's?

_____

_____

_____

_____

_____

_____

_____

_____

_____

In the underlined sentence, the narrator does something she has never done before. What is her **character's motivation** for taking the quilts away from Dee (Wangero) and giving them to Maggie?

_____

_____

_____

_____

_____

_____

_____

Maggie by now was standing in the door. I could almost hear the sound her feet made as they scraped over each other.

"She can have them, Mama," she said, like somebody used to never winning anything, or having anything reserved for her. "I can 'member Grandma Dee without the quilts."

I looked at her hard. She had filled her bottom lip with checkerberry snuff and it gave her face a kind of dopey, hangdog look. It was Grandma Dee and Big Dee who taught her how to quilt herself. She stood there with her scarred hands hidden in the folds of her skirt. She looked at her sister with something like fear but she wasn't mad at her. This was Maggie's portion. This was the way she knew God to work.

When I looked at her like that something hit me in the top of my head and ran down to the soles of my feet. Just like when I'm in church and the spirit of God touches me and I get happy and shout. I did something I never had done before: hugged Maggie to me, then dragged her on into the room, snatched the quilts out of Miss Wangero's hands and dumped them into Maggie's lap. Maggie just sat there on my bed with her mouth open.

"Take one or two of the others," I said to Dee.

But she turned without a word and went out to Hakim-a-barber.

"You just don't understand," she said, as Maggie and I came out to the car.

"What don't I understand?" I wanted to know.

"Your heritage," she said. And then she turned to Maggie, kissed her, and said, "You ought to try to make something of yourself, too, Maggie. It's really a new day for us. But from the way you and Mama still live you'd never know it."

She put on some sunglasses that hid everything above the tip of her nose and her chin.

Maggie smiled; maybe at the sunglasses. But a real smile, not scared. After we watched the car dust settle I asked Maggie to bring me a dip of snuff. And then the two of us sat there just enjoying, until it was time to go in the house and go to bed.

Reader's Response: Which character in this story do you sympathize with—the narrator, Dee, or Maggie? Why?

_____

_____

Thinking About the Skill: How did contrasting the characters of Maggie and Dee in this story help you understand the story better?

_____

_____

_____

Everyday Use

1. **Take a Position:** Should Dee's mother have given the quilts to Dee? Explain.

_____

_____

2. **Literary Analysis:** What seems to **motivate** Dee's interest in her heritage?

_____

_____

3. **Literary Analysis:** Use this chart to analyze the narrator's feelings.

Attitudes Toward Dee	Attitudes Toward Maggie

Evidence	Evidence

4. **Reading Strategy: Contrast** the two sisters. How has Dee learned about her heritage?

_____

_____

How has Maggie learned about her heritage?

_____

_____

BUILD SKILLS

The Woman Warrior

LITERARY ANALYSIS

Most **memoirs** are first-person nonfiction narratives that tell historically or personally significant events in which the writer was a participant or an eye-witness. The following excerpt from Kingston's memoir blends the historical and the personal:

> To while away time, she and her niece talked about the Chinese passengers. These new immigrants had it easy. On Ellis Island the people were thin after forty days at sea and had no fancy luggage.

Kingston includes details of culture and time period into an account of a memorable day in her life.

She uses the **limited third-person point of view** to tell the story. This story is related by a narrator who uses the pronoun *she* to describe herself. The unusual use of point of view helps to blur the line between fact and fiction.

READING STRATEGY

Look for **background information** on a book jacket, in an introduction, or in a footnote. Background information can help you fully appreciate a literary work. In this textbook for example, you can find background information from the author biography, the Build Skills page, and the Background. As you read, record the information you learn from these features in the chart.

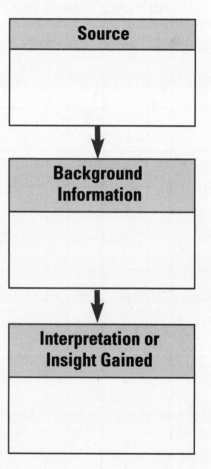

Source

Background Information

Interpretation or Insight Gained

The Woman Warrior

Maxine Hong Kingston

Summary Brave Orchid goes to the San Francisco airport. She waits for her sister to arrive from Hong Kong. The sisters have not seen each other in thirty years. Brave Orchid has brought her niece and two of her children. They wait at the airport for more than nine hours. Finally, the plane lands. Then, they must wait another four hours. Finally, the sisters greet each other. Neither can believe how old the other looks.

Note-taking Guide

Use this chart to find details in the memoir that show what Brave Orchid is like.

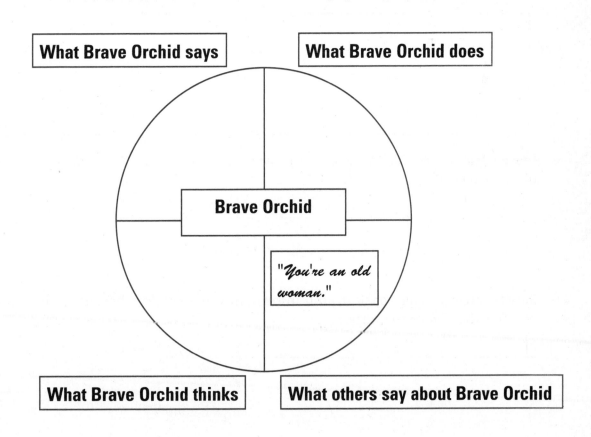

The Woman Warrior

1. **Infer:** What does Brave Orchid's attitude toward America and American culture seem to be? Give an example to support your answer.

   _____

   _____

2. **Draw Conclusions:** Why do the two sister call each other old and speak to each other as they do?

   _____

   _____

3. **Literary Analysis:** List three historical details and three personal details from the **memoir**. Write your information in this chart.

Historical Details	Personal Details

4. **Literary Analysis:** Whose impressions provide the **limited third-person point of view** of this excerpt?

   _____

   _____

5. **Reading Strategy:** Apply **background information** to explain where the family might go after they leave the airport.

   _____

   _____

Antojos

LITERARY ANALYSIS

Plot is the sequence of events in a literary work. In most stories or novels, the plot involves characters and a central conflict. Most plots follow a specific order, often referred to as the dramatic arc:

- **Exposition:** Introduces the basic situation.

- **Inciting incident:** Reveals the central conflict or struggle.

- **Development:** The conflict increases in intensity.

- **Climax:** The conflict reaches its most intense point.

- **Resolution, or Denouement:** The conflict is resolved, and the main character reveals some insight or a change.

Plot events that lead to the climax make up the **rising action**. The events that follow the climax are called the **falling action.**

READING STRATEGY

You can get more out of literature if you **identify with a character** who appears in the work. Think about what you and the character have in common. For example, as you read "Antojos," note qualities you share with the main character, Yolanda. List similarities in this chart.

Yolanda	Me
Background	
Personality	
Attitudes	
Motives	
Behavior	

Antojos

Julia Alvarez

Summary Yolanda's aunts warn her not to take a trip north by herself. She goes anyway. Yolanda stops to ask some boys to help her pick guavas. Yolanda finishes picking. By this time all the boys except Jose have left. She and Jose find that she has a flat tire. Jose goes for help. Yolanda stays alone with the car. Suddenly two men with machetes appear. Yolanda is frightened, but the men change her tire. They refuse any payment. Yolanda finds Jose walking on the road. He says that no one would help him because they did not believe his story.

Note-taking Guide

Use this chart to record key story events in the order in which they occur.

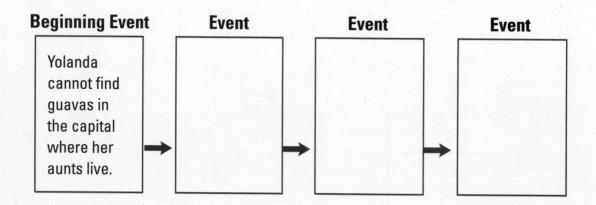

Beginning Event	Event	Event	Event
Yolanda cannot find guavas in the capital where her aunts live.			

Antojos

1. **Analyze:** Why does Yolanda pretend not to speak Spanish?

   _____

   _____

2. **Literary Analysis:** Use this chart to list events that are part of the **plot**.

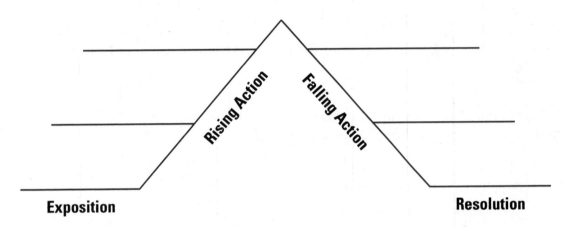

   Climax:

   Rising Action

   Falling Action

   Exposition

   Resolution

3. **Reading Strategy:** Yolanda loves her aunts, but feels they can be overprotective. Do you **identify** with these feelings? Explain.

   _____

   _____

   _____

4. **Reading Strategy:** Think about how you might feel if someone warns you that an activity is dangerous before you do it. How might her aunts' fears about traveling alone have affected Yolanda?

   _____

   _____

   _____

Who Burns for the Perfection of Paper • Most Satisfied by Snow • Hunger in New York City • What For

LITERARY ANALYSIS

Just as each person has a distinctive way of speaking, every poet has a unique **voice**, or literary personality. A poet's voice is based on word choice, tone, sound devices, rhyme (or its absence), pace, attitude, and even the patterns of vowels and consonants. Consider these examples:

- *Espada*: "No gloves: fingertips required / for the perfection of paper. . ."
- *Chang*: "Against my windows, / fog knows / what to do, too"

As you read these poems, note the distinctive voice each one reveals.

READING STRATEGY

Sometimes, you can understand a poem better if you briefly restate the main points in a summary. A **summary** should:

- include content from the beginning, middle, and end.
- be concise—no longer than a single sentence.
- convey the poem's essence.

Use this chart to create summaries for each poem.

Poem	Main Points (Beginning)	Main Points (Middle)	Main Points (End)		Summary
"Perfection of Paper"				→	
"Most Satisfied by Snow"				→	
"Hunger in New York City"				→	
"What For"				→	

Who Burns for the Perfection of Paper • Most Satisfied by Snow • Hunger in New York City • What For

Martín Espada, Diana Chang, Simon J. Ortiz, Garrett Hongo

Summaries In "Who Burns for the Perfection of Paper," the speaker describes the physical labor of an after-school job. In "Most Satisfied by Snow," the poet contrasts the empty spaces of fog with the physical presence of snow. In "Hunger in New York City," the speaker thinks about home, which is far from the city. In "What For," the speaker recalls his childhood in Hawaii and the power of his heritage.

Note-taking Guide

Use this chart to identify the subject and important details in each poem.

Poem	Subject of the Poem	Important details
"Who Burns for the Perfection of Paper"		
"Most Satisfied by Snow"		
"Hunger in New York City"		
"What For"		

Who Burns for the Perfection of Paper • Most Satisfied by Snow • Hunger in New York City • What For

1. **Interpret:** What key words in "Hunger in New York City" does the speaker use to paint a harsh picture of New York City?

   _____

2. **Literary Analysis:** Use the following chart to select the adjectives that best describe each poet's **voice.**

Adjectives: angry, thoughtful, regretful, yearning, respectful

Poet	Voice	Evidence
Espada		
Chang		
Ortiz		
Hongo		

3. **Literary Analysis:** A poet's voice may reflect his cultural background. In what way does the voice of Ortiz reflect his cultural background?

   _____

   _____

4. **Reading Strategy:** Write a **summary** of "Who Burns for the Perfection of Paper."

   _____

   _____

5. **Reading Strategy:** What poetic effects and meanings are lost in the summary you wrote?

   _____

   _____

Onomatopoeia • Coyote v. Acme • Loneliness . . . An American Malady • One Day, Now Broken in Two

LITERARY ANALYSIS

An **essay** is a short piece of nonfiction in which a writer expresses a personal view on a topic. The many types of essays include

- the **analytical essay,** which breaks down and interprets various elements of a topic.

- the **expository essay,** which explains a topic.

- the **satirical essay,** which uses irony, ridicule, parody, or sarcasm to comment on a topic.

- the **reflective essay,** which explores the meaning of a personal experience or pivotal event.

Look for the elements of these essays that will help you decide how to classify each one.

The greatest difference in the essays you are going to read is in their tone. **Tone** is the author's attitude toward the subject or audience. You can hear that tone—humorous, critical, or serious—in each writer's choice of words and details.

READING STRATEGY

A person who writes an essay offers a **line of reasoning** to convince readers that his or her ideas are sound. As you read these essays, identify the key points and note the reasons, facts, and examples that support them. Record each line of reasoning, and its evidence, in the chart.

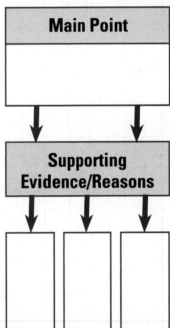

Onomatopoeia

William Safire

Summary "Onomatopoeia" is a humorous essay. In it, William Safire explains the meaning and history of the term *onomatopoeia*. Onomatopoeia refers to words that sound like the action they describe, such as *buzz* or *hiss*. He then talks about the word *zap*, which takes the concept one step further. It imitates an imaginary noise—the sound of a paralyzing ray gun.

Note-taking Guide

Use this word map to explore the meaning of *onomatopoeia*.

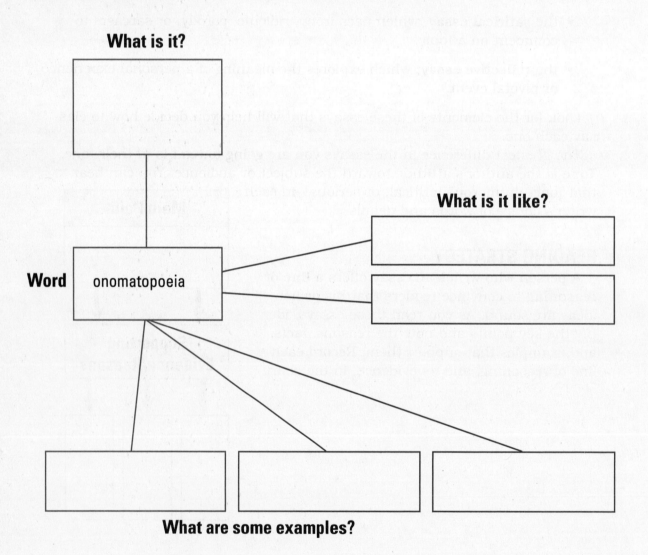

Coyote v. Acme

Ian Frazier

Summary "Coyote v. Acme" is the opening statement of a fictional lawsuit by Wile E. Coyote against the Acme Company. The lawsuit charges that Acme's faulty equipment caused Coyote to injure himself while chasing the Road Runner. These characters come from the Warner Brothers cartoon "Road Runner and Coyote," which made its debut in 1949.

Note-taking Guide

Use this diagram to draw conclusions about "Coyote v. Acme."

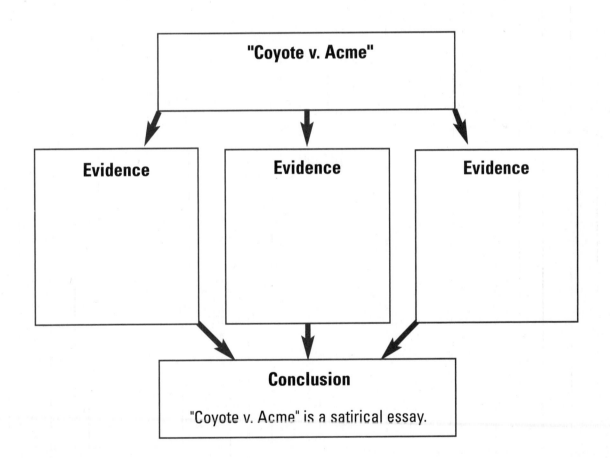

Loneliness . . . An American Malady

Carson McCullers

Summary In this essay, McCullers looks at the nature of loneliness. She concludes that humans need to fit in, but that American individualism makes people lonely.

Note-taking Guide Use this web to identify the nature of loneliness.

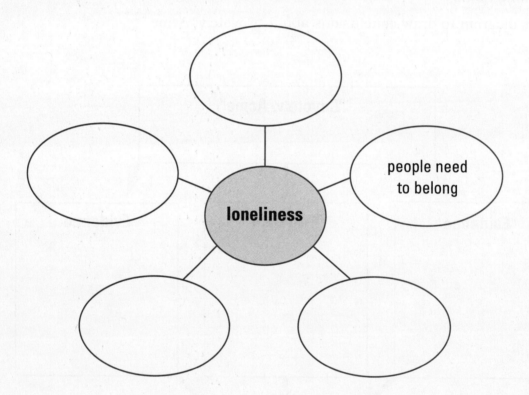

loneliness

people need to belong

One Day, Now Broken in Two

Anna Quindlen

Summary In this essay, Anna Quindlen examines the impact of the events of 9-11 on Americans. She concludes that Americans have become better people as a result of having to face this tragedy.

Note-taking Guide Use this chart to analyze the effects of 9-11.

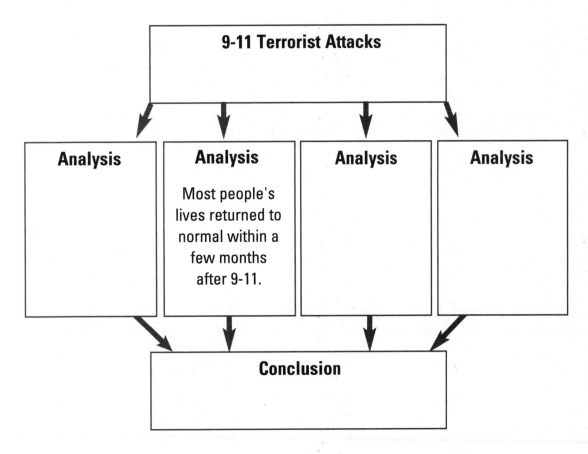

9-11 Terrorist Attacks

Analysis	Analysis	Analysis	Analysis
	Most people's lives returned to normal within a few months after 9-11.		

Conclusion

Onomatopoeia • Coyote v. Acme • Loneliness. . . An American Malady • One Day, Now Broken in Two

1. **Support:** Why does Wile E. Coyote continue to buy products from the Acme company despite some bad outcomes? Support your answer.

_____

_____

2. **Literary Analysis:** What type of **essay** you think "Onomatopoeia" is? Give examples from the essay to support your answer.

_____

_____

3. **Literary Analysis:** **Tone** is the author's attitude toward his or her subject. Use this chart to gather information about the author's tone. Choose one of the essays. Then, explain what attitude the author's tone reveals about his or her subject.

Summary of first paragraph	Words/details that indicate tone	Tone

4. **Reading Strategy:** "In Loneliness . . . An American Malady," what supporting information does McCullers give to show that love is a means of overcoming loneliness?

_____

_____

Straw Into Gold: The Metamorphosis of Everyday Things • For the Love of Books • Mother Tongue

LITERARY ANALYSIS

An essay is a short piece of nonfiction in which a writer expresses a personal view of a topic. In a **reflective essay**, the writer uses an informal tone to explore the meaning of a personal experience or critical event. In her essay, Rita Dove focuses on her love of books:

> . . . always, I have been passionate about books. . . . I loved to feel their heft in my hand.

An essay writer often explores an experience in order to arrive at a deeper understanding of its significance. To help you track each writer's reflections, complete the chart as you read.

Essay	Straw Into Gold	For the Love of Books	Mother Tongue
Experiences			
Feelings/ Significance			
Understanding			

READING STRATEGY

As a reader, your job is not only to get a writer's point, but also to decide what you think about it. When you **evaluate a writer's message**, you assess the validity of the writer's ideas and decide whether you agree or disagree with them. As you read these essays, identify and then evaluate the message of each writer.

Straw Into Gold: The Metamorphosis of the Everyday

Sandra Cisneros

Summary In this essay, Cisneros shares anecdotes about her childhood in a Mexican American family. The excerpt opens with a humorous story about the first time she tried to make tortillas. She compares this to spinning a roomful of straw into gold. She lists other things she has done that she didn't think she could. She describes her travels through Europe trying to be a writer. While telling her stories, Cisneros discusses her strengths that she did not even know she had.

Note-taking Guide

Use the web below to list experiences that shaped Sandra Cisneros's life and career.

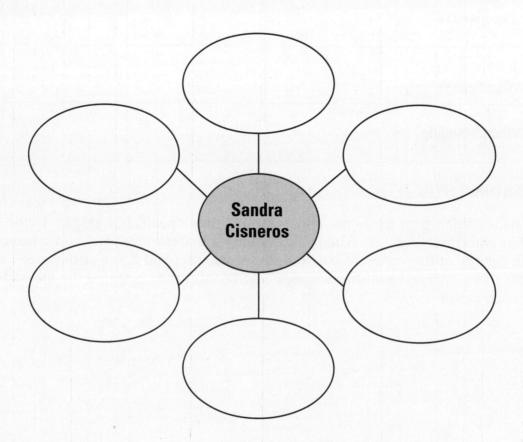

For the Love of Books

Rita Dove

Summary In "For the Love of Books," Rita Dove says her career as a writer came from her love of books. Since childhood, Dove loved to read books. She not only loved to read them, she loved holding them, smelling them, and turning their pages. She read everything from Shakespeare to science fiction. When her eleventh-grade English teacher took her to a book-signing, she realized writers were real people.

Note-taking Guide

Use the chart below to list experiences that influenced Rita Dove's life and career.

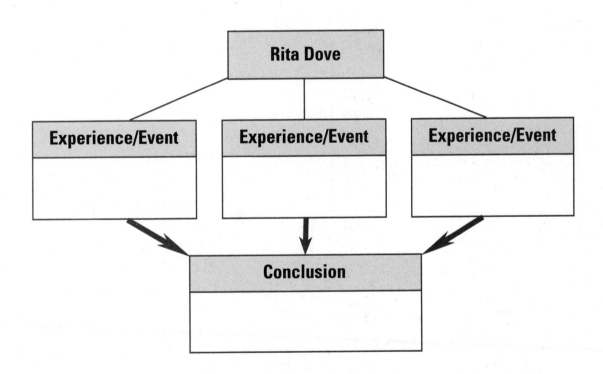

Mother Tongue

Amy Tan

Summary In "Mother Tongue," Amy Tan describes her mother as an intelligent and perceptive woman. However, her mother is regularly confronted by problems because of her non-standard English. Tan writes about the differences between the lessons she has learned from her mother with the English-speaking world's view of her mother. Tan explains that when she began to think of her mother as her reader, she found her voice as a writer.

Note-taking Guide

Use the following cluster diagram to take notes about Amy Tan's mother.

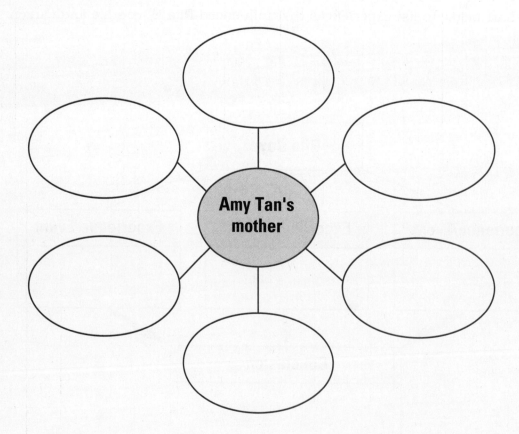

Mother Tongue

Amy Tan

Even people who speak the same language speak differently in different situations. In school, you use formal English that is grammatically correct. With your friends, you probably use slang and less formal English. At home you may have certain phrases or expressions that no one outside your family would understand. It's even more complicated when parents don't speak English well and their children speak English fluently. In this essay, Amy Tan tells how "all the Englishes" she grew up with made her a better writer.

I am not a scholar of English or literature. I cannot give you much more than personal opinions on the English language and its variations in this country or others.

I am a writer. And by that definition, I am someone who has always loved language. I am fascinated by language in daily life. I spend a great deal of my time thinking about the power of language—the way it can evoke an emotion, a visual image, a complex idea, or a simple truth. Language is the tool of my trade. And I use them all—all the Englishes I grew up with.

Recently, I was made keenly aware of the different Englishes I do use. I was giving a talk to a large group of people, the same talk I had already given to half a dozen other groups. The nature of the talk was about my writing, my life, and my book, *The Joy Luck Club.* The talk was going along well enough, until I remembered one major difference that made the whole talk sound wrong. My mother was in the room. And it was perhaps the first time she had heard me give a lengthy speech, using the kind of English I have never used with her. I was saying things like, "The intersection of memory upon imagination" and "There is an aspect of my fiction that relates to thus-and-thus"—a speech filled with carefully wrought grammatical phrases, burdened, it suddenly seemed to me, with nominalized forms, past perfect tenses, conditional phrases, all the forms of standard English that I had learned in school and through books, the forms of English I did not use at home with my mother.

Just last week, I was walking down the street with my mother, and I again found myself conscious of the English I was using, the English I do use with her. We were talking about the price of new and used furniture and I heard myself saying this: "Not waste money that way." My husband was with us as well, and he didn't notice any switch in my English. And then I realized why. It's because over the twenty years we've been together I've often used the same kind of English with him, and sometimes he even uses it with me. It has become our language of intimacy, a different sort of English that relates to family talk, the language I grew up with.

© Pearson Education, Inc., publishing as Pearson Prentice Hall.

Reading Check

The bracketed paragraph quotes Tan's mother exactly. That means the English may be hard to understand.

- Reread the paragraph slowly.
- Make notes in the paragraph to help you.
- Check the paragraph before it for information.

Then rewrite the paragraph in standard English on a separate piece of paper.

Literary Analysis

Because this essay is a **reflective essay**, or a short nonfiction writing in which a writer describes personal experiences, Tan shares her feelings about the way her mother speaks English.

1. How much of Tan's mother's English do Tan's friends understand?

_____

_____

_____

_____

2. How much of her mother's English does Tan herself understand?

_____

_____

_____

_____

So you'll have some idea of what this family talk I heard sounds like, I'll quote what my mother said during a recent conversation which I videotaped and then <u>transcribed</u>.

During this conversation, my mother was talking about a political gangster in Shanghai[1] who had the same last name as her family's, Du, and how the gangster in his early years wanted to be adopted by her family, which was rich by comparison. Later, the gangster became more powerful, far richer than my mother's family, and one day showed up at my mother's wedding to pay his respects. Here's what she said in part:

"Du Yusong having business like fruit stand. Like off the street kind. He is Du like Du Zong—but not Tsung-ming Island people. The local people call putong, the river east side, he belong to that side local people. That man want to ask Du Zong father take him in like become own family. Du Zong father wasn't look down on him, but didn't take seriously, until that man big like become a mafia. Now important person, very hard to inviting him. Chinese way, come only to show respect, don't stay for dinner. Respect for making big celebration, he shows up. Mean gives lots of respect. Chinese custom. Chinese social life that way. If too important won't have to stay too long. He come to my wedding. I didn't see, I heard it. I gone to boy's side, they have YMCA[2] dinner. Chinese age I was nineteen."

You should know that my mother's expressive command of English belies how much she actually understands. She reads the *Forbes*[3] report, listens to *Wall Street Week*,[4] converses daily with her stockbroker, reads all of Shirley MacLaine's[5] books with ease—all kinds of things I can't begin to understand. Yet some of my friends tell me they understand 50 percent of what my mother says. Some say they understand 80 to 90 percent. Some say they under-stand none of it, as if she were speaking pure Chinese. But to me, my mother's English is perfectly clear, perfectly natural. It's my mother tongue. Her language, as I hear it, is vivid, direct, full of observation and imagery. That was the language that helped shape the way I saw things, expressed things, made sense of the world.

Lately, I've been giving more thought to the kind of

Vocabulary Development

transcribed (tran SKRYBD) *v.* wrote or typed a copy of

---

1. **Shanghai** (shang HY) seaport in eastern China.
2. **YMCA** Young Men's Christian Association.
3. *Forbes* magazine of business and finance.
4. *Wall Street Week* weekly television program that reports business and investment news.
5. **Shirley MacLaine's** (MUHK laynz) Shirley MacLaine is an American actress who has written several books.

English my mother speaks. Like others, I have described it to people as "broken," or "fractured" English. But I wince when I say that. It has always bothered me that I can think of no way to describe it other than "broken," as if it were damaged and needed to be fixed, as if it lacked a certain wholeness and soundness. I've heard other terms used, "limited English," for example. But they seem just as bad, as if everything is limited, including people's perceptions of the limited English speaker.

I know this for a fact, because when I was growing up, my mother's "limited" English limited my perception of her. I was ashamed of her English. I believed that her English reflected the quality of what she had to say. That is, because she expressed them imperfectly her thoughts were imperfect. And I had plenty of <u>empirical</u> evidence to support me: the fact that people in department stores, at banks, and at restaurants did not take her seriously, did not give her good service, pretended not to understand her, or even acted as if they did not hear her.

My mother has long realized the limitations of her English as well. When I was fifteen, she used to have me call people on the phone to pretend I was she. In this guise, I was forced to ask for information or even to complain and yell at people who had been rude to her. One time it was a call to her stockbroker in New York. She had cashed out her small portfolio and it just so happened we were going to go to New York the next week, our very first trip outside California. I had to get on the phone and say in an adolescent voice that was not very convincing, "This is Mrs. Tan."

And my mother was standing in the back whispering loudly, "Why he don't send me check, already two weeks late. So mad he lie to me, losing me money."

And then I said in perfect English, "Yes, I'm getting rather concerned. You had agreed to send the check two weeks ago, but it hasn't arrived."

Then she began to talk more loudly. "What he want, I come to New York tell him front of his boss, you cheating me?" And I was trying to calm her down, make her be quiet, while telling the stockbroker, "I can't tolerate any more excuses. If I don't receive the check immediately, I am going to have to speak to your manager when I'm in New York next week." And sure enough, the following week there we were in front of this astonished stockbroker, and I was sitting there red-faced and quiet, and my mother, the real Mrs. Tan, was shouting at his boss in her impeccable broken English.

Vocabulary Development

empirical (em PIR i khul) *adj.* obtained from observation or experiment

---

TAKE NOTES

Reading Check

Underline the sentence that tells you how Tan felt about her mother's English when she was growing up. How did other people react to her mother's English?

_____

_____

_____

_____

Literary Analysis

This **reflective essay** describes Tan's personal experiences. Why does Tan's mother have Tan make phone calls for her?

_____

_____

_____

_____

_____

Short Story

What do you think it feels like for Mrs. Tan not to be able to make herself understood? How would you feel if people couldn't understand you?

_____

_____

_____

Mrs. Tan's limited English has serious consequences as well as amusing ones. What happens to her at the hospital?

_____

_____

_____

_____

_____

_____

When you read nonfiction, it is important to **evaluate a writer's message**. That means that you want to understand the writer's ideas, but you also want to decide whether you agree with those ideas. On this page, Tan says that the language spoken in her home affected her results on achievement tests, IQ tests, and SATs. Does Tan provide enough evidence for you to agree with this part of her message? Explain your answer.

_____

_____

_____

_____

_____

We used a similar routine just five days ago, for a situation that was far less humorous. My mother had gone to the hospital for an appointment, to find out about a benign brain tumor a CAT scan[6] had revealed a month ago. She said she had spoken very good English, her best English, no mistakes. Still, she said, the hospital did not apologize when they said they had lost the CAT scan and she had come for nothing. She said they did not seem to have any sympathy when she told them she was anxious to know the exact diagnosis, since her husband and son had both died of brain tumors. She said they would not give her any more information until the next time and she would have to make another appointment for that. So she said she would not leave until the doctor called her daughter. She wouldn't budge. And when the doctor finally called her daughter, me, who spoke in perfect English—lo and behold—we had assurances the CAT scan would be found, promises that a conference call on Monday would be held, and apologies for any suffering my mother had gone through for a most regrettable mistake.

I think my mother's English almost had an effect on limiting my possibilities in life as well. Sociologists and linguists probably will tell you that a person's developing language skills are more influenced by peers. But I do think that the language spoken in the family, especially in immigrant families which are more insular, plays a large role in shaping the language of the child. And I believe that it affected my results on achievement tests, IQ tests, and the SAT.[7] While my English skills were never judged as poor, compared to math, English could not be considered my strong suit. In grade school I did moderately well, getting perhaps B's, sometimes B-pluses, in English and scoring perhaps in the sixtieth or seventieth percentile on achievement tests. But those scores were not good enough to override the opinion that my true abilities lay in math and science, because in those areas I achieved A's and scored in the ninetieth percentile or higher.

This was understandable. Math is precise; there is only one correct answer. Whereas, for me at least, the answers on English tests were always a judgment call, a matter of opinion and personal experience. Those tests were constructed around items like fill-in-the-blank sentence completion, such as, "Even though Tom was _____, Mary thought he was _____." And the correct answer always seemed to be the most bland combinations of thoughts, for example, "Even though Tom was shy, Mary thought he was charming," with

---

Vocabulary Development

benign (bi NYN) *adj.* not injurious or malignant; not cancerous

---

6. **CAT scan** method used by doctors to diagnose brain disorders.
7. **SAT** Scholastic Aptitude Test; national college entrance exam.

the grammatical structure "even though" limiting the correct answer to some sort of <u>semantic</u> opposites, so you wouldn't get answers like, "Even though Tom was foolish, Mary thought he was ridiculous." Well, according to my mother, there were very few limitations as to what Tom could have been and what Mary might have thought of him. So I never did well on tests like that.

The same was true with word analogies, pairs of words in which you were supposed to find some sort of logical, semantic relationship—for example, "*Sunset* is to *nightfall* as _____ is to _____." And here you would be presented with a list of four possible pairs, one of which showed the same kind of relationship: *red* is to *stoplight, bus* is to *arrival, chills* is to *fever, yawn* is to *boring.* Well, I could never think that way. I knew what the tests were asking, but I could not block out of my mind the images already created by the first pair, "*sunset* is to *nightfall*"—and I would see a burst of colors against a darkening sky, the moon rising, the lowering of a curtain of stars. And all the other pairs of words—red, bus, stoplight, boring—just threw up a mass of confusing images, making it impossible for me to sort out something as logical as saying: "A sunset precedes nightfall" is the same as "a chill precedes a fever." The only way I would have gotten that answer right would have been to imagine an associative situation, for example, my being disobedient and staying out past sunset, catching a chill at night, which turns into feverish pneumonia as punishment, which indeed did happen to me.

I have been thinking about all this lately, about my mother's English, about achievement tests. Because lately I've been asked, as a writer, why there are not more Asian Americans represented in American literature. Why are there few Asian Americans enrolled in creative writing programs? Why do so many Chinese students go into engineering? Well, these are broad sociological questions I can't begin to answer. But I have noticed in surveys—in fact, just last week—that Asian students, as a whole, always do significantly better on math achievement tests than in English. And this makes me think that there are other Asian-American students whose English spoken in the home might also be described as "broken" or "limited." And perhaps they also have teachers who are steering them away from writing and into math and science, which is what happened to me.

Fortunately, I happen to be rebellious in nature and enjoy the challenge of disproving assumptions made about me. I became an English major my first year in college, after being enrolled as pre-med. I started writing nonfiction as a freelancer

---

TAKE NOTES

Literary Analysis

Throughout this **reflective essay,** Tan describes her personal experiences. What is her reaction to word analogies?

_____

_____

_____

_____

_____

_____

_____

_____

_____

_____

_____

Reading Check

Underline the section of the bracketed paragraph that explains why Tan has been thinking about her mother's English and her own achievement tests.

Vocabulary Development

semantic (suh MAN tik) *adj.* pertaining to meaning in language

Evaluate the writer's message about envisioning, or imagining, a reader for her writing. Do you agree with her ideas about who her reader should be? Why or why not?

_____

_____

_____

_____

_____

_____

_____

Reading Check

Circle the praise that Tan's mother gives her for her first book.

the week after I was told by my former boss that writing was my worst skill and I should hone my talents toward account management.

But it wasn't until 1985 that I finally began to write fiction. And at first I wrote using what I thought to be wittily crafted sentences, sentences that would finally prove I had mastery over the English language. Here's an example from the first draft of a story that later made its way into *The Joy Luck Club*, but without this line: "That was my mental quandary in its nascent state." A terrible line, which I can barely pronounce.

Fortunately, for reasons I won't get into today, I later decided I should envision a reader for the stories I would write. And the reader I decided upon was my mother, because these were stories about mothers. So with this reader in mind—and in fact she did read my early drafts—I began to write stories using all the Englishes I grew up with: the English I spoke to my mother, which for lack of a better term might be described as "simple"; the English she used with me, which for lack of a better term might be described as "broken"; my translation of her Chinese, which could certainly be described as "watered down"; and what I imagined to be her translation of her Chinese if she could speak in perfect English, her internal language, and for that I sought to preserve the essence, but neither an English nor a Chinese structure. I wanted to capture what language ability tests can never reveal: her intent, her passion, her imagery, the rhythms of her speech and the nature of her thoughts.

Apart from what any critic had to say about my writing, I knew I had succeeded where it counted when my mother finished reading my book and gave me her verdict: "So easy to read."

Vocabulary Development

quandary (KWAHN duh ree) *n.* state of uncertainty; dilemma
nascent (NAYS uhnt) *adj.* coming into existence; emerging

Reader's Response: What was the most interesting part of this essay for you? Why did you find it so interesting?

_____

_____

Thinking About the Skill: How did evaluating the writer's message help you understand Tan's points in this reflective essay?

_____

_____

_____

Straw Into Gold: The Metamorphosis of the Everyday • For the Love of Books • Mother Tongue

1. **Analyze:** When Cisneros left home for a reason other than getting married, she broke an important taboo. Who was the enemy in the "quiet war" that she had begun? Explain.

   _____

   _____

2. **Infer:** When Tan gives a speech to a crowd that includes her mother, she realizes that she is using a kind of complex standard English that she would never use at home with her mother. What circumstances account for Tan's having developed more than one "English."

   _____

3. **Literary Analysis:** Based on her **reflective essay,** how do you think Rita Dove feels about her childhood?

   _____

   _____

4. **Reading Strategy:** Use this chart to **evaluate each author's message.** For each, list their message, their supporting reasons, and then tell whether you agree with their message.

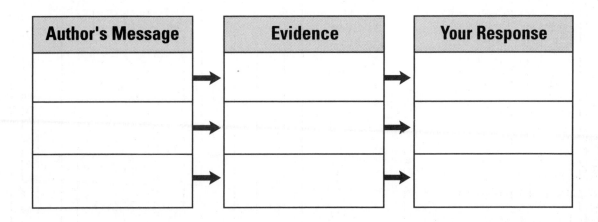

Author's Message	Evidence	Your Response

The Rockpile

LITERARY ANALYSIS

The **setting** of a story is the time and place in which events occur. The setting may include details about the weather, physical features of the landscape, and other elements of an environment. "The Rockpile" is set in Harlem, a section of New York City, during the 1930s. Life in that place and time was influenced by the difficult economic and social realities that people faced. As you read, think about how the setting helps to shape the characters' personalities and actions.

READING STRATEGY

In this story, a child's disobedience reveals a complicated family dynamic. You will understand the characters in the story better if you **identify cause-and-effect** relationships among them. Use this chart to determine the motives for characters' actions and their effects on others.

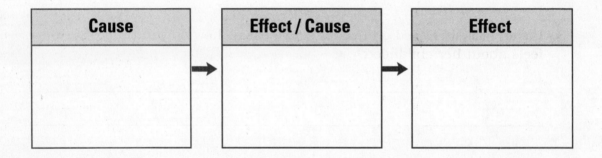

Cause	Effect / Cause	Effect

The Rockpile

James Baldwin

Summary This story is about a boy who disobeys his mother. When he is hurt, his father, a pastor, blames his older stepbrother for not watching him. His mother does not blame the older boy. The conflict between the parents shows that each parent has different expectations for each of the boys.

Note-taking Guide

Use this chart to record the reasons why the neighborhood is dangerous.

The danger	Why it is dangerous
There is a rockpile in the neighborhood.	

The Rockpile

1. **Deduce:** Why is the street "forbidden"?

   _____

   _____

2. **Literary Analysis:** Name three details that describe the **setting** of the neighborhood.

   _____

   _____

   _____

3. **Literary Analysis:** Use the chart below to analyze the rockpile and to tell what it symbolizes, or represents.

The Rockpile			What It Means
What people say about it	Events linked with it	Details used to describe it	

4. **Reading Strategy:** What **causes** John to avoid telling his mother that Roy went to the rockpile?

   _____

   _____

from Hiroshima • Losses • The Death of the Ball Turret Gunner

LITERARY ANALYSIS

The **theme** is the central idea that a writer conveys in a work of literature. Most often a theme is **implied**, or revealed indirectly, through the writer's choice of details, use of literary devices, and portrayal of characters and events. These selections all offer implied themes about war.

READING STRATEGY

When the theme of a literary work is conveyed indirectly, it is up to the reader to **draw inferences**, or conclusions, by looking closely at the writer's choice of details, events, and characters. As you read, use this chart to note important details that point to an implied theme.

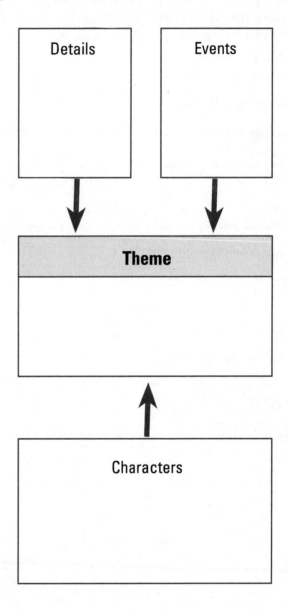

from Hiroshima

John Hersey

Summary On August 6, 1945, at 8:15 in the morning, the United States dropped an atomic bomb on Hiroshima, Japan. More than 100,000 people died as a result of the bombing. Miss Toshiko Sasaki, Dr. Masakazu Fujii, Mrs. Hatsuyo Nakamura, and Mr. Kiyoshi Tanimoto survived. This excerpt tells part of their story.

Note-taking Guide

Use this chart to record what each person was doing when the bomb exploded.

	What were they doing?	How did they experience the blast?
Mr. Kiyoshi Tanimoto		
Mrs. Hatsuyo Nakamura		
Dr. Masakazu Fujii		
Miss Toshiko Sasaki		

Losses • The Death of the Ball Turret Gunner

Randall Jarrell

Summaries: In **"Losses,"** the speaker talks about the sacrifice of human life in war. According to the speaker, death is almost casual and routine. In **"The Death of the Ball Turret Gunner,"** the speaker uses images to show how deadly war is. The powerful final line shows the violence and finality of death in war.

Note-taking Guide:

As you read, use this chart to list striking words and phrases from the two poems.

Poem	Striking words	Striking phrases
"Losses"		
"The Death of the Ball Turret Gunner"		

from Hiroshima • Losses • The Death of the Ball Turret Gunner

1. **Analyze:** Why does Hersey spend so much time describing Hiroshima before the blast?

   _____

   _____

2. **Literary Analysis:** The **implied theme** in *Hiroshima* is the destructive power of the atomic bomb. Which details in the text give clues to the implied theme?

   _____

   _____

3. **Literary Analysis:** Use the diagram below to show similarities and differences in Hersey's and Jarrell's portrayal of those killed during war.

   Hersey   **Jarrell**

4. **Reading Strategy:** How does this line from *Hiroshima* communicate the theme?

   . . . the night before the bomb was dropped, an announcer . . . advised the population . . . to evacuate to their designated 'safe areas.'

   _____

   _____

5. **Reading Strategy:** In "Losses," the speaker says, "We died like aunts or pets or foreigners." **Draw inferences** from this line. What does it suggest about the theme?

   _____

   _____

Mirror • In a Classroom • The Explorer • Frederick Douglass • Runagate Runagate

LITERARY ANALYSIS

A poem's **theme** is its central idea. Poets suggest themes through the **connotations**, or emotional associations, of the words and images they choose. For example, in these lines about aging by Sylvia Plath, the words *drowned* and *terrible* have negative associations:

> In me she has drowned a young girl, and in me an old woman
> Rises toward her day after day, like a terrible fish.

A reader could then infer that the theme is connected with the fear of growing old. As you read these poems, find clues to the themes in words and images that trigger either negative or positive responses.

READING STRATEGY

In most poems, the central message is not directly stated. It is up to you to **interpret** it by looking for an underlying meaning in the words and images. Consider the connotations of the words, and then try to determine what common thread ties them together. Use this chart to record words and images that will help you interpret the theme of a poem.

Poem	Words and Images	Potential Meaning
Mirror		
In a Classroom		
The Explorer		
Frederick Douglass		
Runagate Runagate		

Mirror • In a Classroom • The Explorer • Frederick Douglass • Runagate Runagate

Sylvia Plath, Adrienne Rich, Gwendolyn Brooks, Robert Hayden

Summaries "Mirror" shows a woman's feelings about growing older, as reflected by a mirror. In "In a Classroom," the speaker describes the reaction of her students to a poetry lesson. The speaker in "The Explorer" searches for peace in a noisy apartment building. In "Frederick Douglass," the speaker longs for true freedom that will honor Douglass, one of the leading voices opposing slavery. "Runagate Runagate" uses rhythm and detail to bring the voices, feelings, risks, and rewards of the Underground Railroad to the reader. The Underground Railroad was a route of safe houses operated by people opposed to slavery who helped slaves escape to the North before the Civil War.

Note-taking Guide

Sometimes rewriting a line of poetry will help you to understand its meaning. Use this chart to rewrite one line from each poem in your own words.

Poem	Line	Rewritten Line
Mirror		
In a Classroom		
The Explorer		
Frederick Douglass		
Runagate Runagate		

Mirror • In a Classroom • The Explorer • Frederick Douglass • Runagate Runagate

1. **Infer:** In "Mirror," who is the speaker? How do you know? _____

_____

2. **Literary Analysis:** In "Runagate Runagate," the speaker uses sensory images to express the **theme** that a journey on the Underground Railroad was full of risk, danger, reward, and emotion. Use this chart to list images that support this theme by appealing to the five senses.

Sight	Hearing	Smell	Touch	Taste

3. **Literary Analysis:** In "Frederick Douglass," Hayden describes Frederick Douglass as "visioning a world where none is lonely, none hunted." Based on the **connotations** of these words, what would you say is the theme of the poem?

_____

_____

4. **Literary Analysis:** How can the theme of "Frederick Douglass" be seen as a criticism of society?

_____

_____

5. **Reading Strategy:** Interpret the meaning of the word *swallow* in the poem, "Mirror." How does this word contribute to the poem's message?

_____

_____

Inaugural Address • *from* Letter from Birmingham City Jail

LITERARY ANALYSIS

Parallelism is the repetition of words, phrases, or sentences that have the same grammatical structure or the same meaning. Also known as **parallel structure**, it is a device used in poetry, speeches, and other types of writing. Parallel structure is used to balance related ideas, to stress contrasting ones, or to create a memorable rhythm.

> ...the torch has been passed to a new generation of Americans—born in this century, <u>tempered</u> by war, <u>disciplined</u> by a hard and bitter peace, <u>proud</u> of our ancient heritage...

READING STRATEGY

The **main ideas** in a selection are the key points that the writer wants to convey. The **supporting details** consist of the facts, examples, or reasons that support these ideas. Use this chart to identify main ideas and supporting details as you read these selections.

	Main Idea	Facts, Examples, and Reasons
Inaugural Address		
Letter from Birmingham City Jail		

Inaugural Address

John F. Kennedy

Summary An inaugural address is the speech a president gives when he takes office. John F. Kennedy delivered his inaugural address in 1961. Tensions were high between the United States and the Soviet Union. The possibility of a nuclear war was real. In his speech, Kennedy spoke to the fears of both the nation and the world. He reminded Americans that they had inherited a responsibility to defend freedom. The new President urged Americans to serve their country with the famous words, "Ask not what your country can do for you—ask what you can do for your country." Then, he called on the citizens of the world to work together for the freedom of people everywhere

Note-taking Guide

In his speech, Kennedy calls on many groups of people to take action. In the chart, write what he asks each group to do.

	Actions Kennedy Requests
Enemies of the U.S.	
American Citizens	
People of Other Nations	

Letter from Birmingham City Jail

Martin Luther King, Jr.

Summary Martin Luther King, Jr., was a civil rights leader. In April 1963, he was arrested for protesting segregation in Birmingham, Alabama. While in jail, King read a newspaper article that was critical of the civil rights movement. He responded to the article in this letter. In it, King criticized the police for their actions against protestors. He celebrated the real heroes who had the courage to take a stand against segregation. He also expressed confidence that the struggle for freedom would have a positive outcome.

Note-taking Guide

Answer the questions in the chart to keep track of the ideas King expresses in his letter.

Question	Answer from King's Letter
Why will African Americans win freedom?	
Why doesn't King agree that the police deserve praise?	
How does King feel about the "sit-inners" and demonstrators?	

Inaugural Address •
from Letter from Birmingham City Jail

1. **Respond:** If you had heard Kennedy's speech, which of his ideas would have sparked the strongest response in you? Explain.

   _____

   _____

2. **Evaluate:** Do you think the final paragraph of King's letter is an effective conclusion? Why or why not?

   _____

   _____

3. **Literary Analysis:** Reread the nineteenth paragraph in Kennedy's inaugural that begins "And if a beachhead of cooperation. . . ." Using this chart, identify the **parallel** words and phrases.

Parallel Words	Parallel Phrases

4. **Reading Strategy:** What **details** support Kennedy's **main idea** that the task of defending freedom should be welcomed?

   _____

   _____

5. **Reading Strategy:** According to King, who will eventually be recognized as the "real heroes" of the South?

   _____

   _____

For My Children • Bidwell Ghost • Camouflaging the Chimera

LITERARY ANALYSIS

Lyric poetry is melodic poetry that expresses the observations and feelings of a single speaker. Lyric poems were originally meant to be sung. Though rarely set to music today, lyric poems are still brief and melodic. Unlike narrative poems that tell stories, lyric poems focus on producing a single effect. In these lines from "Bidwell Ghost," for example, the speaker recalls vivid impressions of a fiery tragedy.

> It has been twenty years
> since her house surged and burst in the dark trees

As you read each poem, use this chart to record the words and phrases that contribute to a single unifying effect.

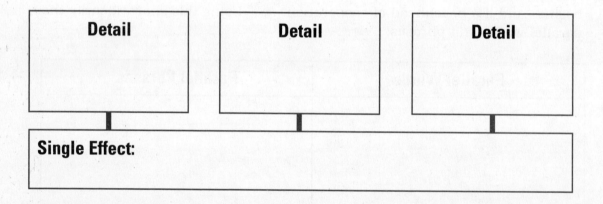

READING STRATEGY

Like prose, many poems are written in sentences. They are also written in lines, but poets do not always complete sentences at the end of a line. Instead, a sentence may extend for several lines and then end in the middle of a line so that the poet can keep a rhythm and rhyme scheme. To understand the meaning of a poem, **read in sentences**. Notice the punctuation. Do not make a full stop at the end of a line unless there is a period, colon, semicolon, or dash.

PREVIEW

For My Children •
Bidwell Ghost •
Camouflaging the Chimera

Colleen McElroy • Louise Erdrich • Yusef Komunyakaa

Summaries In "For My Children," the speaker tells of her memories of the stories of her ancestors. She looks for connections between these stories and the realities of present-day life. In "Bidwell Ghost," the speaker describes a ghost that "waits by the road." In "Camouflaging the Chimera," the poet describes his experiences during the Vietnam War. He tells how soldiers used branches, mud, and grass to camouflage themselves. He relates his memories of being in combat.

Note-taking Guide

Use this chart to record information about the memory of the past in each poem.

	Memory of the Past	**Explanation**
"For My Children"		
"Bidwell Ghost"		
"Camouflaging the Chimera"		

For My Children • Bidwell Ghost • Camouflaging the Chimera

1. **Infer:** In "For My Children," the speaker is addressing her children. What is the speaker's reason for addressing the poem to them?

   _____

   _____

2. **Contrast:** In what way are the ghosts in Komunyakaa's poem different from the ghost in Erdrich's poem?

   _____

   _____

3. **Literary Analysis:** Describe in your own words the thoughts that the speaker expresses in the opening stanza of "For My Children."

   _____

   _____

4. **Reading Strategy:** Why do you think Erdrich chose to punctuate her poem as she did?

   _____

   _____

5. **Reading Strategy:** Using this chart, identify the figurative language in the last stanza of "For My Children."

Sentence 1	Sentence 2	Sentence 3	Interpretation

The Crucible, Act I

LITERARY ANALYSIS

The written script of a drama is made up of dialogue and stage directions:

- **Dialogue** refers to the words characters speak. Dialogue both advances the plot and reveals the characters' personalities and backgrounds.

- **Stage directions** usually indicate where a scene takes place, what it should look like, and how the characters should move and speak. Stage directions are usually set in italic type to distinguish them from dialogue.

As you read Act I of *The Crucible*, look for information about characters and events in the stage directions and the dialogue.

READING STRATEGY

Like people in real life, characters in plays are not always what they seem. Often, we must **question the characters' motives**—their reasons for behaving as they do. Fear, greed, guilt, love, loyalty, and revenge are some of the driving forces behind human behavior. Use this chart to examine the motives of at least three characters in Act I

Character	Words and Actions	Motive

The Crucible, Act I

Arthur Miller

Summary It is 1692 in Salem, Massachusetts. The Reverend Parris is praying for his daughter Betty, who is ill. He says he saw his niece Abigail and Betty dancing in the woods. He asks Abigail why no one will hire her as a mother's helper since Mrs. Proctor fired her. Mary Warren comes in and says the village is accusing the girls of witchcraft. John Proctor comes for Mary and sends her back to his farm, where she works. Parris and all the girls but Abigail leave. Betty begins to wail. Others rush in, including kindly Rebecca Nurse, who calms Betty. Reverend Hale, an expert in witchcraft, enters. He questions Abigail, and she shifts the blame to Tituba, Reverend Parris's slave. Frightened, Tituba says that she saw Sarah Good and Goody Osburn with the Devil. Abby cries out other names, and soon all the girls are crying out names.

Note-taking Guide

Use this chart to record information about the setting, characters, and social or historical background of the play.

Setting	Characters	Background

The Crucible, Act I

1. **Infer:** What seems to be the main **motive** for Reverend Parris's concern about the girls' behavior in the forest?

_____

_____

_____

2. **Literary Analysis:** Use this chart to analyze the character of Abigail Williams. To respond, combine details from her **dialogue** with Miller's descriptions of her in the **stage directions**.

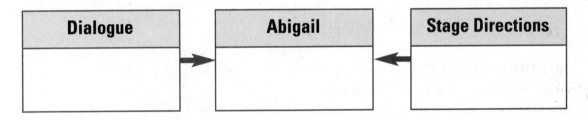

Dialogue		Abigail		Stage Directions
	→		←	

3. **Reading Strategy:** What do Reverend Parris's comments and actions reveal about his motivation?

_____

_____

_____

4. **Reading Strategy:** What do Abigail's actions in the forest and her threat to the girls reveal about her motives?

_____

_____

_____

The Crucible, Act II

LITERARY ANALYSIS

An **allusion** is a brief reference within a work to something outside the work. An allusion usually refers to one of the following:

- Another literary work

- A well-known person

- A place

- A historical event

The Crucible makes many biblical allusions. For example, Act I contains a reference to the New Jerusalem, a term for the holy city of heaven. Use this chart to record biblical allusions in Act II.

READING STRATEGY

When you **read a drama** instead of watching the action and staging, you read the stage directions. Stage directions often interrupt the dialogue, but they provide critical information. As you read, pay close attention to the stage directions to understand the thoughts, attitudes, and behavior of the characters.

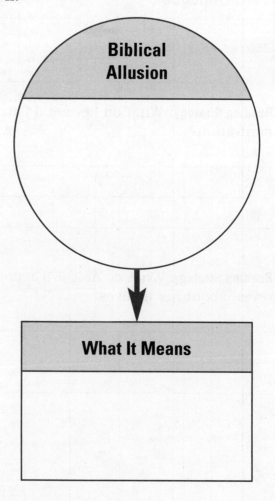

Biblical Allusion

What It Means

The Crucible, Act II

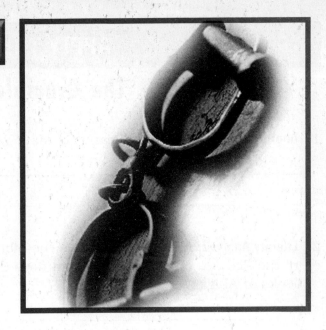

Summary Act II opens in the Proctor home, eight days later. Elizabeth Proctor says fourteen people have been arrested for witchcraft, based on what Abigail and the other girls said. She urges John to testify that the girls are frauds. They quarrel over his previous affair with Abigail. Mary, back from court, gives Elizabeth a small doll. Mary says those who confess will not be hanged. She says that Elizabeth's name has been mentioned. Elizabeth says she is sure that Abigail wants her dead. Hale appears at the door. To test John, Hale asks him to list the Ten Commandments. Ironically, John forgets the one about adultery. Then, two men burst in. They say their wives have been arrested. The marshal arrives and arrests Elizabeth. Over John's protests, she is taken away in chains.

Note-taking Guide

Use this chart to record information that you learn about characters in Act II from stage directions.

Character	Stage Direction	What It Says About the Character

The Crucible, Act II

1. **Interpret:** What is the significance of Mary Warren's gift to Elizabeth Proctor?

   _____

   _____

2. **Literary Analysis:** A footnote explains the biblical **allusion** to Moses and the parting of the Red Sea on page 1293. What does the allusion suggest about how the crowd looks at Abigail?

   _____

   _____

3. **Literary Analysis:** What does John Proctor's allusion to Pontius Pilate on page 1309 imply about the witchcraft proceedings in Salem?

   _____

   _____

4. **Reading Strategy:** Using this chart, cite three examples of dialogue in which a character's attitudes would have been unclear to you if you had not **read** the stage directions.

Dialogue	Attitude Revealed in Stage Direction

5. **Reading Strategy:** In addition to characters' attitudes, what other significant information do the stage directions in Act II reveal to you?

   _____

   _____

The Crucible, Act III

LITERARY ANALYSIS

Irony involves a contrast between what is stated and what is meant, or between what is expected to happen and what actually happens.

- In **dramatic irony**, there is a contradiction between what a character thinks and what the audience knows to be true.

- In **verbal irony**, a character says one thing but means something quite different.

Look for both forms of irony as you read Act III.

READING STRATEGY

The introduction of many characters in a drama can become confusing. It may be helpful to **categorize the characters**. One way you can categorize, or classify, characters in *The Crucible* is by the roles they play in the community. Use this chart to identify the characters and their positions in Salem Village.

Category	Names of characters in category
Court Supporters	
Court Officers	
Ministers and Judges	
The Accused	
Court Witness	
Court Opponents	

The Crucible, Act III

Arthur Miller

Summary Act III opens with Giles Corey pleading for his wife's life. Then, Francis Nurse says the girls are lying. Proctor leads in a terrified Mary. Mary admits that she never saw any spirits. Danforth tells John that Elizabeth is pregnant. He says that she will not be executed until after the baby is born. Abigail swears that Mary is lying. To stop Abigail, John admits his infidelity. Elizabeth is brought in to back up John's claim. To protect John, she lies, so John is not believed. Abigail begins pretending that Mary's spirit is bewitching her. Mary hysterically takes back her confession. John is arrested. Hale condemns the court and leaves.

Note-taking Guide

As you read, use this diagram to track the events in Act III.

Beginning Event	Event	Event	Event	Event	Final Outcome
Mary Warren confesses to lying					

The Crucible, Act III

1. **Apply:** Imagine that Elizabeth Proctor had told Danforth the truth. In what way might the outcome of the trials have been different?

   _____

   _____

2. **Literary Analysis:** Use this chart to list three examples of **dramatic** and **verbal irony** from Act III. Identify the type of irony and explain what each speaker really means.

Passage	Type of Irony	What the Speaker Means

3. **Literary Analysis:** Mary Warren says, "I—have no power," when she is questioned in front of Abigail Williams. What is ironic about her statement?

   _____

   _____

4. **Reading Strategy:** Which characters would you **categorize**, or classify, as static (unchanging)? Explain.

   _____

   _____

5. **Reading Strategy:** Which characters would you categorize, or classify, as dynamic (changing or growing)? Explain.

   _____

   _____

The Crucible, Act IV

LITERARY ANALYSIS

A **theme** is the central idea or insight into life that a writer strives to convey in a work of literature. Like many longer works, *The Crucible* has several themes. One of them is that fear and suspicion are infectious and can turn into mass hysteria. Miller also touches upon the destructive power of guilt, revenge, and the failure of a judicial system fueled by ideology instead of justice. As you read Act IV, use this chart to consider these and other themes that Miller conveys.

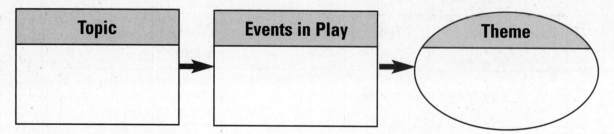

An **extended metaphor** is a comparison that develops throughout the course of a literary work. Miller's imagery of the seventeenth-century witch hunt in Salem builds a comparison to the McCarthy hearings in the 1950s in America. Notice Miller's ability to explore the events of his own era within the parallel context of the Salem witchcraft trials.

READING STRATEGY

The parallel between the events in Salem, as Miller depicts them, and ongoing events in Congress at the time Miller wrote the play are clear. As you read Act IV, think about what themes or messages Miller was conveying that specifically related to contemporary events.

The Crucible, Act IV

Arthur Miller

Summary Act IV opens in the Salem jail. Danforth and Hathorne enter. Parris enters and tells the judges that Abigail and Mercy Lewis have stolen his money and run away. Parris, hoping that John or Rebecca will confess, asks for a postponement of their hangings. Danforth refuses. Hale enters to ask Danforth to pardon the condemned. Elizabeth is brought in. Hale asks her to urge John to confess. John is brought in and the couple is left alone. They express their love, but Elizabeth refuses to advise John about whether he should confess. John decides to confess but refuses to name others. He signs the confession but will not give it to Danforth. In a fury, he rips the paper, crying that he will not destroy his good name. He is taken away to be hanged.

Note-taking Guide

Use this diagram to record themes, or central ideas, of *The Crucible*.

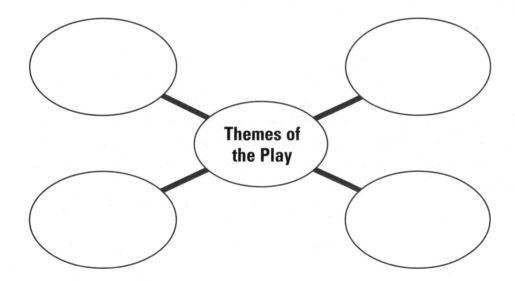

The Crucible, Act IV

1. **Apply:** Why does Elizabeth say that her husband has "his goodness" as he is about to be hanged?

   _____

   _____

2. **Literary Analysis:** Use evidence from the play to show how Arthur Miller conveys the **theme** that fear and suspicion are infectious and can produce a mass hysteria that destroys public order and rationality.

   _____

   _____

3. **Literary Analysis:** Use this chart to cite examples from the play that show how ideas, such as witchcraft and "the work of the Devil," function in *The Crucible* as extended metaphors for Communism.

Passage from the Text	How It Relates to Communism

4. **Reading Strategy:** Based on the play's details, what criticisms might Miller be making about the way McCarthy's Senate committee dealt with those it questioned and those who criticized it?

   _____

   _____

5. **Reading Strategy:** What does the play suggest about the motives behind Senator Joseph McCarthy's political "witch hunts"? Explain.

   _____

   _____

CRITICAL REVIEWS

About Critical Reviews

A **critical review** is a piece of writing that analyzes and evaluates a work of literature, art, or culture. Critical reviews usually include:

- a brief summary of the work
- strong opinions
- evidence and reasons that support the opinions

The purpose of a critical review is to persuade readers to accept the reviewer's opinions. Effective critical reviews have strong arguments and powerful, persuasive language.

Reading Strategy

Comparing and Contrasting Critical Reviews Reviewers often have different opinions about the same work. If possible, read several critical reviews on the same subject. Look for points of agreement and disagreement. **Comparing and contrasting critical reviews** can help you make your own decisions. Both Brooks Atkinson and Howard Kissel reviewed *The Crucible*. To compare and contrast their reviews, complete the chart below.

Critical Reviews		
Critic	Brooks Atkinson	Howard Kissel
Script		
Leading Actors/ Actresses		
Director, Sets, Costumes, Lighting		
Overall Evaluation (+ or −)		

The New York Times

January 23, 1953

The Crucible

By Brooks Atkinson

Atkinson begins by presenting his overall opinion of both the play and the performance. He then provides historical content about the play's subject matter.

Arthur Miller has written another powerful play. *The Crucible,* it is called, and it opened at the Martin Beck last evening in an equally powerful performance. Riffling back the pages of American history, he has written the drama of the witch trials and hangings in Salem in 1692. Neither Mr. Miller nor his audiences are unaware of certain similarities between the perversions of justice then and today.

But Mr. Miller is not pleading a cause in dramatic form. For *The Crucible,* despite its current implications, is a self-contained play about a terrible period in American history. Silly accusations of witchcraft by some mischievous girls in Puritan dress gradually take possession of Salem. Before the play is over good people of pious nature and responsible temper are condemning other good people to the gallows.

This paragraph provides a brief plot summary.

Having a sure instinct for dramatic form, Mr. Miller goes bluntly to essential situations. John Proctor and his wife, farm people, are the central characters of the play. At first the idea that Goodie Proctor is a witch is only an absurd rumor. But *The Crucible* carries the Proctors through the whole ordeal—first vague suspicion, then the arrest, the implacable, highly wrought trial in the church vestry, the final opportunity for John Proctor to save his neck by confessing to something he knows is a lie, and finally the baleful roll of the drums at the foot of the gallows.

Atkinson argues that *The Crucible* is not as good as one of Miller's previous plays.

Although *The Crucible* is a powerful drama, it stands second to *Death of a Salesman* as a work of art. Mr. Miller has had more trouble with this one, perhaps because he is too conscious of its implications. The literary style is cruder. . . .

It may be that Mr. Miller . . . has permitted himself to be concerned more with the technique of the witch hunt than with its humanity. For all its power generated on the surface, *The Crucible* is most moving in the simple, quiet scenes between John Proctor and his wife. By the standards of *Death of a Salesman,* there is too much excitement and not enough emotion in *The Crucible.*

As the director, Jed Harris has given it a driving performance in which the clashes are fierce and clamorous. Inside Boris Aronson's gaunt, pitiless sets of rude buildings, the acting is at a high pitch of bitterness, anger and fear. As the patriarchal deputy Governor, Walter Hampden gives one of his most vivid performances in which righteousness and ferocity are unctuously mated. Fred Stewart as a vindictive parson, E. G. Marshall as a parson who finally rebels at the indiscriminate ruthlessness of the trial, Jean Adair as an aging woman of God . . . all give able performances.

This evaluation of the leading actor and the leading actress is extremely positive.

As John Proctor and his wife, Arthur Kennedy and Beatrice Straight have the most attractive roles in the drama. . . . They are superb—Mr. Kennedy clear and resolute, full of fire, searching his own mind; Miss Straight, reserved, detached, above and beyond the contention. Like all the members of the cast, they are dressed in the chaste and lovely costumes Edith Lutyens has designed from old prints of early Massachusetts.

After the experience of *Death of a Salesman* we probably expect Mr. Miller to write a masterpiece every time. *The Crucible* is not of that stature and it lacks that universality. On a lower level of dramatic history with considerable pertinence for today, it is a powerful play and a genuine contribution to the season.

The reviewer concludes by stating his mixed evaluation of the play.

NEW YORK'S HOMETOWN CONNECTION   WWW.NYDAILYNEWS.COM

DAILY◉NEWS

NEESON & CO. CAST A POWERFUL SPELL

By Howard Kissel

Four years after Arthur Miller wrote a play about a louse—a man who was a failure as a husband, a father and a salesman—he wrote a play about a hero.

The hero was a man in Puritan Massachusetts who redeemed his failures as a husband by his courageous, self-sacrificial commitment to honesty in a world gone berserk.

The louse, of course, was Willy Loman, whose name has become a by word for the failure of the American dream in the mid-20th century.

John Proctor, the hero of Miller's 1953 *The Crucible,* should be every bit as emblematic as Loman. If he isn't, it may be because he is rarely played as powerfully as he is by Liam Neeson in the current revival, which also stars Laura Linney.

Miller's play about the witch hunts in 17th-century Salem draws much of its power from its subtext. It was written when the country was in the grip of another witch hunt: Congress' attempt to find American Communists in the early years of the Cold War.

This has given the play a longer life than it might have had on its own.

The Crucible is, after all, a melodrama.

An Honest Family Before the play begins, Proctor had been an upstanding citizen. His one failing was a brief fling with a servant girl, Abigail Williams, whom his wife dismissed when she learned of the affair.

Shortly afterward, Mary Warren, a servant who replaced Abigail, joined a band of girls accusing townspeople of witchcraft, often as a way of settling old scores.

The pivot point of the play comes when Proctor's longsuffering wife is called on to denounce him for adultery. Not knowing that he has already confessed, she refuses to condemn him. She thus unwittingly seals his fate, implying to the court that he has lied. Such plotting would normally be dismissed as quaint and old-fashioned, but here the subtext makes it acceptable.

Neeson's haunted, brooding look is perfect for Proctor. Moreover, his easy sensuality brings his difficult past effortlessly onto the stage, making his transformation into a man of unassailable character all the more dramatic and thrilling.

Linney gives a performance of disarming simplicity. She is a woman wronged not only by her husband but by his villainous accusers. But she responds to a mountain of cruel torments with a dignity that is profoundly moving. . . .

Jennifer Carpenter gives a wrenching performance as the ultimately disloyal Mary, and Angela Bettis is wonderfully ruthless as Abigail, the leader of the accusing girls. As the judge who brings about the deaths of innocent people, Brian Murray falls into the trap of signaling us that he knows his character is evil, making the melodramatic aspects of the writing too apparent.

Tim Hatley's costumes and sets, beautifully lit by Paul Gallo, have muted colors that suggest a world desperately trying to keep sensuality at bay. Under Richard Eyre's direction, the large cast handles Miller's artful creation of 17th-century language and inflections with great ease.

The Crucible is one of Miller's most-revived plays, but it is seldom as impressive as this.

APPLY THE SKILLS

THINKING ABOUT THE CRITICAL REVIEWS

1. Which play does Atkinson prefer, *Death of a Salesman* or *The Crucible*? Explain your answer.

_____

Write words from the review that support your answer.

_____

_____

READING STRATEGY: COMPARING AND CONTRASTING CRITICAL REVIEWS

2. What does each reviewer think is most powerful about *The Crucible?*

_____

_____

3. Which reviewer liked the play more? Explain.

_____

Give evidence from both reviews to support your answer.

_____

TIMED WRITING: EVALUATION (30 minutes)

Write a critical review of a movie, television show, or other performance. Support your opinion with evidence and reasons. The chart below will help you organize your writing.

Element	Opinion	Evidence/Reasons
script		
acting		
direction		
costumes		
music		

PART 2: TURBO VOCABULARY

The exercises and tools presented here are designed to help you increase your vocabulary. Review the instruction and complete the exercises to build your vocabulary knowledge. Throughout the year, you can apply these skills and strategies to improve your reading, writing, speaking, and listening vocabulary.

PREFIXES

The following list contains common prefixes with meanings and examples. On the blank lines, write other words you know that begin with the same prefixes. Write the meanings of the new words.

Prefix	Meaning	Example and Meaning	Your Words	Meanings
Anglo-Saxon *fore-*	before	*foretell:* to tell beforehand; predict		
Greek *auto-*	self	*autobiography:* the story of one's own life written by one-self		
Greek *di-*	away; apart	*digress:* to move away from a subject		
Greek *dys-*	difficult; bad	*dystopia:* a place with dreadful condi-tions		
Greek *mono-*	alone; one; single	*monologue:* a long speech by one speaker		
Latin *con-*	with; together	*conference:* a meeting for discussion		
Latin *dis-*	apart; not	*dishonest:* not honest		
Latin *ex-*	out	*extort:* to squeeze out		

Prefix	Meaning	Example and Meaning	Your Words	Meanings
Latin in-	in; into; not; without	*inescapable:* that cannot be escaped		
Latin mal-	bad	*malice:* desire to harm another		
Latin multi-	many; much	*multiply:* to increase in number		
Latin ob-	against	*object:* showing disapproval		
Latin omni-	all; every	*omnipotent:* all-powerful		
Latin pro-	forward	*protruded:* thrust forward		
Latin re-	again; back	*revolve:* to move in a circle around a point		
Latin trans-	across; through	*transportation:* means of moving passengers or goods		

WORD ROOTS

The following list contains common word roots with meanings and examples. On the blank lines, write other words you know that have the same roots. Write the meanings of the new words.

Root	Meaning	Example and Meaning	Your Words	Meanings
Greek -archy-	to rule	*anarchy:* without government; without rule		
Greek -psych-	soul; mind	*psychology:* the science that deals with the mind		
Latin -aud-	hearing, sound	*auditorium:* a room for gathering an audience to hear concerts or speeches		
Latin -bene-	good	*benefit:* to do good for		
Latin -equi-	equal	*equivalent:* equal in quantity, value, or meaning		
Latin -fid-	faith; trust	*confident:* full of certainty or trust		
Latin -grat-	pleasing	*grateful:* expressing thankfulness		
Latin -ject-	to throw	*eject:* to throw out		

Root	Meaning	Example and Meaning	Your Words	Meanings
Latin -lib-	free	*liberty:* freedom		
Latin -mort-	death	*mortuary:* a place where dead bodies are kept		
Latin -patr-	father	*paternal:* fatherly		
Latin -press-	push	*compress:* to squeeze or push together; make compact		
Latin -scrib-	write	*transcribe:* to write out or type out in full		
Latin -sol-	alone	*solitary:* being alone; without others		
Latin -terr-	earth; land	*terrarium:* a glass container holding small plants or small land animals		
Latin -vid-	to see	*video:* the process of recording and show-ing television programs, movies, and real events		

SUFFIXES

The following list contains common suffixes with meanings and examples. On the blank lines, write other words you know that have the same suffixes. Write the meanings of the new words.

Suffix	Meaning	Example and Meaning	Your Words	Meanings
Anglo-Saxon -fold	a specific number of times or ways	*tenfold:* ten times		
Anglo-Saxon -ful	full of	*joyful:* happy; full of joy		
Anglo-Saxon -hood	state or quality of	*parenthood:* the state of being a parent		
Anglo-Saxon -less	without	*helpless:* not able to help oneself		
Anglo-Saxon -ness	the state of being	*handedness:* the quality of using one hand more skillfully than the other		
Anglo-Saxon -some	tending toward being	*awesome:* impressive; inspiring awe		
Greek -ate	forms verbs	*evaporate:* to change into a vapor		
Greek -ic	forms adjectives	*hypnotic:* causing sleep		

Suffix	Meaning	Example and Meaning	Your Words	Meanings
Greek -itis	disease; inflammation	bronchitis: inflammation of the bronchial tubes		
Greek -logy	the science or study of	biology: the study of living organisms		
Latin -able/-ible	capable of being	lovable: able to be loved		
Latin -al	of, like, suitable for	theatrical: having to do with the theater		
Latin -ance/-ence	quality of; state of being	permanence: the state of being permanent; remaining		
Latin -er	one who	geographer: one whose profession deals with the study of geography		
Latin -ity	turns adjectives into nouns	complexity: the state of being complex or difficult		
Latin -tion	turns a noun into a verb	deliberation: the act of deliberating or thinking about very carefully		

Etymology is the history of a word. It shows where the word came from, or its **origin**. It also shows how it got its present meaning and spelling. Understanding word origins, or etymology, can help you understand and remember the meanings of words you add to your vocabulary.

A good dictionary will tell you the etymology of a word. The word's etymology usually appears in brackets, parentheses, or slashes near the beginning or the end of the dictionary entry. Part of the etymology is the language from which the word comes.

Abbreviations for Languages	
Abbreviation	**Language**
OE	Old English
ME	Middle English
F	French
Gr	Greek
L	Latin

You can find these abbreviations and more in a dictionary's key to abbreviations.

Words from other languages

The English that you speak today began in about the year 500. Tribes from Europe settled in Britain. These tribes, called the Angles, the Saxons, and the Jutes, spoke a Germanic language. Later, when the Vikings attacked Britain, their language added words from Danish and Norse. Then, when Christian missionaries came to Britain, they added words from Latin. The resulting language is called Old English, and it looks very different from modern English.

For example, to say "Listen!" in Old English, you would have said "Hwaet!"

The Normans conquered Britain in 1066. They spoke Old French, and the addition of this language changed Old English dramatically. The resulting language, called Middle English, looks much more like modern English, but the spellings of words are very different.

For example, the word *knight* in Middle English was spelled *knyght*, and the word *time* was spelled *tyme*.

During the Renaissance, interest in classical cultures added Greek and Latin words to English. At this time, English started to look more like the English you know. This language, called Modern English, is the language we still speak.

Modern English continues to add words from other languages. As immigrants have moved to the United States, they have added new words to the language.

For example, the word *boycott* comes from Ireland and the word *burrito* comes from Mexico.

Note-taking Using a dictionary, identify the language from which each of the following words came into English. Also identify the word's original and current meaning.

Word	Original language	Original meaning	Current meaning
comb			
costume			
guess			
mile			
panther			

Words that change meaning over time

English is a living language. It grows by giving new meanings to existing words and by incorporating words that have changed their meaning over time and through usage.

For example, the word *dear* used to mean "expensive."

Note-taking Using a dictionary, identify the original meaning and the current meaning of each of the following words.

	original meaning	current meaning
1. havoc	_____	_____
2. magazine	_____	_____

Words that have been invented, or *coined*, to serve new purposes.

New products or discoveries need new words.

For example, the words *paperback* and *quiz* are coined words.

Note-taking Identify one word that has been coined in each of the following categories.

Category	Coined word
sports	
technology	
transportation	
space travel	
medicine	

Words that are combinations of words or shortened versions of longer words

New words can be added to the language by combining words or by shortening words.

For example, the word *greenback* is a combination of the words *green* and *back*, and the word *flu* is a shortened version of the word *influenza*.

Note-taking Generate a word to fill in the blanks in each of the following sentences correctly. Your word should be a combination of two words or a shortened version of a longer word.

Jerome served one of our favorite dinners, spaghetti and _____.

Many years ago, people might take an omnibus to work, but today they would call that vehicle a _____.

We took the most direct route to Aunt Anna's house, which meant driving forty miles on the _____.

We thought we could get to shelter before the storm started, but we did not quite make it. A few _____ dampened our jackets.

A dictionary lists words in alphabetical order. Look at this sample dictionary entry. Notice the types of information about a word it gives.

Example of a Dictionary Entry

dictionary (dik´ shə ner´ ē) n., pl. –aries [ML *dictionarium* < LL *dictio*) 1 a book of alphabetically listed words in a language, with definitions, etymologies, pronunciations, and other information 2 a book of alphabetically listed words in a language with their equivalents in another language [a Spanish-English *dictionary*]

Answer the questions based on the dictionary entry.

1. What is the correct spelling?_____

2. How do you form the plural? _____

3. What language does the word come from? _____

4. How many definitions are there? _____

5. What example is given? _____

Here are some abbreviations you will find in dictionary entries.

Pronunciation Symbols	Parts of Speech	Origins of Words
´ means emphasize this syllable as you say the word	adj. = adjective	Fr = French
¯ means pronounce vowel with a long sound, such as -*ay*- for a and -*ee*- for e	adv. = adverb	Ger = German
ə means a sound like -*uh*-	n. = noun	L = classical Latin
o͞o means the sound of *u* in *cute*	v. = verb	ME = Middle English OE = Old English

As you read, look up new words in a dictionary. Enter information about the words on this chart.

My Words

New Word	Pronunciation	Part of Speech	Origin	Meanings and Sample Sentence

ACADEMIC WORDS

Academic words are words you use often in your schoolwork. Knowing what these words mean and how to use them will help you think and write better.

The following chart provides definitions and pronunciations for academic words. When you come across one of these words in your reading, write the sentence in which it appears in the middle column. In the right column, use your own words to explain what these sentences mean.

Academic Word	Example You Find	Meaning of Example
analyze (AN uh LYZ) break down into parts and explain		
apply (uh PLY) tell how you use information in a specific situation		
categorize (KAT uh gaw ryz) group similar items together		
clarify (KLA ri FY) make something more understandable		
conclude (KUHN klood) use reasoning to reach a decision or opinion		
deduce (dee DOOS) figure something out by applying a general idea		
define (dee FYN) tell the qualities that make something what it is		
demonstrate (DEM uhn STRAYT) use examples to prove a point		
differentiate (dif er EN shee AYT) explain what makes two things different		

Academic Word	Example You Find	Meaning of Example
evaluate (ee VAL yoo AYT) determine the value or importance of something		
identify (y DEN ti FY) name or show you recognize something		
illustrate (IL uhs TRAYT) give examples that show you know what something means		
interpret (in TER pret) explain the underlying meaning of something		
judge (JUHJ) assess or form an opinion about something		
label (LAY bel) attach the correct name to something		
predict (pree DIKT) tell what will happen based on details you know		
recall (ri KAWL) tell details that you remember		

When you are reading, you will find many unfamiliar words. Here are some tools that you can use to help you read unfamiliar words.

PHONICS

Phonics is the science or study of sound. When you learn to read, you learn to associate certain sounds with certain letters or letter combinations. You know most of the sounds that letters can represent in English. When letters are combined, however, it is not always so easy to know what sound is represented. In English, there are some rules and patterns that will help you determine how to pronounce a word. This chart shows you some of the common **vowel digraphs**, which are combinations like *ea* and *oa*. Two vowels together are called vowel digraphs. Usually, vowel digraphs represent the long sound of the first vowel.

Vowel Digraphs	Examples of Usual Sounds	Exceptions
ee and *ea*	steep, each, treat, sea	head, sweat, dread
ai and *ay*	plain, paid, may, betray	aisle
oa, ow, and *oe*	soak, slow, doe	
ie, igh, and *y*	lie, night, delight, my	myth

As you read, sometimes the only way to know how to pronounce a word with an *ea* spelling is to see if the word makes sense in the sentence. Look at this example:

The water pipes were made of *lead*.

First, try out the long sound "ee." Ask yourself if it sounds right. It does not. Then try the short sound "e." You will find that the short sound is correct in that sentence. Now try this example.

Where you *lead*, I will follow.

WORD PATTERNS

Recognizing different vowel-consonant patterns will help you read longer words. In the following section, the **V** stands for "vowel" and the **C** stands for "consonant."

Single-syllable Words

CV–go: In two letter words with a consonant followed by a vowel, the vowel is usually long. For example, the word *go* is pronounced wiht a long o sound.

In a single syllable word, a vowel followed only by a single consonant is usually short.

CVC-got: If you add a consonant to the word *go*, such as the *t* in *got*, the vowel sound is a short *o*. Say the words *go* and *got* aloud and notice the difference in pronunciation.

Multi-syllable Words

In words of more than one syllable, notice the letters that follow a vowel.

VCCV–robber: A single vowel followed by two consonants is usually short.

VCV–begin: A single vowel followed by a single consonant is usually long.

VCe–beside: An extension of the VCV pattern is vowel-consonant-silent *e*. In these words, the vowel is long and the *e* is not pronounced.

When you see a word with the VCV pattern, try the long vowel sound first. If the word does not make sense, try the short sound. Pronounce the words *model, camel,* and *closet.* First, try the long vowel sound. That does not sound correct, so try the short vowel sound. The short vowel sound is correct in those words.

Remember that patterns help you get started on figuring out a word. You will sometimes need to try a different sound or find the word in a dictionary.

As you read and find unfamiliar words, look the pronunciations up in a dictionary. Write the words in this chart in the correct column, to help you notice patterns and remember pronunciations.

Syllables	Example	New Words	Vowel Sound
CV	go		long
CVC	got		short
VCC	robber		short
VCV	begin open		long long
VCe	beside		long

FAQS ABOUT THE SAT®

What is the SAT®?

- The SAT® is a national test intended to predict how well you will do with college-level material.

What does the SAT® test?

- The SAT® tests vocabulary, math, and reasoning skills in three sections:
  - Critical Reading: two 25-minute sections and one 20-minute section
  - Math: two 25-minute sections and one 20-minute section
  - Writing: one 35-minute multiple-choice section and one 25-minute essay

Why should you take the SAT®?

- Many colleges and universities require you to submit your SAT® scores when you apply. They use your scores, along with other information about your ability and your achievements, to evaluate you for admission.

How can studying vocabulary help improve your SAT® scores?

- The Critical Reading section of the SAT® asks two types of questions that evaluate your vocabulary.
  - Sentence Completions ask you to fill in one or more blanks in a sentence with the correct word or words. To fill in the blanks correctly, you need to know the meaning of the words offered as answers.
  - Vocabulary in Context questions in Passage-based Reading ask you to determine what a word means based on its context in a reading passage.
- With a strong vocabulary and good strategies for using context clues, you will improve the likelihood that you will score well on the SAT®.

Using Context Clues on the SAT®

When you do not know the meaning of a word, nearby words or phrases can help you. These words or phrases are called *context clues*.

Guidelines for Using Context Clues

1. Read the sentence or paragraph, concentrating on the unfamiliar word.
2. Look for clues in the surrounding words.
3. Guess the possible meaning of the unfamiliar word.
4. Substitute your guess for the word.
5. When you are reviewing for a test, you can check the word's meaning in a dictionary.

Types of Context Clues

Here are the most common types of context clues:

- formal definitions that give the meaning of the unfamiliar word
- familiar words that you may know that give hints to the unfamiliar word's meaning
- comparisons or contrasts that present ideas or concepts either clearly similar or clearly opposite to the unfamiliar word
- synonyms, or words with the same meaning as the unfamiliar word
- antonyms, or words with a meaning opposite to that of the unfamiliar word
- key words used to clarify a word's meaning

Note-taking List several new words that you have learned recently by figuring out their meanings in context. Then, explain how you used context to decide what the word meant.

New Word	How You Used Context to Understand the Word

Sample SAT® Questions

Here are some examples of the kinds of questions you will find on the SAT®. Read the samples carefully. Then, do the Practice exercises that follow.

Sample Sentence Completion Question:

Directions: The sentence that follows has one blank indicating that something has been omitted. Beneath the sentence are five words or sets of words labeled A through E. Choose the word or set of words that, when inserted in the sentence, best fits the meaning of the sentence as a whole.

1. Though he is _____, his nephew still invites him to Thanksgiving dinner every year.

   A cheerful

   B entertaining

   C misanthropic

   D agile

   E healthy

The correct answer is *C*. The uncle is *misanthropic*. You can use the context clues "though" and "invites him" to infer that the uncle has some negative quality. Next, you can apply your knowledge of the prefix *mis-* to determine that *misanthropic*, like *mistake* and *misfortune*, is a word indicating something negative. Eliminate the other answer choices, which indicate positive or neutral qualities in this context.

Sample Vocabulary in Context Question:

Directions: Read the following sentence. Then, read the question that follows it. Decide which is the best answer to the question.

Martin Luther King, Jr., whose methods motivated many to demand equal rights in a peaceful manner, was an <u>inspiration</u> to all.

1. In this sentence, the word *inspiration* means—

    A politician

    B motivation to a high level of activity

    C the process of inhaling

    D figurehead

The correct answer is *B*. Both *B* and *C* are correct definitions of the word *inspiration*, but the only meaning that applies in the context of the sentence is "motivation to a high level of activity."

Practice for SAT Questions

Practice Read the following passage. Then, read each question that follows the passage. Decide which is the best answer to each question.

Many people are becoming Internet <u>savvy</u>, exhibiting their skills at mastering the Web. The Internet is also becoming a more *reliable* source of factual information. A <u>Web-surfer</u> can find information provided by <u>reputable</u> sources, such as government organizations and universities.

1. In this passage, the word *savvy* means—

    A incompetent

    B competent

    C users

    D nonusers

2. The word *reliable* in this passage means—

    A existing

    B available

    C dependable

    D relevant

3. In this passage, the term *Web-surfer* means—

A someone who uses the Internet

B a person who uses a surfboard

C a person who know a great deal about technology

D a student

4. The word *reputable* in this passage means—

A an approved Internet provider

B well-known and of good reputation

C purely academic

D costly

Practice Each sentence that follows has one or two blanks indicating that something has been omitted. Beneath the sentence are five words or sets of words labeled A through E. Choose the word or set of words that, when inserted in the sentence, best fits the meaning of the sentence as a whole.

1. "I wish I had a longer _____ between performances," complained the pianist. "My fingers need a rest."

A post-mortem   C prelude   E solo

B circumlocution   D interval

2. Instead of revolving around the sun in a circle, this asteroid has a(n) _____ orbit.

A rapid   C interplanetary   E regular

B eccentric   D circular

3. He was the first historian to translate the _____ on the stone.

A impulsion   C excavation   E inscription

B aversion   D circumspection

4. To correct your spelling error, simply _____ the *i* and the *e*.

A translate   C transcent   E integrate

B transpose   D interpolate

5. Spilling soda all over myself just when the movie got to the good part was a(n) _____ event.

A fortunate   C tenacious   E constructive

B premature   D infelicitous

COMMUNICATION GUIDE: DICTION AND ETIQUETTE

Diction

Diction is a writer's or a speaker's word choice. The vocabulary, the vividness of the language, and the appropriateness of the words all contribute to diction, which is part of a writing or speaking **style**.

- Hey, buddy! What's up?
- Hi, how're you doing?
- Hello, how are you?
- Good morning. How are you?

These four phrases all function as greetings. You would use each one, however, in very different situations. This word choice is called *diction*, and for different situations, you use different *levels of diction*.

Note-taking Here are some examples of levels of diction. Fill in the blanks with the opposite level of diction.

Level of Diction	Formal	Informal
Example	Good afternoon. Welcome to the meeting.	
Level of Diction	**Ornate**	**Plain**
Example		I need more coffee.
Level of Diction	**Abstract**	**Concrete**
Example		The mayor has asked for volunteers to pick up litter along the river next Saturday.
Level of Diction	**Technical**	**Ordinary**
Example	My brother is employed as a computer system design manager.	
Level of Diction	**Sophisticated**	**Down-to-Earth**
Example	Thank you very much. I appreciate your help.	
Level of Diction	**Old-fashioned**	**Modern/Slangy**
Example	Yes, it is I. Shall we sample the bill of fare?	

With close friends and family, most of your conversations will probably be informal, down-to-earth, even slangy. In school or in elegant surroundings, or among people you do not know well or people who are much older than you, you will probably choose language that is more formal. Sometimes the distinctions can be subtle, so try to take your cues from others and adjust your diction accordingly.

Note-taking Complete the following activities.

1. Make a list of words and phrases that would be appropriate for you to use as you escort a visiting school board member on a tour of your school.

_____

_____

_____

_____

2. Make a second list of words and phrases that you might use as you escort your teenage cousin on a tour of your school.

_____

_____

_____

_____

3. Study the following pairs of phrases. Then, identify one phrase in each pair as formal and the other as informal.

	Phrase	Formal / Informal	Phrase	Formal / Informal
1.	Hello, it's nice to meet you		How do you do?	
2.	What is your opinion, Professor Hughes?		What do you think, Pat?	
3.	Please accept my deepest sympathy.		That's too bad.	
4.	Sorry. I didn't hear you.		I beg your pardon. Please repeat the question	
5.	I don't get it.		I do not quite understand.	

4. List several common phrases. Then, identify whether each phrase is formal or informal, and give its formal or informal opposite.

	Phrase	Formal / Informal	Phrase	Formal / Informal
1.				
2.				
3.				
4.				
5.				

Etiquette: Using the Vocabulary of Politeness

No matter how many words you know, the way you use those words will impact how your friends, your family, your teachers, and all the people in your life react to you. For almost every interaction you have, choosing a vocabulary of politeness will help you avoid conflicts and communicate your ideas, thoughts, and feelings effectively to others.

When in doubt, always choose the polite word or phrase.

Formal or Informal?

Polite vocabulary does not have to be formal. In fact, the definition of the word *polite* is "behaving or speaking in a way that is correct for the social situation." People often think that *etiquette*, which consists of rules for polite behavior, applies only in formal situations. All interactions with other people, though, should follow the etiquette that is appropriate for the situation.

Etiquette for Classroom Discussions

Use the following sentences starters to help you express yourself clearly and politely in classroom discussions.

To Express an Opinion

- I think that _____.
- I believe that _____.
- It seems to me that _____.
- In my opinion, _____.

To Agree

- I agree with _____ that _____.
- I see what you mean.
- That's an interesting idea.
- My idea is similar to _____'s idea.
- I hadn't thought of that.

To Disagree

- I don't completely agree with _____ because _____.
- My opinion is different from yours.
- My idea is slightly different from yours.
- I see it a different way.

To Report the Ideas of a Group

- We agreed that _____.
- We concluded that _____.
- We had a similar idea.
- We had a different approach.

To Predict or Infer

- I predict that _____.
- Based on _____, I infer that _____.
- I hypothesize that _____.

To Paraphrase

- So you are saying that _____.
- In other words, you think _____.
- What I hear you saying is _____.

To Offer a Suggestion

- Maybe we could _____.
- What if we _____.
- Here's something we might try.

To Ask for Clarification

- Could you explain that another way?
- I have a question about that.
- Can you give me another example of that?

To Ask for a Response

- What do you think?
- Do you agree?
- What answer did you get?

Practice With a partner, discuss an issue about which you disagree. At the end of five minutes, list five or more polite words or phrases that you used to communicate your conflicting opinions.

_____

_____

Use this page to write down academic words you come across in other subjects, such as social studies or science. When you are reading your textbooks, you may find words that you need to learn. Following the example, write down the word, the part of speech, and an explanation of the word. You may want to write an example sentence to help you remember the word.

dissolve *verb* to make something solid become part of a liquid by putting it in a liquid and mixing it

The sugar *dissolved* in the hot tea.

_____
_____
_____
_____
_____
_____
_____
_____
_____
_____
_____
_____
_____
_____
_____
_____
_____
_____
_____
_____
_____
_____
_____

VOCABULARY FLASH CARDS

Use these flash cards to study words you want to remember. The words on this page come from Unit 1. Cut along the dotted lines on pages V29 through V32 to create your own flash cards or use index cards. Write the word on the front of the card. On the back, write the word's part of speech and definition. Then, write a sentence that shows the meaning of the word.

confederate	entreated	subsisted
protruded	deliberation	mortality
ablutions	disposition	feigned

adjective
united with others for a common purpose

The *confederate* Iroquois nations worked well together.

---

verb
begged; pleaded

The children *entreated* the parents not to be angry with them.

---

verb
remained alive; were sustained

The lost hunters *subsisted* on berries and tree bark.

---

verb
jutted out

A tuft of hair *protruded* from under her hat.

---

noun
careful consideration

After much *deliberation*, we decided to go to the Grand Canyon for our vacation.

---

noun
death on a large scale

The infant *mortality* rate has been on the increase in certain areas.

---

noun
cleansing the body as part of a religious rite

The people performed their *ablutions* before beginning the scared dance.

---

noun
an inclination or tendency

Neither side shows a *disposition* to compromise in the conflict.

---

verb
pretended; faked

Joe *feigned* sleep so that his brother would not talk to him.

VOCABULARY FLASH CARDS

Use these flash cards to study words you want to remember. Cut along the dotted lines on pages V29 through V32 to create your own flash cards or use index cards. Write the word on the front of the card. On the back, write the word's part of speech and definition. Then, write a sentence that shows the meaning of the word.

VOCABULARY FLASH CARDS

Use these flash cards to study words you want to remember. Cut along the dotted lines on pages V27 through V32 to create your own flash cards or use index cards. Write the word on the front of the card. On the back, write the word's part of speech and definition. Then, write a sentence that shows the meaning of the word.

VOCABULARY FOLD-A-LIST

Use a fold-a-list to study the definitions of words. The words on this page come from Unit 1. Write the definition for each word on the lines. Fold the paper along the dotted line to check your definition. Create your own fold-a-lists on pages V35 through V38.

exquisite _____

_____

affliction _____

_____

indications _____

_____

abundance _____

_____

pilfer _____

_____

palisades _____

_____

conceits _____

_____

mollified _____

_____

peril _____

_____

loath _____

_____

Fold ←

VOCABULARY FOLD-A-LIST

Write the word that matches the definition on each line.
Fold the paper along the dotted line to check your work.

very beautiful; delicate;
carefully wrought

_____

something causing
pain or suffering

_____

signs; things that point
out or signify

_____

a great supply;
more than enough

_____

steal

_____

large, pointed stakes set
in the ground to form a
fence used for defense

_____

strange or fanciful ideas

_____

soothed; calmed

_____

danger

_____

reluctant; unwilling

_____

Fold

VOCABULARY FOLD-A-LIST

Write the words you want to study on this side of the page. Write the definitions on the back. Then, test yourself. Fold the paper along the dotted line to check your answers.

Word: _____

_____

Word: _____

_____

Word: _____

_____

Word: _____

_____

Word: _____

_____

Word: _____

_____

Word: _____

_____

Word: _____

_____

Word: _____

_____

Word: _____

_____

Fold →

VOCABULARY FOLD-A-LIST

Write the word that matches the definition on each line.
Fold the paper along the dotted line to check your work.

Definition: _____

_____

Definition: _____

_____

Definition: _____

_____

Definition: _____

_____

Definition: _____

_____

Definition: _____

_____

Definition: _____

_____

Definition: _____

_____

Definition: _____

_____

Definition: _____

Fold

VOCABULARY FOLD-A-LIST

Write the words you want to study on this side of the page. Write the definitions on the back. Then, test yourself. Fold the paper along the dotted line to check your answers.

Word: _____

Word: _____

Word: _____

Word: _____

Word: _____

Word: _____

Word: _____

Word: _____

Word: _____

Word: _____

Fold →

VOCABULARY FOLD-A-LIST

Write the word that matches the definition on each line.
Fold the paper along the dotted line to check your work.

Definition: _____

_____

Definition: _____

_____

Definition: _____

_____

Definition: _____

_____

Definition: _____

_____

Definition: _____

_____

Definition: _____

_____

Definition: _____

_____

Definition: _____

_____

Definition: _____

Fold →

COMMONLY MISSPELLED WORDS

The list on these pages presents words that cause problems for many people. Some of these words are spelled according to set rules, but others follow no specific rules. As you review this list, check to see how many of the words give you trouble in your own writing. Then, add your own commonly misspelled words on the lines that follow.

abbreviate	auxiliary	census	deficient
absence	awkward	certain	definitely
absolutely	bandage	changeable	delinquent
abundance	banquet	characteristic	dependent
accelerate	bargain	chauffeur	descendant
accidentally	barrel	chief	description
accumulate	battery	clothes	desert
accurate	beautiful	coincidence	desirable
ache	beggar	colonel	dessert
achievement	beginning	column	deteriorate
acquaintance	behavior	commercial	dining
adequate	believe	commission	disappointed
admittance	benefit	commitment	disastrous
advertisement	bicycle	committee	discipline
aerial	biscuit	competitor	dissatisfied
affect	bookkeeper	concede	distinguish
aggravate	bought	condemn	effect
aggressive	boulevard	congratulate	eighth
agreeable	brief	connoisseur	eligible
aisle	brilliant	conscience	embarrass
all right	bruise	conscientious	enthusiastic
allowance	bulletin	conscious	entrepreneur
aluminum	buoyant	contemporary	envelope
amateur	bureau	continuous	environment
analysis	bury	controversy	equipped
analyze	buses	convenience	equivalent
ancient	business	coolly	especially
anecdote	cafeteria	cooperate	exaggerate
anniversary	calendar	cordially	exceed
anonymous	campaign	correspondence	excellent
answer	canceled	counterfeit	exercise
anticipate	candidate	courageous	exhibition
anxiety	capacity	courteous	existence
apologize	capital	courtesy	experience
appall	capitol	criticism	explanation
appearance	captain	criticize	extension
appreciate	career	curiosity	extraordinary
appropriate	carriage	curious	familiar
architecture	cashier	cylinder	fascinating
argument	catastrophe	deceive	February
associate	category	decision	fiery
athletic	ceiling	deductible	financial
attendance	cemetery	defendant	fluorescent

foreign
fourth
fragile
gauge
generally
genius
genuine
government
grammar
grievance
guarantee
guard
guidance
handkerchief
harass
height
humorous
hygiene
ignorant
immediately
immigrant
independence
independent
indispensable
individual
inflammable
intelligence
interfere
irrelevant
irritable
jewelry
judgment
knowledge
lawyer
legible
legislature
leisure
liable
library
license
lieutenant
lightning
likable
liquefy
literature
loneliness
magnificent
maintenance
marriage
mathematics
maximum
meanness
mediocre
mileage
millionaire
minimum

minuscule
miscellaneous
mischievous
misspell
mortgage
naturally
necessary
neighbor
neutral
nickel
niece
ninety
noticeable
nuisance
obstacle
occasion
occasionally
occur
occurred
occurrence
omitted
opinion
opportunity
optimistic
outrageous
pamphlet
parallel
paralyze
parentheses
particularly
patience
permanent
permissible
perseverance
persistent
personally
perspiration
persuade
phenomenal
phenomenon
physician
pleasant
pneumonia
possess
possession
possibility
prairie
precede
preferable
prejudice
preparation
previous
primitive
privilege
probably
procedure

proceed
prominent
pronunciation
psychology
publicly
pursue
questionnaire
realize
really
recede
receipt
receive
recognize
recommend
reference
referred
rehearse
relevant
reminiscence
renowned
repetition
restaurant
rhythm
ridiculous
sandwich
satellite
schedule
scissors
secretary
siege
solely
sponsor
subtle
subtlety
superintendent
supersede
surveillance
susceptible
tariff
temperamental
theater
threshold
truly
unmanageable
unwieldy
usage
usually
valuable
various
vegetable
voluntary
weight
weird
whale
wield
yield

PHOTO AND ART CREDITS

Cover: *Flag on Orange Field*, 1957, oil on canvas, Johns, Jasper (b.1930)/Ludwig Museum, Cologne, Germany, Lauros/ Giraudon; /www.bridgeman.co.uk/Cover art © Jasper Johns/Licensed by VAGA, New York, NY; **3:** Nicole Galeazzi/Omni-Photo Communications, Inc.; **4:** Corel Professional Photos CD-ROM™; **5:** Silver Burdett Ginn; **6:** *Red Jacket*, George Catlin, From the Collection of Gilcrease Museum, Tulsa; **13:** Jeff Greenberg/Photo Researchers, Inc. 16 Erich Lessing/Art Resource, NY; **19:** *The First Day at Jamestown, 14th May 1607*, from "The Romance and Tragedy of Pioneer Life" by Augustus L. Mason, 1883, William Ludlow Sheppard/Bridgeman Art Library, London/New York; **25:** *The Coming of the Mayflower*, N.C. Wyeth, from the Collection of Metropolitan Life Insurance Company, New York City, photograph by Malcolm Varon; **32:** *Anne Bradstreet, The Tenth Muse Lately Sprung Up in America*, Ladonna Gulley Warrick, Courtesy of the artist; **35:** Bettmann/CORBIS; **44:** The Granger Collection, New York; **51:** The Granger Collection, New York; **54:** National Maritime Museum, London; **60:** Courtesy National Archives; **61:** ©Archive Photos; **67:** Liberty and Washington, New York State Historical Association, Cooperstown; **76:** *Patrick Henry Before the Virginia House of Burgesses 1851*, Peter F. Rothermel, Red Hill, The Patrick Henry National Memorial, Brookneal, Virginia; **81:** Bettmann/CORBIS; **84:** *Building the First White House*, 1930, N.C. Wyeth, Copyrighted © by the White House Historical Association, photo by the National Geographical Society; **88:** *Independence (Squire Jack Porter)*, 1858, Frank Blackwell Mayer, National Museum of American Art, Smithsonian Institution, Bequest of Harriet Lane Johnson, Art Resource, New York; **94:** Leonard Lee Rue III/Stock, Boston; **108:** *Seashore in Normandy*, 1893, Maximilien Luce, Erich Lessing/Art Resource, NY; **117:** *Lewis and Clark with Sacajawea at the Great Falls of the Missouri*, Olaf Seltzer, #0137.871. The Thomas Gilcrease Institute of Art, Tulsa, Oklahoma; **118:** Corel Professional Photos CD-ROM™; **121** "I at length...,"

Edgar Allan Poe's Tales of Mystery and Imagination (London: George G. Harrap, 1935), Arthur Rackham, Print Collection, Miriam and Ira D. Wallach Division of Art, Prints and Photographs, The New York Public Library; Astor, Lenox and Tilden Foundations; **130:** New York State Historical Association, Cooperstown, New York; **133:** *Moby-Dick*, 1930, pen and ink drawing, The Granger Collection, New York; **136:** Ralph Waldo Emerson (detail), Frederick Gutekunst/National Portrait Gallery, Smithsonian Institution, Washington D.C./Art Resource, NY; **137:** Tom Bean/ CORBIS; **138:** Frank Whitney/Getty Images; **141:** ©Lee Snider/CORBIS **150:** Getty Images; **153:** eStock Photography, LLC; **156:** Courtesy of the Library of Congress; **160:** Courtesy National Archives; **166:** *Young Soldier: Separate Study of a Soldier Giving Water to a Wounded Companion*, (detail) 1861, Winslow Homer, Oil, gouache, black crayon on canvas, 36x17.5 cm., United States, 1836-1910, Cooper-Hewitt, National Museum of Design, Smithsonian Institution, Gift of Charles Savage Homer, Jr., 1912-12-110, Photo by Ken Pelka, Courtesy of Art Resource, New York; **169:** Courtesy of the Library of Congress; **172:** Frederick Douglass (detail), c.1844, Attributed to Elisha Hammond, The National Portrait Gallery, Smithsonian Institution, Washington, D.C./Art Resource, New York; **184:** CORBIS; **189:** Courtesy of the Library of Congress; **189:** Courtesy of the Library of Congress; **192:** Courtesy of the Library of Congress; **195:** Pearson Education/PH School Division; **204:** *Edge of Town*, Charles Ephraim Burchfield, The Nelson-Atkins Museum of Art, Kansas City, Missouri; **207:** Kansas State Historical Society; **208:** National Museum of American History, Smithsonian Institution; **211:** Annie Griffiths/DRK Photo; **214:** Corel Professional Photos CD-ROM™; **220:** Stock Montage, Inc.; **223:** Joel Greenstein/Omni-Photo Communications, Inc.; **226:** George Schreiber (1904-1977), *From Arkansas*, 1939, oil on canvas, Sheldon Swope Art Museum, Terre Haute, Indiana; **230:** Corel Professional Photos CD-ROM™;